W9-CHR-481

About Island Press

Island Press is the only nonprofit organization in the United States whose principal purpose is the publication of books on environmental issues and natural resource management. We provide solutions-oriented information to professionals, public officials, business and community leaders, and concerned citizens who are shaping responses to environmental problems.

In 2000, Island Press celebrates its sixteenth anniversary as the leading provider of timely and practical books that take a multidisciplinary approach to critical environmental concerns. Our growing list of titles reflects our commitment to bringing the best of an expanding body of literature to the environmental community throughout North America and the world.

Support for Island Press is provided by The Jenifer Altman Foundation, The Bullitt Foundation, The Mary Flagler Cary Charitable Trust, The Nathan Cummins Foundation, The Geraldine R. Dodge Foundation, The Charles Engelhard Foundation, The Ford Foundation, The Vira I. Heinz Endowment, The W. Alton Jones Foundation, The John D. and Catherine T. MacArthur Foundation, The Andrew W. Mellon Foundation, The Charles Stewart Mott Foundation, The Curtis and Edith Munson Foundation, The National Fish and Wildlife Foundation, The National Science Foundation, The New-Land Foundation, The David and Lucile Packard Foundation, The Pew Charitable Trusts, The Surdna Foundation, The Winslow Foundation, and individual donors.

About The Global Development And Environment Institute

The Global Development And Environment Institute (G-DAE) is a research institute at Tufts University that is dedicated to promoting a better understanding of how societies can pursue their economic goals in an environmentally and socially sustainable manner. G-DAE pursues its mission through original research, policy work, publication projects, curriculum development, conferences, and other activities directed toward the development of academic programs at Tufts University and elsewhere. Founded in 1993 and directed by Dr. Neva Goodwin and Dr. William Moomaw, G-DAE is jointly administered by the Fletcher School of Law & Diplomacy and the Tufts Graduate School of Arts & Sciences.

THE
POLITICAL ECONOMY
OF INEQUALITY

FRONTIER ISSUES IN ECONOMIC THOUGHT
VOLUME 5
NEVA R. GOODWIN, SERIES EDITOR

The Political Economy of Inequality

Edited by
Frank Ackerman,
Neva R. Goodwin,
Laurie Dougherty,
and Kevin Gallagher

The Global Development
And Environment Institute
Tufts University

ISLAND PRESS

Washington, D.C. ■ Covelo, California

Copyright © 2000 by Island Press

All rights reserved under International and Pan-American Copyright Conventions. No part of this book may be reproduced in any form or by any means
without permission in writing from the publisher: Island Press, 1718 Connecticut Avenue, N.W., Suite 300, Washington, DC 20009.

ISLAND PRESS is a trademark of The Center for Resource Economics.

Library of Congress Cataloging-in-Publication Data
The political economy of inequality / edited by Frank Ackerman . . . [et al.].
    p. cm. — (Frontier issues in economic thought ; v. 5)
    A literature survey of books and articles, with summaries of 70–90 selections, and
introductory essays by the editors.
    Includes bibliographical references and indexes.
    ISBN 1-55963-797-8 (cloth) — ISBN 1-55963-798-6 (pbk.)
    1. Economics—Moral and ethical aspects. 2. International trade—Moral and ethical
aspects. 3. Income distribution. 4. Distributive justice. 5. Welfare economics. I.
Ackerman, Frank. II. Series

HB72 .P62 2000
330—dc21   99-048264

Printed on recycled, acid-free paper

Printed in Canada
10 9 8 7 6 5 4 3 2 1

For Bennett Harrison and David Gordon

Note to the Reader

In general, the summaries presented here do not repeat material from the original articles verbatim. In a few instances it has seemed appropriate to include in the summaries direct quotations from the original text ranging from a phrase to a few sentences. Where this has been done, the page reference to the original article is given in square brackets. The complete citation for the article always appears at the beginning of the summary. References to other books or articles appear in the Bibliography.

Contents

PART V
Poverty, Inequality, and Power

PART VI
Intrahousehold Dynamics and Changing Household Composition

PART X
Responses to Inequality: The Welfare State

On Targeting and Family Benefits   357
Anthony B. Atkinson

Authors of Original Articles

Walter Adams Deceased

Irma Adelman Dept. of Agriculture and Resource Economics, University of California, Berkeley, California

Anthony B. Atkinson Nuffield College, Oxford University, Oxford, United Kingdom

Vicki Been School of Law, New York University, New York, New York

Ajit S. Bhalla Sidney Sussex College, The University of Cambridge, Cambridge, United Kingdom

Anders Bjorklund Dept. of Economics, Swedish Institute for Social Research, Stockholm University, Stockholm, Sweden

Francine D. Blau School of Industrial Relations, Cornell University, Ithaca, New York

Barry Bluestone Dept. of Sociology, Northeastern University, Boston, Massachusetts

Derek C. Bok John F. Kennedy School of Government, Harvard University, Cambridge, Massachusetts

George Borjas John F. Kennedy School of Government, Harvard University, Cambridge, Massachusetts

Samuel Bowles Dept. of Economics, University of Massachusetts, Amherst, Massachusetts

Gary Burtless Economic Studies, Brookings Institution, Washington, D.C.

David Card Dept. of Economics, University of California, Berkeley, California

Dan Clawson Dept. of Sociology, University of Massachusetts, Amherst, Massachusetts

Paul Cook Institute for Development Policy and Management, The University of Manchester, Manchester, United Kingdom

Sheldon H. Danziger Poverty Research and Training Center, School of Social Work, University of Michigan, Ann Arbor, Michigan

William A. Darity, Jr. Dept. of Economics, University of North Carolina, Chapel Hill, North Carolina

G. William Domhoff Dept. of Psychlogy, University of California, Santa Cruz, California

Ralph Estes American University, Washington, D.C.

Gary S. Fields Dept. of Labor Economics, Cornell University, Ithaca, New York

Nancy Folbre Dept. of Economics, University of Massachusetts, Amherst, Massachusetts

Robert H. Frank Dept. of Economics, Cornell University, Ithaca, New York

Richard B. Freeman Dept. of Economics, Harvard University, Cambridge, Massachusetts

James K. Galbraith Dean of Lyndon B. Johnson School of Public Affairs, University of Texas, Austin, Texas

Herbert Gintis Dept. of Economics, University of Massachusetts, Amherst, Massachusetts

Claudia Goldin Dept. of Economics, Harvard University, Cambridge, Massachusetts

David Gordon Deceased

Ian R. Gordon Dept. of Geography, University of Reading, Whiteknights, Reading, United Kingdom

Siv Gustafsson Comparative Population and Gender Economics, University of Amsterdam, Amsterdam, The Netherlands

Bennett Harrison Deceased

Jerome L. Himmelstein Dept. of Sociology, Amherst College, Amherst, Massachusetts

Michael Hout Director of Survey Research Center, University of California, Berkeley, California

David R. Howell Urban Policy Analysis and Management (UPAM), Robert J. Milano School of Management and Urban Policy, New School for Social Research, New York, New York

Kwan S. Kim Dept. of Economics, University of Notre Dame, Notre Dame, Indiana

Robert Kuttner Editor, American Prospect Magazine, Brookline, Massachusetts

Henry M. Levin School of Education, Stanford University, Stanford, California

Elaine McCrate Dept. of Economics, University of Vermont, Burlington, Vermont

Stephen J. Machin Centre for Economic Performance, London School of Economics, London, United Kingdom

Birgit Mahnkopf School of Business (Wissenschaftzentrum), Berlin, Germany

Brian G. M. Main Dept. of Economics, The University of Edinburgh, Edinburg, United Kingdom

Douglas S. Massey Dept. of Sociology and Population Studies Center, University of Pennsylvania, Philadelphia, Pennsylvania

Karl Ove Moene Sosialokonomisk institutt, University of Oslo, Blindern, Oslo, Norway

Brian Nolan Economic and Social Research Institute, Dublin, Ireland

Melvin L. Oliver Asset Building and Community Development Program, Ford Foundation, New York, New York

Dale Oorlog Lincoln, Nebraska

Frances Fox Piven CUNY Graduate Center, New York, New York

Lant Pritchett Vice President of Development Economics and Senior Economist, World Bank, Washington, D.C.

James Quirk Sequim, Washington

Martha Roldan Departamente Economia, University of Buenos Aires, Argentina

John Scott Dept. of Sociology, University of Essex, Essex, United Kingdom

Ardeshir Sepehri Dept. of Economics, University of Manitoba, Manitoba, Canada

Ronnie J. Steinberg Dept. of Sociology and Director of Woman's Studies Program, Vanderbilt University, Nashville, Tennessee

Susan P. Sturm School of Law, University of Pennsylvania, Philadelphia, Pennsylvania

Duncan Thomas Dept. of Economics, University of California, Los Angeles, California

Chris Tilly Dept. of Policy and Planning, University of Massachusetts, Lowell, Massachusetts

Catherine J. Weinberger   Goleta, California

Jeffrey G. Williamson   Dept. of Economics, Harvard University, Cambridge, Massachusetts

William Julius Wilson   Dept. of African American Policy, Harvard University, Cambridge, Massachusetts

Edward N. Wolff   Dept. of Economics, New York University, New York, New York

Adrian Wood   Institute of Development Studies, University of Sussex, Brighton, United Kingdom

Foreword

Derek Bok

This volume is the latest in a series devoted to widening the lense of neoclassical economics to encompass a variety of other factors—social, institutional, cultural, political—that often bear importantly on the behavior of the economy. It would be hard to imagine a better subject for such analysis than inequality, for efforts to explain unequal earnings and wealth in economic terms alone are almost certain to be inadequate.

In his fascinating study of inequality in Sweden, Japan, and the United States, Sidney Verba shows how differently the leaders of these three countries look at how much inequality ought to exist in their society.[1] In the early 1980s, when Verba conducted his study, Swedish business leaders believed that CEOs should receive approximately four times the earnings of the average worker, while their American counterparts felt that executive salaries of twenty-seven times the average worker's pay would be appropriate. It would be difficult to argue that these contrasting attitudes—repeated in equally large differences of view for other leadership groups in the two societies—did not have a substantial effect on the actual distribution of earnings. At the time Verba wrote, Swedish CEOs received less than three times the earnings of the average worker, while the comparable ratio in the United States was more than ten times greater. (The U.S. ratio would rise much higher still after the explosion of top corporate salaries in the past fifteen years.)

It is equally hard to explain in economic terms alone why the pay of Japanese executives was drawing closer to that of their workers during the 1970s and 1980s, while in America corporate CEOs saw their pay skyrocket even as the wages of their workers stagnated. These trends are scarcely a reflection of supply and demand, since the salaries of lesser executives in the United States were not rising nearly so rapidly as those of CEOs. Nor can comparative economic performance account for the results. After all, these were the years in which Japanese corporations seemed to be outperforming their American counterparts in a whole host of industries.

Such puzzling developments are not confined to big business. How does one account for the fact that in 1990 American physicians earned on average more than three times as much as their counterparts in Britain, France, Sweden, or Japan? This is hardly a difference explainable in traditional economic terms. Neither the supply of nor the demand for doctors' services is determined solely by market forces alone.

It is equally interesting to observe what happened to the earnings in the legal profession in the 1970s and 1980s. Having experienced a long period of moderate growth during the economic boom following World War II, the compensation of partners and associates in large corporate law firms began to rise dramatically after 1975. It would be difficult to explain this sudden growth by economic factors alone. After all, the economy was growing far less rapidly than it did in preceding decades and the supply of new lawyers had risen sharply as a result of the rapid influx of women and baby boomers into the profession. In addition to economic forces, I suspect that one must look carefully at such matters as changes in the organization of large firms and in the motivations of their partners, as well as at the ways corporations choose their outside counsel if one is to comprehend fully what happened to their levels of compensation.

Whatever the causes of inequality may be, it is welcome news to see attention being focused on a broader range of factors to illuminate the study of important economic issues. Such an effort is a necessary antidote to the constant pressure to narrow the framework of analysis not only in economics but in most of the social sciences. Two tendencies in particular push young social scientists in this direction. The first is the familiar desire to achieve greater rigor with the aid of sharper analytical tools by introducing simplifying assumptions that brush aside the messier, less manipulable influences of culture, politics, and human psychology. Such simplification often leads to important insights and intellectual advances that would not be possible by trying to grapple with all the complexities of human behavior and institutions. Nevertheless, if we are to achieve a more complete understanding of human affairs, it is important to balance these technical efforts with attempts to incorporate more of the complexity of life into the analysis.

The other tendency that works to narrow social science is the sheer volume of relevant material that fledgling scholars need to study. When I was much younger and had a chance to talk with an earlier generation of economists— Gunnar Myrdal, Jacob Viner, Wassily Leontieff, and others—I was always struck by their mastery of all the great texts of social science—Adam Smith, Alfred Marshall and Karl Marx, as well as Locke, Mill, Bentham, Weber, Mannheim, and many others. Their understanding of the great intellectual tradition of social science gave these economists a broad perspective even when they wrote about technical subjects. Today, even the introductory course in the history of economic thought is no longer a requirement in most Ph.D. programs. Few doctoral students can afford to linger over the great traditional texts of economics, let alone of social science and political philosophy, in their hectic attempts to gain a reasonable grasp of the mountain of technical literature that has appeared in the last fifty years.

Because there is something so attractive about the power of highly quantitative analysis and simplified models, it is well to be reminded of how easy it is for these techniques to give a distorted and incomplete picture of the world it purports to describe. Thus, it is salutary to have economists such as those summarized in this volume remind us of just how much is lost by disregarding all the other less tangible, less predictable aspects of human, social, and institutional behavior. What Gunnar Myrdal pointed out in 1971 remains equally true today:

> What all social sciences are dealing with is, in the last instance, human behavior. And human behavior is not constant like the movement of celestial bodies or molecules. It is dependent upon, and determined by, the complex of living conditions, the institutions in which people exist, and by their attitudes as those who have been molded by, at the same time as they are reacting against, those living conditions. . . . The isolation of one part of social reality by demarcating it as "economic" is logically not feasible. In reality, there are no "economic," "sociological," or "psychological," problems, but just problems and they are all complex.[2]

As this volume attests, that is certainly true of the problem of inequality.

Notes

1. Sidney Verba, *Elites and the Idea of Equality: A Comparison of Japan, Sweden, and the United States* (1987).
2. *Against the Stream: Critical Essays on Economics* (1972), 139, 142.

Acknowledgments

Putting together the Frontiers volumes is not an easy task. This volume has benefited immensely from the efforts of a number of individuals who we wish to thank.

A number of expert researchers in the field commented on the ever-evolving table of contents for this volume. Most notable were Randy Albelda, Sam Bowles, William Darity, the late Bennett Harrison, Katherine McFate, Dani Rodrik, Chris Tilly, William Julius Wilson, and Edward Wolff.

Early in 1998 we met with colleagues in the Tufts community who have related research interests. We received valuable feedback from Ann Helwege, Rachel Bratt, Molly Mead, and Lisa Lynch.

Our G-DAE colleague Jonathan Harris played a very important role as kibitzer during our marathon staff meetings to review the literature on inequality. Jonathan will take over as director of the final volume in this series.

Graduate research assistants Johanna Meyer and Vijaya Divurri researched a great deal of the early literature for the volume. Johanna will be acting in the same capacity for the final volume of the series. Graduate research assistant Kim Barry did an excellent job compiling data for the overview essays and helping the staff assemble relevant tables.

Part of the secret of our success is hard-working undergraduate library assistant Stacie Bowman, whose meticulous skills and sense of cheer keep the office humming.

Essential backup and support for all of our activities is supplied by the G-DAE office administrator, David Plancon.

We have also been fortunate in receiving institutional support of many kinds. We wish to single out the interlibrary loan office at Tisch Library, which has made possible the retrieval of an astonishing amount of material for this project. Tufts University in general provides an excellent environment for G-DAE's research. We have also benefited from the support of Island Press, and Todd Baldwin in particular.

The funders of the Frontiers project, along with those who support the core activities of G-DAE, provide another, essential type of institutional support. We are indebted to the following funders of volume 5: the Philanthropic Collaborative, the Andrew Mellon Foundation, Fund for the Future, Ford Foundation, Mrs. George O'Neill, the Richard Lounsbery Foundation, and the John D. and Catherine T. MacArthur Foundation.

Volume Introduction

by Neva Goodwin and Frank Ackerman

The hope that economic growth alone will cure poverty, that "a rising tide will lift all boats," has been refuted by events of the late twentieth century. Defying gravity, recent economic tides have flowed uphill, primarily helping those who were already on top. There is, therefore, a need for a deeper examination of the economic theory of the causes, consequences, and cures for inequality.

The goal of *The Political Economy of Inequality* is to bring together the disparate analyses of inequality in economics and related fields, to identify areas where more work is most needed, and to lay the groundwork for an integrated understanding of the causes and consequences of inequality in the United States and the world.

This introduction will begin with some notes on our approach to inequality in particular and to economics in general. The second and third sections discuss the contents of the book from two perspectives: what is excluded and what is included. Some readers may worry that well-known, important articles on inequality have been overlooked; in fact, a number of articles have been intentionally omitted. A positive description of what is included will then provide a more conventional introduction to the contents and organization of the book. The fourth section explains the place of this book within the six-volume series, Frontier Issues in Economic Thought. Many related issues are dealt with in other volumes, especially the previous one, *The Changing Nature of Work*.

A final section of the introduction explains the statistical measures and terminology that appear in much of this book. Skip that section if you are comfortable with discussion of Gini coefficients and income deciles, and you understand what is meant by the ratio of the 90th percentile to the 10th percentile of personal incomes (and why it is a measure of inequality). If you are puzzled by any of the terms or concepts in the previous sentence, read the last part of the introduction.

Why Political Economy?

The analysis of inequality in this book starts from the tradition of political economy—a discipline whose name and roots go back to Adam Smith. In its early days, the name of the field reflected an awareness that political and economic issues and institutions were closely connected. Today, the term "political economy," having largely fallen out of fashion, is used at times to refer to any of three schools of thought: older approaches to macroeconomics in general; radical or Marxian economics in particular; or a new style of theory that incorporates selected, usually quantifiable, pieces of political science into economics. We would be happy to encourage exploration of all of these directions (though the third, as argued later in this book, runs the risk of reducing politics to a narrow formal scheme).

Our reason for adopting the unfashionable term is to emphasize the close connection between the politics and the economics of inequality. Our approach thus differs from the standard approach of the discipline, which, for most of the twentieth century, has shed its overt interest in politics and simply called itself "economics." Sometimes the name is extended to "neoclassical economics" in contradistinction to the "classical" eighteenth and nineteenth century precursors of the field.

The tools of neoclassical economics are recognized by all concerned to be far more powerful for addressing issues of efficiency than for those of equity. As regards the political economist's concerns, the neoclassical economist deals with the distribution of income in a rather gingerly fashion, focusing on those aspects of the subject that are most amenable to the neoclassical methodology.

Even more striking is the difference with respect to power. While there is relatively little room for this topic in neoclassical economics, a characteristic assumption of political economy is that behind, or connected to, most significant issues of inequality one can expect to find inequalities of power. A related assumption is the expectation that power is often used by its possessors to get more of it. This can involve a competitive struggle among titans, or it can be a process of taking power and other things away from those who have less to start with.

How power will be used depends, in large part, on where it is lodged: in private hands, in impersonal institutions (such as the market), or in more obviously political institutions (such as government). The political dimension introduces the issue of rights, standards of fairness, and ethical judgments. An individual, a firm, or a market may have no direct, formal obligations to other individuals, save to avoid doing harm. In contrast, a government is almost certain to have more extensive obligations to individuals. What rights and entitlements should the government, acting on behalf of society, guarantee to all?

Debate over the questions of rights and entitlements is at the heart of the political process. The fundamental problem of inequality—the reason for articles, books, and analyses on the subject—is that *many people believe that developed societies such as the United States have an ethically unacceptable level of poverty and inequality.* This is, as economists love to point out, a value judgment and not a testable scientific hypothesis. Yet it has inspired vast amounts of scientific and scholarly work on income distribution and related topics—far more than most properly proscribed, testable hypotheses. In particular, that judgment has inspired the editors to produce this book and has, we believe, inspired most or all of the authors whose work is summarized here.

Seeking to avoid controversial or "unscientific" value judgments, economic theorists have relied heavily on the Pareto principle: *A change can only be regarded as an improvement if no one experiences a loss, while at least one person gains.* This principle is only superficially neutral and value-free, as an extensive debate has shown (see our earlier volume, *Human Well-Being and Economic Goals*). In the attempt to avoid unscientific judgments, neoclassical economics has accepted a principle that gives overwhelming priority to the status quo.

The concerns represented in this volume are, therefore, propelled from outside of economic theory. Community and labor organizations, many religious groups, journalists, and much of the general public see the wide and widening gap in access to resources between the top and bottom of society as a critical defect of the modern market economy. However, the economics profession has tended to restrict its analysis of inequality, paying too little attention to why the topic matters or to serious proposals for action. When economists view inequality as a technical consequence of differences in factor endowments and marginal productivity, it emerges as an inevitable fact of life that is not subject to moral judgment. When they look at inequality as an issue of social preferences, economists sometimes discuss lump-sum redistribution as a possible, theoretically interesting, response—but one that bears little or no relationship to the world of practical policy.

Fortunately this narrow framework has begun to loosen up. In the 1990s, parts of the economics mainstream gave a good deal of attention to issues of inequality; we will say more about the mainstream contributions in a moment. The recent high-water mark for recognition of alternative approaches was the award of the 1998 Nobel Prize in economics to Amartya Sen. Sen's contributions to the economics and philosophy of poverty and inequality are mentioned in several places in this book, and were discussed in depth in our earlier volume, *Human Well-Being and Economic Goals.*

What Is Not Included in This Book

It would not be possible for one book to include everything important that has been written about the economics of inequality. In any case, we have not attempted to produce such a book. Our goal is to draw attention to new contributions on the frontiers of economics, highlighting analyses and theories that deserve a wider audience. At the same time we want to acknowledge the importance of many articles on inequality that have appeared in the most widely circulated economics journals in recent years. If we had simply selected prominent recent treatments of inequality, we could have filled this book with articles from the top journals. That might have been a valuable book to produce, but it would have been a different one.

We suspect that most readers of this book can obtain access to the most widely circulated economics journals. Full text of many of them is available for downloading at www.jstor.org, with a delay of a few years after publication. Therefore we have decided not to summarize articles in *American Economic Review, Journal of Economic Literature, Journal of Economic Perspectives, Quarterly Journal of Economics,* and *Journal of Political Economy.*[1] Major contributions that appear in these journals are discussed in our overview essays throughout this book, particularly in Part I. The bibliography at the end of the book contains complete citations for these and other works mentioned in our essays, as well as for the works we have summarized.

The subject of inequality is an inherently quantitative one, more so than the topics of our earlier volumes. We have included tables and graphs in each of our overview essays to illustrate the issues of inequality, but we have not come close to providing a comprehensive set of data on any of the problems discussed here. That, too, would require an entire, different book. An excellent source for data on inequality in the United States is *The State of Working America,* published every two years by the Economic Policy Institute (Mishel et al. 1999). We have relied heavily on it for our tables and graphs, and we thank the authors for permission to reprint many selections from their work. Other data sources are noted on the tables and graphs.

A number of economists, including Anthony Atkinson, Amartya Sen, and others, have analyzed the characteristics of different possible measures of poverty and inequality. This literature typically suggests that the standard measures are inadequate, and that other, less familiar measures would be theoretically preferable. The argument is often persuasive as a matter of pure theory, but it remains disjointed from empirical work on inequality. In practice, a few familiar measures of inequality, above all the Gini coefficient and percentile ratios (both of which are explained at the end of this introduction), are almost universally used; data limitations generally preclude the use of more sophisticated measures. Therefore we have omitted most of the literature on alternative formulas for measuring inequality. Galbraith (1998), summarized in Part I, uses one of the alternative measures for wage inequality; yet recognizing its unfamiliarity, he shows that it is highly correlated with the Gini coefficient, in order to justify its use. Nolan and Whelan (1996), summarized in Part V, discuss interesting new approaches to the definition and measurement of poverty, related to some of Sen's theories.

The boundaries of the literature reviewed and considered for inclusion in this book remain similar to those that applied in our previous volumes. We have attempted to survey books and journals published in English that relate to the political economy of inequality. In a few cases we cite working papers from research institutes, but we have not attempted to survey the universe of working papers in general. The time lags for publication are unfortunately long; our research was almost entirely conducted in 1998.

What Is Included in This Book

What remains after all these exclusions is, hopefully, a coherent story about the theory and reality of inequality. The fundamental problem motivating our work, and the work we discuss, is the abrupt increase in income inequality in the United States, Britain, and many other countries in the last quarter of the twentieth century. That trend is all the more striking in contrast to the preceding period. In the 25 to 30 years after World War II, average incomes rose rapidly while the distribution of income grew slightly more equal. In retrospect, some economists have called that earlier era "the golden age"—a name that should be interpreted as referring only to aggregate economic performance, not to the more tarnished details of society, culture, or even the distribution of economic resources.

It was easier to be optimistic about the pursuit of equity in the earlier period. Economic growth was lifting the poorest members of society (and everyone else) up to steadily higher levels of consumption. Some inequities of the past would, it appeared, be automatically eliminated by growth; and the rising prosperity seemed to be creating the resources needed to tackle more stubborn problems. All of that changed in the 1970s, in a transformation that Bennett Harrison and Barry Bluestone dubbed "the great U-turn" (Harrison and Bluestone 1988). Suddenly the much slower growth of average incomes, combined with a rapidly widening gap between rich and poor, meant that many experienced declining real incomes. At the same time there was a "revolution of declining expectations" regarding the ability of the public sector to cure social ills. In short, the political economy of inequality is a problem much farther from solution than it used to be.

Our treatment of inequality is divided into ten parts. We begin in Part I with *the distribution of earnings,* the largest and most often studied component of personal income. Here the mainstream literature makes a substantial contribution, including extensive empirical studies that delineate the problem of rising inequality. However, that literature relies too heavily on unexplained technological change as the deus ex machina that is expected to resolve the mystery. Similar technologies are used in countries with very different degrees of inequality. Institutional factors such as the strength of the labor movement and labor legislation are too often neglected, as is the change in corporate strategy in the 1970s—a theme that will recur in several parts of the book. Intergenerational persistence of inequality, a topic that draws on analyses of the labor market, the family, and the educational system, deserves greater attention.

A major source of intergenerational inequality is, of course, the inheritance of wealth. Part II turns to *the distribution of wealth*, which is far more unequal than the distribution of income. The wealthiest 1 percent of the population holds literally half to two-thirds of many categories of personal wealth; the assets of millions of small investors, and millions of small business owners, pale by comparison. The inequality of wealth differs from one country to another and changes significantly over time, proving that it is not an immutable constant of a market economy. Wealth is important because it generates income, because it provides economic security, and because it is a source of economic power. The relationship of wealth to economic power raises a classic debate: Do stock owners or managers control corporations? The sociologists who have written about this (economists have not, in recent years) suggest that owners and top management are socialized into a network of common interests, rather than being separate, competitive groups.

Not everyone at the top of the income distribution got there through success in business or through inheritance. There are numerous celebrities and chief executive officers (CEOs) of businesses who receive multimillion dollar annual compensation. These new paths to the top, or celebrity and CEO incomes, are the subject of Part III. "Winner-take-all" markets are increasingly common in business, professions, sports, and other forms of entertainment. Ever-escalating payments to CEOs are defended by the claim that top managers need to own stock in order to identify with stockholders—but the theoretical and empirical literature reaches ambiguous conclusions, and the only certain result is the enrichment of the CEOs. The "economics of superstars" suggests that those who dominate the entertainment world may have little or no greater talent than the second-tier performers. In major league sports, free agency and burgeoning broadcast revenues have allowed star players to command greater and greater salaries, based on measurable but small differences in ability. The common thread through all these stories is that while superstar and CEO salaries may sometimes reflect the individual's marginal revenue, that revenue results from a monopoly position, not from a competitive market-based determination of the value of a person's efforts. The new structure of monopoly positions created in winner-take-all markets is a fundamental source of inequality and a challenge to standard economic theory.

We complete our look at the top of the distribution of power and income in Part IV, with a discussion of *the effects of corporate power*. Neoclassical economics ignores the issue of power, assuming that it cannot exist in a competitive market. A new approach to economic theory is needed, in which unequal power is recognized as a normal, endogenous result of market relationships. Corporations clearly do exert vast power over their workers, communities, the environment, and the workings of government. A change in corporate strategy in the 1970s, pursuing increased competitiveness by slashing costs and squeezing labor, was the basis for the "great U-turn" and a major cause of the subsequent increase in inequality. At the same time, corporations became more politically engaged, switching from usually passive support of a business-friendly, bipartisan status quo to active backing of extremely partisan conservative interests. Despite the abundant bad news, corporations have been known to do good things—for the environment, for example, or for their customers. A provocative new line of discussion calls for identifying the circumstances under which corporations behave in socially desirable ways, and developing policies to promote and expand those circumstances.

At the bottom of the income distribution we encounter the problems of *poverty*, the subject of Part V. The definition of poverty and the description of its effects raise surprisingly complex theoretical issues; deprivation of a society's basic consumption goods may be a better indicator of poverty than lack of money alone. European discussion of poverty has focused on the concept of exclusion, a related but broader measure of nonparticipation in the economic, social, and political mainstream of society. Poverty in the United States has worsened since the 1970s, accompanied by an increasingly unsympathetic climate of public opinion and a retreat or reversal of government anti-poverty efforts. Effective responses will require a broad understanding of the political economy of inequality—along with renewed public sector initiatives, a subject we return to at the end of the book.

There are many dimensions of inequality beyond the obvious categories of rich and poor. Part VI takes up the crucial questions of *household roles and family structure.* One branch of neoclassical economics, following Gary Becker, has romanticized the dynamics within the household: an all-powerful household head, normally male, earns the market income and distributes it altruistically to meet the needs of all family members. In contrast, feminist economists emphasize the likelihood of divergent goals, inequalities of power and bargaining strength, and the reality of conflict among household members. Empirical research in many cultures shows that family incomes are not always pooled, and that women are more likely than men to spend a pay raise on their children's welfare. Family structure has a clear link to poverty: Families headed by single mothers are far more likely to be poor in most cultures; in the United States most poor children are in single-mother families. Other countries such as Sweden have done far better in alleviating poverty among children and single mothers, through a variety of labor force, child care, and welfare policies.

Hypotheses about changes in *skills and technologies* play a large role in the economics of inequality; as a result, policies that address inequality often stress *education* as a route to increased skills. Part VII addresses these questions. In the 1980s the supply of college-educated workers grew faster than the labor force as a whole, while the earnings of college-educated workers grew faster than average earnings. According to most economists, this proves the existence of technical change that increased the relative demand for skilled work. Yet identifying the precise relationship is difficult: While those who use computers or other new technologies are paid well, correlation does not imply causation. The upsurge in computerization of workplaces came some years after the biggest increases in wage inequality. Similarly, education is widely seen as a route to upward mobility, but it is equally possible for the educational system to preserve preexisting inequalities. The role of wage-setting institutions and labor legislation must be addressed along with education in order to have a lasting effect on the distribution of earnings.

Categorical inequalities such as those based on race, gender, or ethnicity are the subject of Part VIII. The inegalitarian legacies of the long traditions of racial segregation and patriarchal society continue to shape the distribution of income today. Racial inequality is increasingly correlated with geographical segregation into separate and unequal communities, where differential resources lead to unequal outcomes for the next generation. Environmental hazards are disproportionately likely to be found in minority communities—not necessarily by cynical choice, but perhaps because the arrival of a hazardous facility makes any neighborhood unattractive, leading those with any resources to move out and those with the fewest alternatives to move in. Cynical choices are more evident in the recent revival of claims of a genetic basis for existing racial differences in income and education; these are no more substantial than in past discredited episodes of pseudo-scientific racism.

Segregation by gender poses some similar and some different issues. The female/male income ratio has been rising, though more of the change in recent years is due to men's average decline than to women's advances. Occupational segregation by gender remains strong almost everywhere, though the definition of men's and women's jobs varies from one country to another. Wage differentials by gender vary as well, with Scandinavian countries having quite narrow wage differentials despite the persistence of occupational segregation. The pursuit of remedies for gender inequality leads to the complex questions of comparable worth and affirmative action; the backlash against affirmative action threatens to undermine the progress that has been made toward both gender and racial inequality.

Inequality on a global scale is the subject of an extensive literature, which we examine in Part IX. The vast differences in average income from one country to another are dramatized in a classic illustration that is updated in Figure IX.1. There is an ongoing debate as to whether countries are converging in income over time; both sides of this debate are represented in interesting analyses summarized in Part IX. Regarding income distribution within countries, Simon Kuznets hypothesized that in the course of development a country would first become less equal, then more. Evidence on the resulting Kuznets curve is weak at best, with persistent differences between developing countries far greater than changes over time within any one nation. The related "environmental Kuznets curve," hypothesizing that pollution first gets worse, then better as a country develops, has led to a literature that is still in its infancy. The prescriptions of conventional economic theory for developing countries, including free trade, privatization, and, when necessary, structural adjustment programs, have varied or ambiguous implications for inequality, as shown in a wide range of research. Political strategies that explicitly pursue equality need not hurt, and if adopted skillfully may even help, the process of development.

Finally, in Part X we turn to political responses to inequality, as represented in *the welfare state*. The rise of inequality in the late twentieth century, as noted earlier, was accompanied by a retreat from belief in the efficacy of state intervention. There are no solid theoretical grounds for this retreat; an inherently imperfect world leaves ample room for conscious intervention and improvement. In the real world, welfare state programs do equalize incomes, and many forms of "interference" with markets, such as minimum wage laws, do not paralyze the private sector. The Anglo-American, continental European, and Scandinavian varieties of welfare states have differing implications for income redistribution, poverty, and welfare, with the first and last, epitomized by the United States and Sweden, as polar cases. Sweden's far more humane approach nearly eliminates poverty, incorporating as many people as possible into the world of jobs, social services, and institutional supports. In the United States the government spends less and accomplishes less in the area of income redistribution, allowing shockingly high levels of child poverty to persist in the midst of affluence. There are many differences between the two countries, notably including the strength of the labor movement; the labor-based Social Democratic Party, which has governed Sweden almost continuously for more than 60 years, is the architect of its welfare state policies. The only important argument for the minimalist American approach to welfare is that it reduces taxes and thereby stimulates growth. Yet Sweden and other Scandinavian countries have not fallen into permanent stagnation, and have recovered from earlier economic slumps with only moderate cutbacks in their public programs. Thus there remains, in practice as well as in theory, a viable choice about the extent and generosity of public efforts to redistribute income.

Frontiers of Economics: The Series

This book is the fifth in a six-volume series, Frontier Issues in Economic Thought. Each volume focuses on a "frontier" area where important new work is being done but has not yet been incorporated into the standard definition of economics.

A Survey of Ecological Economics (Krishnan et al. 1995), our first volume, ex-

plores the new field that is emerging at the intersection of economics and ecological concerns. Important work is being done toward the construction of an
economics that recognizes resource constraints and requirements, incorporates
the concept of natural capital, and locates economic activity within a biosphere
of finite carrying capacity.

The Consumer Society (Goodwin et al. 1996) examines the process and the
meaning of consumption, topics that have become the subject of creative recent
analyses in many social sciences other than economics. Well-known work by unconventional economists such as Thorstein Veblen and John Kenneth Galbraith
has become part of the common understanding of consumption in other social
sciences, but ironically has been ignored in mainstream economics.

Human Well-Being and Economic Goals (Ackerman et al. 1997) addresses the
underlying philosophical question: Which economic goals and activities actually
contribute to human well-being? Beyond a minimal level, which developed
countries on average have surely exceeded, it is far from obvious that increased
consumption of material goods is what people fundamentally need or want.
The view of human well-being that is implicit in neoclassical economics rests on
a thin and shaky philosophical foundation, which is at odds with virtually all
major ethical and religious beliefs.

The Changing Nature of Work (Ackerman et al. 1998) discusses new developments in labor economics and industrial relations, viewed in the light of the
ongoing transformation of work in the late twentieth century. It can be considered a companion to the present volume, addressing many of the same themes.
The shift toward greater inequality beginning in the 1970s, and the debate over
the relative importance of trade, technology, and labor market institutions,
make their appearance in *The Changing Nature of Work* and continue in this
book. The relative lack of emphasis on labor and the work process in *The Political Economy of Inequality* reflects the fact that we treated these subjects at
length in our previous volume.

Our final volume, on the economics of sustainable development, is scheduled
for publication in 2001.

Each book has the same format as the one you are reading, and is produced
by the same process. We begin with an extensive review of thousands of possible books and articles on our subject, ultimately leading to the selection of 70
to 90 leading articles and chapters. We summarize them in short, usually 3-page
summaries, longer than abstracts but much shorter than the full text. This format allows the reader to get an overview of a range of articles in the field that
would be close to inaccessible. We try to represent the authors' points of view,
and often phrasing, as accurately as possible, but the summaries are written by
us, not the original authors. We have, however, obtained the authors' approval
of the summaries, and have incorporated any changes requested by the authors.
Introductory essays by the editors review the field, cite other literature that we

have not summarized, and situate the summarized articles within our overview of the subject.

In this volume, for the first time, we have created a combined bibliography of all cited and summarized works at the end of the book. Names of authors whose works are summarized appear in boldface the first time they are mentioned in overview essays.

Measures of Inequality

Inequality is an inherently quantitative subject. The articles and empirical results presented in this book frequently discuss numerical measures of inequality in order to summarize and compare one distribution of income or wealth to another. As in previous Frontiers volumes, we have attempted to avoid mathematical and statistical jargon, and to summarize in prose the significance of mathematically complex analyses. However, it is impossible to avoid using the standard statistical measures of inequality. The remainder of this introduction explains those measures, for readers who are unfamiliar with them.

How can one measure the degree of inequality in one country's income distribution, and compare it to another country, or to the same country at another time? Theorists have proposed many possible measures and have debated their relative merits. Yet only two measures are in widespread use: percentile ratios and Gini coefficients. These two measures, and some related terminology, are all you need to know about statistics to understand the discussion of inequality in this book.

Both measures of inequality are best understood by imagining that the population is lined up, say from left to right, in order of increasing income. Positions along that line are often expressed in percentiles (hundredths) of the distance from left to right. At the 50th percentile, or halfway along the line, is the person with the median income; that is the definition of the median. To refer to categories of people at different income levels, it is common to divide the line into quintiles (fifths) or deciles (tenths).[2] The leftmost, or poorest, quintile is the group of people between the 0 and 20th percentile positions. The rightmost, or richest, decile is the group of people between the 90th and 100th percentiles. Many of the articles in this book discuss the shares of total income going to various quintiles or deciles of the population.

The simpler of the standard measures, the percentile ratio, takes the income of a person at one position in the line and divides by the income of the person at another position. Most common is the ratio of the income at the 90th percentile to the income at the 10th percentile, sometimes abbreviated P_{90}/P_{10}. An alternative is P_{80}/P_{20}, the ratio of the 80th to 20th percentile. In either case, a bigger ratio means a greater spread between someone near the top and someone near the bottom of the income distribution; that is, a larger ratio means

more inequality. Other ratios can easily be created. Some analyses have compared top, middle, and bottom incomes by calculating both the P_{90}/P_{50} and
the P_{50}/P_{10} ratios.

A drawback of percentile ratios is that they use information on only two, or a
few, points in the income distribution. The other standard measure, the Gini
coefficient, uses the whole income distribution in the following manner. First,
find the cumulative share of total income received by everyone up to each income level. That is, for each person in line, calculate the share of total income
received by that person and everyone to his/her left. Then plot these shares, as
shown in the accompanying graph.

If income were perfectly equally distributed, the graph would look like the
diagonal line in the figure: The first 20 percent of the population would receive
20 percent of total income, 40 percent of the population would receive 40 percent, and so on. On the other hand, if the distribution were perfectly unequal,
so that one person got everything, the graph would follow the horizontal axis
(indicating no income) until it reached the last person, and then shoot up along
the vertical line shown in the figure. Neither of these extremes ever occurs; instead, the graph falls somewhere in between, typically looking somewhat like
the curved line in the figure.

The Gini coefficient, or Gini ratio (the terms are used interchangeably), is the
ratio of area A to area A+B. It ranges from a minimum of 0 at perfect equality
to a maximum of 1 at perfect inequality. A larger Gini coefficient indicates a society that is farther away from perfect equality, or in other words a more unequal society. The shape of the entire curve—that is, the pattern of income distribution at every level—clearly affects the relative sizes of A and B, and hence
affects the Gini coefficient. The actual Gini coefficients for income distribution
reported in this book range from 0.23 for the most equal European countries
to about 0.60 for Brazil, the most unequal major country.

Since the Gini coefficient conveys more complete information about the distribution of income, why would anyone choose to use percentile ratios? The

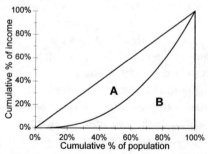

The Gini Coefficient: Defined as Area A/(A+B)

weakness of the Gini coefficient is that it is sensitive to data on the extremes of the distribution, where underreporting and measurement errors are thought to be most common. Income data in the United States, and probably in most countries, are affected by the so-called "top-coding" problem. Census Bureau surveys, from which most income distribution data are derived, have limited categories and a fixed number of digits for recording individual incomes. Incomes above the highest category are arbitrarily coded as falling at the top of that category. Years ago, when six-figure salaries were almost unheard of, incomes were top-coded at $99,999. In 1993 the top code was raised from $299,999 to $999,999, causing an artificial jump in the Gini coefficient due to more complete reporting on the highest-income households. (Some incomes at the very bottom may suffer from problems of intentional or accidental underreporting, although this is less widely discussed.)

Percentile ratios avoid the problems of top-coding and of sensitivity to the extremes of the distribution in general. The individual at the 90th percentile of the income distribution is far below the level at which top-coding occurs. Thus the P_{90}/P_{10} ratio, although reflecting much less information about the overall distribution, is more reliable and entirely based on actual income measurements, free of statistical quirks.

For many purposes these two measures yield qualitatively similar results. Table I.4 presents both Gini coefficients and P_{90}/P_{10} ratios for many countries, allowing a comparison of the two standards. The ranking of countries by the two measures is very similar, though not quite identical.

Notes

1. One exception, for a valuable and little-noticed argument that does not appear elsewhere, is included in Part IX.
2. There is a slight inconsistency in the terminology as it is typically used. A percentile could conceivably refer to a range; for example, the 50th percentile could refer to everyone who is between 49 percent and 50 percent of the way from left to right. In common usage, however, the 50th percentile refers to the one person who is exactly 50 percent of the way along the line; that is, percentiles are interpreted as points, not ranges. Quintiles and deciles, on the other hand, typically refer to ranges, not points. The fifth decile is understood to mean everyone who is between the 40 percent and 50 percent positions, and similarly for other deciles and quintiles.

PART I

Unequal Earnings: Theory versus Reality

Overview Essay

by Frank Ackerman

Thirty years ago, economists had relatively little to say about the distribution of income. U.S. data for the first few decades after World War II showed that nearly constant shares of personal income were received by those at the top, middle, and bottom of the economic ladder. The small changes that did occur were in the direction of greater equality. Under such conditions, income distribution did not seem like an urgent or dramatic topic. Little research was done on the economics of this apparently unchanging pattern.

What a difference a generation makes. In the last quarter of the twentieth century the distribution of income became far more unequal—particularly in the United States but also, to varying degrees, in many other developed countries. The rapid rise of income inequality is documented in many sources, such as the biannual "State of Working America," published by the Economic Policy Institute (Lawrence Mishel, Jared Bernstein, and John Schmitt 1998). Table I.1 shows both the near constancy of the distribution of family income from 1947 through the 1970s and the clear growth in inequality since then.

The question about inequality is no longer, "Why is it nearly constant?," but rather, "Why has it changed so dramatically?" A growing number of economists have focused on the dynamics of income distribution, examining many pieces of the puzzling picture of inequality. Since wages and salaries account for the bulk of household income, much of the analysis has focused on the distribution of earnings. Table I.2 demonstrates that real wages have declined for most workers but have risen for those at the top, resulting in a widening disparity: In 1979 the 90th-percentile worker's hourly wage was 3.5 times that of the 10th-percentile worker; by 1997 the same ratio had risen to 4.4.

An increase in inequality of the magnitude shown in Tables I.1 and I.2 has profound implications. It leads to the hollowing out of the middle-income strata, as shown in Table I.3. The share of the population falling between 50 and 200 percent of the median income has declined from 71 percent to 62 per-

1

Table I.1. Shares of Family Income, 1947–1997

	Lowest fifth (%)	Second fifth (%)	Middle fifth (%)	Fourth fifth (%)	Top fifth (%)	Within the top fifth		Gini ratio
						Bottom 15 percent	Top 5 percent	
1947	5.0	11.09	17.0	23.1	43.0	25.5	17.5	0.376
1967	5.4	12.2	17.5	23.5	41.4	25.0	16.4	0.358
1973	5.5	11.9	17.5	24.0	41.1	25.6	15.5	0.356
1979	5.4	11.6	17.5	24.1	41.4	26.1	15.3	0.365
1989	4.6	10.6	16.5	23.7	44.6	26.7	17.9	0.401
1997	4.2	9.9	15.7	23.0	47.2	26.5	20.7	0.429

Source: Excerpt from Table 1.6, p. 49 in Mishel, Lawrence, Jared Bernstein, and John Schmitt. *The State of Working America 1998–1999*. Ithaca, NY: Cornell University Press, 1999.

Table I.2. Real Hourly Wages for all Workers by Percentile, 1973–97

	Percentile									Ratio of 90th/10th
	10th	20th	30th	40th	50th	60th	70th	80th	90th	
Hourly wage (in 1997 $)										
1973	6.07	7.33	8.70	10.13	11.61	13.32	15.46	17.68	22.22	3.66
1979	6.42	7.33	8.61	10.13	11.46	13.27	15.69	18.29	22.46	3.5
1989	5.39	6.71	8.05	9.62	11.18	13.05	15.53	18.57	23.46	4.35
1997	5.46	6.74	7.94	9.25	10.82	12.59	15.08	18.37	23.90	4.38
Percent Change										
1973–79	5.8	0.0	-1.0	0.0	-1.3	-0.4	1.5	3.5	1.1	-4.4
1979–89	-16.0	-8.5	-6.5	-5.0	-2.4	-1.7	-1.0	1.5	4.5	24.4
1989–97	1.3	0.4	-1.4	-3.8	-3.2	-2.8	-2.9	-1.1	1.9	0.6

Source: Excerpt from Table 3.6, p. 131 in Mishel, Lawrence, Jared Bernstein, and John Schmitt. *The State of Working America 1998–1999*. Ithaca, NY: Cornell University Press, 1999.

cent since 1969. As a result, there has been a loss of economic status and security for those forced to move downward, and an interruption of upward career paths and possibilities for those just starting out. Beyond the statistical details there are moral and philosophical questions: How much inequality is ethically tolerable in a humane and affluent society? There are social and political dilemmas of the costs and objectives of social welfare, and of the impacts of poverty and crime. In economics, the rise of inequality calls for at least creative extension, if not fundamental revision, of standard theories.

The economic analysis of inequality is the subject of this book as a whole. This part focuses on the distribution of earnings; later parts will examine other sources of income, such as property income in Part II. Other parts will also provide a more detailed look at categories and causes of inequality in earnings. This essay begins with a survey of the treatment of inequality in mainstream economics, and then opens four areas for further discussion: models of intergenerational mobility; the corporate initiatives, beginning in the 1970s, that have

Table I.3. Distribution of Persons Relative to Income Level, 1969–97

Percent of Median Income	1969	1979	1989	1997
0–50	18.0	20.1	22.1	22.3
50–200	71.2	68.0	63.2	61.6
200+	10.8	11.9	14.7	16.1
Total	100.0	100.0	100.0	100.0

Source: Excerpt from Table 1.11, p. 61 in Mishel, Lawrence, Jared Bernstein, and John Schmitt. *The State of Working America 1998–1999*. Ithaca, NY: Cornell University Press, 1999).

promoted inequality; the importance of an institutional perspective on inequality; and the changing role of family structures as a key to some of the puzzles about income distribution.

The View from the Mainstream

The subject of income inequality has not been ignored by economists. Indeed, it has received high-profile attention, including two major survey articles in the *Journal of Economic Literature* (Frank Levy and Richard Murnane 1992, Peter Gottschalk and Timothy Smeeding 1997) and a symposium in the *Journal of Economic Perspectives* (Gottschalk 1997, George Johnson 1997, Robert Topel 1997, Nicole Fortin and Thomas Lemieux 1997).

The mainstream consensus includes a recognition of the rise in inequality, and makes at least the following points:

- The wage premium for skill and/or education has increased, even while the labor force was becoming more skilled and educated. That is, both the price and the quantity of skilled labor have been increasing at the same time. Thus there must have been a shift in demand favoring skilled labor.

- Globalization and trade competition can explain only a small part of this shift. The growth of inequality began before trade was very important, and it affects sectors producing nontradeable as well as tradeable goods and services.

- The shift must therefore involve skill-biased technical change, which has emerged as a favorite, widely cited explanation.[1] For example, "Wage inequality has risen in modern economies because rising demands for skills have made talented people more scarce." (Topel 1997, p.69) This key point is discussed further in Part VII.

- "Residual" inequality within homogeneous skill and demographic groups has grown, including (but not limited to) industry-specific and firm-specific wage differentials. The rise of residual inequality demonstrates the growing importance of unobserved skills and/or the need for more research.

Institutions must affect the distribution of income, as suggested by the contrast between Anglo-American experience and the much more egalitarian outcomes in Europe; however, the role of institutions is hard to measure. (Among the authors cited earlier, a much greater emphasis is given to institutions by Fortin and Lemieux. It may not be coincidental that they are Canadians, viewing the United States from the outside.)

The mainstream literature on income distribution makes a substantial contribution to our understanding of the problem. Detailed empirical studies have isolated many demographic and other aspects of inequality, and have illuminated a number of mechanisms that lead to unequal labor market outcomes. The leading literature reviews, cited earlier, discuss a number of the issues and authors presented in this book, though often giving the more challenging new perspectives a modest role. In short, we want to recognize the good intentions and the thoughtful contributions of many mainstream authors writing about income distribution—while still objecting to the theoretical and methodological limitations that constrain their work. The consensus view of the economics profession assumes that income distribution, like many other issues, is best understood as a result of the workings of supply and demand, combined with exogenous technological change. These factors are assumed to be expressed through efficient markets, with little reference to history, institutions, or location; institutional factors are unquantifiable and, for the most part, are therefore ignored.

In contrast, the articles summarized here extend, build on, and argue with the consensus, developing a richer picture of inequality as rooted in real-world economic institutions (which are far more complex than efficient markets) and reflecting the exercise of political and economic power within those institutions. Some of the issues raised here were addressed in our previous volume, *The Changing Nature of Work*, which is in many ways a companion to this book.

Models and Mobility

The first article summarized here is by **Anthony Atkinson**,[2] an economist who is well-known for his numerous studies of income distribution. Atkinson emphasizes that there is more to income distribution than the patterns of labor earnings; capital income and government taxes and transfers are also important. The sharpest increase in inequality in Britain, in the late 1980s, occurred when inequality of earnings was not growing—but capital income, received disproportionately by the rich, was rising, and government policy was becoming more regressive. In Atkinson's view, the standard story about skill-biased technical change is important but incomplete as an account of wage determination. Other themes, many of them drawn from sociology or political science, are needed as well.

As an example of the positive contribution of economic theory, Atkinson cites a model of the role of education costs in determining intergenerational mobility—if unskilled workers can afford to educate their children to a high level of skills, society will converge toward equality in the long run; if not, inequality will persist indefinitely. Another model in which educational costs are the key to the persistence of inequality is presented by Steven Durlauf (1996). Rich families can afford to buy more expensive houses in communities with better schools, so their children receive a better education—which enables them to earn higher incomes. Local financing of schools, combined with the initial inequality of resources, allows the endogenous creation and perpetuation of inequality in this model.

Modeling intergenerational mobility, while assuming that many features of the economic system will remain unchanged across a span of lifetimes, may seem like an extreme in implausible abstraction. Yet the intergenerational persistence of inequality is a serious challenge to many theories that rely on an opposite, implausible premise—the implicit or explicit assumption that everyone begins life with equal opportunities. George Borjas (1994) finds that economic inequalities among early twentieth-century immigrants to America remain detectable for at least two generations. Nancy Stokey (1998) surveys the empirical evidence on mobility and explains how methodological flaws in some past studies have led to misleadingly low estimates of the persistence of inequality.

You Take the High Road and I'll Take the Low Road

The wide scope and long historical sweep of the studies of intergenerational mobility is valuable for many purposes. Yet such theories cannot easily explain the shift from relatively stable to rapidly growing inequality in the late twentieth century. For that we must turn to more specific investigations of recent political and economic changes.

The loss of traditional blue-collar employment since the early 1970s and the associated decline in earnings, particularly for men without college education, is a central theme in *The Changing Nature of Work*. The discussion there identified three broad hypotheses that have been advanced to explain the changes in the workplace, each of which has an obvious parallel in the discussion of inequality. The loss of traditional jobs and earnings could be due to computerization and other changes in workplace technology; or to globalization and intensified trade competition; or to political and institutional factors that are reshaping the labor market. Strong arguments were presented for the importance of all three hypotheses in that volume, and all three reappear in this book as well. The role of technology is a major topic in Part VII, and issues of globalization are addressed in Part IX. The three hypotheses need not be mutually exclusive; for example, Barry Bluestone (1994) argues that global competition could cause both skill-biased technical change and declines in unionization.

This part presents several authors who support the third hypothesis. That is, they attribute the change in the U.S. distribution of earnings to the visible exercise of economic power and to an abrupt change in the prevailing pattern of labor relations. **Bennett Harrison and Barry Bluestone** were among the first to draw attention to "the great U-turn" in average wages and the shrinking of the middle class—as seen, for example, in Table I.3. The article summarized here was published in 1990, before their thesis was as well known as it is today; they make their case persuasively for the magnitude and duration of the changes in distribution, and relate these changes to new trends in the workplace.

David Gordon makes a related argument in more popular, less technical terms, emphasizing that major corporations have chosen the "low road" in labor relations as a competitive strategy. Layoffs, wage cuts, and outsourcing are unattractive to workers, but are one way for employers to restore profits in the face of growing competition. Other chapters of Gordon's book present his reasons for maintaining that growing inequality is not primarily a result of trends in technology or trade. Rather, he argues that inequality results from a conscious, strategic response to economic problems by leading businesses. Companies could choose to take the "high road," investing in retraining workers when needed, and seeking cooperative, high-wage, high-productivity routes to competitiveness. But, as Gordon observes, there is a strong temptation to take the low road and pursue short-term cost reduction. America is largely lacking in the legal and institutional restraints on the labor market that might support the choice of the high road.

The corporate strategies described by Gordon result in an intensification of the dualism or segmentation of the labor market into distinct primary and secondary sectors. The primary sector offers jobs with good wages and working conditions, opportunity for advancement, returns to education and training, and formalized labor relations that circumscribe supervisors' authority. The secondary sector offers the opposite in most or all of these respects. Workers clearly prefer primary sector jobs; there is generally an excess supply of labor willing to work in the primary sector at the prevailing wages. The low road corporate strategy consists in large part of forcing more workers into the secondary sector in order to lower labor costs. Early research on dual labor markets, some of it by Gordon, provoked technical controversies that led some economists to dismiss the concept. A revised dual labor market theory, responding to earlier critiques and presenting new empirical research, can be found in William Dickens and Kevin Lang (1985). A much more complete but less widely available publication of their work (Dickens and Lang 1993) is summarized in *The Changing Nature of Work*.

Institutionalizing Inequality

Technology and trade have affected most developed countries in relatively similar ways. Yet the levels of inequality differ sharply from one country to another, as shown in Table I.4. The ratio of the 90th percentile to the 10th percentile individual's income was 3 or less in several northern European countries, compared to almost 6 in the United States. (The similar-sounding ratio in Table I.2 referred to hourly wages, rather than annual income.[3]) Such striking contrasts among similarly affluent, industrialized countries suggest the importance of differing national institutions. This argument makes occasional appearances in many leading articles on income distribution; it is the principal topic of Fortin and Lemieux (1997).

The pattern of national differences in labor market institutions is also the starting point for **Richard Freeman and Lawrence Katz,** who seek to integrate the role of institutions into the supply-demand framework used by most economists. They conclude that two strategies allowed some countries to avoid the Anglo-American outcome and to experience little or no increase in inequality in the 1980s: first, centralized bargaining and strong minimum wage and

Table I.4. Levels of Inequality in Selected Countries

	Ratio of 90th/10th percentiles of personal income	Gini coefficient for personal income
Finland	2.74	0.227
Sweden	2.78	0.229
Belgium	2.79	0.230
Norway	2.80	0.230
Denmark	2.86	0.239
Austria	2.89	0.227
Luxembourg	2.95	0.238
Germany (W)	3.01	0.249
Netherlands	3.05	0.268
Italy	3.14	0.255
Switzerland	3.43	0.311
France	3.48	0.294
Canada	3.90	0.285
Spain	4.02	0.306
Israel	4.12	0.305
Ireland	4.23	0.328
Australia	4.30	0.308
United Kingdom	4.67	0.335
United States	5.78	0.350
Unweighted average	3.52	0.274

Source: Excerpt from Figure 2, p. 661 in Gottschalk, Peter and Timothy M. Smeeding. "Cross-National Comparisons of Earnings and Income Inequality." *Journal of Economic Literature* 35 (1997): 633–687.

other labor market regulations; and second, investment in education and training of non-college-educated workers, as in Germany and Japan. This conclusion
is consistent with Freeman's numerous other writings on the economic importance of unions and related labor market institutions.

The centrality of institutions to economic analysis is of course a theme of traditional institutionalist economics; for an application to the recent growth in inequality see Charles Clark (1996). A different institutional analysis, offering a
novel, interdisciplinary perspective on labor markets, is provided by Jill Rubery
(1997). She notes that wage structures are simultaneously expected to allocate
labor to high-productivity occupations, to provide legitimacy to patterns of social stratification or cohesion, and to create workplace incentives for exerting effort on the job. Wage structures have never been smoothly successful in ac-
complishing all three objectives at once, according to Rubery, and are even less
able to do so in a time of widespread restructuring of labor relations.

Like his father, **James Galbraith** is an iconoclastic liberal economist and elo-
quent writer who focuses on the importance of corporate power. His recent
book has drawn attention for its controversial conclusion that the U.S. government, specifically the Federal Reserve, is to blame for much of the rise in inequality. This is the endpoint of a unique and complex chain of reasoning: For
Galbraith, unemployment is a key determinant of inequality, and the Federal
Reserve is responsible since it is so deeply engaged in trying to manage the business cycle.

Other portions of his book critique the skill-biased technical change argument and other standard theories. For instance, he shows that most of the U.S.
increase in wage inequality occurred before the mid-1980s—before computers
and related electronic technologies had a significant effect on the workplace.
(This is consistent with Atkinson's timing of the rise of British wage inequality,
mentioned earlier.) The growth of wage inequality slowed as computerization
of the workplace accelerated in the late 1980s, casting doubt on the theory that
these technical changes were important causes of inequality.

Galbraith's own theory focuses on one crucial component of income inequality, namely the dispersion, or interindustry variation, of hourly wages
within manufacturing. A measure of that dispersion turns out to be highly correlated with the Gini ratio for family incomes. In difficult or uncertain times,
high-wage, relatively monopolized and unionized industries will fare better
than low-wage, competitive ones, increasing the interindustry wage spread.
Both unemployment and inflation create such circumstances and are therefore
positively related to inequality, as are several other macroeconomic variables.
Unemployment is the most important causal factor of all; its effect can be traced
through many decades of data. Based on that historical record, Galbraith estimates that when unemployment is above 5.5 percent, wage inequality grows,
while below 5.5 percent it declines. The rising trend of inequality does appear

to have reversed itself around 1996, which is when the unemployment rate fell below the 5.5 percent line.

While he is at odds with current styles of explanation of inequality, Galbraith is not the only economist to raise these themes. David Card and Alan Krueger, in their analysis of the minimum wage (see Part X), discuss the role of monopoly power and of unemployment in wage determination. The "wage curve" found in the empirical work of David Blanchflower and Andrew Oswald (1995), summarized in *The Changing Nature of Work*, embodies a relationship between unemployment and wages that is inconsistent with conventional models of the labor market.

Markets and Marriages

Finally, in an article that deserves to be better known, **Gary Burtless** makes two contributions to the discussion of inequality. First, he reconciles the widely reported statistics that show that real per capita consumption is growing rapidly while median real family income is stagnant. Paradoxically, both are true at once, at least for 1973 to 1993, the period Burtless examines. The rise of inequality plays a major part, but is far from the whole story, as he explains in intriguing detail.

Second, Burtless demonstrates that growing inequality of family income does not just reflect the fact that male earnings and female earnings are each becoming more unequal. The covariance between men's and women's incomes has also risen. In the 1970s richer men were more likely to have stay-at-home wives, so there was, on average, a negative relationship between husbands' and wives' incomes. By the 1990s richer men were more likely to have wives with higher earnings—and indeed, were much more likely to be married than poorer men. Thus the inequality of family incomes grew even faster than the inequality of either male or female incomes. (The complex relationship between men's and women's earnings and patterns of family inequality is also discussed in Bernstein and Mishel 1997.)

In conclusion, the themes discussed in this essay suggest several directions for the further development of the political economy of inequality.

- New behavioral models, drawing on other social sciences, are important to consider.

- Analysis of the intergenerational persistence of inequality calls for new approaches.

- Explanation of the surge in inequality in the last quarter of the twentieth century requires not only the conventional treatment of supply, demand, and technological change, but also a new look at the role of corporate strategies and government macroeconomic policies.

- Differing labor market institutions lead to very different outcomes among the leading industrial nations, with far more equality in northern Europe than in America or Britain.

- Finally, changing family structures cannot be ignored in disentangling the web of income distribution today.

These and other new directions for economic research on inequality are explored in the subsequent parts of this book.

Notes

1. The argument about skill-biased technical change threatens to be circular: it often deduces the existence of such changes from labor market outcomes, which is different from observing the actual process of technical change and then proving that it is skill-biased. Deducing the existence and importance of unobserved skills is, of course, going even further in the same slippery direction.
2. Summarized authors are cited in boldface when first mentioned.
3. It is not surprising that the U.S. "90/10" percentile ratio is higher—i.e., there is greater inequality—in personal income (Table I.4) than in hourly wages (Table I.2). By definition,

Personal Income = (Hourly Wage X Annual Hours of Work) + Nonlabor Income

All three quantities on the right-hand side of this equation are unequally distributed, in ways that reinforce one another: On average, those with higher hourly wages tend to have more hours of work per year and also more nonlabor income.

Summary of

Bringing Income Distribution In from the Cold

by Anthony B. Atkinson

[Published in *Economic Journal* 107, 441 (March 1997), 297–321.]

What is the connection between income inequality and the macroeconomic variables that are center stage in most economic debate? What is the interrelationship between economic performance and income distribution? How can we use economic theory to explain what is happening to the incomes of individuals, families, and households? [299]

This article examines and interprets recent evidence on income distribution, focusing on the British experience. It identifies the related roles of earnings inequality, the workings of capital markets, and the impact of government transfers, suggesting the ways in which economic theory contributes to an understanding of each of these areas—and the ways in which economics needs to be enriched by new approaches.

The Unparalleled Rise in Income Inequality

The celebrated Kuznets curve, proposed in the 1950s, seemed to imply that inequality would continue to fall, steadily if not rapidly, in developed countries. It was still possible to hold this belief as recently as the 1970s; since then, the evidence has contradicted the earlier optimism. Inequality in the distribution of household income has increased since the 1970s in many developed countries. The increase was most spectacular in the United Kingdom, where the Gini coefficient for household income rose by 10 percentage points between 1977 and 1991.

Not only has the Kuznets curve been confounded by recent events; it has become clear that there is no lasting trend in the distribution of income. In both the United States and the United Kingdom, changes in inequality are easily matched with changes in government policy. It may be better to speak of well-defined episodes in which inequality falls or increases. Most of the increase in inequality in the United Kingdom happened between 1984 and 1991; the latter year is, so far, the high-water mark of British inequality.

The Sources of Inequality

Earnings from work (employment and self-employment) are the most important source of British household income, although they declined from 83 percent of the total in 1973 to 73 percent in 1993. There is plain evidence of widening dispersion of earnings: From 1979 to 1995 the real earnings of the bottom decile of full-time workers grew by 11 percent, compared with 50 percent for the top decile. There is a close relationship between trends in earnings inequality and in overall household income inequality during the 1970s and early 1980s. However, in the late 1980s the trends diverged, with household income inequality rising much faster. Part of the explanation is the divergence in employment experience, with rising numbers of both workless and two-income families.

Capital income, another source of inequality, also increased. Real rates of interest rose in the early 1980s and remained high a decade later; real dividends and share prices also climbed. The rise in expected real interest rates may have affected household decisions about savings, investment in human capital, and other financial matters.

The main source of nonwork income is social security. In the past, the system of taxes and transfers has sharply reduced inequality; this effect was weakened by numerous changes in the late 1980s. Application of the 1978/79 tax and benefit system, indexed for the growth in per capita GNP, to the 1994/95 distribution of household incomes would have reduced the tax burden for all groups below the top decile; the Gini coefficient would have been about five percentage points lower.

Explanations of Earnings Dispersion

A lively literature on earnings dispersion, in both the United States and the United Kingdom, begins from a point of apparently widespread agreement: There has been a shift in demand away from unskilled labor in favor of skilled workers, leading to a growing skill differential in earnings. Since the premium for skilled workers increased at a time when their relative numbers also rose, there must have been an increase in the relative demand for skilled labor.

Why should the demand curve for skills have shifted? One popular explanation attributes the shift to international trade with countries where unskilled labor is abundant. Another theory is that technological change has been biased toward skilled labor with the introduction of automation and information technology. However, the skill-based explanation is often extended to include not only observable job characteristics, but also unobserved skill components. This is necessary to explain the increasing inequality of earnings even within narrowly defined, seemingly homogeneous categories: The dispersion of British male earnings grew significantly during the 1980s in 34 out of 38 detailed occupational groups. Faced with such evidence, one must conclude either that there is a growing demand for unobserved skills or that other explanations are needed.

Earlier writing on wage differentials included a creative tension between market forces and alternative explanatory factors, which are missing in more recent accounts. For example, sociological or labor relations approaches emphasize interactions through institutions such as collective bargaining and government intervention. Some analysts have estimated that the decline in unionization might account for 15 to 20 percent of the increased earnings dispersion in the 1980s. The direct impact of the British government in the 1980s included the removal of wage standards for government contractors and the abolition of wage protection for lower-paid workers. These and other government policies had an important effect, although there is debate on the effectiveness of the redistributive government incomes policies of the 1970s.

A useful earlier approach, too hastily discarded by recent theorists, emphasized the role of social customs and norms in wage determination. In a monopolistic or oligopolistic setting, supply and demand may only place broad limits on the range of possible wage differentials, with other factors such as social norms determining wages within those limits. This institutional approach allowed analysis of notions of fairness or equity, a line of investigation that has been reopened by a handful of recent writers. Work by George Akerlof and by Robert Solow has shown how observance of social norms can be consistent with individual rationality, in cases where long-term reputation is important to economic success. In these terms, it is possible that the 1980s witnessed a weakening of conventional norms, and a shift from one equilibrium with low wage differentials to another with higher differentials.

Other Parts of the Puzzle

If there is a persistent, widened skill differential, what effect will this ultimately have on the supply of workers with different skills? Although there is little empirical evidence bearing on this question, its importance can be seen from theoretical models. Assuming that education is the only requirement for skill, and that everyone can borrow at the same interest rate to finance education, then the equilibrium wage differential for skill will be just enough to compensate for the costs of education, leaving workers indifferent between skilled and unskilled jobs. If the same conditions persist over multiple generations, the income distribution converges toward equality.

This result, however, depends on the details, and can be reversed by minor modifications in the assumptions. Unequal inheritance in the form of primogeniture can lead to sustained inequality. So, too, can nonconvexity, or increasing returns, in the accumulation of wealth. An interesting recent theory applies this idea to the economics of education and income distribution. Suppose that people make bequests to the next generation that are proportional to their lifetime wealth, and that only those who receive more than a critical level of bequest can afford the education required to become skilled, high-paid workers. If the critical level (i.e., the cost of education) is high enough, then only the descendants of skilled workers can themselves afford to acquire skills, and inequality will persist across generations. In contrast, if the critical level is low enough so that unskilled workers can often leave bequests sufficient to educate their descendants, then there will be long-term convergence toward equality.

This model highlights the significance of the cost of education, indirectly raising the issue of the importance of state transfers for the distribution of income. There has been a recent resurgence of interest among economists in the politics of income redistribution. Unfortunately, much of the discussion has adopted models of political equilibrium based on simplistic theories of the expected behavior of the median voter. "In my view, this understates what economists can usefully learn from political scientists. . . . The median voter theory is far from being 'standard.'" [316] Modeling the preferences of voters is a matter of some subtlety, even on simple economic choices. When unemployment increases, so that the total cost of unemployment benefits rises, do employed voters prefer to spend less on benefits, since unemployment insurance is now more expensive—or more, since the perceived risk of their own unemployment is now greater? "[T]he explanation of trends in the income distribution cannot be complete without an analysis of public choice, and this cannot be treated simply as a routine application of a well-tried theory." [317]

In conclusion, current economic theory offers insights into parts of the story of inequality, but still needs a framework within which to fit the different mechanisms. The skill shift explanation for wage differentials, for example, is a valuable but incomplete insight. The good news is that income distribution is beginning to receive again the attention that it deserves, and that economics is beginning to learn from other social sciences in this crucial area.

Summary of

Wage Polarization in the U.S. and the "Flexibility" Debate

by Bennett Harrison and Barry Bluestone

[Published in *Cambridge Journal of Economics* 14, 3 (1990), 351–373.]

In the 1980s, the rapid rise of income inequality led to debate about the nature and the causes of the new trends. The authors of this article were among the initiators of that debate, maintaining that the American economy had taken a "great U-turn" and that the middle-income population was now shrinking, leading to increased polarization between rich and poor. The article summarized here reviews the evidence for wage polarization in the 1980s and argues that rising inequality was caused by a change in management strategy that reshaped labor relations.

Income Distribution and Economic Growth

Growing inequality raises obvious normative concerns. It also has troubling economic consequences. In macroeconomic terms, it has been suggested that low incomes for a growing fraction of the workforce could lead to insufficient aggregate demand to sustain economic growth. In microeconomic terms, a growing pool of low-wage labor sends precisely the wrong signal to firms, encouraging them to compete on the basis of cheap labor rather than technological improvement and skill upgrading. Firms that survive despite obsolete technology, because they can use low-wage workers, become caught in a low-level productivity trap from which there is no easy escape.

Overall productivity growth in the United States averaged about 1 percent annually in the 1970s and 1980s, compared to well over 2 percent in the 1950s and 1960s. Given this productivity performance, it is not surprising that average weekly wages stopped growing in the early 1970s. After reaching an all-time peak in 1973, real average weekly wages fell by 9 to 16 percent, depending on how they are measured, by 1987. Of course, stagnation of the average wage need not lead to increased inequality; but in the United States the two trends have occurred together. The United States was not alone in experiencing this pattern; trends in inequality exhibit a similar "U-turn" at about the same time in Canada and in several European countries for which data is available.

Inequality and Polarization

The growing inequality of earnings could, in theory, result from increasingly unequal distribution of hours of work. While there has been growth in part-time employment, the rise in inequality does not primarily result from the distribution of hours. In fact, it can be seen in the earnings of year-round, full-time workers, who usually represent 55 to 60 percent of the U.S. labor force.

To illustrate the polarization of earnings among year-round, full-time workers, consider the proportions of this group with particularly high or low earnings. The proportion earning less than 50 percent of the 1973 median, in real terms, was roughly constant throughout most of the 1970s, then rose steeply after 1978. The proportion earning more than 200 percent of the 1973 median fell slightly during the 1970s, then began rising after 1981. As a result, the middle group, earning between 50 and 200 percent of the 1973 median, was shrinking in the 1980s.

Disentangling Stagnation from Redistribution

There is a risk of some confusion in using a fixed median wage, such as from 1973, to define high- and low-wage workers over time. Yearly changes in the average wage, as well as the redistribution of earnings, will affect the numbers in the high- and low-wage groups. Moreover, the experience of men and women should be examined separately, since they have very different average wages and average rates of growth in earnings.

To address these issues, low and high wages can be defined as less than 50 percent and more than 200 percent, respectively, of current year medians, separately for each gender. On this basis, mid-wage workers dropped from 81.0 percent of male year-round full-time workers in 1979 to 76.3 percent in 1987, a drop of 4.7 percent. Among women the drop was even steeper, from 88.2 percent in 1979 to 81.7 percent in 1987, or 6.4 percentage points. The majority of those who left the mid-wage group fell into the low-wage group, for both men and women. Thus "downward redistribution has clearly been the prime cause of the growth in low-wage employment." [361]

Explaining the U-turn in Inequality

There are several possible causes of the rise in earnings inequality. A sustained slowdown in growth could cause a breakdown in union wage agreements that formerly equalized earnings, as appears to have occurred in Sweden in the 1980s. Or, as in the United States in the 1980s, stagnation could cause a breakdown in traditional wage contours—the widespread follow-the-leader patterns of wage setting that prevailed after World War II. Technology could have changed in ways that promote dualism between leading and lagging sectors. Demography could be blamed, at least in the 1970s, as the baby-boom generation of inexperienced young workers flooded the labor market, lowering entry-level wages. Another popular theory attributes the change to deindustrialization: Since manufacturing has relatively high means and low variances of wages, increased inequality would result from the shift of labor from manufacturing into services, where there is a relatively low average and high variance of wages.

A simple statistical test finds that wage dispersion is related to productivity growth and to manufacturing employment, just as expected (more productivity and more manufacturing jobs both tend to create more equal earnings). However, once these factors and the business cycle are taken into account, demographic variables do not add meaningfully to the relationship. A full explanation for the U-turn in wage inequality requires consideration of other factors.

The Flexibility Debate and Wage Dispersion

What is missing from the mainstream debate over the U-turn is the possible role of management's attempts to increase labor market flexibility. Growing inequality of earnings could result from corporate responses to the "profit squeeze" of the 1970s. By any of several measures, corporate profits fell throughout the developed world after the mid-1960s; the fall was particularly severe in manufacturing. A variety of explanations have been proposed for the decline in profits, but whatever the underlying causes, lower profit rates led to new corporate strategies.

Many of these strategies have been described as the pursuit of flexibility in different aspects of business operations. Some authors have argued that businesses are responding to fast-changing markets by adopting "flexible specialization," with customized, small-scale production allowing rapid response to shifts in demand. Businesses are also seeking flexibility in the definition of work tasks, the deployment of resources, relationships with suppliers (as in the "just-in-time" inventory system), and other areas. The growing importance of part-time and other contingent workers of course allows employers added flexibility in controlling the labor process. Finally, the widespread attempts to reduce wages and avoid unions embody the most extreme vision of flexibility for management.

A few aspects of this process can be quantified. An international comparative study found that average plant size was shrinking in the 1970s and 1980s, especially in manufacturing. Meanwhile, the average number of plants per firm and the number of legally distinct firms were growing. Smaller firms, on average, pay lower wages and benefits, have lower levels of unionization, and in some cases are exempt from protective legislation; thus the move to smaller firms has significant risks for workers.

Of perhaps even greater significance is the wave of corporate demands for wage concessions. Initially justified as a response to the recession of the early 1980s, wage freezes or outright reductions were written into many collective bargaining agreements and continued to expand long after the 1982 trough of the business cycle. Other "innovations" in the employment relation have included two-tiered pay scales, increased use of pay-for-performance or bonus schemes, contracting out, and restructuring of full-time into part-time jobs. All of these changes are likely to increase inequality in the distribution of earnings.

The "Low Road" to Profitability

Why have so many American (and British, though usually not other European) managers taken the low road to resolving the profit squeeze? Part of the answer is the current weakness of the labor movement. Stronger unions would have pressured employers to adopt productivity-enhancing, rather than wage-cutting, strategies. The absence of unions does not cause companies to abandon the high road of innovation and productivity growth, but it allows them to choose the easy way out.

Other factors promoting the low road include: the fluctuating and uncertain economic environment, in which it appears safer to cut back than to make bold new investments; the growing dependence on equity finance, with its demands for short-term profits; and the chronically high interest rates of the period, which were an attempt to control inflation and other macroeconomic turmoil.

It is by no means certain that the negative trends of the 1980s will all continue. But it is clear that the rise of wage inequality and polarization were not simply cyclical phenomena that would disappear with sufficiently strong economic recovery. "Whatever structural changes have conjoined to produce the growing disparities between well paid and poorly paid workers in the United States and elsewhere, there is no longer any reason to doubt that these socially and economically disruptive trends are likely to be with us for a long time to come." [370]

Summary of

Wielding the Stick

by David M. Gordon

[Published in *Fat and Mean: The Corporate Squeeze of Working Americans and the Myth of Managerial "Downsizing"* (New York: Free Press, 1996), Ch. 8, 204–237.]

In the mid-1970s, faced with falling profits and intensified competition, many businesses chose the "low road" of confrontation with labor in an attempt to squeeze wages and benefits. In earlier books and in previous chapters of this book, the author has argued that this shift in corporate strategy, rather than changes in technology or trade, is the primary cause of the decline in real wages and the increase in income inequality of the late twentieth century. [See, for example, the chapter summarized in *The Changing Nature of Work*.] The chapter summarized here provides a more detailed look at the "low road" strategy, describing three key institutional changes that resulted from this strategy and estimating their quantitative impacts.

The Management Offensive

Business faced a crisis of profitability in the 1970s, as the after-tax rate of profit for nonfinancial corporations fell from 9.6 percent in 1966 to 6.4 percent in 1973. In principle, corporations could have responded by taking the high road, providing workers with increased real wages and job security, and more cooperative work relations, as a means to boost productivity and profits. Most, however, chose the low road of coercive attempts to lower labor costs.

Businesses quite explicitly changed their strategies, hiring antiunion consultants, lowering nonunionized workers' real wages, and demanding unprecedented concessions in bargaining with unions. One management consulting firm advertising its services to a corporate audience in the late 1970s said, "We will show you how to screw your employees (before they screw you)—how to keep them smiling on low pay—how to maneuver them into low-pay jobs they are afraid to walk away from—how to hire and fire so you always make money." [208] Surveys of corporate practices in 1978 and 1983 reflected a change in the factors influencing wage-setting: In the earlier survey, the factors most often mentioned were industry patterns and local labor market conditions; in the later survey, the top two factors were the company's own productivity or labor trends, and profits.

With the arrival of a conservative in the White House in 1981, the corporate campaign against labor gained the support of the federal government. President Reagan's dramatic defeat of the air traffic controllers' strike, and the choice of more conservative appointees throughout the government, brought a more frigid atmosphere to labor relations. The proportion of National Labor Relations Board cases decided in favor of unions dropped precipitously.

Some of the effects of the management offensive are hard to measure. However, three important institutional changes can be identified and analyzed: the collapse of the real value of the minimum wage, the decline in union membership and power, and the emergence of the "disposable" worker.

The Falling Wage Floor

The real value of the minimum wage plummeted throughout the 1980s, resulting in a constantly falling floor for wages in general. In a longer historical view, this decline is the third stage in the postwar record: first, from 1948 to 1968 the real minimum wage increased by nearly 50 percent; then from 1968 through 1979 the minimum wage was raised frequently, but rapid inflation meant that it still declined 8 percent in real value. After 1979, there were no increases for a decade, while inflation cut the real value of the minimum wage by nearly a third.

It is often observed that few workers earn as little as the minimum wage; this is mistakenly taken to mean that minimum wage legislation has little effect on other workers. In 1991, 5.7 percent of the workforce earned at or below the minimum wage; however, 16.8 percent of the workforce earned at or below the real value of the 1979 minimum wage. That is, the bottom one-sixth of the workforce would have been directly affected if the minimum wage had kept up with inflation since 1979.

Changes in the minimum wage, upward or downward, have a ripple effect on workers who make only slightly more than the minimum. Including this effect, the author estimates that the decline in the real minimum wage from 1979 through 1993 affected 23.5 percent of all private nonfarm workers. Another study found that the decline in the real minimum wage accounted for a quarter to a third of the increase in income inequality between 1979 and 1988, with a greater effect on women than men. [See also Card and Krueger, summarized in Part X.]

Unions on the Run

The management offensive against organized labor was strikingly successful. By the 1980s, the union movement was suffering obvious and widespread defeats. The decline of union representation and power contributed to the wage squeeze in three ways.

First, fewer workers enjoyed the benefits of union membership. Unionized workers earn higher wages and receive better benefits than comparable nonunionized employees. The unionized share of the labor force, which has been falling since 1954, declined even more precipitously in the 1980s. By the early 1990s, only 14 percent of all nonfarm workers, and 11 percent of those in the private sector, belonged to unions. Almost all of the decline has been among men (where the sharpest drops in income have also occurred); the percentage of women employees who are unionized has been virtually constant since the early 1970s.

Second, unions have become increasingly defensive in the face of the management offensive. Demands for concessions and rollbacks in previously negotiated wages, benefits, and other contractual provisions became nearly universal in bargaining in the 1980s. As a result, the union wage premium was shrinking, for those who remained members of unions. And third, there is some indirect spillover effect of union contracts on wages in the nonunion sector. As unions became less powerful, this spillover effect must have diminished.

It is easiest to measure the first of these effects. Three separate studies, using very different methodologies, found remarkably similar results: Lower unionization rates can account for 21 percent of the increase in wage inequality in the 1980s. Regarding the second effect, the author estimates that the union wage premium in the private sector declined from $1.87 an hour (in 1993 dollars) in 1983 to $1.47 an hour in 1993. The third effect, although undoubtedly important, is difficult to measure.

The Disposable Worker

The much-celebrated new age of "flexibility" at work has a dark side involving insecure, unpredictable employment for millions of people who would prefer steadier work. However, the category of "contingent" workers, sometimes said to include one quarter to one third of all American workers, is too broad, including many who are voluntarily self-employed or part-time. A narrower category of "disposable" workers includes those who expect their current job to last less than a year, plus others who are involuntarily working part-time, and day laborers, temp agency employees and others with involuntary, nontraditional arrangements. In 1995 there were 9.2 million disposable workers, amounting to 9.9 percent of private nonfarm employees.

Involuntary part-time workers earned roughly one-quarter less than comparable other workers in 1993. If this wage penalty applies to all disposable workers, then the rapid growth in the number of disposable workers could have accounted for about one-fifth of the decline in average real wages from 1979 to 1994—roughly on a par with the decline of unionization. Moreover, disposable workers almost never receive employee benefits such as health care, which causes an added squeeze on workers and labor costs.

The Combined Effects of the Offensive

One study estimated that the change in the real minimum wage and in union membership together could explain between 39 percent and 74 percent of the increased wage inequality among men for various time periods since 1973 (the estimates were somewhat lower for women). This conclusion is reinforced by a comparison of male earnings inequality in the United States and Canada in the 1980s; in contrast to the U.S. experience, inequality among Canadian men was roughly constant during this period. Differences in union strength and the minimum wage accounted for two-thirds of the difference between the countries (DiNardo and LeMieux 1994). Similarly, the author estimates that much of the decline in average real wages since the 1970s can be explained by the three institutional changes discussed earlier.

The low-road hypothesis provides a better explanation of the wage squeeze than the competing "skills mismatch" and globalization theories. The alternative theories have problems of timing: Rapid technological changes in the workplace arise after the wage squeeze is well under way [see Howell article summarized in Part VI], while the trade deficit, which soared in the early 1980s, shrank substantially in the late 1980s without visibly lessening the wage squeeze. The management offensive not only began at the same time as the wage squeeze, but also is broadly applicable across the economy: It affects industries pressured by import competition, and those that are unaffected by trade; it is relevant to industries with rapid technological change, and to those that have remained stagnant. Moreover, the low-road hypothesis provides a natural explanation of the difference between the United States and other countries, particularly in continental Europe, which have more cooperative labor relations and less inequality.

Summary of

Rising Wage Inequality: The United States versus Other Advanced Countries

by Richard B. Freeman and Lawrence F. Katz

[Published in *Working Under Different Rules*, ed. Richard B. Freeman (New York: Russell Sage Foundation, 1993), Ch. 2, 29–62.]

Was the twist in the job market against less educated workers [beginning in the 1980s] unique to the United States, or was it part of a general pattern of decline in the well-being of the less skilled in advanced countries? . . . Have other advanced countries avoided or ameliorated the rise in wage inequality that has characterized the United States? [30]

Earnings inequality grew most rapidly in the 1980s in the United States and the United Kingdom. Other advanced countries generally had modest increases in inequality, and a few apparently had no change. This article argues that the familiar forces of supply and demand are important in wage determination, but had similar effects on all countries, and hence cannot explain most international differences in inequality. Institutional differences, on the other hand, have a clear relationship to the international patterns of inequality.

Changes in the United States and Other Advanced Countries

In the United States, overall wage dispersion grew rapidly in the 1980s, as real earnings rose for high-income workers but fell sharply for those at the bottom. Pay differentials by education, age, and experience increased; the only major differential that decreased was that between men and women. Most of these changes were breaks from the past, contrasting with the trends of the 1970s and earlier decades. In addition, wage dispersion increased within demographic and skill groups, a trend that began earlier and continued through the 1980s.

Did other industrial nations experience similar trends? In the 1970s, educational and skill differentials narrowed substantially in all the countries for which data is available. In the 1980s the same differentials narrowed by a lot in South Korea, and by a little in the Netherlands; other countries ranged from no noticeable change (France, Germany, Italy) to modest increases in inequality (Australia, Canada, Japan, Sweden), and large increases (United States, United Kingdom). However, in Britain real wages increased for all groups; inequality rose because wages rose faster at the top than at the bottom. Only in the United States did low-wage workers as a group suffer a serious drop in economic well-being. Women's wages rose relative to men in the 1970s and 1980s in 15 out of 16 major industrial countries (all except Japan).

Explaining the Changes

An analysis of supply and demand factors offers an important but incomplete explanation of the rise in inequality. Supply and demand do not operate in a vacuum; wages must respond to market forces within an existing institutional setting that shapes and constrains the market. Moreover, supply and demand move in roughly similar ways in all advanced countries. Developed countries operate in the same world markets, using similar technologies in similar industries. Thus the demand for skills should not differ significantly among these countries. Labor supply changes will diverge more, but there is a trend toward a greater proportion of workers obtaining college degrees everywhere. So to understand international differences in labor market outcomes, something beyond supply and demand is needed.

That "something" is the pattern of wage setting, training, and other labor market institutions that varies from one country to another. "The stronger the role of institutions in wage determination, the smaller will be the effect of shifts in supply and demand on relative wages and, as a consequence, the greater will be their effect on relative employment." [44] A greater effort in education and training leads to a more egalitarian distribution of skills, dampening the effects of market shifts. Other institutions such as social insurance and income maintenance programs also affect the wage distribution, by allowing workers to remain unemployed when necessary rather than taking pay cuts to stay employed.

Does the Explanation Fit the United States?

Supply-side changes alone cannot explain the U.S. wage trends of the 1980s. Groups with relative wage increases, such as college graduates and women, also had increases in their relative numbers in the labor force. Declining wages for those at the bottom cannot be explained in terms of the declining quality of education received by young workers, since inequality increased in a similar fashion for all cohorts, including those educated in earlier decades. The surge in immigration explains only part of the decline in relative wages for those at the lowest levels (high school dropouts).

Therefore, there must have been a shift in demand that favored more educated and skilled workers. Part of the demand shift resulted from the loss of high-wage, blue-collar jobs as goods-producing industries contracted and professions and other services expanded. Most of the change in job structure, however, occurred within narrowly defined industries, as the use of professional, managerial, and technical workers rose and production workers declined almost everywhere. But most of these demand factors also affected European countries, where the resulting trend in inequality was far more muted.

Institutional factors, which differ from country to country, also play a role in determining how market forces affect wages. The major institutional factor that affected the U.S. wage structure was the decline of unionism. The precipitous drop in the rate of union membership explains one-fifth of the growth in wage dispersion among male workers.

For young blue-collar men, the proportion who were in unions fell by 15 percentage points in the 1980s. Thus 15 percent of less-skilled young men lost the 20 to 25 percent wage advantage associated with union membership, the lower dispersion of wages in union workplaces, and the better pensions and other fringe benefits under union contracts. The effect may be even greater,

since many analysts believe that lower unionization rates reduce the pressure on
nonunion employers to pay high wages and benefits.

Why Other Countries Fared Differently

Demand factors, as noted earlier, explain little of the international difference in
wage inequality. The same technologies and occupational shifts emerged virtually everywhere; the share of employment in manufacturing declined in all developed countries except Japan. Supply shifts are of greater significance: While
the supply of highly educated workers increased rapidly in all developed countries in the 1970s, the rates of growth diverged thereafter. The United States
was alone in having a sharp deceleration of growth in the college-educated
work force in the 1980s, and had the sharpest increase in the college wage premium as a result. At the other extreme, South Korea had exceptionally fast
growth in the college-educated share of its work force, and saw a huge drop in
the college wage premium. Most countries fell between these extremes.

Just as in the United States, institutional factors are critical in determining
the trends in wage inequality. Wage-setting institutions vary greatly from one
country to another. Austria and Sweden have historically had national wage set-
tlements reached between union confederations and employer organizations.
National bargaining also determines the rate of wage increases in Japan, though
the implementation of the resulting increases is quite decentralized. In Germany, the results of industry or regional collective bargaining are often extended to other workers by the Ministry of Labor. In France, the high minimum wage is important in determining the wage structure, and the Ministry of
Labor also extends contracts to other workers. Italy's Scala Mobile, a negotiated nationwide system of wage raises, decreased wage differentials throughout
the 1980s.

In several cases these institutions were changed, in ways that weakened or decentralized wage-setting mechanisms, in the 1980s and early 1990s. Sweden,
for example, retreated from nationwide wage bargaining in 1983; Italy ultimately dropped the Scala Mobile. However, there remains a clear difference between the United States and other countries. Nowhere else are unions so weak,
or is government intervention in wage determination so rare. The only other
country that saw a comparable decline in union membership and a simultaneous weakening of other wage-setting institutions was the United Kingdom, the
other country where inequality rose sharply. The decline in unionization accounts for about one-fourth of the British increase in inequality, comparable to
estimates for the United States. Union membership also fell significantly in the
1980s in France, Austria, and the Netherlands, but other wage-setting institutions remained strong in these countries. Thus they did not follow the Anglo-
American pattern of rising inequality.

Market forces do appear to be gradually weakening wage-setting institutions and pressing for greater decentralization throughout the world. However, there can be many different responses to this pressure. Few if any countries, other than the United Kingdom, are likely to approach American levels of inequality, given existing institutional structures. The institutions that matter most, in ameliorating trends toward inequality, include both European-style collective bargaining and regulation of wages, and institutions that invest heavily in education and training of non-college-educated workers. German and Japanese do far more to provide on-the-job training than do their American or British counterparts. Such training should be combined with investment in higher education, and with institutions that protect workers' interests in the labor market, to develop a long-term solution to the rise of inequality.

Summary of

Inequality, Unemployment, Inflation, and Growth
by James K. Galbraith

[Published in *Created Unequal: The Crisis in American Pay* (New York: The Free Press, 1998), Ch. 8, 133–149.]

High inequality is a well-known fact of life in America today. Much less well-known are the sources of change: What causes inequality to increase or decrease? This chapter seeks to answer that question. It presents a measure of inequality in the manufacturing wage structure and analyzes changes in that measure. The causes of rising inequality turn out to be mainly macroeconomic: Unemployment, inflation, rapid economic growth, the exchange rate of the dollar, and the minimum wage all contribute to an explanation of the pattern of inequality over time. Such factors are reversible; that is, this analysis leads to a prescription for reducing inequality in the future.

Measuring Jobs, Not People

Many studies of inequality rely on the Census Bureau's Current Population Survey, in which a representative cross-section of the population is asked to report on their personal incomes (and other information). For many purposes, such as analysis of family incomes or racial or gender income differentials, population surveys are essential. But for analysis of the underlying wage structure, there are better alternatives. (As argued in an earlier chapter, the effects of the wage structure and of discrimination are complementary: Imagining the income distribution as a multistory building, discrimination may limit who gets into the upper floors, while the wage structure sets the shape of the building, determining how narrow the upper floors are relative to the ground floor.)

There is a high error rate in workers' responses to survey questions about their wages, and even to questions about the industry in which they work. For information about jobs, as opposed to workers, surveys of employers are much more accurate and can provide consistent data for many years. In particular, the Annual Survey of Manufactures provides data on manufacturing back to 1958. In an earlier chapter, the author examines detailed data on manufacturing industries (at the 3-digit level) and classifies them into twenty-three groups on the basis of trends in productivity; in most cases, industries within the same group have similar production technologies as well as productivity trends. Here the focus is on a measure of inequality in the average hourly wages paid to workers in each of the twenty-three manufacturing groups, weighted by the groups' employment, calculated annually from 1958 through 1992.

Inequality in Manufacturing Wages

The dispersion of average hourly wages across the twenty-three industrial groups captures only a portion of inequality, even within the manufacturing sector. There is, of course, substantial wage inequality within the individual groups. And much of income inequality originates outside of manufacturing. Yet the factors that affect interindustry wage differentials are likely to have parallel effects on other aspects of the income distribution. The author's measure of interindustry wage inequality in manufacturing has a correlation of .77 with the Census Bureau's Gini ratio for family incomes, confirming the importance of this measure of wage structure.

A significant difference between the two measures appears in the late 1980s. Both the manufacturing wage inequality measure and the family income Gini ratio reach a trough in 1968 and then begin a fairly steady rise. However, the inequality of wages stabilizes (at a high level) after the mid-1980s, while the inequality of family incomes continues to rise. This pattern, which has been confirmed in other studies of wages, poses a problem for the argument that computer use is a major source of income inequality. Certainly computer use should affect the wage structure, rather than other aspects of the income distribution; however, computers became most important after the mid-1980s, when wage inequality had stopped growing.

Macroeconomics and Market Power

My lead hypothesis is that macroeconomic events will largely determine the movement of a wage inequality measure through time. In a world of organizations—firms, industries, and unions—with greater and lesser degrees of market power, we should expect that events will differentiate the strong from the weak. [138–139]

Under the conventional model of supply and demand in competitive markets, wages should depend on the value of each worker's marginal product, not on macroeconomic variables. Aggregate unemployment or inflation should not have a systematic effect on the (real, inflation-adjusted) value of a product, and hence should not affect the pay scale.

Very different predictions emerge from a model that highlights the importance of market power. Firms and unions with monopolistic power are better able to protect themselves in bad times, cushioning workers with stable, long-term employment and pay. In good times, however, the same long-term stability inhibits the strongest sectors from taking immediate advantage of favorable economic circumstances. Weaker, more competitive parts of the economy will react more quickly to upturns as well as downturns.

Statistical tests strongly favor the market power model, finding that several macroeconomic variables have the expected relationship to inequality. As shown in an appendix, similar conclusions are reached if inequality is measured by the Gini ratio for family incomes, or by another published index of wage inequality, rather than the author's preferred wage inequality measure.

Unemployment is the most important single influence on manufacturing wage inequality. Low-wage, weakly organized, competitive industries are more likely to lower wages when unemployment is high and raise wages as full employment approaches. High-wage, unionized, monopolistic or oligopolistic industries are more insulated from business cycle pressures. Unemployment also affects family incomes because low-wage workers are more at risk of being laid off; while the causes are similar, this effect is distinct from the effect on the wage structure for those who remain employed.

Inflation boosts wage inequality, since unionized, high-wage workers are more likely to have cost-of-living adjustments that protect their pay against price increases. "Thus, like a rise in unemployment, a rise in inflation drives a wedge between the strong and the weak, and so raises inequality in the system as a whole." [140] In the period being analyzed, inflation was most important in the 1970s, a time when union contracts that provided cost-of-living adjustments were more common than they are today.

Rapid economic growth, perhaps surprisingly, increases inequality. The sectors that expand most at times of rapid growth are those producing investment goods, such as construction, machinery, and transport equipment; these tend to be high-wage industries. Rapid growth is good for almost everyone's income, but it is differentially better for some of those who were already doing well.

A rise in the real exchange rate of the dollar relative to other currencies also boosts inequality, by making imports cheaper and weakening the position of industries that compete with imports. A stronger dollar also makes American exports more expensive abroad; but exporting industries, such as aircraft, computers, pharmaceuticals, and machinery, tend to have a degree of worldwide monopoly power that partially protects them from exchange rate problems. The industries that compete with imports include many competitive, low-wage sectors. The exchange rate had a statistically significant effect on manufacturing wage inequality only after 1981, when trade pressures intensified.

The minimum wage has the expected effect on inequality: Higher minimum wages cause a reduction in inequality. Since many minimum-wage workers are in services rather than manufacturing, this effect is stronger when all workers are included; yet it is statistically significant even when the analysis is restricted to manufacturing wages.

Technology and Unemployment

Almost all of the year-to-year changes in manufacturing wage inequality from 1958 to 1992 can be accounted for by the factors listed here (r^2 = .87). There is little left over for other forces, such as changes in education or the supply of skills, to explain. This does not mean that technology is unimportant; it does, however, suggest a switch away from the benign view of technology as "skill enhancing," and back to the old-fashioned idea that technological change is mainly aimed at saving labor. To the extent that technology leads to unemployment, its effects have already been included here.

Taking a longer historical view, the measure of inequality in the wage structure can be extended back to 1920 (with a bit of creative extrapolation, explained in the appendix). This measure of inequality abruptly shot up in the depression of the 1930s, then plummeted downward during World War II. Movements of the unemployment rate alone explain almost all of the variation in wage inequality (r^2 = 0.79) over the entire period of more than 70 years.

Since high unemployment increases inequality, and low unemployment decreases it, where is the break-even point? A final computation using the long historical series shows that inequality tends to increase whenever unemployment is above 5.5 percent and to decrease when unemployment is below that level. In the autumn of 1996, as unemployment fell below 5.5 percent for the first time in many years, inequality also began to fall.

Ironically, 5.5 percent is close to many economists' current estimates of the lowest unemployment rate that is compatible with price stability—the so-called natural rate of unemployment, or nonaccelerating inflation rate of unemployment (NAIRU). "Yet if we care about inequality in America, a 5.5 percent rate of unemployment should assuredly be a ceiling, not a floor."
[149]

Summary of

Trends in the Level and Distribution of U.S. Living Standards: 1973–1993

by Gary Burtless

[Published in *Eastern Economic Journal* 22, 3 (Summer 1996), 271–290.]

Americans who want to know whether living standards have improved or stagnated during the past twenty years are faced with a puzzle. . . . [Real] personal consumption expenditures per person . . . climbed 37.3 percent between 1973 and 1993. . . . however [other data suggest] that real median family income was essentially the same in both 1973 and 1993. [273]

This article offers a solution to the puzzle, reconciling the two sets of data (see Table of Alternative Measures of Change in U.S. Living Standards 1973–1993) and revealing that growing income inequality is one among several factors causing the divergence between per capita consumption and median family income. It then examines some of the changing patterns of income distribution that have led to rising inequality.

Alternative Measures of Change in U.S. Living Standards, 1973–1993

Measure	% change, 1973–93	Explanation for difference from preceding line
Per capita consumption	37.3	
Per capita disposable income	30.2	Decline in personal savings
Per capita income net of employer and government health purchases	22.4	Increased employer and government-sponsored health spending
Average money income, all persons	22.9	(Different data source from above)
Average money income, persons in families	21.6	Growth in the number of unrelated individuals
Income per person in median-income family	7.4	Growth in inequality, median grows slower than average
Median family income	0.0	Decline in average family size

Source: Adapted from article, page 272; all figures in real terms. The first three lines are based on national income and product account statistics, while the last four are based on the Census Bureau's current population surveys.

Understanding the Trend in Living Standards

There are five parts to the reconciliation of growing per capita consumption with stagnant median family income. First, consumption grew faster than income, because the savings rate declined. Personal savings fell from 9.0 percent of disposable (after-tax) income in 1973 to 4.1 percent in 1993. Thus, as seen in the top two rows of the table, real per capita consumption climbed by 37.3 percent, while per capita income rose just 30.2 percent.

A second important difference is that some consumption is not financed out of family income. A large portion of health care expenditure is financed by employers or government agencies. Employer and government reimbursements for medical services climbed from 6.2 percent of personal income in 1973 to 11.8 percent in 1993. The national income and product accounts, the data source for the first three lines of the table, includes such expenditures in personal income. If health care reimbursements are excluded, then net personal income grew by 22.4 percent (third row of table)—which is quite similar to the 22.9 percent real increase in per capita money income that households reported to census interviewers (fourth row of table).

Third, the percentage of the population living outside of families has increased, from 8.8 percent in 1973 to 14.7 percent in 1993. Because there are so many unrelated individuals, it is possible for average income growth to be different for all individuals versus those who live in families. However, this is a small effect in practice, as seen by comparing the fourth and fifth rows of the table.

Fourth, and much more important, is the increase in income inequality. Virtually all of the income gains between 1973 and 1993 went to the top 40 percent of the population, with an overwhelming share going to the top 20 percent. As a result, the average income of family members rose by 21.6 percent (fifth row of table), while the median income rose only 7.4 percent (sixth row).

Finally, the average size of families decreased from 3.44 persons in 1973 to 3.20 in 1993. Coincidentally, this was exactly enough to offset the growth in the median family's per capita income. As a result, median family income showed no change in real terms (last row of table).

Which of these numbers describes the experience of the typical family? The median family saw its real income per family member rise just 7.4 percent over 20 years. It is possible that something should be added for employer- and government-financed health benefits, though it is unclear if most people experienced an improvement in the quantity or quality of health care. Even with an allowance for health benefits, "it is unlikely that the median family enjoyed income or consumption gains exceeding 0.7 percent a year after 1973. This rate of improvement is roughly one-quarter the pace of median income growth from 1947 through 1973." [276]

Trends in Income by Source

As the intricacies of the data in the table suggest, there is a need for careful adjustment for family size and other factors in analysis of income distribution.

Using a common system of adjustment for family size, the Gini ratio for adjusted personal income rose from 0.358 in 1973 to 0.419 in 1993, a 17 percent increase. These data are based on public-use census files, which lack accurate information on the top 3 percent of the population; thus the analysis presented here (and in other census-based studies) refers only to people below the 97th percentile.

Examination of the sources of household income reveals growing inequality in all major areas. A household's income may include male head earnings, female head earnings (both parents are counted as heads in two-parent families), other family members' earnings (which are small and declining at all income levels), and nonlabor income of several types. From 1973 to 1993, the bottom income quintile saw a sharp decline in male head earnings (both due to the declining number of low-income households with male heads, and to declining earnings for low-income men), only a small increase in female head earnings, and a drop in nonlabor income due to the decline in per capita public retirement payments to this group. All other groups saw rapid increases in both female head earnings and nonlabor income. Male head earnings declined modestly in the middle three quintiles and inched upward in the top quintile.

In other research the author has analyzed the effect of these and related factors on the Gini coefficient, finding four main factors that account for its 17 percent rise from 1973 to 1993: the sharp decline in the proportion of people who live in families with a male head; increased earnings inequality among men; the growing positive correlation of female earnings with male earnings; and the increase in unearned income, such as interest, dividends, and private retirement payments, that are correlated with other income sources. The first three are particularly important for working-age families, while the last is most important for those over 65.

The next section focuses on the third of these factors, the male-female income correlation.

Earnings Inequality

Inequality rose among women and among men between 1973 and 1993. On average, women fared better, experiencing rising median real wages while the male median declined. Common explanations for rising inequality of wages include the effects of technology and trade. However, the change in earnings disparities cannot by itself account for the jump in family income inequality since 1973. Equally important is the changing relationship between male and female earnings within the family.

If men are ranked by decile, their real earnings change from 1973 to 1993 rises monotonically, from a 40 percent drop in the bottom decile to no change in the ninth decile and a small gain in the top group. The change in the average wife's real earnings can also be calculated for each male decile, counting zero wife's earnings both for unmarried men and for those with nonworking wives. This figure rises smoothly from roughly zero in the second decile to 157 percent in the top decile. As a result, male and female earnings changes reinforce each other, and family incomes grow faster in higher deciles. In the bottom six deciles, increases in women's earnings were too small to offset the decline in men's earnings, so family earnings fell.

Three factors determine the average wife's earnings: the percentage of men who are married, the percentage of married men who have working wives, and the average earnings of employed wives. Change in all three factors has tilted in the direction of greater inequality. The percentage of men who are married has declined at all income levels, but it has fallen much faster among lower-income men. The percentage of wives who work has increased at all levels, but it has increased fastest among wives of higher-income men. And the change in earnings among wives who work has likewise been positively correlated with their husband's earnings. Overall, in 1973 the correlation between male- and female-head earnings was negative; by 1993 it had become strongly positive.

In conclusion, there are several components to the rise of inequality after 1973. The much-discussed trend toward male earnings inequality and declining prospects for low-income male workers is only one part of the story. Changes in family composition have deprived an increasing proportion of families of the presence of a working male head. Less often noticed is the effect of rising employment and earnings among married women; this increase has been particularly concentrated among wives of high-wage husbands, further contributing to inequality. Trends in unearned income have also boosted inequality, with rising income from capital assets among upper-income groups. Meanwhile, government transfer payments had little effect in ameliorating the trend toward inequality. So long as the benefits of prosperity are so unevenly distributed, "a large minority—perhaps even a majority—of Americans will remain convinced that U.S. living standards are languishing."

PART II

The Distribution of
Wealth and Power

Overview Essay

by Frank Ackerman

In a casual description of inequality it is easy to blur the distinction between wealth and income. At the extremes the difference hardly seems to matter: In the simplest terms, the rich have both money in the bank and more coming in all the time, while the poor have neither. Yet the distinction between accumulated assets and current income is fundamental for the analysis of inequality.

The distribution of wealth is highly unequal, far more so than the distribution of income. The Gini ratio for the distribution of household net worth in the United States was 0.83 in 1995; for financial assets—that is, net worth excluding the value of owner-occupied homes—it was 0.91 (Wolff 1998). These are remarkably high numbers. Imagine a spectrum of possibilities ranging from perfect equality on the left, where everyone has the same amount, to perfect inequality on the right, where one person has everything. A Gini ratio of 0.91 means that the distribution of financial wealth is more than nine-tenths of the way toward the right-hand end of the spectrum. (See "Introduction" for the definition of the Gini ratio.) In contrast, income is far more equally distributed; the Gini ratio for U.S. household income is a bit above 0.4. In Brazil, the world's most unequal major economy, the Gini ratio for income is roughly 0.6, still far below the levels for wealth in the United States.

There are at least three reasons why the distribution of wealth is important. First, ownership of financial wealth is a significant source of income; inequity in the distribution of wealth implies a corresponding inequity in the distribution of dividends, interest, rent, and other income received by wealth owners. Second, wealth provides security; a wealthier household is better able to survive interruptions in income or expensive emergencies. Finally, wealth brings its owners political and economic power in several forms—although, as we will see, the exact nature of that power remains controversial.

This essay begins with a review of the evidence on the U.S. distribution of wealth. It then discusses several theoretical models of the wealth distribution, chosen for their ability to explain or predict highly unequal outcomes. The last two sections examine the relationship between wealth and power, first in general terms and then more specifically in relation to stocks and the ownership of corporations.

The View from the Top

The amounts of income derived from property—that is, from the ownership of stocks, bonds, real estate, and small businesses—are substantial. For the United States in 1997, 60 percent of personal income consisted of labor earnings, while 17 percent came from capital ownership, in the form of dividends, interest, and rent. Another 8 percent was the income of self-employed proprietors, a category which messily combines their earnings as workers and their profits as business owners. The remainder of personal income was transfer payments, largely from the government to the elderly and the poor.[1]

Capital income thus represents one-sixth of all personal income, or perhaps one-fifth if part of proprietors' income is viewed as a return on their capital. While labor income, as emphasized in Part I, is somewhat unequally distributed, capital, and hence capital income, is much more so. Table II.1 illustrates the extraordinary concentration of net worth, and particularly of financial wealth. It is taken from a valuable 1998 survey article by Edward Wolff, the leading economist writing about the distribution of wealth in America today.

With such pronounced inequality, it is exaggerating only slightly to say that the poor have no net assets, the middle class owns its homes and has modest retirement accounts, and the rich own everything else. The bottom 40 percent of the population (hidden within the last column in Table II.1) has less than 1 percent of all net worth and negative net financial wealth. As shown in Table II.2, the top 1 percent, those with net worth over $2.4 million in 1995, own half of all individually owned stocks and bank trusts, two-thirds of bonds and other financial securities, two-thirds of unincorporated business equity, and one-third of nonhome real estate.

Table II.1. The Size Distribution of Wealth, 1983 and 1995

	Percentage Share of Net Worth of Financial Wealth Held by				
	Top 1%	Next 4%	Next 5%	Next 10%	Bottom 8%
Net Worth					
1983	33.8	22.3	12.1	13.1	18.7
1992	38.5	21.8	11.5	12.1	16.1
Financial Wealth					
1983	42.9	24.6	12.3	11.0	8.7
1992	47.2	24.6	11.2	10.1	7.0

Source: Excerpted from Table 2 in Edward N. Wolff, "Recent Trends in the Size Distribution of Household Wealth." *Journal of Economic Perspectives* 12 (Summer 1998), 131–150.

Table II.2. The Percent of Total Assets Held by Wealth Class, 1995

Asset Type	Top 1.0%	Next 9.0%	Bottom 90.0%
Assets held primarily by the wealthy			
Stocks and mutuals	51.4	37.0	11.6
Financial securities	65.9	23.9	10.2
Trusts	49.6	38.9	11.5
Business equity	69.5	22.2	8.3
Nonhome real estate	35.1	43.6	21.3
Total group	55.5	32.1	12.5
Assets and liabilities held primarily by the nonwealthy			
Principal residence	7.1	24.6	68.3
Deposits	29.4	32.9	37.7
Life insurance	16.4	28.5	55.1
Pension accounts	17.7	44.7	37.7
Total for group	12.8	29.7	57.5
Total Debt	9.4	18.9	71.7

Source: Reprint of Table 6, p. 140 in Wolff, Edward N. "Recent Trends in the Size Distribution of Household Wealth." *Journal of Economic Perspectives* 12 (Summer 1998), 13–150.

For some purposes it is relevant to count the present value of an individual's expected retirement benefits as wealth; for other purposes, human capital can be viewed as a form of educational wealth. Inclusion of either of these categories would sharply reduce wealth inequality, although wealth by any definition would remain less equitably distributed than income. However, neither future retirement benefits nor human capital represents marketable wealth. You can sell your home and buy a new one, but you cannot do the same with your college degree. In most analyses, net worth is taken as synonymous with marketable wealth.

The first article summarized here, by **Edward Wolff,** contrasts wealth distributions in several different countries where data are available. The comparison of fairly long time series for the United States, the United Kingdom, and Sweden shows that there is nothing fixed or inevitable about the inequality of wealth: all three countries have changed, exhibiting very different patterns over time. Before 1950 the United States and Sweden had similar degrees of wealth inequality, but in the second half of the twentieth century the United States became rapidly more unequal. In the early twentieth century the United Kingdom was the most unequal of the three, but it moved rapidly toward equality, reaching the American level by the 1960s and the Swedish level of equality by the 1980s. The British experience reveals the surprising fact that a country can simultaneously move toward equality of wealth and toward inequality of income. Other international comparisons, for selected years in the mid-1980s, are

Table II.3. The Inequality of Household Wealth in
Selected Countries, mid-1980s

	Percent of total wealth held by	
	Top 1%	Top 15%
United States, 1983	35	56
Canada, 1984	17	38
France, 1986	26	43
Japan, 1984		25
Sweden, 1985/86	16	31
Statistics Sweden, 1985/86	16.5	37
United Kingdom, 1983	25	
United Kingdom, 1986	22	

Source: Reprint of Table 12, p. 149 in Wolff, Edward N. "Recent
Trends in the Size Distribution of Household Wealth." *Journal of Economic
Perspectives* 12 (Summer 1998): 131–150.

shown in Table II.3. Japan is the most equal, and the U.S. is the most unequal, of the six countries shown there.

Wealth data are reported less frequently and less completely than income data; recent analyses of wealth rely on a survey of consumer finances that has lately been performed every three years. However, economic historians have collected an impressive amount of information about the distribution of wealth in the past. A detailed study by **Jeffrey Williamson and Peter Lindert** surveys the historical record. Estate records, describing a person's assets at the time of death, are available for varying times and places; and questions about assets have occasionally been included in the census. Williamson and Lindert conclude that there was little change in the distribution of wealth during the colonial era, but then a noticeable increase in inequality between the American Revolution and the Civil War, probably associated with the beginnings of industrialization. After emancipation, which clearly boosted equality in the South, there was little obvious change until the Depression and World War II, which was an era of rapid movement toward equality. The more recent trend toward inequality is beyond the scope of Williamson and Lindert's article. For a shorter "long-term" analysis, examining twentieth-century trends in detail, see Wolff and Marley (1989).

Theories of Inequality

What causes the dramatically unequal distribution of wealth? Wolff (1998) offers a simple statistical analysis of trends in wealth inequality, measured by the share of marketable wealth held by the top 1 percent of households. Most of the variation in the share of the top 1 percent from 1922 to 1995 can be explained by two variables, the inequality of income and the ratio of stock prices to median housing prices. Income inequality affects wealth inequality because the savings of the rich account for many of the changes in wealth. The ratio of stock prices to housing prices is significant because stocks are disproportionately owned by upper-income groups while housing is owned by the middle class. Income inequality rose in the 1980s, and stock prices surged upward much faster than real estate, so both factors contributed to the decade's rising wealth inequality.

A more detailed analysis, seeking to explain the shape of the wealth distribution curve—or the pattern of data in Table II.1—appears in the sociology literature, in the work of John Angle (e.g., Angle 1996, Angle 1993, and earlier work cited there). Like neoclassical economists, Angle starts with a simple model of individual maximizing behavior and proceeds to draw rigorous, highly mathematical conclusions about the expected distribution of resources. His basic behavioral premise is that once people are producing a surplus above subsistence, there is a tendency for those who are already wealthier to obtain a greater share of the surplus produced by others. In his model, individuals continually engage in pairwise competitions in which the winner gains a fixed fraction of the loser's assets. The probability that the richer person will win each competition is greater than 50 percent but less than 100 percent.

From these simple assumptions Angle derives the expected distribution of wealth, yielding curves that bear a strong resemblance to the empirical data for many societies. His behavioral model, like that of neoclassical economics, is obviously oversimplified; among other limitations, it makes no provision for group interactions or categorical inequalities. (In an extension of the model in Angle 1992, he allows coalitions among individuals, simulating several features of racial inequality.) However, it is a model in which inequality is a natural, endogenous result, even among individuals of identical abilities and preferences. Angle attributes the origins of his behavioral hypothesis, in part, to the economics of Adam Smith and Karl Marx, as well as to developments in sociology, anthropology, and evolutionary biology.

Economic theory has, of course, fundamentally changed since the days when Adam Smith and Karl Marx could inspire the sociological imagination. Today the more common microeconomic behavioral model involves well-informed, utility-maximizing individuals participating in perfectly competitive markets (in which they frequently solve complex mathematical optimization problems). There are, of course, numerous theoretical analyses that attempt to modify aspects of this model while maintaining its mathematical rigor. One that is particularly relevant to the distribution of wealth, by Arthur Robson (1992), assumes that people care about their relative status as well as their absolute wealth—adopting an idea that has lingered on the margins of economic theory at least since the days of Thorstein Veblen. Robson's model solves some anomalies in the standard theory and makes the predicted wealth distribution appear somewhat more realistic; it also allows multiple equilibria and implies that the equilibrium wealth distribution need not be socially optimal.

Another possible modification of standard economic theories leads to remarkable quantitative success in modeling the distribution of wealth. Mark Huggett (1996) argues that people do not only save to meet their predictable life-cycle (retirement) needs; they also save for precautionary reasons, based on uncertainty about their own future earnings, health, and longevity. There is no market that offers insurance for future earnings uncertainty; variations in luck among otherwise identical individuals will lead to differing income and wealth levels over time. The remarkable point is that Huggett not only develops an abstract mathematical model representing these ideas, but also goes to great lengths to calibrate the model with actual U.S. data, and asks whether it can replicate the observed inequalities of wealth. Some of his simulations provide a reasonably close match to the Gini ratio for wealth and to the shares in total wealth of the top 5 percent and 20 percent. However, his predictions all fall well short of the actual share of the top 1 percent and understate the extent of within-age-group inequality. He concludes with speculations about modifications to the model that might make it even more realistic.

The precautionary reasons for saving and the importance of personal wealth as a source of security are vividly illustrated in the survey research on race and wealth by **Melvin Oliver and Thomas Shapiro.** Oliver and Shapiro document the fact that at every income level, age, and family status, blacks have far less wealth than comparable whites.[2] In numerous anecdotes describing people they interviewed (found in the original, not in the summary), the authors describe how modest personal wealth makes it possible to overcome the economic problems of temporary unemployment, illness, or accident, while the absence of wealth allows small crises to turn into long-term losses. Their book is primarily a stark statement of the economic realities of race in America. However, it can also be read as a description of the personal meaning of economic security, currently available only to some whites and few blacks, which an equitable society should strive to provide for all.

Why Wealth Wields Power

The statement that wealth creates power may seem obviously true, a part of common knowledge of life in an unequal society. But exactly how does power arise from wealth? There are at least three answers, of which the third calls for the most detailed exploration.

First, those with more wealth or income inevitably have more power over resource allocation in a market economy. A smoothly functioning competitive market produces whatever is profitable to sell; in the ancient but applicable textbook metaphor, the market makes its decisions on the basis of "dollar votes." To be wealthy is to have more votes in the economic election. This power exists independently of any institutional role, or indeed of any conscious intention or planning to influence events. The rich, simply by being rich and going shopping, divert resources into the production of whatever luxuries they currently desire. Traditionally, conservatives have seen this unequal exercise of power as an acceptable price to pay for the efficiency of the market, while liberals have often viewed the same phenomenon as an argument for redistributive policies such as progressive taxation.

In addition to the pervasive and passive market power that accrues to wealth, there are more active ways in which wealth influences economic outcomes. Samuel Bowles and Herbert Gintis (1992) describe the power of lenders, analogously to the power of employers, in terms of their "contested exchange" model. (The model is usually applied to the labor market; see the summary of their work in *The Changing Nature of Work.*) Just as employers pay a little more than the worker's marginal product to ensure loyalty and effort, so lenders offer terms a little better than a market-clearing interest rate to ensure that borrowers will remain motivated to repay their loans. For this reason, lenders prefer to lend to those who can post collateral or otherwise demonstrate likelihood of repayment. In short, credit is differentially made available to those who already have assets, thereby recreating existing inequalities. Using a similar theoretical framework, Karla Hoff (1996) maintains that, if high levels of entrepreneurship and risk-taking are socially desirable, then it is efficient as well as equitable to increase access to credit and insurance, which will encourage the poor to take such risks. Hoff's strongest empirical examples of this effect involve tenant farmers in developing countries.

The arguments raised so far—the disproportionate purchasing power of the wealthy and the differential access to credit of those with collateral—suggest two ways in which aspects of power associated with wealth can readily be incorporated into economic theory. However, they fail to address the form of power that many noneconomists would consider of primary importance, namely the ownership and control of businesses. Marxists, populists, and antitrust economists have in the past focused on this question, although it has nearly vanished from the consciousness of the economics profession at present.

Recalling the statistics presented in Table II.2, the top 1 percent of U.S. households own most bonds and other financial assets and, surprisingly, dominate unincorporated business even more completely than corporate stock holdings. Two-thirds of all equity in unincorporated businesses is held by the top 1 percent, compared to about half of all stocks owned by individuals. The mythology of small-town America, allegedly populated by countless hard-working, middle-class proprietors of stores, restaurants, and gas stations, is deeply ingrained in our thinking; few of the facts about wealth are as unexpected as the monopolization of "small business" equity by the rich. A survey of the wealth distribution by John Weicher (1997) explores this statistical anomaly, identifying professional practices of lawyers, doctors, accountants and architects, and real estate and insurance agencies, as among the most important unincorporated businesses owned by the richest Americans.

Ownership of small businesses may give rise to significant forms of power in local economic and political life, though that subject will not be pursued here. The fact that the same upper income stratum predominates in small business and corporate stock ownership certainly challenges the assumption that big and small businesses represent different interest groups (the commonality of interests between local and national business elites is examined in Domhoff, 1998, in chapters not summarized here). Much more important is the question of ownership of major corporations, the subject of the last two summaries included here. The power *of* corporations is addressed in Part IV; the remainder of this essay deals with the question of who has power *over* corporations.

Who Owns Corporate America?

In the not-too-distant past, stock ownership was almost entirely in the hands of households; today it is split between them and a variety of institutions. As shown in Table II.4, in 1950 households owned more than 90 percent; by 1994 their share had fallen to just over half. The other half is largely owned by institutional investors, particularly pension funds, mutual funds, and insurance companies. The richest 1 percent of households own half of personally owned stock, or a quarter of all corporate stock.

Does the concentration in ownership of corporate stocks still create real power over major corporations, or has ownership become diffused, as it has passed into financial intermediaries and/or managerial control? This issue, once

Table II.4. Percentage Ownership of U.S. Equities, 1950–1994

	1950	1960	1970	1980	1990	1994
Households	91.6	87.7	80.4	68.3	54.0	50.8
Private Pension Funds	0.8	3.7	7.4	14.6	18.6	17.3
Mutual Funds	2.0	3.3	4.4	2.8	6.6	12.2
Public Pension Funds	0.0	0.1	1.1	2.9	8.4	8.6
Insurance Companies	3.2	3.8	3.2	5.1	5.0	4.4
Foreign Holders	2.0	2.1	3.0	4.2	6.3	5.6
All Others	0.5	0.4	0.5	2.2	1.1	1.2
Total	100.00	100.00	100.00	100.00	100.00	100.00

Source: Benjamin M. Friedman, "Economic Impicationsd of Changing Share Ownership." *Journal of Portfolio Management* 22 (spring 1996), 59–70.

Notes: Values are percentages of year-end dollar holdings, at market prices. Households include bank-managed personal trusts. Details may not add to total because of rounding.

hotly debated, has slipped out of academic discourse in recent years—for no apparent reason. Berle and Means initiated the controversy, back in 1932, with their argument that ownership had already become so diffuse that managers exercised effective control over major corporations. While their view was debated at the time and into the 1960s and 1970s, it appears to be widely accepted today. Certainly the evidence for diffusion of ownership is stronger now than it was when Berle and Means wrote. Two of the works summarized in Part III, by Derek Bok and by Michael Jacobs, attribute the recent explosion of CEO salaries to the final triumph of managerial control.

Despite the obvious economic importance of the question of the control of corporations, most recent writing on the subject has been done by sociologists. Our two summaries are of chapters from books published in 1997 and 1998; each, however, is the third edition of an earlier work, and the sections summarized here largely seem to date from the 1980s. There is apparently no newer research on the subject, so that it is impossible to tell whether the old patterns still apply—for example, the available research cannot tell us whether the emergence of junk bonds and the rise in hostile takeovers in the 1980s caused much of a change in corporate ownership patterns.

G. William Domhoff defends the unfashionable view that individual families do exert real control over corporations—especially outside of the few hundred biggest corporations. Some wealthy families go to great lengths to conceal their still-concentrated ownership, as shown in an interesting example involving the Weyerhaeusers. The individuals who sit on corporate boards, particularly those on more than one major corporate board, form an elite, wealthy group that communicates and coordinates among corporations. Rising executives gain enough stock options to become part of the upper class and are socialized into elite charitable, social, and recreational institutions as they rise. This implies that managerial control is not necessarily something distinct from ownership control, but may reflect socialization of a new group of owners.

John Scott reviews similar evidence, and similarly rejects the idea of managerial control as defined by Berle and Means. Scott argues, however, that financial institutions, particularly banks, now are the dominant owners of major corporations. The share of the top 1–5 stockholders may be declining, but at the same time the share of the top 20, many of them institutions, can be increasing, as occurs in a provocative example involving Union Pacific. If banks own corporations, who owns the banks? To a large degree, the answer is other banks. Scott sees a dense network of interconnected ownership interests between financial and other businesses. In other chapters (not summarized) he finds somewhat different patterns in other leading capitalist economies.

Scott's network of interconnections bears a strong resemblance to the role of those who serve on multiple corporate boards for Domhoff. And both authors, as sociologists, agree that it is more useful to look at the socialization of rising executives into the world of stock owners, rather than counterposing owners versus managers as economists tend to do. To answer the big question, concentrated stock ownership occasionally brings direct control, particularly of smaller corporations; more often it brings only indirect influence. But the sociologists who examine the question see an ongoing community of interests and experience between the large network of active owner/managers who run and coordinate the corporate economy and the even larger group of passive stock-owners of similar socioeconomic backgrounds—an important type of connection that is missing from traditional economics.

In short, wealth brings power over the corporate economy—occasionally in the form of direct personal control, more frequently involving participation in a broad network of owners and managers. Wealth also provides security, as Oliver and Shapiro emphasize, in the face of planned and unplanned changes in a household's economic circumstances. And wealth also generates income in the form of dividends, interest, and rent. For all these reasons, wealth plays a leading role in the story of inequality. The extremely unequal distribution of wealth helps to create and perpetuate the more obvious inequalities of income and power.

Notes

1. U.S. Census Bureau, *Statistical Abstract of the United States: 1998,* Table 724.
2. Black wealth grew somewhat faster than white wealth in the 1990s, a period too recent to appear in Oliver and Shapiro's data; see Mishel, Bernstein, and Schmitt (1999), Table 5.8, p. 267. However, the gap is still immense, and the broad conclusions about racial differences in wealth remain unchanged.

Summary of

International Comparisons of Wealth Inequality

by Edward N. Wolff

[Published in *Review of Income and Wealth* 42, 4 (December 1996), 433–451.]

Many international comparisons of the distribution of income have appeared in the recent economics literature. Such comparisons are often based on the Luxembourg Income Study, which provides data for many countries based on standardized definitions of income. No such international database is available, however, for comparisons of wealth. This article, by an economist known for his extensive studies of the distribution of wealth, assembles wealth data for eight different countries, including relatively long time series for three of them. It summarizes the changes in the U.S. wealth distribution over time and contrasts it with other countries. The author's careful discussion of data comparability problems is omitted from this summary; interested readers should consult the original article.

Trends in Household Wealth Inequality

Two definitions of household wealth are useful in assessing long-term trends. Marketable wealth, or net worth, is the sum of all financial assets, real estate, consumer durables, and equity in unincorporated businesses, net of mortgage, consumer, and other debts. Augmented wealth is the sum of net worth plus the present value of discounted future pension and social security benefits. Augmented wealth is distributed more equally than net worth, because pensions and especially social security benefits are distributed more broadly than financial assets.

U.S. data are available for the share of household wealth, by both definitions, held by the top one percent of households in nineteen different years from 1922 through 1992. The peak year for both series was 1929, when the richest one percent held 44 percent of marketable wealth and 41 percent of augmented wealth. After several sizeable fluctuations up and down, including a particularly rapid drop after 1965, the share of the top one percent reached its low point of 20 percent of marketable wealth and 13 percent of augmented wealth in 1976–1979. This low level was due in part to the depressed stock market prices of the late 1970s, which reduced the assets of the wealthiest households more than others. The top group's share then climbed rapidly until 1989, followed by a slight dip to reach 34 percent of marketable wealth and 20 percent of augmented wealth in 1992, the latest available figures.

Two other countries, the United Kingdom and Sweden, have data on household wealth beginning in the 1920s. In both countries, the share of the top one percent in net worth declines relatively steadily from the 1920s through the 1970s. In more recent years there is virtually no change in the U.K. data and a slight increase in the share of Sweden's top percentile in the 1980s. Based on these figures, the concentration of wealth was similar in Sweden and the United States before about 1950 and again, briefly, in the late 1970s. For the rest of the time since 1950, Sweden has had noticeably less inequality than the United States. The United Kingdom, initially the most unequal of the three, has moved most rapidly toward equality; its concentration of wealth was comparable to the United States from about 1960 to 1980, but is now similar to Sweden.

More limited data on trends in wealth inequality are available for Canada and France. In Canada, there was a small decline in the concentration of wealth from 1970 to 1977 and virtually no change from 1977 to 1984. In

France there was virtually no change from 1975 to 1980 to 1986, then a decline in concentration to 1992. Unfortunately, the data in these countries cannot be directly compared to the U.S., Swedish, and British figures. However, it is clear that there is no single pattern of changes in the distribution of wealth that is typical of all developed countries; none of the other countries' data shows the sharp rise in inequality in the 1980s that is found in the United States.

Direct Comparisons of Wealth Inequality

Surveys of the distribution of wealth for various years in the 1980s can be found for Germany, Japan, and Australia, in addition to the countries discussed so far. The definitions of wealth used in the surveys, and the measures of distribution that they report, are similar but not strictly comparable. Bearing these qualifications in mind, it is possible to create a rough international comparison of the degree of inequality, with almost all of the data referring to 1983–1988.

Several studies report Gini coefficients for wealth distribution, a measure that ranges from 0 for perfect equality to 1 for maximum possible inequality. The Gini coefficient for the U.S. distribution of wealth in the mid-1980s ranged from 0.76 to 0.79 in four different surveys, compared to 0.71 in France, 0.69 in both Germany and Canada, and 0.52–0.58 in two Japanese surveys.

Some of these studies, and others, also report the share of net worth (with slight variations in definitions) held by the top 1 percent or 5 percent. The share of the top 5 percent was from 54 to 56 percent in U.S. studies, compared to 43 percent in France, 41 percent in Australia, 38 to 46 percent in Canada, 24 to 37 percent in Sweden, and 25 percent in Japan.

It is interesting to compare the findings reported here to the better-known international patterns of income distributions. The most striking fact about both income and wealth comparisons among developed countries is that the United States is now the most unequal and experienced the most rapid rise in inequality in the 1980s. In other respects, there is less correspondence between changes in income and wealth distributions. For example, Australia, Canada, France, Sweden, and the United Kingdom were roughly comparable in terms of wealth distribution in the mid-1980s; yet Australia and Canada had distinctly more income inequality, and Sweden less, than France and Britain. In terms of changes over the course of the 1980s, Sweden experienced a small rise in inequality of both income and wealth; however, the United Kingdom had rising income inequality with virtually no change in the distribution of wealth.

Summary of

Long-Term Trends in American Wealth Inequality

by Jeffrey G. Williamson and Peter H. Lindert

[Published in *Modeling the Distribution and Intergenerational Transmission of Wealth*, ed. James D. Smith (University of Chicago Press, 1980), Ch. 1, 9–93.]

The distribution of wealth has undergone marked changes in the course of American history. This article analyzes and synthesizes work by many economic historians, creating a composite picture of wealth inequality over three centuries, from early colonial times to the twentieth century. It finds, in brief, little change during the colonial era, then a sharp rise in inequality between the Revolution and the Civil War, followed by a high but little-changing concentration of wealth from about 1860 to 1929, giving way to a pronounced decline in concentration through mid-century. From the 1950s to the early 1970s (the latest period covered in this article) there was little change in wealth inequality.

The Distribution of Wealth in Colonial America

There are three competing hypotheses about the trends in inequality in colonial America. Some historians hold that a European class structure and unequal distribution of property were initially exported to America, but that the expanding frontier undercut the European model, creating an egalitarian trend. Others maintain that the frontier initially allowed a very equal distribution of land and other resources, but that economic growth in settled regions then led toward greater inequality.

In contrast to these views, the third hypothesis is best supported by the data: "Trends were mixed, but *in the aggregate* colonial inequality was stable at low levels." [14] Inequality did rise in the cities and in some settled agrarian areas, but this was offset by the expansion of newer, more egalitarian rural areas.

There are twenty-nine available local data series on the distribution of wealth in New England and the Middle colonies, with Connecticut and Massachusetts particularly well represented. These data series are drawn from tax and probate records, raising difficult questions about selectivity or bias in reporting. (See the original article for detailed treatment of these questions.) Some of the data suggest that the 1680s and 1690s were a period of lower inequality than the years before or after; thus comparisons beginning in 1690 or 1700 have sometimes found growing inequality in the colonial period. However, most of the data series that begin before 1680 show little if any change from the earliest years through the mid-1700s.

Two major exceptions to this pattern are the cities of Boston and Philadelphia, where inequality was clearly growing in the colonial period. Yet the importance of these cities should not be overstated. Boston accounted for a small and declining share of the population of the New England colonies, as did Philadelphia in the Middle colonies. On balance, rising inequality in the leading colonial cities barely affects the regional averages, which show little change in the share of top wealth holders.

The First Century of Independence

The first reliable nationwide wealth estimates are for the thirteen colonies in 1774. These estimates can be compared to data from the 1860 Census, which asked questions about wealth. The comparison shows that there was a sharp rise in inequality in the first century of independence. The top 1 percent of free adult males held 12 percent of all assets in 1774 and 29 percent in 1860; the share of the top 10 percent rose from 49 percent in 1774 to 73 percent in 1860. The Gini ratio for the distribution of total assets among free adult males rose from 0.632 to 0.832. Dramatic increases in inequality occurred both in the South and in the rest of the country. The qualitative conclusion—the existence of a strong trend toward inequality—remains valid under a number of possible adjustments for sampling bias or differences between the earlier and later data sources.

Several demographic shifts could have affected the postindependence distribution of wealth. On average, the population aged quite markedly; the percentage of adults in the youngest age groups dropped, while older groups rose in importance. However, average wealth was lowest, and the distribution of wealth was most unequal among the youngest groups of adults. Thus if all else remained equal, the aging of the population should have led to reduced overall inequality, the opposite of the observed trend.

Rising immigration could have led to increased inequality. Immigrants had lower average wealth and a more unequal distribution than did native-born free adults. However, the fragmentary available evidence suggests that the effect was not large. In 1860 the Gini coefficient for wealth was 0.832 for all free adult males versus 0.816 for those who were native born. By 1870 even this small difference had essentially vanished; the Gini coefficient was 0.833 for all adult males and 0.831 for the native born.

Urbanization had a stronger, but still minor, impact on inequality. The urban share of the Northern population rose from 8 percent in 1790 to more than 25 percent in 1860. Urban wealth was higher on average, and more unequally distributed, than rural wealth. Yet if the variance within urban and rural areas had remained constant, urbanization would have raised the Gini coefficient for Northern wealth by only 4 percent from 1790 to 1860. The vast majority of the

surge in inequality in antebellum America occurred within (rather than between) sectors and regions.

When and where did wealth become more concentrated? There is little direct
evidence. One relatively well-studied topic is the ownership of slaves. Slaveholdings grew slightly more concentrated in the hands of the biggest slave-
holders after 1830, while the share of Southern families that owned any slaves
declined; the combination of these trends led to a pronounced rise in the inequality of slaveholdings among all families.

Other available observations are mainly from tax and probate data for Northeastern cities. Some show a trough in inequality in the 1810s and 1820s; all
show a steep increase after 1830. The average rate of increase in inequality in
these data series is broadly consistent with the change in national data between
1774 and 1860, as cited earlier. However, census data on ownership of real estate, the largest component of personal wealth at the time, shows essentially no
increase in inequality between 1850 and 1860. The tentative conclusion, therefore, is that the concentration of wealth rose especially steeply from the 1820s
to the late 1840s, coinciding with the first wave of industrialization.

Civil War to Great Depression

"The seven decades following the Civil War mark a period for which wealth inequality remained very high and exhibited no significant long-term trend."
[56] Between the 1860 and 1870 censuses, the concentration of wealth in the
North was virtually unchanged, while the concentration of wealth among white
Southerners dropped sharply due to emancipation. Subsequent censuses do not
include comparable information. A set of guesses about wealth distribution
based on the partial data in the 1890 census suggest little change from 1870.

Estate data for 1912 to 1923 for twenty-three selected counties in thirteen
states plus the District of Columbia show a sharp drop in wealth inequality
across World War I, consistent with other findings on income equalization in
the war years. In the 1920s, the decade in which extensive wealth data first become available, inequality rose rapidly, with the top wealthholders apparently
regaining their pre-World War I position by 1929. The all-time peak of inequality was at some point between 1860 and 1929, but we do not know exactly when it occurred.

The Twentieth-Century Leveling

The share of top wealthholders dropped precipitously over the two decades
after 1929, hitting a trough around 1949 but then rising only slightly through
1972 (the latest data in this article). The top 1 percent of adults held 36 percent

of all personal wealth in 1929, but only 21 percent in 1949. While wealth data is somewhat more abundant in the twentieth century, it is not necessarily of better quality. The new problem of tax evasion distorts all voluntary reporting of wealth in recent years. If twentieth-century taxes have stimulated successful efforts to conceal large wealthholdings, then reported data may understate inequality.

Two other trends imply that reported wealth data may overstate the extent of inequality. First, human capital is of rising importance and is distributed more equally than property. For male cohorts aged 35 to 44 around the mid-twentieth century, the Gini coefficient averaged 0.45 for human capital versus 0.71 for conventional wealth. Estimates of the aggregate value of human capital suggest that, at least since 1929, it has been growing more rapidly than other forms of wealth. Moreover, human capital is often held by younger individuals who are less likely to own conventional forms of wealth, implying that it equalizes the distribution of resources.

Second, social security and pension benefits have expanded rapidly, and are distributed much more equally than conventional wealth. One study calculated that for 1962, the share of the top 1 percent of wealthholders aged 35 to 64 is reduced from 28 percent of conventional wealth to 19 percent when the present value of social security benefits is included. The reduction would be smaller if based on adults of all ages, but it would be larger if pensions as well as social security were included.

Summary of

A Story of Two Nations: Race and Wealth

by Melvin L. Oliver and Thomas M. Shapiro

[Published in *Black Wealth/White Wealth: A New Perspective on Racial Inequality* (New York: Routledge, 1995), Ch. 5, 91–125.]

Analyses of racial inequality frequently focus on the gap between black and white incomes, implicitly or explicitly assuming that income is a good measure of economic well-being. This book emphasizes the separate importance of wealth, arguing that assets as well as income are required for economic security and stability. Using statistical results from an extensive 1988 survey, the chapter summarized here finds that the disparity between black and white households is far greater in terms of wealth than in terms of incomes. The ratio of black to white median incomes was 0.62; the ratio for median net worth was 0.08. Similar racial gaps, though not always equally extreme, can be found within many socioeconomic and demographic subgroups of the population.

The Black Middle Class

Membership in the "middle class" is an ambiguous concept, at times referring to a certain level of income, education, occupation, or self-employment status. Three possible definitions of the middle class, which are useful for statistical analysis, are: those earning between $25,000 and $50,000 (in 1988); those with college degrees; and those in white-collar jobs. By any definition, the black middle class is much farther behind its white counterparts in wealth than in income.

The ratio of median black to white incomes is 0.70 for white-collar workers and 0.76 for college graduates. In contrast, the ratio of median black to white net worth, for the three definitions of middle class, ranges from 0.15 to 0.35. The median white household had a net worth of $44,000 to $75,000, depending on which definition is used; black median net worth was $8,000 to $17,000. In terms of net financial assets (i.e., excluding equity in homes and vehicles), the contrast is even more extreme. Median financial assets ranged from $7,000 to $20,000 for the three white middle-class categories, and from zero to $300 for the corresponding black groups.

The racial income gap is somewhat narrower among married couples (not restricted to the middle class); the ratio of black/white median incomes is 0.80 for all married couples and 0.85 for two-earner couples. Yet the black/white wealth ratio is 0.27 for all married couples and 0.31 for two-earner couples. The wealth difference among couples does not appear to be declining over time; among young (25 to 35) two-earner couples, the income ratio is 0.81, while the wealth ratio is 0.18. In all of these categories, the median black couple has zero net financial assets.

The wealth gap is important because "a middle-class standard of living rests on the twin pillars of income and wealth. The two together create a solid economic foundation that simultaneously safeguards a secure standard of living and enhances future life chances. When either one is lacking, middle-class status is jeopardized." [94]

A Wealth Comparison

By any standard, the black/white wealth gap is substantial. The average black family has modest home and/or car equity, and no other assets; the average white family has more home equity, and financial assets as well. Over time, the gap is getting only slightly narrower in relative terms, and larger in absolute terms. From 1967 to 1988, the net worth of the mean (not median) black family rose from $4,000 to $24,000, compared to an increase from $20,000 to $96,000 for whites. The gap is narrowest, but still significant, at the highest income levels. Among those with 1988 incomes of $50,000 or more, the ratio of black/white median net worth was .52.

Has there been black economic progress in recent years? In the survey used in this study, blacks represented 9.2 percent of the population, and received 7.4 percent of total income. While still short of parity, this figure does represent progress over earlier years. However, blacks owned only 2.9 percent of the nation's net worth and held a mere 1.3 percent of all financial assets. Whites were 82.5 percent of the population and owned 95 percent of all financial assets. Viewed through the prism of wealth, black economic progress is much harder to see.

The Composition of Assets

Not only the size, but also the composition of assets differs between blacks and whites. Home and vehicle equity accounts for 72 percent of black assets, but only 49 percent of white assets. Financial assets of all types are more common among whites: 76 percent of whites, versus 43 percent of blacks, have interest-bearing bank accounts; 27 percent of whites versus 6 percent of blacks have IRA or Keogh pension accounts. White households save more than blacks at the same income level and put a higher proportion of their resources into interest-bearing assets. Such differences are most pronounced at lower incomes; at higher incomes, black and white portfolios and savings rates become increasingly similar.

Home ownership is the most important single asset for both whites and blacks. Blacks own 3.9 percent of all home equity, greater than their share of other forms of wealth, but still far less than proportional to their numbers, or even their incomes. More whites than blacks are homeowners (66 percent versus 42 percent), and median white home equity is greater as well. Again, the gap is greater at lower income levels and narrows but does not vanish for those with incomes over $50,000.

Routes to Wealth and Poverty

Human capital characteristics such as training, skills, and experience have well-known effects on earnings. Intricate patterns of differences can be seen in the data on education. Among those with the lowest level of education (elementary school only), black and white incomes are virtually the same. Then the first several steps up the educational ladder add much more to white than to black incomes. Finishing high school, for example, adds $5,800 to median white income, but only $2,800 for blacks, compared to the incomes of high school dropouts. The rewards of higher education are much more equal; moving from a high school diploma to a college degree increases white income by $18,000 and black income by almost $17,000.

In terms of wealth, each additional level of education is associated with an increase in median net worth, for both whites and blacks. However, the rewards are much greater for whites at every step. High school graduates have median net worth $9,000 greater than dropouts among whites, but only $800 greater among blacks. White college graduates have median net worth $34,000 greater than those with just a high school diploma; among blacks, the corresponding figure is $14,000. The contrast between the nearly equal returns to college graduation in terms of income, and the starkly unequal returns in terms of wealth, "suggests that more complex dynamics are at work than we have yet been able to explain." [110]

Racial disparities also change with age. The racial gap in median incomes narrows from $12,000 for young people to $10,000 in the 50-to-64 age bracket, and less than $3,000 for seniors. The latter figure, however, does not mean that near-equality is reached in retirement; the difference in wealth is so great that blacks are much more likely to have to continue working after age 65. The racial gap in median net worth starts at $7,000 for young households and expands steadily to $70,000 for those who are 50 to 64. The wealth gap grows with age, even though the income gap does not, in part because more whites begin adult life with assets that grow in value—and in part because whites are more likely to inherit wealth from their parents, which typically happens when the children are in their 40s or 50s.

A final factor to consider is family structure. "Explanations of racial inequality often start, and too often end, with a discussion of changes in black family structure." [122] Households headed by single women are far worse off than married couples, among whites as well as among blacks. White single-parent households have low incomes and $4,000 in median net worth; black single-parent households have lower incomes, and, in most cases, no assets whatsoever. As we have seen, black married couples are closer to income parity with whites than the black population in general; yet a huge gap in wealth remains, even among married couples. For every family status—including those who are never married, separated, divorced, or widowed—whites have greater assets and incomes than blacks. One of the starkest racial differences occurs among widows, where whites have median financial assets of over $15,000, while blacks have none.

Since racial gaps in income, and particularly in wealth, exist within every family structure, it is implausible that black family structure alone could explain inequality. The same is true for other socioeconomic and demographic categories such as education, age, and work experience. "[T]he wealth gap that creates two nations, one black and one white, continues to be America's great racial divide." [125]

Summary of

The Corporate Community and the Upper Class

by G. William Domhoff

[Published in *Who Rules America?*, 3d. ed. (Mountain View, Calif.:
Mayfield Publishing, 1998), Ch. 3, 71–116.]

This book, an update of the author's 1967 classic work, documents the existence of a small, wealthy, socially cohesive upper class in America, and shows that the upper class is vastly overrepresented in the top echelons of government, business, and other institutions. The sections of a chapter summarized here argues that, contrary to the conventional wisdom, members of the upper class control many of the largest corporations and banks. Other sections of the chapter, omitted from this summary, discuss other aspects of the sociology of the upper class, including the role of upper-class women (who are rarely involved in business) and patterns of intermarriage and intergenerational persistence of social status.

It is widely believed that direct control of corporations by individual owners has been virtually eliminated by the dispersal of stock ownership. There is often said to be a separation of ownership and control in the modern corporate economy. A four-part response to this popular view, presented here, shows that

> (1) members of the upper class own almost half of all privately held corporate stock in the United States; (2) many large stockholding families in the upper class continue to be involved in the direction of major corporations . . . ; (3) members of the upper class are disproportionately represented on the boards of large corporations . . . ; and (4) the professional managers of middle-level origins are assimilated into the upper class both socially and economically and share the values of upper-class owners. [71–72]

Stock Ownership and Control

While it is true that there are millions of stock owners, systematic studies repeatedly show that most of them own very little stock. Several studies, ranging from the 1920s to the 1990s, found that the top 1 percent of all adults own between 50 percent and 76 percent of all privately held stock. There is significant concentration even within this small group; one study found that in 1969 the top 0.2 percent of adults held one-third of all privately owned stock. The concentration of stock ownership does not by itself settle the question of corporate control; it would still be possible for ownership of each firm to be dispersed within the upper class, preventing the exercise of individual control. However, further evidence shows that such dispersion of ownership is far from universal.

There are important categories of businesses in which there is a clearly visible, close relationship between ownership and control. Many fairly large corporations, such as Mars Candy, Levi Strauss, and Amway, are privately owned by a family or group of families. Several dozen of these would have been in the *Fortune 500* listing of the largest corporations in the mid-1990s, if they had been publicly owned. (Ninety-two of them have made their owners wealthy enough to appear in the Forbes 400 listing of the wealthiest individuals.) Among publicly held corporations just below the 200 or 300 largest firms, several studies show that there are often a few large owners who also serve as directors and top managers. The problem of the relationship between ownership and control thus arises primarily for the very largest of corporations.

Patterns of Family Ownership

Even within firms where no major owners are apparent at first glance, wealthy families or individuals may continue to play significant roles. Wealthy families sometimes create family offices or holding companies to manage their investments. Such devices provide coordination and professional advice to family members, and in some (not all) cases may also serve to conceal the identity of the investors.

For example, a detailed sociological study of the Weyerhaeuser family, whose wealth is concentrated in the lumber industry, showed that in the 1970s they controlled not only the Weyerhaeuser Corporation, but also Potlatch and Arcata National, two other major lumber companies where family control was not immediately apparent. The family office, Fiduciary Counselors, Inc., and two related holding companies, Rock Island Corporation and Green Valley Corporation, coordinated the family's investments as well as its charitable and political contributions. It would not be obvious to the casual observer that these nondescript corporate entities represent vehicles for one family's ownership.

Three major studies providing detailed evidence on the extent of family ownership in large corporations were available as of the early 1980s; all three reached similar conclusions. The most extensive study examined the owners of the 500 largest industrial corporations in 1980. One individual or family held at least 5 percent of the stock in 44 percent of the 423 firms that were not controlled by other corporations or foreign interests; two to four families held at least 5 percent of the stock and were represented on the board of directors in another 7 percent. Among the 50 largest, however, only 17 percent had evidence of significant family ownership.

Such studies may, in fact, represent underestimates of family control. The study of the top 500 industrials found that the Weyerhaeusers owned 5 percent of Arcata in 1980, while the company itself reported that the three Weyerhaeusers on its board owned 7.5 percent of its stock in 1975. When the company decided to buy up its outstanding stock and go private in 1981, it turned out that the Weyerhaeuser family owned about 30 percent of Arcata's common stock.

The Board of Directors

There are cases, particularly among the very largest corporations, where stock is widely dispersed. Often the largest owners are pension funds or other financial institutions, which rarely take any role in influencing management. In such cases, the composition of the board of directors is of great importance. Several sociological studies have found that the directors of the largest corporations have elite social backgrounds, with roughly one-third coming from families listed in the Social Register, attending prestigious private schools, and belonging to exclusive upper-class clubs.

Small groups within the upper class often play important roles in the corporate world, as suggested by the author's study of alumni of Saint Paul's, a small, exclusive private school. Of the several thousand alumni who were over 45 in 1980, 102 were directors of one or more of the 800 largest U.S. corporations. They were particularly concentrated in the financial sector; twenty-one Saint Paul's graduates were officers or directors of Morgan Guaranty Trust, one of the largest banks in the country.

Other social institutions connect top executives and directors. Exclusive clubs such as the Links Club in New York provide meeting places for the elite; in 1970, twenty-one of the top twenty-five industrials and twenty of the top twenty-five banks nationwide had a director who belonged to the Links Club. The Bohemian Grove summer festivities are a famous gathering of the economic elite; in 1980, one officer or director attended Bohemian Grove from 30 percent of the 800 largest corporations, and much higher proportions of the very largest firms.

All measures of upper-class social origins and activity are most pronounced for those who are directors of more than one corporation. In 1970 there were 8623 people on the boards of the 800 largest corporations, of whom 1572 were on two or more boards. Those who serve on multiple boards of directors are often bankers or executives who sit on bank boards; they play a crucial role in coordination and communication among corporations. These interlocking directorates do not represent distinct corporate cliques, but rather interconnections throughout the corporate world as a whole. This role is played largely by members of the upper class: Those on two or more boards of directors are roughly twice as likely as single directors to be in the Social Register, to have attended a prestigious private school, or to belong to an elite social club.

The Assimilation of Rising Executives

Despite the prominent role of upper-class families and individuals, there are many top executives in major corporations who have worked their way up from middle-class origins. These upwardly mobile executives enter a process of assimilation into the upper class that often begins in college—regardless of social origins, a disproportionate number of CEOs attended the most prestigious private colleges—and continues as they rise in the business world. They frequently join elite charitable and cultural organizations and social clubs (as do their spouses). Their children are much more likely to attend private schools and Ivy League colleges than they were.

Assimilation occurs in economic as well as social terms. Rising executives receive generous stock options, making them into owners as well as managers, and ensuring that they will understand the perspective of wealthy investors. In view of this process of assimilation, it is not surprising that there are few, if any, important differences between the behavior of managers in owner-controlled and management-controlled firms. There is no difference in profitability, nor in the managerial interest in profit maximization. When giving public speeches, executives at managerially controlled firms were no more likely than their counterparts in owner-controlled firms to emphasize the social responsibility of corporations; nor were there differences in their attitudes toward government regulation, government spending, or labor relations.

The evidence presented in this chapter leads to the conclusion that

> The upper class is based in the ownership and control of profit-producing investments in stocks, bonds, and real estate. In other words, the nationwide upper class rooted in the corporate community is a capitalist class as well as a social class. Its members are not simply concerned with the interests of one corporation or business sector, but with such matters as the investment climate, the rate of profit, and the overall political climate. [116]

The corporate power of the upper class gives them direct influence over the economic lives of the great majority of Americans and indirect influence over political life as well.

Summary of

Structures of Corporate Control

by John Scott

[Published in *Corporate Business and Capitalist Classes* (New York: Oxford University Press, 1997), Ch. 3, 35–78.]

Large corporations clearly dominate modern industrial economies. But since ownership of the stock of these firms is often widely dispersed, it is not so clear who dominates the corporations. This book explores the patterns of ownership, control, and the exercise of power within the corporate economy. The sections summarized here analyze and contrast several possible systems of control and review the evidence on the ownership of the largest U.S. corporations. Other sections, reviewing comparable data for other countries, find somewhat different patterns of ownership in Japan and in most of Western Europe.

Shareholders, Financiers, and Managers

In analyzing power within the corporation, it is useful to distinguish between the power to set long-run strategic goals and the power to direct day-to-day operations; these can be called control and rule, respectively. The distinction was less important in the classic entrepreneurial firm, where the owner/manager exercised both control and rule. The corporate form separates these two forms of power, giving owners an attenuated form of control—particularly the right to vote on the selection of the top managers, who direct the daily operations of the firm.

There are some cases in which a unified group of shareholders effectively maintains complete control over a corporation. In other cases, however, the power of shareholders may be challenged either by managers, using their position in the organizational hierarchy to rule the corporation for themselves, or by external financiers, who can exercise indirect control by dictating the terms on which credit will be available to the firm.

The patterns of ownership of a corporation range from the case in which one individual or group holds a majority of the stock and hence controls the corporation to completely dispersed stockholdings that allow management to gain control. An important question of judgment arises between these two extremes: What fraction of the company's stock is required for a large minority stockholder to exercise effective control? The answer depends on the dispersal of the remaining shares; estimates of the threshold for minority control have drifted downward over time. Many analysts now suggest that minority control is possible with 10 percent of a company's stock, and a few claim that only 5 percent is needed, if the other 95 percent is scattered widely among numerous small holdings.

A classic picture of the evolution of ownership, due to Berle and Means,[1] assumed that as the original owners sold their shares, stockholdings would become steadily more dispersed. As a result, corporations would tend to progress from majority control to minority control, and finally to management control. However, the process of dispersal is not inexorable. The growth of ownership by pension funds, insurance companies, and other financial institutions has led to a renewed concentration of shareholdings. Even when there is no single dominant investor, the institutional and financial investors as a group may be too large for management to ignore.

This raises the possibility of control through a constellation of interests, a concept suggested by Max Weber in his discussion of power. Institutional investors do not generally act like a cohesive controlling group, yet management knows that it cannot disregard their interests. The corporation may depend on its institutional investors for future capital needs, and their shareholdings are large enough that they could, if provoked, demand changes in policies or personnel.

This pattern, implying corporate control through a constellation of interlocking financial interests, characterizes Anglo-American economies. It can be distinguished both from the Berle and Means model of management control, and from the tighter groupings of interlocked firms, clustered around banks, leading companies, or wealthy families, that can be seen in many European countries and in Japan.

Corporate Power and Control in the United States

Throughout the twentieth century, the average number of shareholders in the largest corporations has risen and the average size of personal shareholdings has fallen. The number of companies with majority or minority control by a leading stockholder has fallen as well. The largest owner held 20 percent or more of the stock in eighteen of the forty largest corporations in 1900, and eighty-four of the largest 200 in 1929. Yet by 1975, the largest owner held 10 percent or more, a lower standard, in only twenty-five of the largest 200 corporations. There are methodological problems with many empirical studies of stock ownership, which may result in a tendency to underestimate family control of corporations. Even when attempts are made to correct for these problems, however, the trend is still toward decreasing family control over major corporations.

A more serious problem concerns the treatment of intercorporate shareholdings. Berle and Means, and many later analysts, have assumed that the decline of family control must imply the rise of management control of corporations. This ignores the role of financial investors, whose stockholdings have risen rapidly; by the 1970s, financial institutions owned one-third of all corporate stock. Could such institutional stockholdings give rise to control through a constellation of interests?

An example of a particular corporation illustrates the growing importance of financial institutions. Union Pacific, a railroad company, was classified by Berle and Means as management controlled in 1929, when the top twenty shareholders owned 10 percent of the company. By 1937 the top twenty held 14 percent; in 1980 the top twenty held 22 percent of the stock. Most of the top twenty shareholders were banks, insurance companies, and pension funds; in 1980, only five were families. No single institution or family approached the level of a controlling interest in Union Pacific; the Harriman family was the largest stockholder in 1937 with 3 percent of the stock, and second largest (just behind Prudential Insurance) with 2 percent in 1980. Nonetheless, there was a growing concentration of ownership in the hands of a constellation of investors.

A study by the author examined the ownership of the 252 largest American corporations in 1980. In sixty-one cases the top investors held sufficient stock for majority or minority control; in 154 others, well over half, there was a controlling constellation of interests (i.e., the top twenty owners held between 10 percent and 50 percent of the stock). None of the enterprises for which information was available had a sufficient dispersion of ownership to qualify as management controlled. Family investors have not disappeared; two-thirds of the controlling constellations included some family interests. Yet institutional investors played a larger part than individuals in these constellations.

Institutional investors have usually preferred to remain passive and uninvolved in corporate management. Unfortunately for them, this is not always possible. Institutions may be unable to sell their stock when they are displeased with management, either because other investors are unwilling to buy because they are displeased for the same reasons, or because the institutional stockholdings are so large that a sudden sale would depress the price. Thus institutions may find themselves locked into a stock and forced to take a more active role in corporate affairs. This can involve seeking representation on the board of directors, or ensuring that the board includes independent, outside influences; in more extreme cases it might include voting against management or attempting to alter the composition of the board. There are scattered signs of growing activism among institutional investors; in 1995 the pension fund TIAA-CREF mobilized other institutions to remove the chairman of W.R. Grace, and to reduce the size of its board and the average age of its directors.

If financial institutions increasingly control nonfinancial corporations, who owns and controls the financials? A 1970 study found intricate patterns of interlocking ownership among banks in the 1960s; for example, in each of the top six New York banks, between 12 and 20 percent of the shares were held by the same six New York banks. Almost half of the top 275 banks nationwide had at least 5 percent of their stock held by other financial institutions. The limited available information suggests that financial institutions are governed by constellations of interests similar to those found in other corporations, connected by extremely dense networks of interlocking and overlapping ownership.

The twentieth-century history of the ownership and control of U.S. corporations begins with a long decline, but not disappearance, of family ownership and a corresponding rise of management control until the 1950s. "Since the 1950s, however, managerial enterprises and surviving family enterprises have declined in number as enterprises in which intercorporate 'institutional' shareholdings are the dominant form of ownership have grown in number. . . . Control through a constellation of interests has become the dominant form of strategic control in the largest American enterprises." [78]

Note

1. A.A. Berle and G.C. Means, *The Modern Corporation and Private Property* (1932).

PART III

New Paths to the Top: CEO and Celebrity Compensation

Overview Essay

by Frank Ackerman

There is an unconventional form of inequality that fascinates the public but fits poorly, if at all, into standard economic theories. A certain number of people with little or no capital, and with only slightly greater skills and abilities than others, become famous, rise to the top of their profession, and receive enormous incomes. Others, nearly or equally as skilled, continue to work hard at similar endeavors and earn very ordinary incomes. The lifestyles of the rich and famous receive endless attention in the mass media; can economists explain the incomes of the rich and famous?

Celebrity and CEO compensation is a significant part of the story of inequality. Many of those at the peak of the income distribution today got to the top by being a star in entertainment or sports, a leader in a profession such as law or medicine, or a top executive in business. In his book *Money*, Andrew Hacker estimates that athletes, movie stars, lawyers, and CEOs account for perhaps 4000 of the 58,000 working-age households with at least $1 million in taxable income in 1994.[1]

This is qualitatively different from the long-standing pattern in which affluence is based on the development and ownership of successful businesses or natural resources. Within that older paradigm, new businesses and newly wealthy owners have frequently emerged. Bill Gates and other computer industry entrepreneurs provide well-known contemporary examples. Yet despite the novelty of his enterprise, Bill Gates has in essence followed the path taken long ago by the Carnegies, Rockefellers, and DuPonts. That is, he has prospered from success in business, based on a monopoly position in a rising industry.

Michael Jordan, Jerry Seinfeld, Oprah Winfrey, Walt Disney executive Michael Eisner, and others like them have also become immensely rich, but not, at least initially, because of their ownership of businesses or corporate stock. Rather, as stars in their fields, they have been successful in winning compensation far beyond what was imaginable a generation ago.

This essay explores the "celebrity/CEO" style of compensation and its implications both for economic theory, and for our understanding of the dynamics of inequality. The discussion begins with general social critiques and theoretical perspectives. It then turns to the separate economic analyses of CEO compensation on the one hand and the salaries of sports stars and entertainment celebrities on the other hand, and concludes with a hypothesis about the economic changes that have allowed these new forms of affluence.

Too Much Competition, or Too Little?

In *The Winner-Take-All Society*, **Robert Frank and Philip Cook** suggest that there is a spreading pattern of huge rewards for being "number one" in some competitive endeavor. This, they argue, is distorting resource allocation, drawing labor skills and effort away from important, productive tasks that receive ordinary levels of compensation.

The pattern Frank and Cook describe as "winner-take-all" markets has been analyzed by economic theorists under the rubric of tournament theory. This theory (originated by Lazear and Rosen 1981) observes that in some occupations, people are paid for their relative, not absolute, performance. A sports tournament with a fixed prize for the first-place contestant is a classic example, but there are many others. Conventional systems of pay based on an absolute measure of productivity can be compared to school grading with a fixed standard of what constitutes an A, B, and so on. Tournament-style pay scales can be compared to grading on a curve, in which the best student is sure to get an A regardless of the level of absolute accomplishment.

Tournament pay is attractive to employers in circumstances where it is difficult to establish appropriate absolute performance standards, or to monitor absolute individual accomplishment. This may explain the popularity of incentives such as bonuses for the sales representative who sells the most. In theory, Lazear and Rosen show that there is a set of tournament "prizes" (for those who do not come in first, as well as those who do) that will inspire exactly the same level of effort and lead to the same allocation of labor as a conventional pay scale. Preferences between equivalent tournament and conventional pay scales depend on the degree of risk aversion, among other factors.

The burgeoning discussion of tournament theory in the economics literature has largely failed to address the question that is central for Frank and Cook: Why are "tournaments" or winner-take-all markets becoming more common, and the top prizes becoming larger? Frank and Cook suggest a range of possible explanations. The declining cost of communication and transportation increases the size of markets, creating economies of scale in production and distribution that allow individual firms (and entertainers) to reach more people. Network economies and learning curves cause "lock-in," so that technologies and producers that gain an early lead are hard to displace. Prestige and reputation are important factors when decisions are made on the basis of limited information; this creates positive feedback, since the best-known individuals become even better known. The "mental shelf space" constraint—that is, the limit on the number of different firms, individuals, and activities that anyone can remember—leads to ever-intensifying competition to be well enough known to be on the shelf.

This list may or may not contain the right answer to the original question. Indeed, the passage from *Winner-Take-All Society* summarized here could perhaps be faulted for offering glimpses of too many different answers, without a clear evaluation or discussion of the relationship among them. However, Frank and Cook unmistakably asked the right question—and for that, their book deserves much greater attention than it has received from the economics profession (see, e.g., the largely dismissive review by Rosen 1996).

While Frank and Cook argue that excessive competition is driving up celebrity and executive salaries, **Derek Bok** reaches an opposite conclusion. Analyzing the escalation of executive and elite professional salaries since the early 1970s, Bok concludes that the problem is that doctors, lawyers, and CEOs have too much control over their own compensation. The services they provide are unique and differentiated, so that there is a potentially large payoff to getting the best possible candidate for the job; but those who make the hiring and salary decisions are inevitably poorly informed about the relevant professional qualifications, or about the pool of alternative candidates. Thus the job-holder often plays a major part in advising his "employers" about how much to pay him. In the extreme, a corporate CEO often picks the members of the compensation committee that sets the salaries for top executives, including the CEO himself. According to Bok, the acceptability of escalating salaries may stem in part from the politics of the Reagan years, which brought greed back into fashion.

Bok's image of collusion at the top leads to conclusions similar to Frank and Cook's picture of excessive competition. According to Bok, top executives and elite professionals are, in general, overpaid. The high salaries in these fields distort the allocation of talent, pulling capable people away from lower-paid but socially important fields such as teaching and public administration. And there is often no effective way to structure a merit pay system to motivate hard work for socially desirable goals. The last of these points is particularly important in the discussion of executive compensation.

The Price of Management

CEO compensation has been rising rapidly in recent decades. As seen in Table III.1, during the stock market boom of the late 1990s a few executives received

Table III.1. The Highest-Paid CEOs in 1998

Rank	Name	Company	Total Compensation (millions of dollars)
1.	Michael Eisner	Walt Disney	576
2.	Mel Karmazin	CBS	202
3.	Sanford Weill	Citigroup	167
4.	Stephen Case	American Online	159
5.	Craig Barrett	Intel	117
6.	John Welsh	General Electric	84
7.	Henry Schacht	Lucent Technologies	67
8.	L. Dennis Kozlowski	Tyco International	65
9.	Henry Silverman	Cendant	64
10.	M. Douglas Ivester	Coca-Cola	57
11.	Charles Heimbold	Briston-Myers Squibb	56
12.	Phillip Purcell	Morgan Stanley Dean Witter	53
13.	Rueben Mark	Colgate-Palmolive	53
14.	Scott McNealy	Sun Microsystems	48
15.	Louis Gerstner	IBM	46

Source: *Business Week,* April 19, 1999.

more than $100 million, and many more received tens of millions of dollars, for a single year's work. Among those shown in the table, only Henry Silverman founded the company he now heads; Cendant is a real estate and business services company, with about $5 billion in revenues in 1998. Although several of the top-earning CEOs are, by now, owners of a significant fraction of their company's stock, it is unlikely that any were when they entered the job. Many of the companies shown in Table III.1 did very well in the 1990s, with returns to stockholders significantly above the market average; however, there were exceptions. In 1998, America Online lost money, while Walt Disney and Citigroup had below-average returns to stockholders. Moreover, there were other companies that did very well in market terms but paid their CEOs much less.

It is not only the handful of CEOs shown in Table III.1 who did exceedingly well. An annual survey by *Business Week* and Compustat reports on the compensation of the highest-paid executives at 365 of the largest U.S. companies. Average CEO compensation rose 36 percent in 1998, compared to 2.7 percent for the average blue-collar worker and 3.9 percent for the average white-collar worker. The average CEO in the survey made $10.6 million, 80 percent of it from long-term compensation (primarily exercised stock options). That is a 442 percent rise above the 1990 average of just under $2 million; virtually all of the increase is due to the soaring value of stock options. However, CEO compensation rose even faster than the stock market in 1998; the Standard & Poor 500 stock index increased 26.7 percent for the year (*Business Week,* April 19, 1999).

The average CEO compensation was also 419 times the pay of the average blue-collar worker in 1998. Similar comparisons of the incomes of CEOs to average workers can be found throughout the literature of the last twenty or thirty years; although observers have routinely been shocked at how high it was, the ratio has continued to rise. A future archaeologist could date late twentieth-century business periodicals quite accurately by referring to their astonished statements that a CEO now makes x times as much as a typical worker—with ever-increasing values of x.

Most analysts agree that salaries have risen far faster than any measure of CEO productivity. One common argument—by now it could be called the new conventional wisdom—says that huge CEO compensation is necessary to overcome the "principal-agent" problem. The problem is that, although the CEO is hired by and works for the stockholders, his incentives are different from theirs: He will tend to choose actions that make executive life more comfortable and better-paid, even at the expense of profits; and they cannot monitor his behavior in enough detail to prevent all such choices. Generous compensation in the form of stock, or stock options, is said to solve the principal-agent problem, making the CEO represent stockholders' interests by making him a stockholder. (Male pronouns are used here in the interests of accuracy: *Forbes* reports that more than 99 percent of the top 800 corporate CEOs are men.)

Michael Jacobs vigorously rebuts the principal-agent argument for high CEO salaries, based in part on his own experience in business. Incentive compensation schemes for management cannot work, in his opinion, for at least three reasons. First, it is hard to apply incentive pay plans to those below top management, although they make many crucial decisions. Second, it is prohibitively expensive to set up rewards big enough to make a significant difference to an already well-paid top executive. Finally, any compensation scheme has unintended consequences due to inescapable areas of divergence between CEO and stockholder interests. As *Business Week* said in its review of 1998 CEO compensation, "No academic has proven that higher pay creates higher performance." For Jacobs the deeper problem is the decline of mechanisms that formerly ensured corporate accountability: Stockholders, banks, and government regulators are all playing weaker roles in corporate governance than they did in the past. As a result, CEOs can drive up their own salaries in the manner described by Bok.

Paying CEOs with stock options may appeal to businesses because it appears to be an easy, costless way to reward their leaders—and, increasingly, other employees as well. Yet, as an article in *Forbes* observes, taking the easy way out does have its costs. Issuing stock options dilutes the equity and the future earnings of other stockholders.[2] By 1998 the 200 largest U.S. corporations had allocated shares to management and employee stock option plans equal to 13.2 percent of their outstanding stock. If stock options were counted as a cost to the companies that issued them, then eleven of the 100 largest U.S. companies, including Microsoft and Intel, would have reported net losses in 1996 (Morgenson 1998).

As serious as the principal-agent problem is the question that top CEO salaries raise in the minds of many people: How much is enough? What could anyone do with tens of millions of dollars, and why would anyone at that level continue striving for more? The paradigm of market incentives threatens to break down when applied to people who can afford to satisfy their every whim, and who have probably bought more toys than they will ever have time to play with.

For those at the top, it is hard to imagine desires for any end uses of additional money. More plausible, for the extremely competitive individuals who make it that far, is a desire for the reputation and status that accrue to those who make more than others. Information like that in Table III.1 is widely available in the business world, and it is likely that CEOs, board members, and others judge an executive's success in part by his standing relative to CEOs elsewhere. While the names listed in the table are not household words to most of us, they are celebrities within their world of business executives, and their gains define what is possible in the field of CEO compensation. Paying "only" half a million dollars a year to someone who runs a major company—a lavish salary by any absolute standards—would be taken as a sign that the company and/or the CEO had fallen far below the prevailing standards of corporate success.

Such considerations, unfortunately, rarely enter the academic literature on CEO compensation. In that literature, a widely discussed article by Jensen and Murphy (1990) takes an iconoclastic stance toward the new conventional wisdom on the principal-agent problem. They argue that CEO pay is remarkably insensitive to stockholder interests; their extensive database shows that in the 1980s the change in CEO net worth averaged only $3.25 per $1,000 change in stockholder wealth. This is not nearly enough to solve the principal-agent problem, since it is still easy for CEO personal interests to diverge from stockholder interests. One possible interpretation of this finding is that CEOs are not paid enough! Principal-agent theory implies, for risk-neutral CEOs, the absurd conclusion that the optimal contract would give 100 percent of any change in stock value to the CEO.

Many articles have responded to Jensen and Murphy on both theoretical and empirical grounds. Theorists reply that principal-agent theory is actually ambiguous or underspecified when it comes to the questions of CEO incentives and preferences. It is possible to hypothesize a set of relatively plausible preferences that might be held by CEOs and others, which would make the Jensen and Murphy findings consistent with principal-agent theory (Haubrich 1994, Garen 1994).

Findings like this suggest that it is hard to pin down just what principal-agent theory has to say about any particular problem. Along these lines Herbert

Simon (1991) offers an interesting critique, building on his well-known advocacy of "satisficing" or bounded rationality models of behavior. Simon criticizes principal-agent and related new theories for maintaining the problematical assumption that everyone really is optimizing, albeit in a much more complicated environment than the one assumed by neoclassical economics. In fact, the added complexity of the new approaches means that, as in the responses to Jensen and Murphy, anything could happen. An impossibly large amount of information would be needed to obtain any definite predictions about the world from such theories.

Empirical research has challenged the Jensen-Murphy finding that CEO pay is insensitive to corporate performance. Companies that are financially distressed do take it out on their CEOs at times, with salary cuts and/or dismissal, often followed by promotion of an inside candidate at lower salary, as shown by Gilson and Vetsuypens (1993). On the other hand, Boschen and Smith (1995) show that while CEO compensation may rise only slightly in the year of performance gains, it remains higher for several years. The cumulative CEO compensation response to a corporate performance gain is roughly ten times the immediate response.

A variant on the link between pay and performance is presented by Yermack (1997), who demonstrates the astonishingly good timing of CEO stock option awards. Such awards typically give the option to buy stock in the future at the price prevailing on the date of issue. Yermack shows that CEO stock options are extremely likely to be awarded shortly before favorable news drives up the price of the company's stock. The only believable explanation is that CEOs use inside information to schedule their stock awards at times when they know there is about to be an increase in the value of the stock (and therefore an increase in the value of their options to buy it).

A piece of the puzzle that fits poorly with many academic analyses is the wide international variation in CEO compensation levels. Table III.2 presents typical CEO compensation for moderate-sized industrial companies in ten countries. The other countries ranged from 14 percent to 65 percent of the U.S. level, with Japanese and German CEOs receiving less than 40 percent as much as their American counterparts.

Kaplan (1994) compares CEO compensation in the U.S. and Japan. Despite great differences in business culture, expectations, and management styles, the response (elasticity) of compensation to measures of firm performance is quite similar in the two countries. Kaplan's finding is expressed in terms of elasticities, or percentage changes—but these are percentage changes around very different average levels. Despite the far lower rate of CEO compensation in Japan, leading Japanese firms are still thought to be world-class competitors in most industries.

Returning to the underlying theoretical issues, **Brian Main, Charles**

Table III.2. CEO Compensation around the World, 1998

Country	Average annual compensation for CEO of industrial company with sales of $250–$500 million (thousands of U.S. dollars)
U.S.	1,072
Brazil	701
Hong Kong	681
Britain	646
France	520
Canada	498
Mexico	457
Japan	421
Germany	398
South Korea	151

Source: *New York Times*, January 18, 1999. Original source: Towers Perrin (a consulting firm).

O'Reilly, and James Wade argue that CEO compensation is far higher than any plausible measure of marginal product. They suggest that CEO pay may intentionally resemble a tournament, with corporations seeking to boost productivity by creating the winner-take-all effect that Frank and Cook deplore. If people like to gamble, or if they overestimate their own relative standing and chance for the prize, then tournament-style competition will induce a large quantity of high-quality effort from all those who think they have a chance at first place. Like Boschen and Smith, this study emphasizes multiyear gains: Becoming CEO has a small initial effect, but a large lifetime present value, compared to remaining a vice-president for the rest of your career. The limit on the tournament mechanism is the need to promote teamwork, or at least restrain cutthroat competition: Too much inequality of rewards makes life too unpleasant for the competitors, or makes them too unpleasant to each other, for the organization to function.

The tournament metaphor fits some, but not all, of the facts of executive life. Main et al. find evidence that a successful corporate career involves many small raises, not just a few big jumps as suggested by the simplest forms of tournament theory. Similarly, in a thoughtful, brief comment, Rees (1992) lists several ways in which the tournament model is not appropriate for executive compensation: The time frame is too long, the nature of the game being played changes as you move up through the ranks, the losers are not free to enter next year's tournament on equal terms, all contestants do not enter at the same level, success depends on external events and on the performance of nonmanagerial employees, and the "prizes" must simultaneously reward past performance and provide incentives for future efforts.

The Price of Celebrity

The winner-take-all model describes celebrity and entertainment at least as well as management. There are three areas of analysis to examine: a theoretical literature on the economics of celebrity; a detailed literature on the salaries in sports; and a much more limited discussion of other forms of entertainment.

The "economics of superstars" (introduced by Rosen 1981; see also MacDonald 1988) offers a possible explanation for the increasing, and increasingly unequal, rewards for top performers. If consumers prefer the best performer, even when quality differences are slight, and all performers face similar, rapidly increasing returns to scale in producing recordings, TV broadcasts, or other output, then small quality differences will explode into huge income differences—a process which, as described by Frank and Cook, often reaches absurd levels.

Are any quality differences at all necessary to explain stardom? Adler (1985) argues that, if people want to talk to other fans of the performers they listen to, and if search time is limited (a concept similar to Frank and Cook's "mental shelf space" constraint), it will be more attractive to listen to performers who are already popular. Small random differences in sales then can snowball into huge inequalities, even if all performers offer identical quality. To explain why there is more than one star at a time, Adler suggests that an offsetting taste for diversity may arise at very high levels of consumption, while the need for abundant fellow fans dominates at low levels.

Similar notions arise more generally in connection with network externalities (see Katz and Shapiro 1994 and literature cited there). Your telephone is more valuable if more people have phones; your computer has more software written for it if more people have the same kind; your car can be serviced in more places if more people own the same make. No quality differences are necessary for the market to tip toward one producer in the presence of strong network externalities. Indeed, as shown by Arthur (1989), the results are path-dependent, and it is possible for society to lock into an inferior technology that gains an early lead.

These arguments can easily be extended to the economics of stardom, although there are also some differences. The costs of switching allegiance to a new star, while not zero, are small in comparison with the costs of switching phone systems or computers. Thus permanent lock-in is less likely, but the market can still tip one way or another, regardless of quality.

One step beyond the economics of stardom is the analysis of "mob goods"—experiences such as rock concerts or sports events, where the performance is enhanced by crowd reaction (DeSerpa and Faith 1996). Suppose that consumers like events better and are willing to pay more if there are more other people there. Then the demand curve slopes upward; if it is steeper than the supply curve, it is possible that there is excess demand for tickets at the going price, even when the suppliers (concert promoters) maximize profits. Audience noise does seem to be part of the experience at big events for performers as well as spectators. In the 1998 World Cup, despite the quite audible cheering of French fans, the captain of the winning French soccer team reportedly said that the crowd was too quiet, since the stands were full of "suits in expensive seats," and the "real fans" couldn't get in.

Sports

It is hard to tell which is more striking in the literature on the economics of sports: the density of jargon and sports babble, presented without apology or explanation—or the obvious passion and enthusiasm of the economists who write about it. Imagine that you were somehow never called in at the end of recess, but stayed out as the school year became an endless summer, and found that the subject of econometrics was used solely to analyze sports statistics. Imagine, that is, that you are a sports economist. What would you choose to study?

In fact, the economics of sports focuses particularly on baseball, presumably reflecting the preferences of the economists involved. Other sports now draw bigger audiences and, as seen in Table III.3, other sports now pay higher top salaries. Michael Jordan, the premier athletic superstar of the 1990s, of course leads the list; but in general, the top pay in basketball, boxing, and auto racing is well ahead of baseball.

Table III.3. The Highest-Paid Athletes in 1997

Rank	Name	Sport	Sports earnings	Endorsements	Total
			(all amounts in millions of dollars)		
1.	Michael Jordan	basketball	31.3	47.0	78.3
2.	Evander Holyfield	boxing	53.0	1.3	54.3
3.	Oscar de la Hoya	boxing	37.0	1.0	38.0
4.	Michael Schumacher	auto racing	25.0	10.0	35.0
5.	Mike Tyson	boxing	27.0	0	27.0
6.	Tiger Woods	golf	2.1	24.0	26.1
7.	Shaquille O'Neal	basketball	12.9	12.5	25.4
8.	Dale Earnhardt	auto racing	3.6	15.5	19.1
9.	Joe Sakic	hockey	17.8	0.1	17.9
10.	Grant Hill	basketball	5.0	12.0	17.0
and top earners in selected other sports:					
15.	Pete Sampras	tennis	6.5	8.0	14.5
17.	Cal Ripken, Jr.	baseball	6.7	6.5	13.2
33.	Barry Sanders	football	8.4	1.8	10.2
—	Rolando (Brazil)	soccer	4.0	NA	NA
—	Laurent Jalabert (France)	cycling	2.1	NA	NA

Source: *Forbes,* December 15, 1997.

It is fortuitous that so many American economists enjoy a sport like baseball, which has such comprehensive, individualized performance statistics. In soccer, in contrast, there is nothing corresponding to batting or pitching averages, and success in scoring goals does not provide a complete measure of individual ability. Thus it would have been difficult for sports economics to develop in Europe or Latin America. Meanwhile, American economists have learned an immense amount about the relationship between major league baseball performance and salary (and other aspects of the "political economy of baseball" as well; see Zimbalist 1992).

As **James Quirk and Rodney Fort** and others show, slight quality differences are important in determining the salaries of sports stars. So is the structure of the market for pro athletes. "Free agency"—the freedom of players to change teams at will in search of a better deal—helps players win larger salaries. Baseball salaries went up sharply after free agency was adopted in 1976; salaries in the 1980s were far higher in baseball and basketball than in pro football, where team owners retained greater control over negotiations.

However, Quirk and Fort argue that it was the growth of television broadcast revenues that made the explosion of baseball salaries possible—the sale of TV rights expanded the pool of money available, and free agency allowed star players to win substantial chunks of it. Their data show a steady rise in attendance at major league sports events, noticeably faster than population growth, perhaps reflecting better marketing, league expansion, and movement of teams into new, growing metropolitan markets. There was also an abrupt explosion in television revenues in the early 1980s, as shown in Figure III.1.[3] The graph also shows that football did even better than baseball in winning much higher payments from television at that time, while basketball followed a few years later. (Football and basketball revenues continued to rise in the 1990s, while the major league baseball strike of 1994 accounts for the dip near the end of the baseball line in the graph. A minor puzzle—broadcast revenues are lower, but salaries are higher, in basketball than in baseball or football—is explained by the fact that basketball teams are smaller, so the players' share of the revenues is divided into fewer salaries.)

Regression analysis shows that there is a clear relationship of baseball salaries to performance variables. Free agency led to an increase in many coefficients (i.e., the value of the same level of performance went up) and in the constant term (i.e., the base salary that players receive independent of performance went up). Interestingly, the amount of salary variation explained by the regression (r^2) drops from 0.8 to 0.5 after free agency. The freer bargaining process may introduce noise, or errors in rewarding performance. And inequality is growing: As the average salaries in major league baseball have risen, so has the spread among those salaries. Before free agency, the Gini coefficient for major league baseball players was comparable to that of the United States as a whole. Today, Baseball Nation is approaching the levels of income inequality found in the

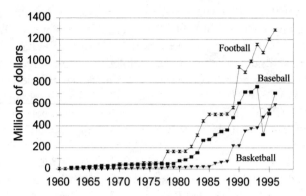

Figure III.1. Sports Broadcast Revenues, 1960–1996

Sources: 1960–1990 data excerpted from pages 505–511 in James Quirk and Rodney Fort, *Pay Dirt: The Business of Professional Sports.* Princeton: Princeton University Press, 1992; 1991–1996 data excerpted from pages 189–193 in James P. Quirk, *Hard Ball: The Abuse of Power in Pro-Team Sports.* Princeton: Princeton University Press, 1999.

world's most unequal countries. (For Gini coefficients for many professional sports leagues, see Scully 1995, p. 74. Hockey is the most equal, and golf the most unequal, of the sports shown there.)

Dale Oorlog offers his own version of the relationship between individual performance and salary, with a focus on the distinction between spectator revenue and broadcast revenue. It is a logically straightforward, though computationally intricate, process to calculate the relationship between individual ballplayer performance and spectator revenue. Attendance is quite sensitive to the number of games won, so a better player helps his team win more and brings in more money at the stadium. Salaries could, therefore, be based on the marginal increase in revenues that each individual earns for the team, as suggested by economic theory.

However, broadcast revenue is large and is growing faster than stadium revenue; for many teams, aggregate players' salaries exceed stadium revenue. Broadcast revenue does not depend on the team's number of wins or other performance measures, so there is no meaning to an individual player's broadcast revenue. Strictly speaking, every player's marginal contribution to broadcast revenue is zero. This means that salaries based solely on marginal contributions to team revenue would lead to the players receiving no share of broadcast revenues. According to Oorlog, this may explain the frequent labor disputes in baseball; collective action is the only way for the players to win part of the teams' fast-growing TV earnings.

What happened to TV in the early 1980s that made possible the jump in payments for sports broadcast rights? This was the period when cable became an effective competitor to the broadcast networks. (See Vogel 1990, the source of much of this account.) To recap the history of TV: The tube arrived in American living rooms in the 1950s, achieving less than 10 percent market saturation at the beginning of the decade but more than 90 percent by the end. From 1965 to 1975, weekly hours of TV viewing per adult increased from 10 to 15, as color TV sets arrived (Robinson and Godbey 1997); sports viewing may have been a big part of the increase for men. But as late as 1970, the dominance of the three traditional broadcast networks was reflected in laws that placed severe, arbitrary restrictions on what could be shown on cable. These laws were challenged and repealed over the course of the 1970s, leading to drastically increased competition for popular programs such as leading sports events. TV rights for U.S. broadcast of the summer Olympics cost a mere $7.5 million in 1972, versus $225 million in 1984 (Vogel 1990, p. 388).

Entertainment

Can a similar story be told about other media, explaining the rise of stardom in other fields? Economists have paid far less attention to music, art, and other forms of entertainment than to sports. However, the top incomes are much greater in the larger entertainment world, as seen in Table III.4. The numbers

Table III.4. Top Entertainment Incomes in 1997

Rank	Name	Principal source	Income (millions of dollars)
1.	Jerry Seinfeld	TV: *Seinfeld* syndication rights	225
2.	Larry David	TV: *Seinfeld* syndication rights	200
3.	Steven Spielberg	Dreamworks movie studio	175
4.	Oprah Winfrey	Talk show	125
5.	James Cameron	*Titanic* director	115
6.	Tim Allen	TV: *Home Improvement* syndication rights	77
7.	Michael Crichton	Movie scripts, books	65
8.	Harrison Ford	Movie actor	58
9.	Rolling Stones	Rock music	57
10.	Master P	Rap music	56.5
11.	Robin Williams	Movie actor	56
12.	Celine Dion	Singer	55.5
13.	Mel Gibson	Movie actor	55
14.	Garth Brooks	Country music	54
15.	Sean (Puffy) Combs	Rap music	53.5
16.	Mike Judge	Cartoons (*Beavis & Butthead*,	53
17.	Greg Daniels	*King of the Hill* co-creators)	53
18.	Chris Carter	TV: X-Files script writer	52
19.	David Copperfield	Special effects	49.5
20.	Spice Girls	Pop music, merchandise	49

Source: *Forbes*, September 21, 1998.

shown here are enormous, even without the extraordinary income received by Jerry Seinfeld and one of his principal writers for multiyear syndication rights. If the *Forbes* lists of the forty best-paid entertainers and athletes were combined, only four athletes would appear above the fortieth entertainer (Julia Roberts, with $28 million). In broad socioeconomic terms, professional athletics could be described as simply a branch of the entertainment industry, and far from the biggest branch at that—although one that is particularly prized by many advertisers for its demographics—its ability to reach an adult male audience.

The explosion of incomes has an obvious economic basis in some cases. For recorded music, the arrival of high-fidelity home stereos in the 1960s, cassette tapes in the 1970s, and CDs in the 1980s allowed steady expansion of the market. The superstars of popular music have a major economic impact by many measures: For example, the annual concerts by the Grateful Dead in Las Vegas in the early 1990s had direct and indirect employment effects equivalent to the creation of 300 to 600 full-time year-round local jobs (Gazel and Schwer 1997).

For films, there is more of a mystery to the rising incomes of the stars. Real U.S. expenditure on movie theater attendance peaked in the early 1940s, fell to about one-third of the peak level by the late 1960s, and remained more or less flat through the 1970s and 1980s (Vogel 1990, p. 38). Videocassette sales, pay cable, and foreign sales allowed some expansion of the market, though less dramatically than for sports or music. Corresponding to the vast outpouring of economic analysis of baseball players' performance, there are apparently just a few studies of the effects of individual movie stars on film revenues (e.g., Wallace, Seigerman, and Holbrook 1993; Prag and Casavant 1994).

Can performance quality be objectively measured in music? An intriguing and slightly discordant note is struck by Hamlen (1991). He claims to measure the voice quality of the top-selling singers of 1955–1987 and finds it has a significant correlation with sales, but far too low an elasticity to fit the superstar model. If, as the model suggests, small quality differences yield big returns, the quality-elasticity of sales should be above 1; Hamlen estimates it at 0.14. His voice quality rankings, though said to be based on objective measurements, are certainly subject to debate: He places Barbra Streisand first, followed by Bing Crosby, Frank Sinatra, George B. Shea, and John Denver. Of these five, only Streisand was among the top ten in sales.

A different study of the sales of best-selling "gold records" from 1958 to 1989 found their distribution to be almost precisely what would be expected from Adler's theory, as discussed above—assuming no quality differences (Chung and Cox 1994). Since the time period for this article and Hamlen's are so similar, it is surprising that there are substantial differences in their lists of the best-selling singers. The Chung and Cox list, which includes Elton John, the Rolling Stones, and Aretha Franklin among the top ten, seems easier to believe than the Hamlen list, which does not include any of these three in the top twenty.

Finally, a unique study deals with the economics of classical singing, by an author who is trained in both fields. Although stardom here may not bring the same financial rewards as in more popular, mass market entertainment, Ruth Towse (1993) finds the analysis of the economics of superstars relevant to classical music, introducing new levels of inequality among performers of similar ability levels. In her view, the market is efficient but cruel; there is no alternative to market-based allocation of labor and rewards, but there is also a need for public subsidies for training in culturally valuable fields such as singing. For an American reader, the most surprising aspect of her analysis may be the extent to which public subsidies to the arts are taken for granted in Britain.

Common Themes

What do these varied new paths to the top of the income distribution have in common? Why are so many activities now structured by winner-take-all markets with explosively growing top prizes? One common cause is the introduction of new technologies in communication, transportation, and other areas, enlarging the effective size of markets and thus creating new economies of scale. Even in the largest industries this may lead to the creation of new, giant competitors, along the lines of DaimlerChrysler. Music and films are increasingly marketed worldwide, allowing bigger audiences and incomes for the most popular performers. In sports, although performances and spectator loyalties are more localized, there is an increasing role for nationwide and worldwide broadcasts of the Olympics, the World Cup, and other championship events.

This expansion of the sphere of competition has a damaging psychological effect on all but the very best contestants. In an earlier era the summit of an individual's ambition might have been to be the most acclaimed singer, dancer, movie star, or athlete in Paris, in Calcutta, or in Philadelphia. Now many performers feel that anything less than "world class" status has little meaning. As the notoriously competitive sound bite on the Olympics puts it, "You don't win the silver, you lose the gold." One result is that the satisfaction of adequate performance and even local fame are overwhelmed by the elusive nature of superstar achievement.

Another common cause is the breakdown of conventional structures and restraints on the market. Before free agency in sports, the owners controlled teams and players, and conventional notions of a reasonable distribution of salaries were easier to enforce. Likewise, before cable TV the three traditional networks controlled television. And in days past, CEOs were restrained by powerful individual stockholders, banks, and government regulators—and rarely jumped from one industry to another. As much as the U.S. economy of 25 to 50 years ago appeared to be dominated by market forces, it now appears in retrospect that an institutional structure of nonmarket conventions (and conventional uses of monopoly power by entrenched owners) still governed many patterns of distribution.

In a process much like that described by Karl Polanyi for earlier times, the spread of market relationships has continued to erode past conventions and to undermine past monopolies. Yet new positions of monopoly power are being created by technological and cultural change, along the lines discussed in this essay. It is hardly surprising that a new wave of self-seeking behavior has resulted; there is no reason to think that it has crested. As winner-take-all markets continue to expand, the identities of the winners may be unexpected, but not the process that allows someone to win.

Does the compensation of celebrities and CEOs violate the tenets of standard economic theory? Superstar salaries may often be consistent with the notion that rates of pay in a competitive market economy are based on the marginal revenue produced by individual workers. Entertainers who are seen and heard by audiences of millions may actually be bringing in revenues that match their soaring salaries. The same could be true for those CEOs who actually lead their companies to new heights of profitability (though this does not describe all well-paid executives).

Yet if bloated pay is based accurately on bloated marginal revenues, a second pillar of the conventional theoretical edifice has been removed. In a perfectly competitive economy, pay is based on marginal revenue, *and* marginal revenue reflects a market-based judgment about the social value of each person's labor. (This may not be the best way to determine social value, but it is the only way that the market provides.) The competitive market's judgment of each person is confirmed by the other available opportunities for employment. Everyone could, in theory, go elsewhere and still earn their current salary; there are no positions of monopoly power that allow the incumbents to earn greater salaries than they would in their next-best alternatives.

Celebrities and CEOs clearly occupy monopoly positions, where the equation of marginal revenue and social value no longer applies. There is no possibility of earning the same salary elsewhere: A pop singer without a microphone, a baseball player without a bat, and a CEO kicked out of the corner office would be just three more faces in the crowd, not multimillionaires. It is not the personalities of the incumbents, but rather the underlying structure of profoundly and needlessly unequal opportunity, that challenges familiar economic theories and violates a sense of fairness.

Notes

1. Hacker (1997), 73–81. There were 68,064 households who filed tax returns with over $1 million in income in 1994, of whom 10,509 received Social Security checks (implying that they were over 70, the age at which Social Security is available regardless of

other earnings). The total of 4000 in identified professions combines several separate estimates made by Hacker. Hacker's lists of identifiable top earners do not include any entertainers other than movie stars, nor any athletes in sports other than baseball, basketball, football, and hockey.

2. If a hypothetical company has 10 shares of stock outstanding, each share is worth 1/10 of the value of the company and receives 1/10 of the dividends. If one more share is then issued to the CEO, each of the other shares drops in value to 1/11 of the company and receives 1/11 of the dividends.

3. The graph combines data from two sources using slightly different definitions, Quirk and Fort (1992) and Quirk (1999). They are in reasonably close agreement for 1990 and 1991, the two years of overlap.

Summary of

How Winner-Take-All Markets Arise *and* The Growth of Winner-Take-All Markets

by Robert H. Frank and Philip J. Cook

[Published in *The Winner-Take-All Society* (New York: The Free Press, 1995), Chs. 2 and 3, 23–60.]

A recent commercial, referring to the Olympics, said, "You don't win the silver medal, you lose the gold." There are increasing numbers of competitions—and not only in athletics—in which winning first place is all that matters to the participants. These chapters, from a well-known book on the subject, analyze the sources of winner-take-all markets and the factors that promote their growth.

Winner-Take-All Markets Defined

Winners in many arenas, including athletic competitions, elections, competitive bidding, and the pursuit of top positions in many institutions, have several characteristics in common. One is that each has prevailed in a contest whose payoffs depend on relative rather than absolute performance. The winner of an athletic or electoral race must come in ahead of everyone else running at the same time, but need not meet any absolute standards of accomplishment. Production workers, in contrast, are often paid for the amount they produce—that is, they are rewarded for their absolute, not relative, performance.

Another common characteristic of winner-take-all competitions is that the rewards are concentrated in the hands of one or a few top performers, with small differences in talent or effort giving rise to potentially enormous differences in results. Only hundredths of a second separate first and second place winners in many Olympic events; only minor differences in musical quality, undetectable to many listeners, separate the most famous and successful classical musicians from the virtually unknown second tier of performers.

These characteristics alone do not give rise to inequalities of income; in unglamorous sports such as handball or horseshoes, even the champions need to have day jobs in remunerative occupations. However, when the prizes in a competition are large, winner-take-all markets can produce immense incomes for the lucky few. Large prizes can arise in mass markets with millions of buyers or viewers, or in "deep-pocket" markets where a few buyers are intensely interested in the winner's performance.

Winner-take-all competition can arise among rival technologies, fashions, political entities, or even universities competing for scarce research funds and famous researchers. The winners can be determined by lottery, auction, majority vote, or coercion. For our purposes, though, the most important are competitions among individuals and firms in the marketplace.

Sources of Winner-Take-All Markets

Several factors, affecting both supply and demand, allow the emergence of winner-take-all markets. On the supply side, economies of scale in production and distribution create a tendency for one product or supplier to dominate the market. The costs (aside from paying the performers) are no greater to record the performances of the very best actors and musicians rather than those who are less famous, or to broadcast tennis matches between the world's top players rather than those of lower rank.

On the demand side, network economies make a product more valuable when more consumers use it. Telephones, fax machines, and DOS/Windows-based computers are all valuable to individuals in large part because so many other people already use them. Choosing a common make of car because it is easy to get it repaired, or reading a best-selling book because it is easy to find people to discuss it with, are also examples of the importance of network economies.

A similar phenomenon on the demand side has been described as "lock-in" to a leading technology. If the rate at which a technology improves and its costs decline is related to its prevalence in use, then the first technology to be adopted gains a head start in cost reduction that becomes larger over time. Eventually it may become impossible for alternate technologies to compete because they must start from so far behind.

Other self-reinforcing processes lead to the formation of prestige and reputation; these also involve positive-feedback effects, in which success breeds success. There are natural limits to the number of names, products, and activities that people can remember and pay attention to—the "mental shelf space" problem—implying that there is a big payoff to becoming famous enough to be on the shelf. The importance of habit formation and the slow development of acquired tastes in most areas of consumption lead to brand loyalty and the persistence of reputations. Similar factors in business create a preference for selecting the most established vendors or hiring the best-known consultants; your boss is less likely to question your judgment if you make the safe, familiar choice.

Positional concerns, such as conspicuous consumption intended to display one's superior wealth and prestige, leads to demand for expensive, high-status goods and services. This is particularly important since wealth and income are already quite unequally distributed; those at the top have substantial resources to spend on public displays of prestige.

The Growth of Winner-Take-All Markets

Winner-take-all markets are hardly new, but they are becoming more important. Several factors have promoted their growth in recent years. The long-term tendency toward falling transportation and tariff costs allows the dominant suppliers to reach ever-larger markets. The rise of telecommunications and electronic computing have created global information flows and encouraged the emergence of global markets, reinforcing the decline in transportation costs. Advances in communication technology also intensify the mental-shelf-space constraints, as the number of sellers competing for our attention has grown, but our capacity for attention has not. Thus a smaller percentage of sellers can hope to win the competition, intensifying the winner-take-all nature of many markets.

Network economies have become of growing importance in the era of electronic communications. English has acquired a de facto status as the language of global communication in business, science, and even entertainment. The growing size of the world market allows an expanded division of labor and more specialized production processes, increasing the power of those producers who understand and can manipulate the new information flows. All these trends promote the expansion and intensification of winner-take-all markets.

In many markets, a variety of formal and informal rules traditionally prevented winner-take-all competition; these rules have been eroded in recent years. The defeat of the reserve clause in baseball was followed by similar changes in other major league sports, providing players with the benefits of free agency and allowing owners to bid for each other's best players. Businesses, in the past, had informal norms that encouraged promotion of executives from within and discouraged competitive recruitment from outside, a system that produced top salaries that were modest by today's standards. As recently as 1984, it was widely viewed as surprising when Apple hired a soft-drink marketing executive to run a computer company. Today, of course, top executives enjoy free agency and the opportunity to change teams frequently, much like professional athletes.

Other competitive pressures that have led to increased bidding for top executives include deregulation of many industries and the threat of outside takeovers financed by junk bonds and other new sources of funds. Within large companies, the shift away from traditional employment contracts toward the use of independent contractors has increased performance-based competition, and driven up the salaries of the best performers.

Changes in the social context also promote positional, or status-oriented, competition. Since the affluence of the richest Americans has grown far faster than average incomes, there have been increases in both the acceptability of public displays of wealth and the share of all consumer spending devoted to elite, positional consumption. Indeed, as winner-take-all markets have become more common, there is a growing tendency for top performers in many fields to compare themselves to other well-known and well-paid individuals, rather than to their own coworkers. Thus winner-take-all markets become a self-reinforcing process, amplifying their effects on society through the process of social comparisons.

Of course, not every trend points in the same direction. New technologies have allowed niche marketing and boutique-style enterprises to flourish in some areas. Microbreweries and specialized cable channels are two well-known cases. The Internet allows extremely narrowly defined groups—dentists interested in scuba diving, for example—to stay in contact with each other. Such trends have potentially contradictory implications. A continuing movement toward boutique retailing might fragment the huge winner-take-all markets and thereby reduce star performers' salaries. On the other hand, the same process also raises the number of competing sellers, which might worsen the mental-shelf-space problem and increase the rewards for being on top. The net effect on the distribution of economic rewards is uncertain, and may vary from one industry to another.

Summary of

The Cost of Talent: Summing Up

by Derek Bok

[Published in *The Cost of Talent: How Executives and Professionals Are Paid and How It Affects America* (New York: The Free Press, 1993), Ch. 11, 223–248.]

The top salaries in management and in some professions have risen extremely rapidly since the 1970s, far exceeding the growth rates of most wages and salaries or of the output of goods and services. This chapter, summarizing a book-length analysis of the escalating standards for managerial and professional compensation, addresses three questions:

Are certain executives and professionals significantly overpaid? Is the supply of intellectually gifted university graduates distributed among the fields in a manner that matches the nation's needs? Do current methods of compensation motivate professionals to work suitably hard for appropriate goals? [223]

Are Some Professionals Overpaid?

It is hard to avoid the impression that top-level salaries are excessive when, for example, the CEOs of General Motors and Ford earn three or four times as much as their counterparts at Honda or Toyota, or when the partners at some large law firms have average individual earnings greater than the combined salaries of all nine Supreme Court justices. In fact, the incomes of medical specialists and the profits per partner at elite law firms have risen sharply since 1970, despite the unusually rapid growth in the number of doctors and lawyers. CEOs of large firms have likewise had soaring incomes at a time when the number of MBAs has jumped upward and when foreign firms have challenged American business more successfully than in the past.

Top executives, doctors, and lawyers have fared so well because they sell their services in labor markets with several unique characteristics. The work that they perform is important and differentiated enough that there is a great incentive to pick the best available candidate—but it is extremely difficult to make such choices well. Seldom are there clear measures of a candidate's past performance; nor do those making the hiring decisions know the identity, let alone the qualifications, of all potential candidates. Under these circumstances it is easy to choose the candidate with the greatest reputation, a process that of course reinforces existing inequalities of reputation and incomes. Price competition is rare; someone who offered to work for less than the going rate might appear to be of lower quality, repelling rather than attracting clients.

Moreover, leading professionals and managers can often keep some control over the level of their earnings. Few clients or patients can judge exactly what they need from their lawyers or doctors. CEOs control the information received by boards of directors that evaluate them; often CEOs even pick the consultants or committee members who recommend executive pay increases. Under these uncompetitive market conditions, publicizing high salaries for CEOs, or high profits per partner at law firms, may have the perverse effect of encouraging others to demand more in an effort to catch up or stay ahead.

Do high salaries matter? Several reasons have been suggested for minimizing the problem, including: the high degree of mobility in and out of the top income groups; the relatively small amounts of money, in aggregate terms, earned by those at the top; the innovative investments and charitable contributions made by the rich; and even the claim that money matters little because it cannot buy happiness. None of these arguments are persuasive. There is limited mobility in and out of top income brackets, especially for the managers and professionals under discussion here; the rapid growth of top incomes has made their aggregate importance greater than it used to be; charitable contributions, even by the very rich, are less than 3 percent of income on average; and survey data suggests that richer people are, in fact, slightly happier than others. Finally, extreme inequality might be morally objectionable on grounds of fairness, regardless of the relationship between income and happiness.

How Well Is Talent Distributed?

Do distortions in the system of executive and professional pay lead to distortions in the allocation of talent to different occupations? Lured in part by hopes of high earnings, students apply to law schools, medical schools, and business schools in much larger numbers than the system can absorb. Similarly, international comparisons suggest that America has many more executives and lawyers per capita than other industrial nations and is near the high end of the range in doctors per capita.

The best students, by any of several measures of academic ability and success, are disproportionately likely to go into medicine, law, or business. They are correspondingly less likely than other students to go into school teaching or other public sector careers; those who do enter such careers often leave after just a few years. Yet it is clear that our society needs an abler, better-educated corps of teachers and public servants than we have had in the recent past.

Even within the best-paid professions, the differential pattern of salaries may lead to misallocation of talent. Large proportions of the best new entrants are attracted to high-tech specialties within medicine, corporate law firms within the legal profession, and careers in finance within the business world. In the early 1970s, graduates from leading law and business schools earned about the same starting salaries in the federal government or on Wall Street, and made about twice as much as a beginning teacher. By 1990, Wall Street salaries were double the starting pay in the federal government and four times the salary of a beginning teacher.

> These large and growing differences are considerably greater than those in most other industrialized countries. They have undoubtedly helped to cause the shift of talented young people from the public to the private sector. There is little reason to suppose that the country will be better off as a result. [242]

How Successful Is Merit Pay?

Many organizations made renewed efforts in the 1970s and 1980s to tie compensation to performance. Merit pay was introduced for teachers and civil servants; boards of directors gave CEOs lucrative incentive pay packages to spur greater efforts; law firms began to pay partners on the basis of current accomplishment rather than seniority; HMOs began to experiment with incentive plans for salaried doctors.

"The striking fact about these attempts is that they have all either failed completely or fallen far short of expectations." [243] Bonus systems in the federal government have been poorly administered or too small to matter. CEOs have manipulated incentive pay schemes so that the link between their compensation and performance is embarrassingly weak. Appropriate incentives for doctors are notoriously difficult to design; simple systems often reward doing too much (when doctors are paid for working harder) or too little (when there are bonuses for cost-consciousness).

All pay-for-performance schemes assume that monetary rewards will motivate people to work harder and more effectively. Although seemingly obvious, this premise is supported by surprisingly little empirical evidence. Financial incentives do seem to have a positive effect on the performance of routine, repetitive tasks, but this effect does not necessarily translate to the more complex, creative jobs expected of managers and professionals. We know very little about the incentive effect on a multimillionaire CEO of a chance to earn another million dollars. Nor do we know how a bonus affects professionals in fields such as teaching or public service, careers which have often been chosen for reasons other than making money.

Even if performance pay were an effective motivator, it would be difficult to implement such methods of compensation. The requirements for an effective incentive pay system are formidable, including: clear, objective procedures for definition, measurement, and evaluation of performance; honest and impartial communication of the results of performance assessments; widespread understanding of the goals of the system; goals high enough to be challenging but not so high as to be frustrating; rewards large enough to provide real motivation, but not so large as to encourage cheating; and recognition of all the behaviors and objectives that are to be encouraged and design of a balanced package of incentives that rewards them in the right proportions.

It is hardly surprising that one or more of these vital elements are often missing, rendering incentive systems ineffective. A failed performance pay plan can leave an organization in worse shape than before, by fostering rivalry among coworkers, disrupting harmonious working relationships, and increasing the focus on making more money instead of doing the best possible job. The lavish paychecks so often given to CEOs of poorly performing companies symbolize the failure of twenty years of attempts to use financial incentives to improve performance.

In conclusion, it is clear that the competitive market that regulates executive and professional compensation has many imperfections. Those who employ professionals, and those who establish their compensation, are often poorly informed. In the private sector, executives and professionals exert great influence over their own compensation because of their knowledge and power within the organizations that employ them. No "unseen hand" guides the relative levels of compensation in the public and private sectors to ensure an adequate flow of talent into such occupations as teaching or government services.

> Under such artificial conditions, there is no reason to suppose that the process of fixing professional compensation will result in just rates of pay, or produce an optimal distribution of talent, or create a system of incentives calculated to elicit the kind of effort needed to excel in the important tasks that professionals perform in our society. [247]

Summary of

Management Compensation Plans— Panacea or Placebo?

by Michael T. Jacobs

[Published in *Short-Term America: The Causes and Cures of Our Business Myopia* (Boston: Harvard Business School Press, 1991), Ch. 7, 197–212.]

The escalating compensation of top corporate executives has been one of the most dramatic and visible sources of new individual wealth in recent years. Huge payments to CEOs often result from performance-based compensation plans, which are said to create incentives for managers to maximize shareholder returns, thereby harmonizing the interests of managers and investors. This chapter examines the practice of performance-based management compensation plans and explains why those plans rarely provide the intended incentives. The author is a business executive who served in the U.S. Treasury Department under the Bush administration; his book presents a broad critique of institutional factors that promote an excessively short-run orientation in corporate decision making.

The Myth of Management Incentives

The system of connections and constraints that once guided corporate management has been seriously weakened as top individual shareholders have come to exert less influence, deregulation has removed many traditional legislative requirements for corporate accountability, and relationships between banks and their corporate clients have grown more distant. [These changes are described in earlier chapters.] There is a need for new approaches to bring the interests of capital users into line with those of capital providers. Performance-based management compensation plans appear to be the most popular solution.

Academic analysts have found that executive compensation has very little relationship to corporate performance, and have suggested that making CEOs substantial owners of their own company's stock will lead them to maximize corporate values on behalf of stockholders in general. Yet despite the intuitive appeal of this argument, the evidence indicates that compensation systems are ineffective in achieving shareholders' objectives. Tinkering with compensation schemes is not the answer. "No management incentive system will unilaterally solve the problem of focusing corporate managers' attention on the long-run value of a business." [197]

The three principal reasons for the failure of management incentive plans are: Performance-based pay is difficult to implement at levels below senior management; it is expensive to provide incentives big enough to affect the decision making of CEOs who are already wealthy; and most existing incentives have side effects that promote unintended results.

Performance Pay Below the Top

The ideal performance-based compensation plan would meet several important criteria: It would rely on performance measures consistent with the goal of maximizing shareholder value; it would judge managers only on factors they can control; it would use simple, accurate, clearly defined, challenging standards that are meaningful to the employee but not excessively expensive to the corporation. In practice, compensation plans typically fail to meet one or more of these criteria.

A critical problem is the definition of the appropriate measure of performance, especially for those below the top of the corporate hierarchy. Incentive plans frequently rely on accounting measures of profits, ignoring a manager's possible contributions to the firm's strategic position, market share, adoption of new technologies, or maintenance of employee morale—all of which contribute to long-run success and therefore are usually reflected in share prices.

An alternative to profit-based incentives, then, might be to tie everyone's pay to share prices. However, mid-level managers (let alone the employees below them) have very little control over either profits or share prices for the corporation as a whole. While they will be delighted with bonuses when the company does well, they will balk at compensation declines based on poor performance in other divisions. This problem has led to the abandonment of some of the most ambitious corporate pay-incentive schemes.

Pay Must Make a Difference

Top executives can reasonably be held responsible for the performance of the corporation as a whole. Yet at this level, it is expensive to provide incentives big enough to affect behavior. Those who have enjoyed six- or seven-figure incomes for years have by now bought anything they want and may be unwilling to take risky or difficult initiatives simply to earn a little more.

The drive to link executive compensation to performance has led to pay packages with huge incentives for success, but usually without any downside for poor performance. Stock options, grants, and bonuses have simply been piled on top of already ample salaries. The result is ever-higher incomes, making it more expensive to obtain noticeable incentive effects in the future. International evidence suggests that U.S. executive compensation levels are not needed for effective corporate performance: As of 1989, top executives at the largest American corporations earned 109 times the average worker's pay; the comparable ratio in other leading industrial countries ranged from 17 in Japan to 35 in Britain, with Germany and France falling below the British level.

Pay Packages Can Have Unexpected Side Effects

Statistically, the correlation between incentive-based executive compensation plans and corporate performance is weak. This is in part because all the typical forms of incentive pay have deficiencies that can reward perverse behavior. Stock options, widely used in incentive plans, are a common example. The owner of stock options benefits only from increases in the stock price, while the stockholder benefits both from price increases and from dividend payments. Thus an executive compensated with stock options will favor reinvestment of profits to boost the stock price, even if a greater dividend payment would have maximized total return to shareholders.

Compensation that is insensitive to performance, or that rewards the wrong outcomes, can reflect the influence that top executives have over the determination of their own pay. Consultants who recommend executive compensation plans are almost always chosen by the CEO; the compensation committee of the board of directors, which approves pay packages, is frequently filled with the CEO's closest allies. Many so-called performance packages that emerge from this system are simply additional income. Cash bonuses are allegedly tied to year-end performance measures; in practice there is little rhyme or reason to bonus levels. In the year after the Exxon Valdez accident, when Exxon's net profit dropped by almost $2 billion, the salary and bonus of Exxon's CEO went up.

Stock options appear to offer, at least, a clear incentive to keep the value of the company's stock as high as possible. If the stock price falls below the fixed "strike price" of the option, then the option becomes worthless. However, boards of directors have been known to reissue options with lower strike prices when the value of the stock declines. Former Continental Airlines CEO Frank Lorenzo received options with a strike price of $29 per share; under his leadership the company's stock fell far below that level. Yet he still made money when he eventually sold his shares at $10 because the board had rewritten his options over the years, reaching a final strike price of less than $5.

An alternative is to provide direct grants of stock, sometimes with the restriction that it cannot be sold for a number of years and is forfeited if the executive leaves the company during that period. Critics claim, however, that restricted stock grants, like options, provide rewards without risk; unlike ordinary stockholders, the recipient does not have any of his own money at stake. Yet requiring an executive to invest much of his own money in the company's stock would leave him with a very undiversified and risky portfolio, and would likely be unworkable.

While the benefits of incentive pay schemes are elusive, the costs are real, if somewhat hidden. Both stock grants and options are methods of providing generous executive compensation without any apparent cost to the company. The hidden cost is the dilution of other stockholders' equity, through the reduction in earnings per share that occurs when the number of shares increases.

Costs to stockholders are even more serious with another common incentive, "golden parachutes" that guarantee large cash payments to executives if there is a change in control of the company. The companies most vulnerable to takeovers are underperformers. Thus golden parachutes eliminate one of the primary risks of poor performance—executives with golden parachutes need not fear job loss due to a hostile takeover. Golden parachutes may even provide a perverse incentive for executives nearing retirement age to encourage takeovers.

In conclusion, "management pay is not an effective motivator. When it does work, it often motivates the wrong kind of behavior. . . . [P]ay alone will never prove to be a substitute for effective accountability." [211–212]

Summary of

Top Executive Pay: Tournament or Teamwork?

by Brian G. M. Main, Charles A. O'Reilly III, and James Wade

[Published in *Journal of Labor Economics* 11, 4 (1993), 608–628.]

Economists often explain the structure of pay among top executives in terms of "tournament theory," in which the lure of a large prize for the winner motivates competition among many contestants. A CEO salary far above the individual's marginal product might be economically efficient if it provides an incentive for other executives to work hard, at salaries below their marginal products, in the hopes of winning promotion.

While tournament theory suggests that large salary differences among top executives may be efficient, an alternative theory suggests just the opposite. If the success of a corporation requires cooperation among its top management, then huge rewards for promotion may inspire excessive rivalry among individual executives. On this interpretation, a more compressed executive pay scale would be more efficient because it would promote teamwork.

This article tests both theories empirically, finding support for tournament theory but failing to demonstrate any efficiency gains from compression of executive pay differentials. The concluding comments suggest changes that are needed to make tournament theory more realistic.

The Tournament Model

Theoretical discussion of the tournament model has identified many situations in which it would be efficient to base remuneration on rank-order, rather than absolute, performance. In terms of the structure of rewards, it has been argued that contestants proceeding through the rounds of a multistage tournament require ever-larger increases in prizes to motivate further effort among the winners of the early stages. This implies that, if executive compensation is viewed as a tournament, there should be greater salary differentials between ranks as one moves toward the top of the corporate hierarchy.

Some empirical work has supported tournament theory. For example, contestants in professional golf tournaments have better (lower) scores when the prize money is skewed toward relatively large prizes for the winner. Evidence on executive compensation supports the theory in some cases, but not others.

Among the contrary evidence is previous work by two of the authors. They found that, after controlling for corporate size and performance, top executive pay is influenced by the level of pay that outside members of the board of directors receive from their own companies—a finding that "is difficult to understand . . . unless one resorts to a nonoptimizing story such as one involving social comparisons." [610] The same study also found that the differential between the pay of CEOs and senior vice presidents—that is, the prize for the final round of the tournament—was not related to the number of vice presidents in a company. This is at odds with the prediction of tournament theory that the prize should increase with the number of contestants.

A New Empirical Test

Survey data on the compensation of top executives at over 200 corporations for the years 1980–1984 provide the basis for a new empirical examination of tournament issues in pay structures. It is true, as predicted, that the average percentage difference in compensation between levels is greatest at the very top of the pyramid. In 1980, for example, the base pay plus bonus for the top level (CEOs) averaged 141 percent greater than that of the second level (largely vice-presidents). The second level's average compensation was 75 percent above the third. The third level was 44 percent above the fourth, which was, in turn, 28 percent above those below them. The data are very similar for other years. This pattern contradicts earlier models of executive compensation, which predicted relatively stable percentage differentials between levels of an organization.

A different and seemingly inconsistent picture emerges from data on actual promotions from vice president to CEO, an event which occurred only 28 times in the survey period. The increase in compensation accompanying these promotions averages less than 20 percent—much less than the 141 percent reported above, and small enough to raise questions about the applicability of the tournament model.

The two pictures can be reconciled if the typical promotion moves an individual from the top of level 2 to the bottom of level 1, receiving a pay increase much smaller than the average difference between levels. This implies that there are important changes in salary within broad organizational levels, as well as between them. It also means that the value of becoming CEO is far greater than the one-year increase in compensation.

In fact, the value to an individual of holding the top job rises quickly over time. A further empirical analysis estimates the gap in pay between the CEO and the average vice president of the same firm, controlling for firm size and other effects. The gap is a rapidly increasing function of both the CEO's total work experience and his tenure as CEO. Using this relationship, it is possible to calculate the expected value of the gap for each CEO in the survey, for every year from the time of his promotion until his assumed retirement at age 65. The present value of the lifetime gap between CEO and vice presidential compensation averaged $4.6 million for those holding the top jobs in 1984. With an added estimate of the value of CEO stock options (most compensation data discussed here do not include stock options), the average present value of the lifetime gap rises to $6.2 million in 1984—surely a large enough prize to motivate many contestants.

Moreover, the present value of the CEO's lifetime pay gap increases when there are more vice presidents, as predicted by tournament theory. For each additional vice president, the pay gap (including stock options) goes up by $186,000.

The Effects of Wage Compression

Alternative theories examine executive pay structures from a different perspective, emphasizing the importance of equity and social comparison processes. In an interdependent, status-conscious group, individuals are more likely to be satisfied with their own pay, on average, if there is less rather than more wage dispersion. More employee satisfaction can lead, in turn, to greater productivity, because better social relations in the workplace should reduce the incidence of unproductive office politics. In short, wage compression can enhance output, by minimizing the loss of productivity due to overly competitive workplace rivalries.

A firm's top management engages in work that requires a high degree of interdependence and encourages social comparison. Moreover, the top executive ranks are filled with extremely competitive people, who may be prone to excessive rivalry. So the benefits of wage compression could be particularly important, perhaps more important than the incentive effects of unequal, tournament-style rewards. This argument leads to a potentially testable proposition: When there is a high degree of executive team interdependence, wage dispersion should have a negative effect on corporate performance; when there is less interdependence among executives, wage dispersion should have a positive effect on performance, through its tournament effects.

Unfortunately, the survey data provide only a very indirect measure of executive team interdependence. Firms in the survey varied widely in the proportion of executives whose titles indicate that they are profit-center heads. If running your own profit center is a sign of relatively separate, independent work, then the higher the proportion of executives who are profit-center heads, the lower the degree of team interdependence. However, this measure of interdependence has no significant effect on the firm's performance, as measured by either stock market returns or accounting calculations of return on assets. In contrast, the dispersion of executive salaries does have a positive effect on the firm's return on assets, consistent with tournament theory.

The lack of empirical support for the wage compression theory could result from the imprecision of the measure of interdependence. It could also reflect the fact that those who make it to the upper echelons of a large company are already so competitive that their behavior is unlikely to be moderated by any simple incentives.

Conclusion

Although arguments can be made for both theories, the evidence provides much stronger support for tournament theory. Yet the unadorned tournament model appears implausible on several grounds. It ignores the fact that top managers must frequently operate as a team, not as competitors. Moreover, it makes the unreasonable assumption that effective long-run motivation for senior executives can emerge from infrequent chances to enter crowded contests for huge additional pay increases.

It is more effective to motivate people with smaller, more frequent raises and promotions—not least because many valuable executives will fail to win the occasional big promotions. Psychological studies have shown that people often prefer a more certain chance of winning a small prize now to a riskier chance of winning a big prize later. The survey data on executive salaries showed that the actual pay increase at the time of promotion to CEO is surprisingly modest, with much of the benefit of the position coming later. This is consistent with the notion that rising through a corporate hierarchy and pay structure involves many small steps, not just a few huge ones.

> None of this denies the existence of tournament structures within managerial career paths, but it does suggest that any tournaments are likely to be of a sequential nature. Winning at one stage leads to pay rewards and enhanced promotion prospects. But losing still permits the loser to try again, with even the prospect of "leapfrogging" earlier winners. Such a model, while lacking the elegance and parsimony of either tournaments or industrial politics, seems consistent with both the data and a large body of sociological and psychological research on pay. [625–626]

Summary of

Why Do Pro Athletes Make So Much Money?

by James Quirk and Rodney D. Fort

[Published in *Pay Dirt: The Business of Professional Team Sports* (Princeton: Princeton University Press, 1992), Ch. 6, 209–239.]

Within the past generation, professional sports have become a well-known new route to the top of the income distribution. Average salaries in major league baseball had reached $850,000 by 1991, about 12 times the $70,000 average (in 1991 dollars) that prevailed in the mid-1950s. This chapter addresses the obvious question, posed in its title, primarily through an analysis of the labor market for baseball players, with occasional comparisons to other sports. It focuses on the implications of the introduction of free agency in baseball in 1976, documenting the subsequent increase in financial rewards for small increments in performance, and finding that overall inequality among baseball players has risen sharply in the free agency era.

Pro Athletes as Entertainers

Since the mid-1970s, average salaries have risen rapidly in professional baseball, basketball, and football and to a lesser extent in hockey. A common perception among sports fans is that pro athletes are wildly overpaid, and that free agency—the players' right to switch to other teams when their contracts expire—is the culprit. However, salaries also rose sharply in football during the 1980s, despite much greater limitations on player mobility in the National Football League than in the baseball and basketball leagues. Other factors must be at work, including the impressive increases in both the demand for tickets to pro sports events and the value of television rights.

Since pro athletes are in fact entertainers, one standard of salary comparison is to the top pay in other forms of entertainment. As of 1991, the most successful singers and movie stars had received much more than any athlete: Sylvester Stallone's $20 million for starring in *Rocky V* and Janet Jackson's $15 million for her latest album dwarfed baseball's top salaries of between $5 million and $6 million per season paid to Roger Clemens of the Boston Red Sox and Bobby Bonilla of the New York Mets.

Interestingly, the equivalent of free agency for movie performers, allowing them to switch studios from one film to the next, was only adopted in the 1950s—amid predictions (quite unfounded, in retrospect) that runaway star salaries would ruin the movie industry. Yet although the top salaries are higher in films and music, public resentment of high salaries is far more pronounced in sports.

The Workings of the Player Market

The market for professional athletes is characterized by extensive monopoly rents. A player's marginal revenue product (MRP), the amount he adds to the team's revenues, is generally greater than his reservation wage, or the amount he would earn in his next-best employment opportunity. The team owner will not pay more than the MRP, while the player will not work for less than his reservation wage; a process of bargaining determines precisely where, between these limits, the player's salary actually falls. The players' union establishes a minimum salary for major league teams but does not negotiate individual salaries.

Before free agency, under the reserve clause that prevailed in baseball until 1976, a player could only negotiate with the team that owned his last contract. Under the reserve clause, therefore, the player's reservation wage was the maximum salary he could earn outside of baseball, or the league minimum salary, whichever is higher. After 1976, the reserve clause applied only to players in their first six years in the major leagues. After six years a player now becomes a free agent, and his reservation wage becomes the amount that another team is willing to pay him. Clearly the reservation wage is much higher, and much closer to MRP, under free agency; this limits the scope for bargaining. Conversely, there is more room for bargaining, and more potential for team owners to insist on salaries far below MRP, under the reserve clause. Today, individual players typically experience a jump in salary after their sixth year, when they become free of the reserve clause.

Ticket Price and Player Salaries

Do high player salaries drive up ticket prices? This common notion rests on an economic misconception. Profit-maximizing prices for tickets depend on fans' willingness to pay for tickets, but are independent of salaries. The owners' demand for inputs used to produce games, such as players, is derived from the ticket revenues. Thus it is more accurate to say that high ticket prices drive up salaries, by increasing players' MRPs.

Evidence against the common view that salaries drive ticket prices is provided by the history of prices before and after the 1976 introduction of free agency. Average salaries began to rise immediately after 1976, as one would expect. But ticket prices remained roughly constant or declined throughout the 1970s. The average real price of tickets was lower in 1980 than in 1971 for all but two major league baseball teams. In the 1980s, as salaries continued their rapid rise, ticket prices changed only modestly, and remained constant or declining in real terms for a number of teams. Players' MRPs rose in the 1980s primarily due to increased broadcast income, which allowed salaries to climb faster than ticket prices.

Salary Determination in Baseball

A simple statistical model shows that baseball salaries are highly correlated with standard measures of playing time, performance, age, experience, and related factors. Playing time is assumed to be an indicator of quality because managers play the better athletes more often. Performance is measured separately for hitters and pitchers (bases from base hits for hitters, ratio of strikeouts to walks for pitchers). Using relatively few variables, the model explains most of the variation in player salaries in each year.

The equation is estimated three times: once using a sample of players from 1965–1974, in the reserve clause era; a second time for 1976–1977, in the initial transition to free agency; and in a final version, for 1986–1990, well into the free agency years. Comparison of the estimates shows that playing time and performance elasticities (the gain in salary from a 1 percent change in playing time or performance) are much larger now than in the reserve clause years. Performance elasticities for players beyond their sixth year are 300 to 400 percent greater for hitters, and 200 to 300 percent greater for pitchers, than they were before 1976. That is, the salary gain for a 1 percent improvement in hitting is now three to four times as great.

The three estimates can also be used to calculate the change in salaries over time for a constant level of performance. For fifteen actual 1990 players, selected to represent a range of salary levels, the model predicts that their 1990 performance would have earned an average salary of $79,000 in 1969, $113,000 in 1976, and $707,000 in 1990 (all expressed in 1991 dollars). The big salary increases did not occur immediately after 1976, as would be expected if they simply reflected the value of free agency. Instead, the substantial increases were spread out over more than a decade, presumably reflecting the effects of free agency combined with the rising demand for baseball.

The Salary Distribution in Sports

A final calculation looks at the degree of inequality in the salary distribution in sports. The Gini coefficient for baseball salaries has risen over time: It averaged 0.354 in 1965–1974, rose to 0.373 in 1976 and 0.457 in 1977, and averaged 0.510 in 1986–1991. For 1991, the last year reported here, the baseball Gini was 0.539. While all players have benefited from free agency, a disproportionate and growing share of the gains have gone to the top players. Those in their first six years of major league play, who remain under the reserve clause, have lost ground relative to their star teammates.

Data are available on the distribution of salaries in other major league sports for various years in the period 1988–1990. During those years, the baseball salary Gini ranged from 0.494 to 0.529. The National Basketball Association had a Gini of 0.427, the National Football League had 0.411, and the National Hockey League was the most egalitarian at 0.284. This pattern is consistent with a ranking of the sports in terms of the degree of free agency, or player mobility, enjoyed by the players at the time. Baseball had the highest degree of mobility, followed by basketball. Football had much more limited free agency, and hockey had nearly none. The degree of free agency, in turn, reflects the relative strengths of the players' unions, ranging from strongest in baseball to weakest in hockey.

Summary of

Marginal Revenue and Labor Strife in Major League Baseball

by Dale R. Oorlog

[Published in *Journal of Labor Research* 16, 1 (Winter 1995), 25–42.]

Professional baseball has a history of intense labor disputes, which have caused games to be canceled or postponed every few years. At the same time, player salaries grew at a compound rate of 13.5 percent per year from 1976 to 1993, reaching an average of $1.1 million in the latter year. Team owners, who are generally extremely wealthy businessmen, complain that players' demands are making the business unprofitable. "This dispute among millionaires leaves most fans confused and disgusted with both sides." [25]

This article offers an economic explanation of labor strife in baseball. While spectator revenue is dependent on individual players' performance and contribution to victories, broadcast revenue is not. There is currently no way for individual players to claim a share of the increasingly important category of broadcast revenue, except through collective action.

The Marginal Spectator Revenue Product

Professional sport is both a cooperative and a competitive industry, the nature of which requires competing teams to cooperate in producing an entertaining contest. Early analyses often viewed sports leagues as cartels, exploring the possibilities of collusion and price fixing. More recent literature on the economics of sports has focused on the competitive aspects of the business.

In studies of baseball, a common methodology involves estimation of two relationships, one between a player's performance and the number of wins for his team, and the second between a team's victories and its total revenue. The combination of the two yields an estimate of the individual player's marginal revenue product, which should in theory be the maximum that a team owner is willing to pay that player.

This article uses new developments in sabermetrics (the study of baseball statistics) to estimate each player's marginal contribution to team victories. By using a formula based on a player's batting statistics, it is possible to estimate how many runs an entire team duplicating those statistics would score, and what percentage of games such a team would win given an average number of runs allowed. This player's "winning percentage" is applied pro rata to the player's share of team at-bats during a season to arrive at "marginal wins created," the number of victories for which that player may take credit beyond the wins expected of a borderline-quality or replacement level player.

The number of marginal wins created is the key to calculating each player's marginal spectator revenue product. Fans are much more likely to attend when their team is winning; each additional game won or lost causes ticket sales to rise or fall dramatically. Annual data for all major league baseball teams for 1970–1992 show that the gain in attendance per win averaged 23,000, or slightly more than 1 percent of the season total. Revenue per fan, at 1993 prices, averaged $13.50, making the net revenue per win roughly $310,000. Multiplying this figure by a player's marginal wins created yields the player's marginal spectator revenue product (MSRP).

Player Performance, Bargaining Power, and Salaries

There is a high correlation between a player's 1992 marginal wins and his 1993 salary, and an even higher correlation between lifetime average marginal wins and current salary. However, salaries generally exceed players' MSRPs. The salary-to-value index (SVI), or ratio of 1993 salary to 1992 MSRP, had a mean value of 2.02, indicating that players on average were paid twice what they contributed to revenues in the stadium. Since baseball salaries are highly skewed, the median SVI was considerably lower, at 1.15.

Examining salaries by years of service, players in their first three years of service had mean SVIs between 0.6 and 0.7, indicating that they were paid roughly two-thirds of the revenue they brought into the stadium. The mean SVI jumps to 1.3 for 4 years of service, and 1.6 for 5 years, reflecting an increase in bargaining power. The players' union has won the right to binding arbitration for salary negotiations, starting after approximately three years in the major leagues. For those who have completed six or more years and hence enjoy free agent status, bargaining power is even greater: The mean SVI jumps again to 3.0 for six years of service and remains between 2.3 and 5.0 for all greater lengths of service.

On the one hand, these results (and others presented in the article) confirm that the salary-to-value index has the expected relationship to seniority and bargaining power. On the other hand, the prevalence of SVIs well above 1 makes it clear that players' salaries exceed the revenues available from fans who attend the actual games. Figures for 1991 show that thirteen of the twenty-six teams paid their players more than the total of all spectator receipts. The bulk of the salaries, particularly for players with four or more years in the major leagues, must come from broadcast revenues.

The Marginal Broadcast Revenue Product

Broadcast revenue is a large and growing part of the income of major league baseball teams. National television rights fees are shared equally, amounting to about $13 million per team in the early 1990s; local media revenues, which are kept by the respective clubs, averaged about $11 million per team in 1992. Performance has no effect on national broadcast revenue; each player's marginal national broadcast revenue is precisely zero.

Potentially, there could be a positive marginal local broadcast revenue, if winning more games attracted a larger viewing audience and justified higher television fees. However, multiyear broadcasting contracts, such as the Yankees' 12-year cable television deal, hide the effects of yearly changes in performance. Estimates of the marginal broadcast revenue from winning an additional game are small and often statistically insignificant. In broadcasting, "the most important determinant of rights fees is clearly potential audience size; winning plays at best a minor role." [38]

If salaries were based simply on marginal revenue products, therefore, broadcast revenue would not be a factor in salary determination. If this were the case, team salaries would be closely related to spectator revenue but unrelated to broadcast revenue. Yet in fact, salaries and broadcast revenue are highly correlated. Over time, salaries have kept almost perfect pace with broadcast revenues. From 1976 to 1986, the first decade of free agency, salaries rose at an average annual rate of 20.8 percent, while broadcast revenues rose by 18.2 percent. In the same years, average ticket prices rose only 6.2 percent annually, and attendance grew by 3.9 percent per year. Spectator revenue cannot explain the growth of salaries; and the marginal revenue product approach cannot account for the relationship between salaries and (nonmarginal) broadcast revenue.

> How do players receive a share of broadcast revenue? . . . Only by credibly threatening a general shutdown of the industry can players induce owners to increase salaries to a level that fairly reflects [broadcast revenue]. . . . Labor discord in baseball arises from the players' need to force owners to disclose the true private value of a jointly-held asset—national broadcast revenues. [39]

Alternatives to Strikes

Unfortunately, repeated strikes and threats of strikes over multimillion-dollar pay packages have a side effect, leading to growing public disgust with both labor and management. Are there alternatives to strikes as a means of sharing broadcast revenues? One avenue would be to pool broadcast revenues and distribute them to teams on the basis of the number of games they win, thereby creating a well-defined marginal broadcast revenue that owners might be willing to pay to the players. Another proposal, briefly considered and rejected in the 1980s, is to establish a salary schedule based on performance. A more palatable alternative, modeled on the practices of the National Basketball Association, is to limit the range of aggregate salaries. The NBA salary cap sets a minimum and maximum range of salaries as a percentage of all revenues, including broadcasting.

Yet to date, none of these plans has been adopted. "As long as baseball owners have an incentive to pay players based only on marginal performance, while some revenues are performance-insensitive, labor strife may become a permanent fixture on the baseball scene." [40]

PART IV

Corporate Power: Why Does It Matter?

Overview Essay

by Neva Goodwin

What kinds of power do corporations have? What are the effects of concentrating economic power within a relatively small number of giant corporations? How does the exercise of corporate power affect the distribution of income and other resources?

To ask such questions is already to ask for a new approach to economic theory. In neoclassical economics the analysis of corporate power is largely restricted to the issue of whether a firm can monopolistically set its prices without worrying about being undercut by other suppliers. Occasionally a beginning economics student may be heard to ask, "Is *that* what it's all about? Is 'how are prices set' really the most important question in economics?" Monopoly power over prices does have distributional impacts, but that is only a narrow part of the broad problem of economic inequality. The political economy approach is of special value in understanding the unequal division of economic power in a system dominated in many ways by huge corporations, and in appreciating how it is that this skewed organization of corporate power can impact large areas of human experience.

The essay begins with an overview of the treatment of the concept of power in mainstream economic theory, followed by a brief empirical demonstration of the size and market power of large corporations. Subsequent sections examine the pervasive and frequently negative effects of corporations on society; the direct impacts of corporate strategies on the distribution of wages and salaries; and the political mobilization of corporate conservatism that began in the late 1970s. A concluding section suggests places to look for theoretical and practical alternatives to corporate business as usual.

Power and Competition

Other social sciences, such as sociology, political science, anthropology, and history, all treat power as a critical variable for understanding human societies. So do alternate schools of economic thought such as Marxian, feminist, and institutional economics. Neoclassical economics stands alone in its dismissive attitude toward the subject.

The treatment of power within the discipline of economics touches on academic and political ideologies; but it is a matter of more than academic interest. Mainstream economics, by giving such scant and narrow attention to the subject, has made it possible to use this discipline to justify a laissez-faire policy toward many (though not all) aspects of the corporate role in society. To be sure, the preference of political and academic conservatives for a laissez-faire government may be suspended when corporations want help: for example, in sheltering them against foreign competition, in underwriting the costs or the risks of natural resource exploitation, or in bailing out failing financial institutions. Such inconsistencies aside (and normally they are simply brushed aside without explanation), it is widely believed that economics has shown that *market economies will produce a good quality of life for societies that allow them to flourish without undue interference.*

This belief is based on a standard picture of how the system works. It is assumed that the overriding goal of all firms is to maximize profits. This goal drives firms to be cost minimizers who must purchase all inputs to production (investment capital, labor, raw materials, and goods and services provided by other firms) at the lowest possible cost. The keystone of the theory is the assumption of competition among producers. They compete in a variety of ways—for example, in the markets for labor and capital—but most important is the idea that firms vie to attract consumers to purchase their products. It is this orientation (often referred to as "consumer sovereignty") that is expected to make corporations the servants of the general public (viewing members of the public solely in their role as consumers), and thus the prime agents by which market economies will produce a good quality of life.

Samuel Bowles and Herbert Gintis argue that the simple neoclassical picture of the world starts from a misunderstanding of the basic relationships that give rise to inequality. They point out that, even in a perfectly competitive economy, the asymmetry of the employer-employee relationship allows employers to exercise power in enforcing employment contracts. A similar asymmetry between lenders and borrowers leads to the exercise of power by financial institutions. Thus even the idealized conditions of the textbook model (which are, in any case, never realized in practice) would not eliminate the unequal distribution of political and economic power.

What use do employers and lenders make of their economic power? One of the most basic and consistent objectives of firms is to grow large and powerful enough that they can escape from perfect competition. The textbook model, in which firms relentlessly drive each other's profits down toward zero as they compete and innovate, offers a more attractive life for consumers than for producers. Every firm would rather be in a monopoly or oligopoly position, able to charge higher prices and receive higher profits—and to enjoy relatively more relaxed working conditions, which are squeezed out by hot competition. The inequalities of power identified by Bowles and Gintis imply that some firms are more able to escape from competition than others. The fact that unequal power would exist even in a perfectly competitive economy is, in a sense, one of the reasons why a perfectly competitive economy does not exist.

What exists instead is an economy dominated by large corporations. The emergence of the modern corporation was not a simple or automatic response to an economic stimulus. Large enterprises of some sort may have been inevitable, but the corporation as we know it is only one of many ways to structure a business. A review of the rapidly growing field of corporate history is beyond the scope of this essay; one noteworthy recent contribution is Roy (1997). Like Bowles and Gintis, Roy is intrigued by the not obviously inevitable manner in which the concepts of "public" and "private" have evolved to their present shapes. He asks, "Is a canal, turnpike, or railroad built to serve the interests of the public at large, or is it built to serve the interests of the stockholders? This is the fundamental difference between public and private property" (Roy, p. 44). Roy's account of the nineteenth-century origins of the corporation emphasizes the efforts of property owners to consolidate and institutionalize their power, and the historical contingency of the legislation and court decisions that have defined corporate law. As he puts it, there is no selection process that ensures that more efficient institutional forms will triumph; the winners depend on the past uses of power and the accidents of history.

The Extent of Corporate Power

By any measure, the biggest corporations are enormous. Ranked according to revenues, in 1997 the world's biggest firm was General Motors. Its sales revenues of over $178 billion were larger than the gross domestic product (GDP) of Norway, Hong Kong, or Saudi Arabia. The world's five largest companies (see Table IV.1) each had sales revenues of at least $128 billion, more than the GDP of Finland or Greece. In fact, only 52 nations were as large as Sears Roebuck, the world's 50th-largest corporation.

According to William Greider, in 1991 the 500 largest companies accounted for one-third of all manufacturing exports in the world, three-fourths of commodity trade, and four-fifths of the trade in technology and management services. In that year the top 300 transnational corporations, excluding financial institutions, owned one-quarter of the world's productive capital. The combined assets of the world's fifty largest commercial banks and diversified financial companies amounted to nearly 60 percent of the estimated $20 trillion global stock of productive capital.[1]

These statistics speak to the sheer size of leading corporations. Corporations of that size are naturally quite powerful in many arenas, as we will demonstrate in a moment. However, in neoclassical economic theory the absolute size of the

Table IV.1. Top 20 and Selected Other Global Corporations, 1997

Rank	Name	1997 Revenues ($ millions)	Country	Industry
1.	General Motors	178,174	U.S.	Automobiles
2.	Ford	153,627	U.S.	Automobiles
3.	Mitsui	142,688	Japan	Conglomerate
4.	Mitsubishi	128,922	Japan	Conglomerate
5.	Royal Dutch Shell	128,142	Netherlands	Petroleum
6.	Itochu	126,632	Japan	Conglomerate
7.	Exxon	122,379	U.S.	Petroleum
8.	Wal-Mart	119,299	U.S.	Petroleum
9.	Marubeni	111,211	Japan	Conglomerate
10.	Sumitomo	102,395	Japan	Conglomerate
11.	Toyota	95,137	Japan	Automobiles
12.	General Motors	90,840	U.S.	Electronics
13.	Nissho Iwai	81,894	Japan	Conglomerate
14.	IBM	78,508	U.S.	Computers
15.	Nippon Telegraph & Telephone	76,984	Japan	Telephones
16.	AXA	76,874	France	Insurance
17.	Daimler-Benz	71,561	Germany	Automobiles
18.	Daewoo	71,526	S. Korea	Automobiles
19.	Nippon Life Insurance	71,388	Japan	Insurance
20.	British Petroleum	71,193	U.K.	Petroleum
50.	Sears Roebuck	41,296	U.S.	Retailing
100.	Vivendi	28,634	France	Construction
200.	Yasuda Mutual Life Insurance	18,805	Japan	Insurance
300.	Karstadt	13,720	Germany	Retailing
400.	Microsoft	11,358	U.S.	Software
500.	Sunoco	8,968	U.S.	Petroleum

Source: *Fortune,* August 3, 1998.

firm is less important than its market share. The power to raise prices above the competitive levels and earn monopoly profits results from being large relative to the market, not from being large relative to the world. Power to set prices, in short, comes from market share.

There are industries in which a few firms dominate the market, raising the neoclassical problem of market power. Selected examples are shown in Table IV.2. Most of the examples are makers of consumer products with well-known brand names; successful promotion of brand names is a leading source of market power today.

The companies shown in Table IV.2 are not small; in fact, ten of the world's largest 100 companies appear there (the five auto companies, Coke, Pepsi, Sony, Philip Morris, and Procter & Gamble). But large size and large market share are not quite the same thing; the criteria for inclusion in Tables IV.1 and IV.2 are different, and the two lists of companies are not identical. Mindful of

Table IV.2. Market Shares of Top Four Firms in Selected Industries

Regular type: U.S. data, 1997
Italics: World data, 1993–94

Industry	Top Four Firms				Share of Market	
	Biggest	Second	Third	Fourth	Biggest	All Four
Beer	Anheuser-Busch	Miller	Coors	Stroh/Heilman	45.8	93.7
	Anheuser-Busch	*Heineken*	*Miller*	*Kirin*	*9.0*	*19.6*
Cars and Trucks	General Motors	Ford	Chrysler		30.6	70.4
	General Motors	*Ford*	*Toyota*	*Volkswagen*	*15.9*	*46.0*
Cosmetics	Revlon	Cover Girl	Maybelline	L'Oreal	21.6	69.4
Drug Stores	Walgreen	CVS	Rite Aid	Eckerd	18.6	65.5
Film Distributors	Disney	Sony	Paramount	Fox	21.0	64.6
Salty Snacks	Frito-Lay	Wise	Procter & Gamble		54.0	62.0
Soft Drinks	Coca-Cola	Pepsi-Cola	Seven-Up/Dr. Pepper		43.9	89.3
	Coca-Cola	*Pepsi-Cola*			*46.0*	*63.0*
Cigarettes	Philip Morris	RJR Nabisco	Brown & Williamson	Lorillard	47.8	97.1
	Philip Morris	*BAT Industries*	*Japan Tobacco*	*RJR Nabisco*	*12.2*	*29.5*

Source: Taub, Amy et al. "Oligopoly! Highly Concentrated Markets Across the U.S. Economy," *Multinational Monitor* 20, no. 4 (November 1998), pg. 9; and Sawinski, Diane M. et al. *Encyclopedia of Global Industries* (New York: Gate Research, 1996).

our earlier set of comparisons, between corporations and nations, we need to be alert to sources of power that may not show up directly in the standard picture of industry concentrations. Especially important is the power of conglomerates, where their overall ability to shape events may be much greater than is suggested by the market share of any of the individual firms collected under the conglomerate umbrella. A huge conglomerate with only a tenth of the market in one of its many activities is a far stronger creature than a firm with the same share of this market and nothing else.

Numerous corporations are clearly big enough to wield substantial power, either based on their absolute size or, in many industries, based on their market share. We will turn now to the uses of that power.

Some Negative Aspects of Corporate Power

Why should the uses of corporate power concern us? What can corporations do that matters to people outside of the business pages of the newspaper? Sociologists **Dan Clawson, Alan Neustadtl, and Denise Scott** describe the varieties of corporate decisions that affect the lives of people inside and outside of the firm. Corporate employment decisions determine who gets jobs and under what conditions—often under quite dictatorial conditions, as they point out. Corporate investment decisions can transform a community's future, for better or worse. The choice of technologies and processes determines the level of pollution experienced by workers and by those who live nearby. Corporate lobbying, campaign contributions, and threats to move in search of a better business climate can reshape the political process. The effects of product design, marketing, and advertising decisions are felt in all of our daily lives.

Walter Adams and James W. Brock argue that corporate bigness leads to two types of disturbingly undemocratic, unaccountable power: Internal corporate planning can displace the market's role in resource allocation; and corporate wealth gives rise to disproportionate influence on government policy. They illustrate the antisocial uses of corporate power with dramatic examples from the automobile industry. The U.S. automakers have actively worked to roll back and replace urban mass transit; they have fought against efforts to reduce automobile emissions; they have resisted safety regulations; and they have refused to produce fuel-efficient cars. To take one particular example, Adams and Brock note that General Motors

> understood at an early date that if urban railways could be eliminated as a viable competitive option, the sale of its buses could be vastly expanded. And if transit systems using buses could subsequently be made to decline or fail, a huge market would open up for additional sales of private automobiles. [Adams and Brock, p. 223]

The destruction of public transportation, it is now recognized, strikes a blow against the viability of communities. To cite another example of the tension between big corporations and the communities in which they establish a foothold, when a giant Wal-Mart store comes to town, as many as a hundred local stores may go out of business. Three jobs in local retailing are lost for every two created at Wal-Mart; yet Wal-Mart wages are rock-bottom, and benefits are meager or nonexistent. Some towns are clobbered again when Wal-Mart later decides to open a new, even bigger supercenter replacing several of the earlier, (comparatively) smaller Wal-Marts. Having already lost most of their local businesses, the townspeople have no choice but to drive long distances to the new, regional Wal-Mart. (Korten 1999, 164–165, drawing on *How Wal-Mart Is Destroying America;* Quinn 1998).

The Corporation and the Worker

One of the major themes of this book (and its predecessor, *The Changing Nature of Work*) is that there was a change in corporate strategy in the 1970s, which has led to a more unequal distribution of wages and salaries. **Bennett Harrison** is one of the economists who analyzed, and vigorously publicized, the change in corporate employment practices. In the chapter summarized here, Harrison explains that big business responded to the increasingly competitive environment of the 1970s by becoming "flexible"—or in Harrison's words, "lean and mean." Full-time jobs with good wages and benefits are offered only to a diminished number of the most crucial employees, while outsourcing to low-wage subcontractors, contingent work, and other cost-cutting measures are the fate of everyone else. Like David Gordon (summarized in Part I), Harrison sees corporations having a choice between the cost-cutting "low road" and the revenue-enhancing "high road" to renewed competitiveness. For the most part, the inegalitarian "low road" has been taken. This choice is not only part of the political economy of the late twentieth century, it is a recurring dilemma for business and will surface again in other contexts.

In general, large employers are often in a position to make a choice between a cost-minimizing versus a revenue-maximizing strategy. Employers adopting the cost-minimizing approach choose to hire labor cheaply, reducing the wage to the minimum level at which vacancies can be filled. The firm is always on the lookout for possibilities for contracting out, replacing a part of its own workforce with lower-paid workers in other firms or other regions who can perform a portion of the work process. Workers are provided with the minimum training needed to complete their tasks. There are few opportunities for promotion; higher-level positions are filled by experienced applicants from outside the firm—applicants who gained their experience at no expense to their new employer. Since workers earning low wages and with few chances to advance have little motivation to work hard or well, the cost-minimizing employer must rely on close supervision (the "stick"), rather than intrinsic motivation, to maintain a basic level of product quality. This level will be low; since it is easier to monitor quantity than quality in most lines of work, the cost-minimizing firm's focus will be on high levels of output.

The revenue-maximizing approach is the opposite on almost every count. Employers adopting this "carrot" strategy are willing to pay for a greater degree of worker quality and commitment, hoping that this will pay off in other ways. The firm will be on the lookout for workers who will make a long-term commitment, who come with a relatively high level of competence, and who are willing to acquire new skills along the way. To get them, the firm will offer a similar commitment of its own, along with higher than average salaries, and it will stress opportunities for on-the-job training and promotion. The revenue-maximizing employer's more highly motivated workforce can be given more autonomy and does not require constant supervision. Conflict is more destructive in a long-term relationship of this sort, so the firm will establish institutions to resolve differences cooperatively. All of these commitments are expensive. In return, the employer expects a high level of performance from the organization, including rigorous quality control, dependability, trust, and creativity that manifests itself in a high rate of innovation. These expenses can be justified when customers are willing to pay more for goods that will meet more exacting specifications and whose supply can be depended on.

A firm's decision on whether to take the "low" or the "high" road partly depends on the nature of the product market it faces. Such decisions are also affected by the history of industrial relations within each corporation and each workplace: Change in employment relations generally takes time and effort, whether it appears to be change for the better or for the worse. Nevertheless, the case is made by both Harrison and Gordon that this choice was available to many large corporations, which, in the 1970s and 1980s especially, opted for the low road. The management theories that became popular during the 1980s and into the 1990s, in the climate of globally heightened competitiveness, gave an emphasis to minimizing the cost of paying workers—an emphasis that had not previously been thought necessary in large corporations that possess the ability to compete on other grounds than price alone.

It is evident that society is powerfully affected by the aggregate choices of many large employers, choosing between strategies that emphasize an educated, self-motivated workforce versus one that offers mostly low-wage, dead-end jobs. The low-wage option is not as cheap as it appears at first glance, as explained by David Gordon (1996).[2] Gordon described the "bureaucratic burden" carried by the United States, the nation that employs the world's largest proportion of supervisors/managers to regular workers. According to his 1996 calculations, 15 to 20 percent of the total private, nonfarm workforce are appropriately categorized as supervisors or managers, with their compensation accounting for nearly a one-fifth of GDP. This amount—$1.3 trillion—was about the size of the total revenue of the federal government in that year. Thus a significant portion of the money that was saved by cutting the compensation and the numbers of production workers was laid out again to hire an army of managers and supervisors for a disaffected workforce.

What changed in the late 1960s and early 1970s to cause the shift in corporate strategies that is associated with The Great U-Turn? Was this change in corporate behavior in fact responsible for ending the period of remarkable economic stability (even growth and declining inequality) of the quarter-century after World War II? **David Gordon, Thomas Weisskopf, and Samuel Bowles** offer a creative neo-Marxian explanation, focusing attention (as Marx and other classical economists did) on the division of national income between capital and labor. Gordon et al. draw a complex picture of the inherent contradictions that gradually emerged in the Golden Age of stability, leading to the breakdown of its implicit contracts and supporting institutions.

Instability can result, in macroeconomic terms, from an imbalance between capital and labor in either direction. For Gordon et al., the economic problem of the late 1960s was that capitalists had lost the power to keep profits high enough to support investment. As we will see in the next section, capital responded by mounting an attack on labor that was so effective that, by the 1980s, the danger was that wages would not be high enough to support consumption.

There is an implicit suggestion in this account (and in many other macroeconomic analyses) of the need for a balance between the interests of capital and labor. Both sides need to have the division of income occur within a band where labor gets enough to support robust demand, and capital gets enough to be able to support progressive investment. Yet it is a famous problem of macroeconomics that the optimal balance is unstable; in the short run, there can be excessive swings in either direction. A traditional textbook image referred to the difficulty of maintaining a knife-edge balance in the process of growth. More recent commentary in the business press has called for maintaining the Goldilocks economy—not too hot, but also not too cold.

Political Action: Corporate Power Bites Back

The legal and institutional definitions of corporations give them a powerful advantage—corporations, unlike individuals, can be immortal. At the same time, corporate representatives have agitated, over the last 100 years, to keep many of the rights and advantages (though not all of the responsibilities) that come with the legal status of personhood. This effort was given its greatest boost in 1886 when the Supreme Court ruled, in *Santa Clara County v. Southern Pacific Rail-*

way, that a private corporation enjoys all of the Constitution's protections of a natural person. This ruling was reaffirmed in the 1976 case, *Buckley v. Valeo,* in which the Supreme Court specified protection of commercial speech under the First Amendment.

The single dissenting voice on the largely Republican Supreme Court at the time of *Buckley v. Valeo* was Justice White, who stated that

> Corporations are artificial entities created by law for the purpose of furthering certain economic goals. . . . It has long been recognized . . . that the special status of corporations has placed them in a position to control vast amounts of economic power which may, if not regulated, dominate, not only the economy but also the very heart of our democracy, the electoral process. (Quoted in Wright 1982, 641.)

The warning was a timely one, for it occurred just as a wave of corporate political activism was rising. According to **Jerome L. Himmelstein,** the political activity of big business helped to turn the tide of increasing equality that had characterized the post–World War II Golden Age. An important enabler of this political activity was the Supreme Court decision, which decided that, for the purposes of the first amendment, "money is speech" (see Wright 1976). This rolled back the efforts, started in the 1970s, to limit the impact of large contributors (such as corporations) on political campaigns. It has also blocked efforts to treat advertising as a form of social manipulation that requires social control.

Individual corporations can achieve some of their goals by acting alone—for example, when they entice cities or regions into a bidding war. However, there is a line of research that focuses on the even greater impact business can have when it acts in unison. The sociologists and others who write about this topic (often referring to it as "corporate unity") sometimes take a defensive tone, insisting that empirical evidence of cooperative behavior among actors from different corporations must be taken seriously, even though it runs counter to the economic assumption of competition. The subject of corporate unity appeared in Part II, particularly in the summaries of articles by Scott and Domhoff, and it appears again here in Part IV, in the article by Clawson et al. The quotation at the head of the latter summary puts the matter very neatly: Corporations will compete among themselves for market share, but they may be expected to unite to advance their common interest in enlarging the pie that they will divide among themselves. (See also Kerbo and Della Fava 1983.)

Himmelstein, like Gordon, Weisskopf, and Bowles, grounds his analysis in the economic slowdown of the 1970s, to which big business responded by mobilizing their political muscle and devoting it to conservative, anti-egalitarian causes—including, importantly, a multipronged attack on the efficacy of labor unions. He has published a subsequent book about corporate philanthropy

(Himmelstein 1997) that makes even sharper distinctions between the right-leaning interests of big business and a far-right "Conservative Vision," which he perceives as lying largely outside the corporate world and often in conflict with big business. Himmelstein characterizes the normal U.S. business philosophy as "pragmatic"—an approach that "accepts the political world as it is and seeks broad influence within it." (Ibid., 127) This use of corporate power—subtler than outright lobbying, the use of corporate PACs, or the funding of conservative think tanks—is "rooted in structural indispensability" (Ibid., p. 142); that is, the raw fact that business controls a large proportion of investment capital. In Himmelstein's view corporations do not necessarily see a dramatic opposition between profits and wages; under certain economic circumstances (e.g., the Golden Age) all can rise together. However, when economic growth slows, corporations lean toward a conservative ideology that regards wage increases, government benefits, and government regulation as enemies to profits.

Making the Best of Corporate Power

Not all corporate decisions have such negative side effects as those emphasized here. Firms can also use their resources (including management and technology) to do things we generally regard as good. At the least, corporations supply jobs to people who need them (though the jobs-to-revenue ratio is markedly lower for large corporations, in general, than for small firms), and they produce products at least some of which are valuable, even essential, for human well-being. They may also support constructive research and make other contributions that go beyond their own obvious self-interest. As we go on, in this final section, to consider how best to deal with the reality of corporate power, we should be aware of the possibility for it to work in positive ways. On the other hand, it is critical to strengthen legal and cultural inhibitions against the harm that corporations can do, reducing their power to pursue their own objectives without regard to their negative externalities.

Examples of corporations that have made serious efforts to take responsibility for their environmental impacts include British Petroleum, which has taken the lead among energy companies in accepting the reality of global warming and pursuing less carbon-intensive sources of energy (Steiner and Steiner 1997, 128); and B&Q, the largest retailer of do-it-yourself furniture in Europe, which requires suppliers to document their timber sources, preferring those that chose sustainable harvesters (Ayres 1997, 11). Merck Pharmaceutical company spent well over $200 million to develop and distribute free a drug that effectively cures and may eradicate river blindness—a disease that has devastated areas of the world that were too poor to pay for the product. (Steiner and Steiner 105).

Which do you trust more: markets or politics? Which is more likely to act in the public interest: a corporation or a government agency? There is a political

divide that is related in obvious ways to the answers to these questions: Markets·
tend to be kinder to the rich than to the poor, while governments, especially
when they attempt to restrain or counterbalance the power of the private economy, are viewed less favorably by the rich. To be sure, when governments are
corrupt, then everyone suffers, and the poor may suffer the most. Even when
governments are honest, they are often criticized (frequently with good reason)
for being inefficient. But at least an honest government is likely to have impacts
that are seen as "fair," whereas that is no concern of the ideally competitive
market.

As the balance in public policy has shifted toward greater and greater reliance
on the market, academic theorists have produced more and more elaborate
grounds for glorifying the private sector and disparaging any efforts of the government. A response to this trend can be found in a chapter in **Robert Kuttner**'s book, *Everything for Sale: the Virtues and Limits of Markets*. Kuttner's the-
oretic contribution is to make explicit the linkages between a conservative
political agenda and a particular strand of academic ideology, "public choice
theory." This theory, as Kuttner describes it, extends to political life the psychological assumptions of neoclassical theory, which simplify all human motivations to self-interest. He shows how the historical American distrust of government has been used to support those who believe that their pockets will be
pilfered for any kind of aid to the less advantaged. In opposition to such views,
he urges that we rethink the balance between the public and private spheres.

Bowles and Gintis similarly relate academic thinking to political positions.
They call on intellectuals to reexamine the distinctions between *public* and *private* that, they say, have been defined so as to support the interests of holders of
wealth (capital). As previously noted, corporate power enables a relatively small
group of individuals to make a large number of decisions that affect the lives of
most members of society. Kuttner, like Bowles and Gintis, proposes that the solution is to strengthen government, giving more power to a democratic system
of "one person, one vote" and less to the system of corporate dominance that
comes down to "one dollar, one vote."

The final summary, which covers two chapters from **Ralph Estes's** recent
book, *Tyranny of the Bottom Line: Why Corporations Make Good People Do Bad
Things*, takes a different tack. Estes does not count on direct action by governments to correct the modern corporation's ability and willingness to externalize
the costs of workplace injuries, deceptive advertising, unhealthy and dangerous
products, toxic wastes and other environmental destruction, defense contract
overcharges, and other white-collar crime. Estes, formerly a senior accountant
with Arthur Anderson & Co., undertakes the task of estimating these external-
ized costs in the United States and comes up with a total (adjusted to 1994 dollars) of over two and a half trillion dollars. He points out that this is over eight

times the total expenditure on education in the United States—almost twice the whole federal budget.

Estes' understanding of why corporations externalize these costs is suggested in the title of his book. He starts from a common assumption, held by both Marxian and neoclassical economists, that individual motivations are normally swamped by the exigencies of market forces. Individual decision makers might wish to behave in a public-spirited way, but if they deviate from a strict profit orientation, their companies will fail or, at least, they will lose their jobs. (Note that this prediction is not always accurate; monopoly power does create slack within which companies can raise CEO salaries above any reasonable estimate of marginal productivity, or offer public services, or engage in other not directly profit-related activities.)

Estes' point does not, in any case, depend on a deterministic vision of corporate behavior. He is interested in figuring out what actions can create an environment in which it is easier for corporate decision makers to act in society's interest—and harder for them to make antisocial moves. This would not be an easy agenda to pursue, even if there existed somewhere a precise and definitive list of which corporate behaviors are good, bad, or indifferent in their social impacts. Unfortunately, no such chart exists. The fallback for Estes, and for those with similar aims, is to promote the idea of *corporate transparency*.

The nascent movement along these lines[3] starts from the premise that there are numerous interested groups (including, but not restricted to, nonprofits) who are aware of corporate influence on their particular areas of concern. Therefore, a great force can be unleashed simply by making much more information about corporations available. An intermediating group of institutions, the "aftermarket" for corporate information, can be expected to expand, as the available information expands, to digest the data for use by NGOs, customers, workers, and communities. When the latter possess more knowledge about a company's past practices, as Estes explains, they will begin, through their choices and actions, to clarify what are the critical elements in corporate responsibility.

Estes' focus on transparency is complementary to, not at odds with, the more traditional emphasis on government regulation of corporations, as represented by Kuttner and Bowles and Gintis. Indeed, he recognizes the need for government action to create a level playing field, by requiring all companies to meet basic standards in what and how they report regarding their impacts on the full range of stakeholders. Such a recognition of the requirement for government involvement to make markets work is a step in the direction of institutional economics—or its older form, political economy.

However, the mechanism that Estes expects will spur corporations to internalize externalities is a complex chain, in which governments mandate transparency and corporations respond by reporting on their own impacts; the "aftermarket" of nonprofit and for-profit institutions analyze and report on the accuracy and completeness of the corporations' reports; and a broad group of stakeholders reacts in ways that affect the corporation's ability to function and to thrive. The forms of these reactions can include, for example, stockholder resolutions, worker actions, community decisions (on what kinds of supports or inducements to offer to a corporation), consumer preferences (e.g., for products with an eco-label), and consumer boycotts. (The last of these, normally requiring organization of an especially diffuse group, can be effective for only a few, very high-profile situations.)

Such a chain of actions and reactions could radically change the motivations that make corporations, and the world, look as they do today. At best, it could link corporate behavior more closely to broad social goals, for the long run as well as for the present. This would be a dramatic change from a system ruled by an economic theory that says that profits and individual self-interest are the only things that can get maximized in a market. Among other import effects, all corporate stakeholders would be required to make conscious decisions about the values they would like to see reflected in the socioeconomic system. If such a process does gather momentum and begins to reshape corporations, it will be interesting to see where equality will rank among the values that will take on more salience for corporate behavior.

Notes

1. Greider, 1997, 21; *The Economist* March 27, 1993, supplement, 6; Korten, 1995, 221.
2. A chapter from Gordon (1996) was summarized in Part I; the discussion here draws on other chapters of the same book.
3. For information about this movement contact CERES (the Coalition for Environmentally Responsible Economies), 11 Arlington St., 6th Floor, Boston, MA 02116-3411; www.ceres.org.

Summary of

Economy: The Political Foundations of Production and Exchange

by Samuel Bowles and Herbert Gintis

[Published in *Democracy and Capitalism: Property, Community, and the Contradictions of Modern Social Thought* (New York: Basic Books, 1986), Ch. 3, 64–91.]

The authors show that power, in the sense of the ability of one agent to control the behavior of other agents, exists in the capitalist economy, even under conditions of widespread competition and voluntary exchange. This poses a problem for democratic political theory: The capitalist economy is political, but is not a democracy. How do we justify this dichotomy in a society dedicated to realizing substantive democracy wherever unaccountable power is found? Liberal economic theory solves the problem by asserting that economic power is nonexistent. "Liberal . . . renders the power of capital invisible: Democrats cannot assail economic power within liberal theory because they lack the tools for making such power visible." [65–66] This chapter makes the power of capital visible, demonstrating that even a perfectly competitive economy would give rise to pervasive, politically significant, and unequally distributed power.

Introduction: The Failure of Liberal Theory

Two political principles delineate rights in liberal theory. The principle of liberty holds that individuals have inviolate personal rights; the principle of democracy upholds equality and collective popular sovereignty. The public sphere can be defined as those aspects of life where the norms of liberty and democracy both apply; the private sphere can be defined as those aspects where only liberty is applicable. In these terms, any socially consequential exercise of power should be in the public sphere.

Liberal democratic theory supports the application of both principles to the state, but applies only the principle of liberty to the economy; that is, it describes the economy as a private sphere devoid of the exercise of power. This overlooks the fact that power in fact exists in the capitalist economy and is wielded by owners and hierarchically well-planned managements.

The classification of the economy as private rather than public rarely receives an explicit defense; an argument can be constructed from two central propositions of neoclasical economics. The first may be called the "labor commodity" proposition: The purchase of labor in an employment relationship has the same character as the purchase of a commodity—there is no exercise of power by buyer or seller in either case. Second is the "asset neutrality" proposition: Ownership of productive assets does not convey power, since the competitive pressure of the market dictates economic outcomes. If true, these propositions would support the idea that economic life is private. Yet both propositions are false.

Understanding Employment

Capitalism is always a system of employment as well as exchange. The asymmetry of the employment relationship has been recognized at least since Thomas Hobbes (at a time when the terms servant and employee were synonymous), who said, "To have servants is to have power." The existence of a structure of command within the firm is central to the neoclassical analysis of the firm by

Ronald Coase; for Coase the existence of firms proves that it is inefficient to conduct all economic transactions through contractual exchange.

Why does it matter that capital hires labor, rather than vice versa? Neoclassical theory has ignored the problem of contract enforcement, which Marx termed the problem of extracting labor (actual productive effort) from labor power (the capacity to work). Employment contracts almost never specify the exact services to be performed; workers are hired to be available for work for a specified time and to submit to the rules and regulations of the workplace during that time. Services delivered by the worker cannot be separated from the person of the worker, and work is almost always a social process involving direct relationships among workers.

These characteristics facilitate worker resistance and thus render contract enforcement problematic for the employer. There is a trade-off for employers between paying higher wages and subjecting workers to more intense (and costly) surveillance; both are means of eliciting greater effort. Such incentive costs would be lower in a worker-controlled enterprise where identification with the goals of the firm would be greater and the desire to resist work would be weaker.

Power, Production, and Competition

The labor commodity proposition justifies undemocratic, hierarchical organization of enterprises; it claims that racial, sexual, and other forms of discrimination will be eliminated by the market; and it interprets unemployment as voluntary. All of these notions are invalid and at variance with empirical evidence.

Hierarchical organization is said to be both efficient and unimportant because production is simply a matter of making the optimal choices dictated by the market and the available technologies. Thus the cost-minimizing price and quantity of labor services to be hired by a firm are determined by the market. However, this implies that owners of capital should have little interest in controlling production, since they perform only an externally dictated, technical management function. In practice, this conclusion is obviously false.

The same competitive pressure toward cost minimization should impel the employer to seek the lowest price for an hour of equivalent labor, hiring women or minorities whenever they are paid less than white men. As neoclassical economists have often noted, the market should therefore eliminate wage discrimination; prejudiced employers who persist in preferring higher-wage workers should be eliminated by competition. Again, this is at variance with the facts.

Likewise, if labor is a commodity, unsold units must have been voluntarily withheld from the market. Yet in reality there is a recurrent tendency toward significant unemployment, even in the absence of wage restraints.

The alternative model of labor exchange as a social process involving the exercise of power easily fits all these facts. Hierarchy is of course important to employers seeking to control the labor process. Racial, sexual, and other divisions are functional for capitalists because they weaken workers' unity and bargaining strength, and thus decrease the chance of effective resistance to workplace incentives for greater effort. Involuntary unemployment raises the cost of job loss to workers, making the employer's ultimate threat of dismissal a more ominous sanction.

An anomaly in the alternative model is that it suggests that democratic worker-owned firms should be more efficient than capitalist firms, and should therefore outcompete traditional enterprises. The actual scarcity of worker-controlled firms reflects the second dimension of capitalist power, the command over investment.

The Power of the Purse

As Joseph Schumpeter argued long ago, the evolution of new technologies and new forms of organization should, in neoclassical theory, be subject to the same rules: Firms that are best able to meet existing market demands will obtain credit, expand their operations, and flourish. In a competitive economy, unsuccessful technologies and organizations, as well as banks that back the unsuccessful, will be squeezed out. Notice that neither financiers nor entrepreneurs exercise real power in this model. If worker-controlled enterprises are efficient, they should thrive.

However, survival in competitive markets is based on profits, not efficiency. Worker-controlled firms may be more efficient in maximizing net output per labor hour but still produce lower profits. And because they generally start with less capital of their own, worker-controlled firms must borrow more and pay more interest. Financial institutions generally demand either control or collateral in return for funds; a worker-controlled enterprise is ill-equipped to meet these demands.

Credit markets routinely violate the asset neutrality proposition. Dealing with their own problems of contract enforcement—ensuring the repayment of loans—financial institutions act in a decidedly nonneutral manner. They prefer to lend to, and offer the best terms to, those who appear to be the best risks (those who are most able to offer collateral and most certain to repay). This reinforces existing inequalities and inhibits the entry of new start-up firms into established markets.

Free to Move

Despite the existence of enormous inequalities of power in economic life, liberal theory suggests that economic power can be held accountable to the democratic state. This notion can be faulted on the empirical grounds that the wealthy exercise disproportionate influence through campaign contributions, political advertising, lobbying, and so on. There is also a deeper problem: Capital exerts a kind of veto power over public policy, deriving from the effectiveness of a "capital strike."

By threatening to withdraw investment and move elsewhere, capital can frequently win concessions from the government; a capital strike would impose much greater costs on the incumbent government and the population than it would on the owners of capital. Labor, in contrast, is much less mobile and is generally constrained to work for some employer in its immediate vicinity. A sovereign state could conceivably change the rules, responding to a capital strike by limiting capital outflow and undertaking public investment. But there are immense practical obstacles to this kind of democratic revolution.

In conclusion,

> Liberal political philosophy is thus curiously at odds with liberal economic theory. The former heralds the individual as an agent empowered to transform his or her world; the latter favors an economic system in which agency is so compromised as to be little more than a false promise for all but the few. . . . By rendering invisible the power of capital, liberal economic theory has contributed more to the legitimation of powerlessness than to making good its claim of universal agency. [90]

Summary of

Business Unity, Business Power

by Dan Clawson, Alan Neustadtl, and Denise Scott

[Published in *Money Talks: Corporate PACs and Political Influence*, (New York: Basic Books, 1992), Ch. 6, 158–190.]

> In the marketplace we're competitors, but when it comes to the halls of Congress or the halls of the legislatures we are allies more than we are opponents. It is bottom-line oriented but it's not who has the biggest share of the market. It's all of us being able to sell our products in a healthy environment, so then we can compete for market share. [Industry spokesperson, quoted on p. 177]

Academic debates over business power have focused on the question of whether business unifies to promote a common agenda. This chapter provides evidence for a strong affirmative to this question, especially in the context of pressure for congressional legislation. The authors examine how such unity is achieved, how it is affected by legislation, and what are its goals and impacts. The chapter ends with a description of the wellspring of corporate power: control over the economy.

Building Business Unity

There is a close commonality of interests among businesses, even when they are also competitors. In fact, the more directly competitive the market relationship, the greater is the likelihood that they share the same interest in shaping the legislative and cultural environment in which they operate.

Industry trade associations take on the issues that are particular to just one industry, such as banking, lumber, automobile manufacturing, and so on. Other associations are more generally representative of business interests, including the Chamber of Commerce and the Business Industry Political Action Committee (BIPAC). Some Political Action Committees (PACs) focus on fundraising and building support for candidates while others are more ideological, advocating for particular issues and causes.

This cooperation is supported by a tightly interlocked social world and a common culture, tied together through interlocking directorates, interlocking PAC activities, overlapping memberships in social and/or political organizations, and so on. More material links include "loans from the same banks, sales and purchases from each other . . . common interests in accumulating capital and avoiding government initiatives that might restrict their power." [161]

Campaign finance laws, instead of reducing the influence of large donors on elected officials, merely skew the impact, magnifying the impact of the largest companies and the force of unified action. The disclosure provision ensures that businesses can keep an eye on one another, making it harder for any one corporation to cut a special political deal at the expense of the rest. The limits on individual and PAC donations makes it impossible for a maverick billionaire or a company in a crisis to finance, alone, even a small fraction of one campaign. This greatly increases the motivation for a kind of cooperative behavior that makes it very clear to candidates that they will be identified as generally pro-business, or not. Their ability to finance their campaigns will be hugely affected by how friendly they are to the business point of view, overall. Examination of donations by the largest corporate PACs revealed that "corporations almost always unify to support one of the two candidates in a race. In about three out of four races business can be classified as unified, giving at least nine times as much to one candidate as to the other . . . and in only one race out of fifteen is business divided (accepting a split of two to one or closer as evidence of division)." [160]

Control of the Economy

> Business's power is magnified and reinforced by its political unity. The real
> bedrock of its power, however, is the pervasive economic inequality in our so-
> ciety and business domination of the economy. [181]

Inequalities in wealth and income translate into inequalities in power through
the ownership of productive assets. The corporate scene in the United States is
dominated by the 500 largest industrial corporations, which control 75 percent of industrial sales, assets, and profits; and by the 500 largest service corporations, which similarly dominate the service sector. The owners and top executives of these thousand corporations may number about 25,000 individuals
(0.001 percent of the U.S. population at the time of writing). These individuals are responsible for a large majority of what we view as the activities of
"business." One of the major goals of business-backed political activity is to
shelter these activities from public scrutiny and regulation, yet these activities
pervade almost every aspect of the lives of the other 0.999 percent of the population.

Business decisions about employment determine the number of people employed, when they go to work and how long they stay, who is laid off and when.
Business controls who works and who doesn't by specifying skill and education
requirements and controlling whether women, minorities, or the disabled receive fair opportunities. Workers rights to form unions, to exercise freedom of
expression on the job, and to enjoy safe working conditions are often subordi-
nated to the freedom of firms to make business decisions. One worker at a
Coca-Cola plant was legally suspended for drinking a Pepsi while at work. A
worker at another firm was fired for refusing to work on a job at which another
worker was killed until improvements were made. The firing was upheld by the
Supreme Court.

Decisions about investments have far-reaching consequences for people and
their communities, yet businesses have sole discretion over whether to open or
expand a facility, or close one down. Firms often make deals for tax abatements
and implicit exemptions from labor and pollution laws. Business decisions determine the amount of pollution in the workplace and in the external environment. Campaign contributions are not the only means that business can use to
influence legislators. They can also threaten to close a plant and move away if
they are not given favorable tax treatment or are subject to environmental regulations they dislike.

Businesses also wield enormous power over products and marketing, including which products to introduce or continue; their cost, quality, and design;
and which elements of design will be stressed, for example safety or style; and
the amount and character of advertising.

Decisions in these areas further agendas that "business" (that is, the 25,000 or so individuals who wield the greatest corporate power) perceives as in its interest—which may not be the interest of the rest of society. One example of such a conflict was the decision of the Ford Motor Company, led by Lee Iacocca, to fight gas tank safety regulations, delaying their implementation for eight years while continuing to sell Ford Pintos whose gas tanks, in Ford's own tests, ruptured in every crash at over 25 miles per hour.

Another category of business power is the decision on how to spend profits, which "implies choices about the kind of society we should have and the activities that should be supported." [188] In the United States in 1988 the total of corporate advertising expenditures equaled more than two-thirds the total spending on public elementary and secondary education. Increasingly large sums are spent on advertising that is not tied to a specific product, but that aims to elevate a company's image (regardless of the social impact of the company's product) or to promote political positions. Government is in many ways controlled by the economy; and the economy is controlled by the tiny minority of powerful individuals who run the largest corporations.

Summary of

Bigness and Social Efficiency: A Case Study of the U.S. Auto Industry

by Walter Adams and James W. Brock

[Published in *Corporations and Society*, eds. Warren J. Samuels and Arthur S. Miller (Westport, Conn.: Greenwood Press, 1987), Ch. 9, 219–237.]

Giant corporations have come to dominate industrial and other economic activity, a fact that many journalists and commentators have noted. "Yet . . . economists have generally declined the challenge of assaying the parameters of corporate bigness and size-based economic power. . . . [D]espite a monumental revolution in industrial organization over the past century, the economists' conception of power—defined as the capacity to influence price in a particular market—has remained remarkably unchanged, unidimensional, and, in all, anemic and innocuous." [219]

At least two other types of power are wielded by large firms. First, big corporations can displace the competitive market as society's primary instrument for planning and resource allocation. The internal coordination of activity and distribution of resources has been central to analyses of corporations by such economists as Alfred Chandler and John Kenneth Galbraith. Some defenders of big business, such as Peter Drucker, have argued that by insulating enterprises from short-term market fluctuations, bigness allows corporations to take the long view and think about society's needs.

Second, corporate giantism gives rise to disproportionate influence on government policy. Big businesses can mobilize massive political resources in lobbying for their objectives. Moreover, big businesses can obstruct public policy by threatening to curtail or close their operations, leading to mass layoffs and unemployment.

This chapter explores these dimensions of size-based power in a case study of the U.S. automobile industry. Rather than the traditional economic issues of cost minimization and the pace of technical progress, it focuses on the question of social efficiency: Does the exercise of power by large corporations represent an efficient way to achieve society's goals? A review of four major areas—urban congestion, pollution, automotive safety, and fuel consumption—shows that the answer is largely negative.

Urban Congestion

In the context of urban transportation, social efficiency would require the ability to transport large numbers of people quickly, comfortably, at low cost, and with a minimum use of scarce urban land and open space. The actual urban transportation system in the United States, overwhelmingly dominated by the private automobile, is in many respects the least socially efficient system that could be created. Traffic congestion is a massive and growing problem, for motorists and nonmotorists alike.

The predominance of the private automobile, its displacement of other modes of transportation, and the resulting adverse impacts on urban communities, are not accidental. Nor are they solely due to passive, impersonal market forces. A 1951 federal court decision in an antitrust case found that General Motors was instrumental in organizing National City Lines, a company that engineered the demise of forty-six electric mass transit systems in sixteen states. Through National City Lines, GM, together with a tire producer and an oil company, gained control of urban rail transit systems, destroyed them, and replaced them with GM buses.

In the 1930s, Los Angeles had clean air and the world's largest electric railway network. Then GM and its allies bought the local transit companies, ripped up the tracks, and replaced the trains with GM buses—and, in effect, with millions of private cars. While the rail transit systems of the early twentieth century, in Los Angeles and elsewhere, did not disappear *only* because General Motors wanted to sell buses, it is also clear that GM was not a passive bystander observing the natural evolution of the market.

Smog and Air Pollution

By the early 1960s the automobile was recognized as a leading cause of air pollution. Yet here, too, "size-based power was hardly conducive to a triumph of social efficiency." [225] At first the auto industry denied the existence of the pollution problem. Later, according to a 1969 antitrust suit (which the industry did not contest), the auto giants conspired to avoid competing in research, development, and commercialization of pollution control devices. They ignored promising inventions, refused to purchase technology developed by outsiders, delayed introducing available technologies, and disciplined individual companies that strayed from the agreement.

Then, under intense government pressure in the 1970s, the industry hastily adopted the catalytic converter, an approach to pollution control that the National Academy of Sciences characterized as the most disadvantageous in terms of cost, fuel economy, maintenance, and durability. A modest investment in research and development over the preceding decade, the academy's scientists pointed out, could have led to a much cheaper, better planned method of emission controls.

Automotive Safety

Tens of thousands of people die annually in highway accidents, and millions are injured. By any measure, automotive safety is a serious public health issue. While many other factors are involved, the design of the automobile itself plays a major role in accidents. Here the power of corporate giantism has been applied on many occasions.

Safety features are often shelved for decades after they are developed and patented. Collapsible steering wheels and padded dashboards were patented by the big auto companies in the 1920s and 1930s but only introduced much later when mandated by the government. Seatbelts were initially offered as extra-cost options and were deliberately made expensive and difficult to install. Airbags were developed in the 1970s and by the early 1980s were known to be very cost-effective in accident reduction. Yet the industry resisted their introduction and actively discouraged air bag sales until recently.

Safety is not an essential design feature for the industry; in fact, automobiles have often become more dangerous in design over time. The auto companies have insisted that safety should be optional, supplied only when consumers demand it. "The industry spent hundreds of millions of dollars extolling raw horsepower and rocket acceleration and then (disingenuously) pleaded that 'safety doesn't sell'—despite evidence to the contrary." [227]

Fuel Consumption and the Small Car

The vast fuel consumption of U.S. automobiles is a major contributor to the nation's total demand for energy. The dependence of the American economy on volatile foreign oil supplies can be traced to the widespread use of fuel-inefficient vehicles. Fuel economy therefore provides a further test of social efficiency in the auto industry—a test in which corporate giantism puts in another disappointing performance.

Traditionally, the Big Three automakers considered neither the fuel efficiency of their cars nor the limits to petroleum supplies to be matters of serious concern. The fuel efficiency of U.S. automobiles steadily worsened from 1958 to 1973, primarily due to the increasing size and weight of cars that resulted from styling innovations. The industry stubbornly refused to produce small, inexpensive, fuel-efficient cars, although the demand for them was evident long before the oil crises of the 1970s. As early as the 1940s, the United Auto Workers advocated building a small, fuel-efficient car, citing opinion polls showing widespread public support for such automobiles. Compacts and subcompacts sold well when they were available, and contributed to the first waves of interest in imported cars.

The industry began serious manufacturing and marketing of small cars only in the 1970s, in the face of oil crises, government-mandated fuel economy standards, and the onslaught of foreign competition. But by then, the industry was actually in crisis, as shown by Chrysler's financial collapse. The industry responded by pressuring the government not only to bail out Chrysler, but also to restrain imports of fuel-efficient foreign cars that consumers wanted to buy. Longer-run results of the crisis included some moves to build small cars, often in combination with foreign partners—and also successful efforts by the industry to weaken government fuel economy standards.

Conclusion

Four key conclusions can be drawn from this analysis. First, corporate giantism does have economic consequences that are far more extensive than the ability to influence price in an isolated market. The power of bigness includes the capacity to influence society's planning, control, and allocation of resources, and the affiliated capacity to pressure the state to favor private interests.

"Second, corporate giantism is basically incompatible with a society steeped in the belief that the only legitimate power is accountable power." [232] The biggest firms are not held accountable by the market, nor by the state; even import competition may not restrain them, if they can manipulate the state to restrain trade.

Third, theoretical rationalizations of the existing industrial power structure on grounds of efficiency are unconvincing. The pursuit of social efficiency, achieving society's goals at the lowest possible cost, is not what companies such as the automakers are doing. Since corporations have substantial control over the options open to consumers, it is impossible to take consumers' choice among those options as an optimal outcome or an expression of true social preference. The choices of urban rail transit, for example, or nonpolluting, safe, fuel-efficient automobiles, are not available in the marketplace, but are perfectly plausible social preferences.

Finally, corporate giantism is thus a valid concern for public policy. Acceptance of mega-mergers rests on the erroneous notion that bigness is benign. Perhaps public policy should block some of the biggest mergers and consider the question of whether there should be any limits on the size of corporations, in order to promote decentralization of economic power.

Summary of

The Dark Side of Flexible Production

by Bennett Harrison

[Published in *Lean and Mean* (New York: Guilford, 1994), Ch. 9, 189–216.]

For almost three decades America has been experiencing a surge in wage polarization. There is now a consensus among economists that since the late 1970s, the lowest wage and highest wage Americans have been growing in number, while the proportion of those earning middle-level wages has been falling. Early assessments of this trend by conventional economists incorrectly attributed wage polarization to a rise in the market value of college education during the 1980s. The wage gap occurred from a decline in wages among the non-college-educated work force, not from a growth in the college wage. The puzzle then remains: What is causing the long-term trend toward increased earnings inequality?

This article argues that businesses' pursuit of "flexibility" to adapt to heightened global competition is creating a new dualism that is proliferating low-wage, insecure employment. This dark side of flexible production is responsible for much of the wage polarization in the United States.

The New Dualism

Segmented or "dual" labor market theory was developed in the late 1960s and 1970s to examine the organization of work. A reconceptualization of this theory can go a long way in explaining flexible production and growth of wage inequality.

Dual labor market theorists saw the economy as consisting of a primary and a secondary labor market. The primary labor market is dominated by large, vertically organized, somewhat oligopolistic firms that earned above average profits and gave out above average wages. Within these firms exist vertical career ladders or internal labor markets. These ladders were quite secure and came with comfortable benefits. Outside of the big firms lay the secondary labor market, those working for smaller firms where wages were lower, benefits were poor or nonexistent, and on the job training was hard to find.

Today the businesses are embarking on vertical disintegration, downsizing, outsourcing, and the formation of networks of companies that span sectors and nations. This new era is breeding a new dualism, between insiders and outsiders of the "lean and mean" flexible firm. On the inside are full-time year-round jobs equipped with health insurance, paid vacations, organizational learning, and opportunities for upward mobility. On the outside are smaller firms that act as suppliers to the lean ones. A growing number of jobs on the outside are involuntary part-time or part-year work that comes with low wages and few benefits. The growing number of those on the outside is contributing to the hourglass shape of wage polarization.

The Erosion of Employment Security and the Growth of Contingent Work

A major distinction between the new and old dualism is the fact that even high-level jobs in the larger firms are no longer secure. This shrinking of internal labor markets is one of the sources of growing wage polarization.

The corporate search for flexibility and cost savings is driving firms to externalize much of the skills training that was performed in the internal labor market. Recent research has shown that there has been a great deal of job growth in the best jobs and the worst jobs, but that middle-level jobs have been on the sharp decline. At the same time, the quality of jobs also declined. These jobs are characterized as low wage, low benefit, low union covered, involuntary, part-time positions. Much of this latter work is "contingent" labor, including part-time, temporary, and contract work.

By 1988 contingent labor is estimated to have employed roughly a quarter to a third of the civilian labor force. Contingent work grew three times as fast as employment as a whole between 1982 and 1988, reaching somewhere between 30 and 37 million by the latter year. This has had a big effect on personal well-being. Between 1979 and 1989 the share of the private sector work force covered by pension plans fell 7 percent, and the share of workers with health insurance fell 8 percent. Are managers consciously creating this dual labor market? In the United States the answer is yes. In a survey of representatives of 521 of the country's largest manufacturing, financial, and nonfinancial services corporations, a significant portion said they used labor as a deliberate "contingent staffing alternative."

Dualism in the Nike Production System: A Case Study

Nike provides an example of how this new dualism can exist even within the boundaries of a single firm. While Nike is a U.S. corporation, not one of the 40 million pairs of running shoes that are annually produced by the company are manufactured in the United States: everything is subcontracted overseas.

Nike operates in a context of concentration without centralization: Production is dispersed but under the control of managers in a relatively small area. Nike connects very low-paying unskilled production jobs with high-skilled research and development jobs, mass production with flexible automated technology, and First World with Third World. The first tier of the Nike system, the design and raw material operations of Nike, consists of "developed partners," "volume producers," and "developing sources." The developed partners are in Taiwan and South Korea and work with R&D personnel in Oregon to design the high-end footwear. The Asian partners then farm out the manufacturing to low-wage subcontractors. The volume producers are large vertical companies with leather tanneries and other facilities that sell to Nike and other producers on more of a spot basis. Developing sources are producers in Thailand, Indonesia, Malaysia, and China. These are the lowest-wage operations in the Nike system.

The second tier of the Nike production network are the material, component, and subassembly sources. The more skills that are required in these operations, the closer they are to Oregon. However, as the human capital and sophistication of those subcontractors in the first tier is developed, Nike sees these operations shifting to the outside as well.

Nike managers tout this form of organization. Their combination of high-tech R&D in Oregon and semi- and unskilled labor overseas allows them to bring products quickly to market and make huge profits. Nike's success derives from its managers ability to set up and manage a dualistic system—a dark side of flexible production. While Nike's low-wage workers are overseas, similar patterns of dualism exist within the U.S. labor force. The division between insiders and outsiders reinforces the long-term trend toward wage polarization.

The High Road or the Low Road to Long-Run Economic Growth?

Managers governing networks like Nike have the power to play one group in a network against another. This can weaken the bargaining power of labor unions, making it more difficult to organize workers and pressure companies for higher wages, benefits, and security. Firms that build their foundation on cheap labor can be seen as the low road to company profitability and growth.

If firms continue along this road, both macro- and microeconomic problems of serious consequence could arise. On the macro level, very low wages at the bottom end of the distribution could begin to be problems with aggregate demand if the workforce is not able to consume from its current income and the demand is not offset by government deficits or household saving. Aggregate demand was sustained despite growing inequality in the United States during the 1980s, but partly because of the accumulation of $2 trillion in added government debt and $500 billion in additional consumer credit. On the micro level, firms that rely on undervalued labor will get the wrong signals about the future. Relying on cheap labor can keep inefficient producers and obsolete technologies competitive. If such firms are competing with more sophisticated firms, their only option will be to further reduce wages to stay alive.

Low-road firms scrimp on training, move operations to low-wage havens in the Third World, outsource work, rely on older capital equipment, and pit suppliers against each other. Part of the reason firms are taking the low road is the weakness of the American labor movement. The fraction of private sector workers in unions is at a pre-1935 low of 12 percent, and no alternatives for worker protection are practically in sight. Another reason is the sheer suddenness with which the U.S. economy opened its international trading system, leaving oligopolistic firms to shed weight quickly. In addition, continually volatile exchange rates caused many firms to abandon revenue enhancing strategies to boost profits and turn to cost reduction instead. Finally, interest rates have also been a factor.

It is time to hit the high road, where reinvigorated labor unions could demand higher wages and working conditions and could demand that companies invest in skills training and new technologies. A combination of technology, training, and technical assistance can increase the productivity of the national economy, and with it the standard of living of the mass of the population.

Summary of

Power, Accumulation, and Crisis: The Rise and Demise of the Postwar Social Structure of Accumulation

by David M. Gordon, Thomas E. Weisskopf, and Samuel Bowles

[Published in *Radical Political Economy: Explorations in Alternate Economic Analysis,* ed. Victor D. Lippit (Armonk, N.Y.: M.E. Sharpe, 1996), Ch. 9, 226–244.]

In the United States, the period immediately after World War II was one of prosperity, rising expectations, and falling inequality. By the end of the 1970s, however, the trends in economic growth, earnings, and productivity that marked this "Golden Age" had faltered. High inflation and sluggish growth in the late 1970s (stagflation) were followed by steep recession in the early 1980s and the resurgence of inequality. The authors of the chapter summarized here trace the reversal of the Golden Age to the mid-1960s, when profitability began to decline. Their analysis, based in a Marxian framework, proposes that the economic regime that gave rise to postwar prosperity was inherently contradictory and ultimately unsustainable.

The Postwar Social Structure of Accumulation

Karl Marx described two sources of crisis in capitalist economies. One results from a shortfall in demand for goods and services. Such a crisis occurs when the capitalist class is too strong and workers, farmers, and other noncapitalists command too little income to absorb the goods and services produced by the economy. The capitalist class is therefore unable to realize gains from its investments. This type of crisis is also well-established in Keynesian macroeconomic theory and represented by the 1930s Depression.

The second type of Marxian crisis arises from the supply, or production, side of the economy and is characteristic of weakness in the capitalist class. When workers, political entities, or foreign trade partners are relatively strong, profitability falls, inducing capitalists to cut back on new investment. In either type of crisis a declining rate of profit leads to lower investment and slower growth. "The pace of the economy is driven by the rate of capital accumulation while capital accumulation is fundamentally conditioned by the level and stability of capitalist profitability. As profits go, in short, so goes the economy." [227]

A typical Keynesian crisis can be resolved through policies that strengthen the position of noncapitalist classes, redistributing income to them and increasing their demand for goods and services. However, the crisis of late twentieth-century capitalism arose from the relative weakness of U.S. capitalists and the strong position of interests antagonistic to them. The profit rate reached a peak in the mid-1960s, then fell sharply. Within a couple of years the rate of accumulation, defined as the rate of change in the net capital stock, also fell.

Power and Profit

"Profits are made possible by the power of the capitalist class over other economic actors which it confronts." [228]

The employment relationship is based in the power of the employer to induce workers to sell their labor power for less than the full value of what they produce. Employers extract the surplus as profits. International terms of trade depend on the exercise of political and military power as well as market forces. The relationship between the capitalist class and the state influences the profit rate through taxation and state policies concerning labor supply, research and development, and other economic issues. The intensity of intercapitalist competition affects the cohesiveness with which the capitalist class fights this three-front war against workers, foreign buyers and sellers, and the state.

The Postwar Social Structure of Accumulation

Capitalists need an expectation of making a profit before they will invest in production. At any given time a particular set of institutions comprises a socioeconomic regime, or social structure of accumulation (SSA), which influences expectations and investment decisions. If the SSA is stable and supportive of their aims, capitalists will be enthusiastic about investing and will expand productive capacity. If the SSA is shaky or its institutions pushed to their limit, "capitalists will be more disposed to put their money to other uses—consumption, financial investments, or assets abroad." [231]

It is not sufficient for the SSA to encourage the expectations of investors; it must also enable adequate demand. This is a daunting task: Capitalists must be in a strong position to be confident of investment, but other classes must command enough income to consume production. Historically the United States has gone through several periods of expansion and contraction, each several decades long and each characterized by a different SSA.

The postwar SSA contained four institutional elements that produced the economic expansion, but then generated contradictory or oppositional forces that eventually led to decline. The *capital-labor accord* governed employment relations. Through explicit and implicit agreements, management held control of business decision making. In return, compensation for workers would rise with productivity. Better working conditions and job security also contributed to labor's sharing in capitalist prosperity. However, corporate control declined after the mid-1960s. Many workers became restive under bureaucratic restrictions and were less vulnerable to corporate discipline as tight labor markets lowered the cost of losing a job.

The *Pax Americana* "was the postwar structure of international economic institutions and political relations that assured the United States a dominant role in the world capitalist economy." [233] The United States enjoyed favorable terms of trade in its dealings with foreign suppliers of goods, materials, and components. Capital mobility enabled U.S. firms to threaten domestic workers with moving plants offshore, therefore strengthening the bargaining position of U.S. employers. By the mid-1960s the United States faced challenges to its hegemony, most notably from Third World resistance to domination. The revolutionary movement in Vietnam and the OPEC oil cartel were two of the most visible examples.

The *capital-citizen accord* established a role for the state in the economic security of its citizens and regulation of business, however profitability was the overriding goal. By the mid-1960s trust in the social accountability of business eroded and movements arose to constrain corporate greed. "With striking speed, these movements led to new government regulations in traffic safety, occupational health and safety, environmental protection, consumer product safety, and nuclear power generation." [234]

The *moderation of intercapitalist rivalry* for U.S. firms occurred because European and Japanese firms were devastated by World War II. The rapidly expanding U.S. economy was able to accommodate many large firms, giving them ample room to grow. After the mid-1960s, both foreign and domestic competition intensified. Japanese and European firms cut into U.S. export markets and supplied more and more imports to the U.S. domestic market. As economic pressure on U.S. capitalists increased on many fronts, internecine competition also increased. Mergers, hostile takeovers, and junk bond buyouts became common events in the corporate scramble to stay on top.

The conservative administrations of the 1980s responded with "a consistent effort to restore corporate profitability by rolling back effective challenges to United States capitalist power: by raising the cost of job loss, improving the terms of trade, more vigorously flexing United States military power, reducing the intensity of government regulation, and dramatically reducing capital's share of the total government tax burden." [237] The strict monetarist policies undertaken as one element of this campaign led to a severe recession in the early 1980s and increased the value of the dollar, making U.S. exports unattractive. Capacity utilization fell to extremely low rates. U.S. capitalists won the battle for control over labor and the state, but still failed to restore profitability, at least by the mid-1980s.

Critique of Alternative Explanations

Mainstream economists attribute the stagnation of the U.S. economy after the Golden Age to exogenous shocks like the rise of oil prices in the 1970s or to macroeconomic mismanagement. However, the relevant indicators began to change in the mid-1960s, well before the oil price shock of 1973. Mainstream accounts ignore the challenges to capitalist control that arose in the 1960s and fail to see that dynamics internal to the prevailing socioeconomic regime led to its decay.

Some Marxists also present alternative views. One stresses a tendency for capital to overinvest; however, factoring in trends in capital intensity does not increase the explanatory power of the statistical model. Others view the late twentieth-century crisis as a typical Keynesian underconsumption crisis; however, profitability fell well before investment, output, or demand. If this were a Keynesian crisis, measures to support demand would also serve to redistribute resources to noncapitalist classes.

The most obvious resolution to the stagnation of this crisis is the one proposed by the right wing: strengthen the capitalist class, restore its profits, and set off a new cycle of accumulation. For other classes, this path leads to economic insecurity and inequality. Progressive solutions may need to be more radical than the New Deal solutions to the 1930s Depression, when both capitalists and noncapitalists could benefit from restorative economic measures. At present, it is not clear that simply beating back the challenges to capitalist control will be enough to build a new social structure of accumulation. Furthermore, it is shortsighted to assume that there is no alternative to capitalism. Democratic socialism provides another model. The focus on political power in the analysis presented above leads to the conclusion that greater power in the hands of the people can lead to social transformation.

Summary of

The Mobilization of Corporate Conservatism

by Jerome L. Himmelstein

[Published in *To the Right: The Transformation of American Conservatism* (Berkeley: University of California Press, 1990), Ch. 5, 129–164.]

The rise of corporate conservatism has played a crucial role in reshaping American politics. "Big business indeed worked successfully from the mid-1970s on to support policies it deemed in its interests: cutting tax rates on profits and investment income, defeating labor law reform, preventing the creation of a consumer protection agency, limiting the growth of government domestic spending, and promoting deregulation of specific industries." [130] This chapter examines the causes of the corporate mobilization, the mechanisms through which it has influenced politics and policy, and the implications of these developments for existing theories of the state.

Why Big Business Mobilized

In the simplest terms, big business mobilized politically in response to a severe and long-lasting slowdown in economic growth. By some measures, the rate of growth in the late 1970s was less than one-third of the average rate from 1948 to 1966. As other countries recovered from World War II and grew at a rapid pace, the United States lost its former position of dominance in world trade and investment.

Domestically, the arrangements that had once led to social peace and economic prosperity were becoming increasingly difficult to maintain. Those arrangements had included a limited "capital-labor accord" that reduced conflict over labor relations in the biggest companies, and included government activism both in managing the business cycle and in providing a set of social welfare programs. From a business perspective, these policies were creating a dangerous sense of popular entitlement that led to a growing demand for wage increases, government benefits, and regulation, while the ability to finance such demands was stagnating in the 1970s. In short, a whole set of social arrangements had ceased to work, both economically and politically.

Interviews with top corporate executives in the 1970s revealed a sense of political impotence and a belief that the American political system was out of their control. The new style of regulation on issues such as environmental protection, health and safety, product liability, and affirmative action, felt more intrusive and threatening to the businessmen than earlier regulatory measures. High taxes and expanding income maintenance programs led them to fear that a rising tide of entitlements was engulfing the nation. Some darkly wondered whether we could still "afford" democracy. In more practical terms, many realized that they had failed to communicate a pro-business point of view to the media, universities, and many politicians. As one executive said, "We have been successful in selling products, but not ourselves." The corporate political mobilization was a response to these problems.

What Big Business Did

The business mobilization included lobbying, electoral activism, and extensive support for conservative advocacy efforts. In contrast to fragmented earlier efforts that had defended the particular interests of individual businesses or industries, the new mobilization was a unified, hegemonic effort that successfully asserted the interests and perspectives of business as a whole.

The new hegemonic style was visible in lobbying with the rise of the Business Roundtable. Founded in 1972/73, it was originally a merger of three smaller business groups concerned with combating unions and maintaining international competitiveness. Membership in the Business Roundtable was restricted to CEOs of major corporations, 160 of whom had joined by 1975. Using CEOs rather than paid lobbyists to lobby members of Congress, the Roundtable played a major role on many issues of broad interest to business. It successfully opposed a consumer protection agency, labor law reform, and new antitrust legislation, while supporting corporate tax cuts and energy deregulation.

In the electoral arena, the campaign finance reform laws of the early 1970s limited individual contributions to candidates, which had the perverse effect of encouraging the growth of political action committees (PACs) to coordinate smaller donations. In the early 1970s there were twice as many labor PACs as corporate and trade association PACs, and their total contributions were roughly equal. By the early 1980s business PACs outnumbered labor PACs by more than four to one, and outspent them by more than two to one.

Business changed not only the amount it spent on elections, but also the way it spent its money. Until the mid-1970s business campaign contributions had been pragmatic, typically directed to entrenched incumbents of either party who held positions that affected the interests of individual companies. By the end of the 1970s business leaders, including the head of the Business Roundtable, were urging a redirection of contributions to pro-business candidates. In House races, incumbent Republicans were heavily favored by business throughout this period, receiving 20 times as much as their opponents in 1976 and 1980. Incumbent Democrats, on the other hand, received four times as much as their challengers in 1972, twice as much in 1976, and actually less than their opponents in 1980.

Businesses of course differed in their contribution strategies. In 1980 Coors Industries gave only 4 percent of its campaign contributions to incumbents, largely following the lead of conservative ideological PACs; McDonnell Douglas gave 93 percent of its money to incumbents, largely to those who were not supported by conservative PACs. Attempts to explain variation in business support for conservatism in terms of size, export orientation, geographical location, or other factors have been unsuccessful: Location in the Sun Belt makes a company only slightly more likely to back conservative candidates, while most other proposed explanatory variables have no relationship to corporate conservatism. Despite variation in corporate philosophies, however, in any particular race it is usually clear who is the pro-business candidate. One candidate received more than two-thirds of all business donations in more than 90 percent of all contested congressional races in 1980; in most of those races, one candidate received more than 90 percent of the corporate money.

Business also stepped up advocacy advertising, ranging from support for Milton Friedman's public television series to Mobil Oil's regular advertising of its corporate opinions in major newspapers. Hundreds of millions of dollars were being spent annually on advocacy advertising by the late 1970s; one estimate suggested that advocacy accounted for one-third of the ad budgets of major corporate advertisers at the time. Union Carbide commissioned a public opinion poll and stretched its results somewhat in a series of ads claiming that the American people endorsed the company's strategy of pursuing economic growth by cutting government spending, regulation, and business taxation.

Perhaps most important was business funding of new or vastly expanded conservative think tanks and research organizations. The American Enterprise Institute, the Hoover Institution at Stanford University, the Heritage Foundation, and other institutions provided well-funded opportunities for conservative intellectuals to write and publicize their views. These initiatives were launched by the most actively conservative corporations and foundations, such as Coors Industries and the Mellon-Scaife, Olin, and Smith Richardson foundations. They soon gained access to broader corporate support; Chase Manhattan Bank, Dow Chemical, Mobil Corporation, and others were major backers of the Heritage Foundation in the 1980s. Through this new institutional network, formerly obscure conservative writers became able to influence public opinion and, in many cases, gained influential positions in government under the Reagan administration.

Implications for Theories of the State

The political mobilization of big business challenges most of the leading theories of the state. Pluralist theories argue that capitalists are not a ruling class and that business has limited political power for several reasons: A diversity of autonomous potential bases for power exists in American society; the source of power is said to be shifting from money and property to technology and communications; and business has such heterogeneous interests that it has very low potential for political unity. This theory might have seemed appropriate in the 1970s to businessmen who then felt powerless, or to others observing them. Yet it remains only partly convincing because it cannot explain where business suddenly found the capacity to mobilize in such an effective and hegemonic manner. Nor can it explain earlier episodes in American history when business also played a powerful political role.

Marxist and other radical theories portray capitalists as a ruling class. There are two different images of how this class rules: structuralist theories, in which capitalist authority is passive because the institutional structures of society embody basic class interests; and instrumentalist theories, in which capitalists are an active ruling class that can and does exercise its authority. Structuralist theories fail to explain why the corporate political mobilization was either necessary or possible. In this respect, instrumentalist theories have advantages over either pluralism or structuralism; instrumentalists at least believe that capitalists have the political power to do what they obviously did. Yet instrumentalists cannot easily explain why big business felt so powerless in the 1970s. Neither instrumentalism nor structuralism can explain why business chose a conservative, antistatist political strategy as opposed to advocating an activist, corporate-dominated state.

In pursuit of a better theory, two assumptions are fundamental. "First, different government policies are best for capitalist interests at different historical moments. Second, capitalists have demonstrated a substantial capacity for hegemonic action, but the degree to which that capacity has been realized has depended on the nature of those policies." [161] Passive support for a Keynesian welfare state may have been appropriate for business interests in the 1950s and 1960s; when conditions changed in the 1970s, corporate support for liberalism fell away quickly.

Liberalism in general involves compromises and trade-offs for business and is never likely to be embraced as wholeheartedly as conservatism. It is thus to be expected that there is less corporate political mobilization in liberal eras and more mobilization of other groups that benefit from liberalism. In contrast, when conditions call for conservative policies, broad-based capitalist mobilization is both required and encouraged. The capacity of business to organize itself and to influence American politics is much greater than implied by pluralism, but more variable and subject to historical contingency than implied by the notion of a ruling class.

Summary of

Markets and Politics

by Robert Kuttner

[Published in *Everything for Sale: the Virtues and Limits of Markets* (New York: Alfred A. Knopf, 1997), Ch. 9, 328–362.]

The 1980s and 1990s have been marked by a crusade to expand market-based activity and reduce the public sector. These efforts reflect a belief that competition and the profit motive generate efficiencies in the allocation of resources and the production of goods and services, resulting in the optimal economic system. The benefits of this system are widely distributed. Any attempt by government to regulate or otherwise intervene in the free workings of the market will only reduce the general welfare.

Challenging this agenda, the chapter summarized here argues that, not only does the unfettered market produce negative externalities and failures of the sort described in many economics texts, it also curtails democracy. As the role of government is attenuated, citizens have less ability to affect economic affairs. This chapter sums up the book's defense of the public sector and critiques Public Choice Theory, which, during the last quarter of the twentieth century, has been an influential intellectual underpinning of the "everything for sale" economy.

Democracy and the Political Arena

> Even a fervently capitalist society . . . requires prior rules. Rules govern everything from basic property rights to the fair terms of engagement in complex mixed markets such as health care and telecommunications." [328]

The regime of rules must evolve to address new dilemmas arising from new products and practices. There must, therefore, be rule makers and rule-making procedures, which can be either democratic or nondemocratic. Allowing the market free rein or displacing decisions from public processes to elites like the Federal Reserve Bank is itself a political decision, one among a range of choices.

No matter what the form of government, there is a need to govern markets. Consumers are not always able to protect their interests effectively. Without regulation, socially undesirable outcomes can be expected in many sectors—for example, health care or pollution control. Law and government protect liberty and property rights and result from a long history of social evolution. "A vacuum of legitimate state authority does not yield efficient laissez-faire; it yields mafias and militias, with whose arbitrary power would-be entrepreneurs must reckon."[330] Nations with competent public administrations have a competitive advantage in the global economy. In addition to formal regulations, norms that encourage trust, civility, and reciprocity can make both markets and society healthier.

The Asian model of government combines a strong state with a weak democracy. European nations, especially in Northern Europe, link strong states with strong democracies and high levels of civic participation. The United States has historically been ambivalent about the role of the state. During the early years of the Republic, the Federalist/anti-Federalist debates posed a dichotomy between a strong democracy and a strong state. At the end of the nineteenth century Woodrow Wilson (while a university professor) drew on the European parliamentary experience to articulate a model of government that combined

democracy with effective public administration. Although the U.S. Constitution presents structural obstacles to strong government, in some periods, such
as the New Deal, "partisan majorities in Congress [were] large enough to constitute *de facto* parliamentary majorities and to bridge over the structural weakness of the American state." [332]

Public Choice

Public Choice is a cynical theory about democracy that applies the self-interest-
based behavioral model of neoclassical economics to political life. Public Choice
idealizes the market and demonizes the state, recognizing only the self-correct-
ing mechanisms in the former and only the self-destructive ones in the latter.

The theory claims that politics aggregates the selfish aims of individuals into
interest groups that vie for power, angling for unearned windfalls at the expense
of the common good. Public Choice is wary of free-riding, the idea that most
people will not engage in political or civic activity because the cost outweighs
the individual gain. Politics, therefore, becomes the domain of a few highly focused groups who trade political favors to gain support for their own narrow
goals, a practice known as logrolling. The theory denies that people can get
what they want through political means because, with multiple preferences,
multiple coalitions are possible and no outcome is predictable or inherently superior. Thus, "the celebration of the market has become an insidious form of
contempt for political democracy. Excluded by definition are the possibility of
deliberation leading to social learning, institutional refinement, and an evolving
conception of the common good."

The predictions and the relevance of this school of thought have suffered
from its emphasis on pure theory with insufficient attention to empirical findings. In reality, history presents a mix of outcomes. Sometimes people get what
they want, sometimes they are frustrated. People do, in fact, vote—in some
countries suffering hardship and risk to do so—even though the costs exceed
the benefits. Throughout the industrial world, national budgets have stopped
growing, even though logrolling should result in unchecked public spending as
interest groups buy support for their projects by supporting the pet projects of
others. Contrary to Public Choice premises, politicians often seek office out of
conviction or a desire to advance a political ideology, rather than pure self-interest.

Despite these empirical failures, Public Choice remains influential among intellectuals because it extends the current infatuation with the economic model
into the political arena; it resonates with a long-standing American strain of
skepticism about politics; and its reliance on laissez-faire preserves the privileged status of powerful elites. When voters without wealth or property mobilize politically, they are likely to choose leaders and policies that reduce their

vulnerability to market forces and alter society's distribution of power and wealth. If political organization among the powerless can be discredited as either economically perverse or politically futile, the position of the elite becomes more secure.

When Public Choice theorists emphasize the selfish behavior of political interest groups, they focus on the "rent-seeking" behavior of such groups as welfare mothers or unemployed workers, while ignoring the disproportionate purchase of influence by moneyed interests. When large contributors gain privileged access while ordinary voters are left out of any real and effective role in the political process, the latter become cynical and apathetic. Grassroots mobilization around legitimate popular interests is driven out by "Astroturf lobbying," which simulates the real thing by underwriting front groups for well-heeled special interests.

Reviving the Polity

Contrary to the propositions of Public Choice theory, markets need to be constrained with effective government. Given the American resistance to authority, this requires democracy. Democracy protects against tyranny, enables citizens to influence the collective experience, keeps markets in their place, and ensures a resilient society.

We need to reclaim a space for politics and public activity, and to revive avenues for public administration and civic engagement. Cynicism and the decay of political institutions discourage voting, particularly among the poor and working classes. Making registration and voting more convenient would be a step in the right direction. Adjustments in work hours to accommodate civic involvement, as well as family leave and child care, would relieve the time pressure that hinders greater participation. Public service corps can expand the sphere of citizenship and civic institutions. "Policy juries" can bring citizens together to learn about and debate difficult policy issues.

In rebuilding vehicles for participation in civil society, we need to strike a balance between public and voluntary endeavors. Social Security and Medicare provide more dignified and comprehensive alternatives to poverty for the elderly than soup kitchens. In turn, financially secure senior citizens can be more involved in community life. Voluntary organizations like the PTA support public schools. Many community-based organizations like economic development corporations and tenant councils began with government assistance.

While Public Choice theorists and other conservative analysts blame the government, others point to the ascendance of television as a corrosive influence on civic involvement. TV steals time from other activities, assembles audiences in order to sell products, encourages passivity, and delivers a sterile version of politics. More broadly, television is the emblem of a marketized society. "Since the early 1970s, widening inequality has been associated with greater commodification . . . many things that were once basic social amenities now depend on private purchasing power, which is increasingly unequal." [356] Increases in working time mean that people have less time for their own families, let alone for community activity and life-affirming sociability.

Recent efforts to "reinvent government" by introducing competition between public and private service providers and by incorporating entrepreneurial practices into government agencies can be beneficial if the goal is greater efficiency, but not if the purpose is to strip government of needed resources. The private sector is sometimes ill-equipped to fulfill public-policy purposes. For example the U.S. Postal Service, which has been partially privatized, competes with delivery companies, but these private corporations do have a public mandate to deliver mail to every address in the country. This responsibility requires cross-subsidy, a practice that violates market pricing principles. Prisons, schools, and social and sanitation services are other areas where the trend toward privatization must be carefully weighed against public purposes. "The grail of a perfect market, purged of illegitimate and inefficient distortions, is a fantasy—and a dangerous one." [329]

Summary of

The Solution: A Better Scorecard *and* What the Scorecard Should Contain

by Ralph Estes

[Published in *Tyranny of the Bottom Line: Why Corporations Make Good People Do Bad Things* (San Francisco: Barret-Koehler Publishers, Inc., 1996), Chs. 9 and 10, 201–231.]

. . . corporate managers make their decisions against the yardstick of the present narrow and deficient definition of profit. Although other standards may from time to time be announced, the bottom line is the only continuous and consistent performance standard to which managers are held accountable. . . . Change the performance evaluation system and you change behavior. [203]

Corporate abuses produce pressure for government regulation, but this alone cannot be the solution. Comprehensive regulation would cost too much, inordinately expand the federal bureaucracy, and restrict corporate flexibility and responsiveness. "In contrast, the approach proposed here would be simple, nonintrusive, and in comparison to the benefits to be gained, inexpensive indeed. It is directly modeled after the prescriptions adopted in the United States in the 1930s to curb abuses in the securities markets." [204–205]

The Prescription

Financial fraud and abuse during the 1920s led Congress to create the SEC (Securities and Exchange Commission) to require firms to disclose the information needed by potential and actual investors. The need today is to go beyond disclosure to stockholders, giving all stakeholders the information they require in order to make informed choices about their relationships with individual businesses.

The most effective response to this need would be for Congress to enact a "Corporate Accountability Act" [a draft version is provided in Appendix 1 of Estes' book], which would redesignate the SEC as the Corporate Accountability Commission, charged with requiring each corporation to provide an annual, comprehensive corporate report.

The new commission could simplify reporting requirements at the same time as it expands their impact. This would be achieved through a comprehensive review of the tangle of federal reporting requirements now in place, to improve their coherence and clarity and reduce redundancy. If most federal reporting requirements were consolidated into a single Corporate Report, filed with a single agency, this would actually reduce the reporting burden for corporations and the administration and oversight functions of government.

Compliance could be reasonably assured through the mechanisms now used to obtain fair financial reporting—independent audits by certified public accountants. . . . New laws would not be required to deal with every new corporate abuse; when full and relevant information is available, then customers, workers, and communities . . . will regulate the corporation by their choices. [211–212]

The government's role in ensuring that corporations produce the required information on their own activities would be assisted by actors in the aftermarket for corporate information. These are the independent enterprises that would arise to assemble, transmit, summarize, and criticize information on pollution, workplace safety, and other indicators of social responsibility—entities like Dow Jones, Moody's, Standard & Poor's, and Value Line, which already digest SED filings for public use.

The suggestions that follow build on a variety of earlier proposals, including several that have been taken seriously in the U.S. Congress but have, so far, been defeated by corporate influence.

What the Scorecard Should Contain

The proposed Corporate Report should help customers decide what to purchase and from what company; it should help workers decide where to work and, once there, what rights to demand or what abuses to protest; it should help communities to balance the costs and benefits associated with attracting a given company, so that they will be better able to judge what concessions, if any, are worth making; and it should give society at large the information necessary to make ongoing decisions about which corporations deserve to keep the corporate charter that permits them to exist, as contributors to (at the very least, as neutral toward) the public weal.

The reporting system now required of corporations is designed, first and foremost, for the needs of owners; that is, stockholders. However they would benefit greatly from a Corporate Report that would not only address the moral concerns expressed by an increasing number of investors, but would also indicate which companies are more, and less, likely to thrive in an environment that holds firms accountable for their social and environmental impacts.

The next group whose information requirements have received some government attention is customers. A number of acts of federal government have required labeling and other means of informing consumers about foods, toxic substances, and a variety of other products and services. These data and more could be built into a Corporate Report that would not replace labeling requirements but that (especially with increasing use of World Wide Web) would enable consumers to make safe and informed market choices. The additional information needs of customers include companies' past record of legal and regulatory actions; claims brought against them; and enhanced product information, including information on environmental impact.

Employees need better information on which to make career and work choices, including data on a company's past history of layoffs, plant closings, employee grievances, and employment stability; its health and safety record; its record in equal employment; the opportunities it offers for training and promotion; its pension program; how technology is affecting workers; and what plans it has for the future. Neither the Equal Employment Opportunity Commission nor OSHA requires adequate transparency in these critical areas, and existing laws, such as that requiring 60 days notice for plant closings, are not being enforced. "The history of the plant-closing law shows how a weak, piecemeal approach to disclosure, with administration by agencies that lack the experience and the enforcement and audit capabilities of the SEC, holds only false promise." [224]

Disclosure of relevant information to communities could have a large and immediate impact. "Corporations routinely seek special tax breaks, zoning exemptions, free utility line extensions, industrial development bonds, and anything else the community may be able to provide." [226] Even without intending to provide special incentives, communities find themselves footing the bill for training the employees of large businesses imposed by the corporation on its neighbors, and often including pollution and wastes that must be disposed of. Yet communities are rarely equipped with enough information to know what risks they take, and what costs they will incur, to balance out the jobs and taxes they believe will come with a company. Elected officials generally lack the business, finance, or accounting backgrounds that would enable them to ask the right questions, or to assess the information that is available. Research indicates, however, that officials and staff will pay attention to relevant information when it is available.

PART V

Poverty, Inequality, and Power

Overview Essay

by Frank Ackerman

What accounts for the persistence of poverty amidst the affluence of the developed countries, particularly the United States, at the end of the twentieth century? The vast and unequal accumulation of wealth, chronicled in the preceding parts of this book, might seem less problematical if everyone had enough to live in comfort. But that is not the case. Great wealth and great poverty have been created at the same time, in a society that has ample resources to provide a much higher minimum standard of living for all.

Most of this essay focuses on poverty in America and other developed countries, but this is not meant to suggest that the problem is less severe elsewhere. (For a useful international review of poverty research, see Øyen, Miller, and Samad 1996.) Material deprivation has long been the plight of most people in most societies. Yet the causes are to some extent different, and more understandable, in circumstances where the average person is not affluent. In the past, and in developing countries today, the absolute scarcity of resources may be a large part of the explanation of widespread poverty (though this is not the only explanation; unequal distribution of income is common in poor nations as well as rich, as discussed in Part IX). When average incomes are low, the simple prescription of conventional economic theory is at least superficially plausible: Economic growth would increase total resources; if the distribution of income becomes no more unequal, then the much-discussed rising tide might indeed lift all boats.

In America today, the rising tide has lifted the average income to a level that is surely sufficient to guarantee material comfort, though not enough to satisfy every new desire emerging from advertising and fashion. Those at upper incomes have done far better, floating away on a sea of ever-greater consumption. It is no longer plausible that further economic growth alone will solve the problems of those who remain anchored at the bottom. Late twentieth-century growth was accompanied by worsening inequality, providing an empirical rebuttal to the rising-tide theory of poverty alleviation. This experience should be an ominous sign for those in Europe and elsewhere contemplating adoption of the U.S. economic model.

Much of the recent United States discussion of poverty centers on categories of race, gender, and family structure, which are the subjects of Parts VII and VIII. This essay and the following summaries focus on more general economic theories and analyses of poverty, topics that received little attention from economists in the 1990s. It is far beyond the scope of this essay to provide a complete review of the extensive literature on poverty, much of it found in fields such as sociology and political science. Instead, the goal here is to identify selected topics that are relevant to an understanding of the economics of inequality. We will begin with questions of the definition and significance of poverty and the related concept of social exclusion, then document the extent and effects of poverty, review the changing political economy of poverty, and conclude with comments on the possibilities for effective antipoverty initiatives (a subject that is examined further in Part X).

What's the Problem?

What exactly is poverty, and why is it a problem? The basic question of the definition of poverty turns out to be surprisingly complex. Poverty in developed countries is not usually a matter of absolute inability to obtain the physiological requirements for survival. As Amartya Sen has pointed out, an income that qualifies as desperate poverty in America can support a princely existence in India. (Conversely, a respected senior professor from a major African university, visiting Boston a few years ago, found in an emergency that he easily qualified for free medical care for the indigent, because his salary—high for his country— was so low in U.S. dollars.)

Therefore, poverty, in any but the poorest countries, must be understood in relative terms. One reason it costs more to live in a richer country is that daily life is structured so that basic services become more expensive. When most people have cars, then the housing stock, food distribution system, and other aspects of life can be reorganized in ways that require ownership of a car. The private automobile has become a necessity for obtaining food and other basic needs in most of the United States, unlike India.

Differences in the cost of obtaining the same basic needs, however, account for only a small part of the income gap between America's poor and India's poor. Our needs themselves are defined in relation to our society and our peers. That is, it takes more goods and services—a higher level of consumption—to escape from poverty when everyone around you is also consuming more. One common approach in international comparisons is to define the poverty line as a fixed percentage, usually 50 percent, of the per capita median income (adjusted for household size). This acknowledges the relativity of poverty, but in an arbitrary manner: Why should 50 percent of the current median income have the same meaning, in terms of the perceived harm of poverty, in all times and places?

A well-known theoretical treatment of these issues is Sen's analysis of functionings and capabilities (discussed in detail in *Human Well-Being and Economic Goals*, the third volume in this series). Individual well-being, according to Sen, cannot be measured in terms of material consumption. Rather, what makes a person well-off is the capability to achieve desirable human functionings. Those functionings include, but are not limited to, physical survival, good health and longevity, and material comfort. Material resources are often required, but may have a variable impact on well-being. For example, different quantities of food are required to achieve the same levels of health and nutrition in different people.

In the first article summarized here, **Brian Nolan and Christopher Whelan** comment that Sen's work has been influential among theorists, but has had relatively little effect on empirical research. One reason, they suggest, is that desirable functionings and capabilities are often defined in very abstract terms. A widely cited example, originally due to Adam Smith, is "the ability to appear in public without shame." It is more expensive to avoid falling shamefully below prevailing standards of appearance in a rich country than in a poor one. Yet shame-free public appearance is an important but vague objective; standard economic data do not make it easy to place a dollar cost on this functioning.

This example comes close to a common definition of poverty, which is used by Nolan and Whelan: Poverty is the exclusion from the normal life of society enforced by the lack of material resources. Poverty researchers employing that definition have attempted to measure material deprivation, though they have often been constrained by data limitations. Nolan and Whelan analyze a very detailed survey of Irish households to identify consumption goods that are considered essential by a majority of respondents. They then contrast two alternate definitions of poverty: one based on income alone, and the other including information on deprivation of basic goods. Those experiencing "deprivation poverty" seem poorer and are more likely to suffer from lack of long-term resources, while many of those experiencing "income poverty" have somewhat greater long-term resources but are suffering current labor market setbacks.

In contrast to such careful research methods, official poverty statistics are often defined in an ad hoc manner. U.S. poverty statistics, first calculated in the 1960s, are based on the cost of a low-priced but nutritionally balanced food "basket"; that cost is then multiplied by three since low-income households often spend one-third of their incomes on food. The poverty line is adjusted each year based on changes in the price of the basket of food. Research into alternative poverty measures, conducted by a panel of the National Academy of Sciences, has suggested use of a broader basket of necessities (and a correspondingly lower multiplier), with annual adjustments in proportion to median household spending on necessities, rather than to inflation (Garner et al. 1998).

The element of social judgment about the definition of poverty, explicit in Nolan and Whelan's research, is still present but implicit in the official statistics. How does one choose the basket of food or other necessities that forms the basis for the poverty line? Once it is chosen, how does the poverty line change over time? The proposal to link future changes to median household spending would formalize the notion that poverty is a social category involving relative position.

Analyzing poverty therefore requires information about popular attitudes toward acceptable patterns of consumption and standards of living, as well as data on incomes and prices. Along these lines, David Miller (1992) discusses survey results on popular views of inequality, relating the findings to philosophical debates on the subject. Americans are more accepting of inequality based on performance, and have more muted class differences in attitudes toward equality, than Europeans. However, the greatest degree of inequality that most Americans would describe as "fair" is far less than what exists today. Many favor some form of minimum income guarantee.

Understanding Exclusion

American and European discussions of poverty and inequality have diverged in many respects. One major difference is the emergence in Europe of the concept of "exclusion," now widely used to describe the plight of those at the bottom of society. In contemporary European parlance, the problem is not simply that some people are poor; more broadly speaking, those at the bottom are suffering from exclusion from normal membership in society. The term has become so popular that it risks becoming a buzzword devoid of content, prompting several attempts to provide rigorous definitions of exclusion.

Hillary Silver (1995) offers three paradigms of exclusion, each of which is the negation of an ideal of inclusion. The *solidarity* paradigm of republicanism (of the traditional French, not the contemporary American, variety) upholds the ideal of moral and social inclusion through community solidarity; exclusion here means social isolation. The *specialization* paradigm of liberalism and market economics offers the ideal of inclusion through free association and the development of valuable, specialized skills; exclusion in this case usually reflects economic discrimination. The *monopoly* paradigm of bureaucratic society offers status and other rewards to those who are inside powerful institutions, with the ideal of social democratic citizenship and rights extending inclusion to all. Exclusion in these terms reflects the incompleteness of social democracy, or the political failure to extend the rights of citizens to outsiders.

In short, permuting the classic French slogan to match Silver's list, the three ideals of inclusion are roughly fraternity, liberty, and equality. The three corresponding failures are social or moral exclusion, economic exclusion, and political exclusion. (For a related discussion of the varieties of exclusion see Strobel 1996.)

Ajit Bhalla and Frédéric Lapeyre survey the various meanings of exclusion, noting the close relationship of the concept to Sen's theories of poverty and to the definition of poverty used by Nolan and Whelan, among many others. Nolan and Whelan, in fact, suggest that poverty means the same thing as exclusion from society due to lack of economic resources. On this interpretation, poverty is a narrower category because it omits cases in which the grounds for exclusion are noneconomic. Acknowledging the multiple dimensions of the problem, Bhalla and Lapeyre call for separate economic, social, and political indicators of inclusion or exclusion. They also highlight the problem of those who are only temporarily or precariously included in society—for instance, workers who are employed in unstable jobs.

The Extent of Poverty in America

Meanwhile in America, poverty, as traditionally defined, remains a pressing concern. Despite the economic growth of the 1980s and 1990s, the officially reported poverty rate has climbed up from the all-time low of 11 percent, achieved in the 1970s. The poverty line is remarkably low: It is an annual income of only $16,276 (or $313 per week) for a family of four in 1997, and equivalent amounts for other household sizes. As shown in Table V.1, more than 13 percent of Americans fell below that level in 1997, including about one out of every nine whites and more than one out of every four African-Americans and Hispanics. The situation is even worse for children under eighteen, with one-fifth of the total—almost one-sixth of white children and more than one-third of African-American and Hispanic children—living in households below the poverty line.

While it is hard enough to imagine maintaining a family of four on a grand total of $313 per week, the problems of poverty extend far beyond the mere lack of money. The poorest people have the worst health (Krieger and Fee 1994). Environmentally damaging facilities are much more likely to be located in poor neighborhoods (see Been summary in Part VIII). Both poverty and income inequality are strongly, positively correlated with a community's rate of violent crime, with some evidence that the economic variables are more closely linked to homicide than to robbery (Hsieh and Pugh 1993).

As Douglas Massey observes, the poor are increasingly likely to be located in predominantly poor neighborhoods. Residential segregation by class, as well as race, is now on the rise, with more and more people living in economically homogeneous communities. In the past, the long post–World War II economic

Table V.1. The Extent of Poverty in American, 1959–1997

Percent of Population Below the Poverty Line
All ages

	Total	White	Black	Hispanic
1959	22.4%	18.1%	55.1%	NA
1967	14.2	11.0	39.3	NA
1973	11.1	8.4	31.4	21.9%
1979	11.7	9.0	31.0	21.8
1989	12.8	10.0	30.7	26.2
1997	13.3	11.0	26.5	27.1

Children under 18

	Total	White	Black	Hispanic
1979	16.4%	11.8%	41.2%	28.0%
1989	19.6	14.8	43.7	36.2
1997	19.9	16.1	37.2	36.8

Source: Tables 6.2, 6.3, pages 280–281 in Lawrence Mishel, Jared Bernstein, and John Schmitt, *The State of Working America, 1998–1999*. Ithaca, N.Y.: Cornell University Press, 1999.

expansion led to some increase in economic integration of neighborhoods, a trend that reversed itself in the 1970s.

Today, in Massey's global view, there is a rapid trend toward urbanization in developed and developing countries alike, combined with a narrowing of the avenues to upward mobility within the cities. The result is that those who are newly arrived at the bottom of the urban economy will probably stay at the bottom. These new arrivals will often find themselves stuck in the worst of neighborhoods, facing multiple social problems that all too frequently accompany urban poverty. (For related discussion of the sociology of urban poverty, see Part VII.)

Excuses for Poverty: A Retrospective

Public policy toward the poor, and the conventional wisdom about the causes of poverty, have undergone dramatic shifts over time. In a 1993 update to their earlier work, **Frances Fox Piven and Richard Cloward** relate the changing attitudes toward welfare to the threat of civil unrest, on the one hand, and the goal of creating a low-wage labor force on the other hand.[1]

Poverty fell rapidly in the economic expansion of the 1960s and early 1970s, as seen in Table V.1. It was a time when liberal optimism prevailed, and the extension of civil rights to all was high on the national agenda. Michael Harrington's much-discussed book, *The Other America*, drew attention to the persistence of poverty in the early 1960s. The War on Poverty, an ambitious-sounding federal program, appeared to commit the nation to finding a solution to the problem. However, the War on Poverty should not be credited with most of the gains of the era. Far more important factors were operating at the same time: The expansion of Social Security and Medicare payments slashed the rates of poverty among the elderly; and the booming labor market continued to draw impoverished rural Southerners (many of them African-Americans) into better-paying Northern jobs.

Unfortunately it was not obvious at the time, particularly to the poor, that poverty was being reduced at a record-breaking rate. By the end of the 1960s, the movement for civil rights had fragmented into disorganization and impatience, while urban riots underscored the urgency of the problems of poverty. The official response, still relatively generous (particularly by more recent standards), was to expand welfare and other payments to the poor. Then, when the economic crisis and structural changes of the 1970s led to a decline in low-skilled employment, the result was a burgeoning welfare population and rising welfare costs.

The dominant corporate response to the crisis of the 1970s, as discussed in Parts I and IV, relied on cutting labor costs to restore profitability and competitiveness. Lowering labor costs required cutbacks in welfare, unemployment compensation, and other nonwage sources of income that were available to potential low-wage workers. In concert with this strategic shift, there was a change in the public discourse about poverty. Concern about the plight of "the other America" or about racism and poverty as causes of urban violence gave way to critiques of affirmative action, advocacy of "benign neglect," and discovery of the "culture of poverty" and the supposed long-term pathology of the black family. Research on that pathology had seemed less urgent in the years when large numbers of black workers were needed to make automobiles and steel.

(The ever-popular idea that there are multiple generations of welfare-dependent families, who have passed on a culture of dependency from mother to daughter, seems to date from this era. It is hard to reconcile the image of long-term welfare dependency with the broad facts of economic history. Many African-American families experienced three distinct economic environments in the course of the twentieth century: They were initially employed in Southern agriculture, moved north for industrial employment around mid-century, and then were trapped in long-term unemployment or underemployment in the last quarter of the century. They may have been poor in all three stages, though somewhat less so in the second. However, it is only the last stage that undermines the traditional economic role of the male breadwinner and promotes welfare dependency. A stereotypical family that lost its connection to the industrial economy in the 1970s and became reliant on welfare would barely have had time to start a second welfare generation before the federal government put an end to "welfare as we know it.")

With the election of Ronald Reagan in 1980, the attacks on labor and the poor reached their peak. This was the time of the most rapid increases in inequality, as shown in Part I. The combination of tax cuts for the rich and a massive military build-up left far too little funding for numerous civilian government functions. New justifications were needed for the curtailment of all remaining charitable impulses and the elimination of the surviving programs that benefited the poor. Moving beyond the benign neglect and "culture of poverty" theories of the 1970s, the conservative theorists of the 1980s hypothesized that useful government intervention was in general impossible. Instead, there was a revival of genetic interpretations of inequality, an ancient and discredited form of pseudo-scientific prejudice. (See the discussion of *The Bell Curve*, the best-known work of the new genetic theorists, in Part VII.) Repressive responses to crime grew rapidly, replacing other policies that once hoped to address the root causes of crime—and indeed, replacing many social programs in federal and state government budgets.

In the 1990s, the growth of inequality slowed down and even reversed late in the decade. But the government was trapped by the debt and deficits created in the 1980s, and by the antigovernment, antiegalitarian ideology that had become hegemonic in policy-making circles. A Democratic administration, pursing policies that would have been advocated only by Republicans a generation earlier, put an end to welfare and made only marginal changes in other programs for the poor, while maintaining the fundamental Reagan-era commitments to low taxes and high military spending. With those commitments in place, it does not matter whether the president wishes he could help the poor—since he has ensured that he cannot afford to. Despite occasional calls for a renewed conversation about race in America, there is a great silence about the poor, who will, under current policies, always be with us.

Policies and Possibilities

What can and should be done about poverty? The starting point is the recognition that growth does not automatically bring an end to poverty. Nor is there a fixed trade-off between equality and efficiency. Industrial countries at similar levels of development have very different degrees of equality and very different policies toward the poor. A nation's political and institutional framework and the choices made about public policy evidently have a substantial impact. As **Chris Tilly and Randy Albelda** explain in the final summary in Part V, an adequate understanding of income inequality and potential policy responses requires not only insights from a variety of economic theories, but also a broadened perspective on the role of institutions such as class, family, and the state. Our discussion of these topics continues throughout the later parts of this book, ending with a focus on the role of the state and the significance of public sector activism in Part X.

Throughout most of history, and in much of the world today, poverty (at least by contemporary developed-world standards) has been the inescapable fate of the majority. Today, in the midst of affluence, the persistence of poverty is a result of the political and economic strategies that society adopts, the shape of the wage structure, and the extent of the public sector programs that buffer those in need. Looking at America in the Depression, Franklin D. Roosevelt saw "one-third of a nation ill-housed, ill-clad, ill-nourished"[1] and attempted to respond with numerous initiatives large and small. More than fifty years later, according to Piven and Cloward, a reasonable standard of poverty (which they set at about 150 percent of the official poverty line) found a quarter of the nation still in need. The subtle critiques and budgetary constraints that inhibit antipoverty programs today should be measured against a moral standard articulated by FDR: "Better the occasional faults of a government that lives in a spirit of charity than the consistent omissions of a government frozen in the ice of its own indifference."[2]

Notes

1. As quoted in Albelda, Folbre, et al. (1996), 103.
2. Ackerman (1984), 99.

Summary of

Income, Deprivation, and Poverty *and* Implications for Conceptualizing and Measuring Poverty

by Brian Nolan and Christopher T. Whelan

[Published in *Resources, Deprivation, and Poverty* (Oxford: Oxford University Press, 1996), Chs. 6 and 8, 115–151, 179–201.]

Theoretical and empirical analyses of poverty often seem to be dealing with different concepts. While theorists emphasize the importance of considering deprivation, rights, and capabilities as well as the money incomes of the poor, most empirical studies continue to rely on income data as the sole or primary measure of poverty. This book attempts to bridge the gap, applying a multidimensional definition of poverty to a survey of Irish households, and drawing out the implications of the empirical findings for ongoing theoretical debates. The first chapter summarized here explores the survey results, while the second addresses related theoretical issues.

Income, Deprivation, and Poverty

A widely accepted definition, proposed by Townsend, says that poverty consists of exclusion from ordinary living standards arising from lack of resources. Under this definition, income alone is not a satisfactory measure of poverty, since the correlation between low income and deprivation in consumption is far from perfect. A few analysts have attempted to apply this idea in practice, but have usually been hampered by the lack of adequate data on consumption or by ad hoc definitions of deprivation.

A survey of a random sample of more than 3000 Irish households in 1987 (described in earlier chapters) provides detailed information on consumption patterns and attitudes as well as standard economic and demographic data. Of the twenty-four indicators of consumption available in the study, eight are regarded as necessities by most people in the survey and tend to cluster together statistically. (Examples include being able to afford two pairs of shoes, or being able to eat meat or fish every other day.) Being deprived of any one of these eight items for lack of resources is taken as the definition of deprivation for most of the analysis.

Two alternate definitions of poverty, corresponding roughly to common notions of what it means to be poor, are (1) an income below 50 percent of the mean and (2) an income below 60 percent of the mean combined with enforced deprivation of at least one of the eight basic items. Overall, 77 percent of the sample is "consistently non-poor,"—not in poverty by either definition— while 10 percent is consistently poor. The remaining, inconsistent group is split almost evenly: 7 percent is poor only by the first definition, or "income-poor only," while 6 percent is poor only by the second definition, or "deprivation-poor only."

The two definitions imply different risks of poverty: farmers and other self-employed people are more likely to be income-poor, while households headed by someone who is ill or disabled, or in "full-time home duties" (e.g., single mothers of young children), are more likely to be deprivation-poor. Current labor force status appears more closely related to income poverty, while long-term lack of household resources (growing up in poverty, experiencing long-term unemployment, being widowed, living in an inner city) is more closely related to deprivation poverty.

Resources of the Inconsistent Groups

By any of several criteria, the consistently nonpoor are doing best, followed by the income-poor-only, then the deprivation-poor-only, with the consistently poor at the bottom. This ranking applies to measures of long-term resources such as average savings, house value, and level of education, and to outcomes such as the percentage reporting difficulty in making ends meet or high levels of psychological distress.

These findings raise several questions about the resources of the inconsistent groups, which can only be partially answered with the survey results. In general, the income-poor have greater resources; some (though certainly not all) of them may be classified as poor due to errors in measurement of income, or to short-term fluctuations. For example, the survey year was an unusually bad one for Irish farmers. One simple adjustment for income fluctuations would reclassify 10 percent of the income-poor as nonpoor.

People experiencing deprivation of at least one of the basic items can be found at every income level; on average they have much smaller savings and less valuable homes than those of the same income who are not deprived. Some of them may have different spending priorities than the majority, whose opinions were used to define the eight basic items. Even among those below 60 percent of the mean income, about 21 percent of the deprivation-poor households own a car and 36 percent own a telephone; in some circumstances these may be more necessary than the "basic" items.

Finally, it is likely that there are individual differences in needs and circumstances, and in strategies for coping with limited resources, that make the income-poor-only households feel less deprived than the deprivation-poor-only; however, such distinctions cannot be made on the basis of the survey data.

Conceptualizing and Measuring Poverty

There appears to be widespread acceptance of the idea that poverty consists of inability to participate in society due to lack of income and other financial resources. To be poor according to this definition, a person must both experience deprivation and be constrained by lack of resources. This implies that income alone is not an adequate measure of poverty. As suggested by the survey results in earlier chapters, both low income and deprivation should be measured, and the definition of poverty should include both criteria.

Amartya Sen's proposed "capability" approach to assessing living standards has been an important feature of recent theoretical debates. Sen highlights the importance of the freedom or ability to achieve desirable "functionings," rather than actual outcomes. However, such views have had little impact on empirical research, in part because the capabilities and functionings discussed by Sen are at a high level of generality. The combined use of income and deprivation data to define poverty could be seen as a small step toward implementing the capability approach.

In measuring deprivation, there is a danger of casting the net too widely, yielding an overly detailed or prescriptive list of activities and possessions that are required to be classified as nonpoor. The aim is to identify those excluded from society and its commonly accepted standard of living because of a lack of resources. Specific deprivation indicators are used, not because they are uniquely important in themselves, but because they are thought to correlate with and reflect an underlying latent variable, the experience of generalized deprivation.

The term "social exclusion" has replaced "poverty" in much of the European discussion of the issue. "Social exclusion is presented as relating to dynamics and processes, to multidimensional disadvantage, and to inadequate social participation, whereas poverty is presented as static and descriptive, unidimensional, and narrowly financial. Our own analysis illustrates how this contrast is based to a significant extent on a caricature of the concept of poverty. . . ." [201] That is, the exclusion literature is critiquing the simple financial measures of poverty that are widely used in practice, not the more sophisticated theories of poverty. The distinction between the two concepts in theory is only that poverty is restricted to exclusion based on lack of financial resources, whereas the newer term may include cases where nonmarket factors are the cause of exclusion from society. The concept of poverty is often analytically preferable for its clarity of focus, while the more fashionable but vague concept of exclusion has a political advantage in mobilizing support for antipoverty programs at present.

There is an important distinction between notions of poverty based on living standards and those based on minimum rights to resources. However, the survey results show that there can be a substantial number of people below a low-income line who are not experiencing basic deprivation, based in part on wide variation in personal circumstances and desires. Are people below the minimum income necessarily deprived of an entitlement, regardless of other circumstances? Even if there is or should be such an entitlement, it is useful to distinguish between the right to a minimum income, based on considerations of equity, and the right to participate in society, which requires elimination of enforced deprivation. The two concepts are closely related, but not identical.

Finally, the concept of the "underclass" has been important in recent American discussions of poverty, drawing on the influential work of William Julius Wilson. The underclass is usually defined as a subset of the poor who experience prolonged labor market marginality, unusually severe deprivation, and the development of a distinctive subculture. The Irish survey data show that those with marginalized labor force histories do have much higher levels of deprivation than the nonmarginalized working class, drawing attention to the particular needs of those who are detached from the world of work. However, in Ireland, those with marginalized work histories who live in rented public housing in large urban centers make up a small proportion of the poor and do not show an unusually high level of fatalism. So adopting the "underclass" terminology may do more harm than good.

Summary of

The Age of Extremes: Concentrated Affluence and Poverty in the Twenty-First Century

by Douglas S. Massey

[Published in *Demography* 33, 4 (November 1996), 395–412.]

The resurgence of inequality at the end of the twentieth century is occurring in tandem with rapid growth in urbanization. The geography of population is at once becoming more dense and more stratified. Increasingly, the poor live in a world of crime, disease, violence, and family breakdown. The world of the rich is more and more one of isolation and privilege.

The article summarized here projects these trends into the twenty-first century, arguing that "we have entered a new age of inequality in which class lines will grow more rigid as they are amplified and reinforced by a powerful process of geographic concentration," [395] and predicting that without positive interventions, the future will be bleak, divided, and violent.

Spatial Concentrations of Poverty and Wealth

In Latin America, the region of the developing world with the best statistics on poverty, there has been a rapid change in the location of the poor. In 1970, nearly two-thirds (64 percent) of the region's poor people lived in the countryside. By 1980, only a narrow majority (54 percent) of the poor lived in rural areas. And by 1990, the urban poor outnumbered their rural counterparts, 60 percent to 40 percent. "The typical poor Latin American of the twenty-first century will not live in a village or town but in a city, and most likely a very large one." [396]

The same process is even more advanced in the United States, where the proportion of the poor living outside of metropolitan areas fell from 44 percent in 1970 to 28 percent in 1990. Geographic concentration of the poor is occurring within cities as well: The proportion of central-city poor people living in predominantly poor neighborhoods has risen sharply; by any of several measures, income segregation is growing in urban America. The average urban poor person lives in a neighborhood where roughly one-quarter of the population is poor.

The affluent traditionally clustered in core cities to enhance their ability to control and administer territory and enterprises. However, before modern advances in transportation and communication, the masses who produced goods and services for the wealthy were situated nearby. New technologies in the nineteenth century enabled separation of work from residence and segregation of classes. The middle and upper classes moved to suburbs, while the working classes stayed near factory jobs in central cities.

The fluid economy of the early post–World War II era began to break down this class stratification. As the middle class grew, residential class segregation dropped. More and more people lived in neighborhoods among people with different occupational status. However, this pattern also reversed in the 1970s. The affluent population became even more concentrated than the poor. In the ten largest metropolitan areas in 1970, the typical affluent person (defined here as someone with an income of more than four times the poverty level) lived in a neighborhood that was 39 percent affluent; by 1990, the figure had risen to 52 percent.

The New World Order

The emerging spatial world order is one in which powerful economic forces drive the poor out of the countryside into the cities and then block their upward economic mobility. Racial and ethnic biases further stymie geographic mobility.

The urbanization of poverty is well advanced in the developed world, where the urban population was 74 percent of the total in 1990 and is projected to reach 82 percent by 2020 (figures for the United States alone are slightly higher in both cases). In the developing world only 35 percent of the population was urban in 1990. These countries are rapidly urbanizing and should become 47 percent urban by 2010.

In the past, rural migrants to the cities could take advantage of numerous routes to eventual upward mobility; studies done in the 1970s documented this, both in developed countries like the United States and in developing countries like Mexico. But since the 1970s the structure of opportunities has changed, with a dwindling proportion of middle-income jobs for the modestly educated. Those entering at the bottom of the urban economy are now more likely to stay there.

Segregation by Class, Race, and Ethnicity

Class-based spatial segregation, which has risen since 1970, is magnified by racial discrimination. Persistent white prejudice and a history of discriminatory real estate and lending practices have left blacks in the United States extremely segregated. The increase in black poverty in the 1970s and 1980s "was absorbed by a small set of racially homogeneous, geographically isolated, densely settled neighborhoods packed densely around the urban core; and because class segregation was increasing as well . . . , a disproportionate share of the economic pain was absorbed by neighborhoods that were not only black but also poor." [404]

In 1990, 83 percent of poor central-city blacks lived in neighborhoods with poverty rates of over 20 percent; the corresponding figure was 43 percent for poor central-city whites. The problem was not confined to central cities: For the fifty largest metropolitan areas as a whole, 64 percent of poor blacks, but only 13 percent of poor whites, lived in neighborhoods with a poverty rate over 20 percent in 1980.

Racial segregation accounts for a large share of the spatial concentration of poverty in the United States. In previous research coauthored by the present author, sixteen metropolitan areas were designated *hypersegregated*, that is, geographically segregated on several dimensions, based on an analysis of 1980 data. Fourteen remained hypersegrated in 1990; the two areas that escaped the list barely did so, while six more areas were added. These twenty areas contain over one-third of the black population of the United States.

Political and Cultural Ecology of Inequality

"In a society where most people live in small towns and villages, rich and poor families must mix socially, share the same public services, and inhabit the same political units. . . . The poor benefit from public institutions to which the rich are committed by reason of self-interest." [406] The trend toward economic segregation fractures this shared polity at the same time as it diminishes shared space. The danger is that advantages and disadvantages will be compounded if political boundaries correspond to class differences. The rich can withdraw from the cost of providing services to the poor by decentralizing government. Rich enclaves will have low tax rates on high property values and abundant public services. Poor communities will have high demand for services and will need high tax rates on low property values in order to support them. School systems are the most significant manifestation of this syndrome. As education becomes increasingly important to success in the global marketplace, disadvantaged children are shunted into resource-poor school systems while rich children attend well-funded learning-oriented schools.

In small communities, informal measures such as ostracism, ridicule, or physical discipline hold crime and violence in check. These devices tend to break down in the anonymity of large-scale settings. Louis Wirth perceived this breakdown as the cause of alienation and antisocial behavior, while other analysts maintained that urban dwellers reconstruct networks based on friendship rather than kinship. As a researcher in Depression-era Chicago, Wirth probably mistook the effects of concentrated poverty for results of urbanism in general.

A more recent theorist, Claude Fischer, proposed that the concentrated spaces in cities are conducive to subculture formation in which intense interaction reinforces behavior that others may consider unconventional. This theory is consonant with the emergence of divergent subcultures of poverty and affluence. Joblessness, crime, family problems, violence, and other social ills concentrate in poor neighborhoods, while the rich share a privileged environment with affluent neighbors.

The most troubling result of concentrated poverty is the reinforcement of criminal and violent behavior. This behavior can become a survival mechanism in response to threatening actions from others. A constant condition of threat may even trigger physiological changes that produce reflexive violence. Poor children will be socialized in an environment in which supervision, respect for education, and successful role models are scarce. The effects will spill over into many areas of life: "Concentrated poverty is a stronger predictor of violent crime than of property crime, and of violence between people known to one another than between strangers." [408] Oppositional subcultures will form in the most impoverished, segregated areas, seeking to preserve self-esteem by legitimizing failure to meet conventional educational and other social standards. Once formed, such subcultures are difficult to change, and contribute independently to the perpetuation of the problems of poverty.

We are facing an age of extremes. Social scientists devote a great deal of attention to the poor. But to understand the new regime, it is necessary to investigate the culture of affluence as well. If present trends continue, the future looks bleak. Self-conscious actions are required to change course; sacrifice by the affluent will inevitably be required to reduce inequality and class segregation.

Summary of

Social Exclusion: Toward an Analytical and Operational Framework

by Ajit S. Bhalla and Frédéric Lapeyre

[Published in *Development and Change* 28, 3 (July 1997), 413–433.]

The term *social exclusion* came into use among French sociologists to describe "a breakdown of the relationship between society and the individual." [414] When these connections are broken the consequence may be poverty, alienation, or disqualification from the rights and benefits of participation in society.

The concept of social exclusion is meaningful in the French context because of the Republican tradition of solidarity, but it has also come into play in two other contexts: the formation of the European Union, and the crisis of the welfare state under the pressure of global economic restructuring. The article summarized here explores whether social exclusion is also a useful lens for examining dimensions of disadvantage in developing countries as well.

Defining Social Exclusion

Social exclusion is related to poverty, but it incorporates social and political matters as well, extending the notions of advantage and disadvantage beyond an immediate accounting of income to issues of economic security, civil rights, and social integration. The French intellectual tradition holds the Republican state responsible for political cohesion, for joining the individual to society. In contrast, the Anglo-Saxon tradition highlights relationships between individuals acting in a competitive marketplace.

Social exclusion is a multidimensional construct, including economic, social, and political elements. The common thread is disadvantage. Several analysts of poverty embrace themes that resonate with social exclusion. Amartya Sen developed a theory based on the presence or absence of capabilities that enable an individual to thrive physically or to engage successfully in community life. Dasgupta's theory, applicable mainly to agrarian societies, maintains that the landless poor are especially vulnerable in the absence of social norms. Those who have land may undercut those with no assets in labor markets so that the landless may not even have nutritional resources adequate for employment. A third theory, developed in the United Kingdom, "defines poverty in terms of 'relative deprivation' as a state of observable and demonstrable disadvantage relative to the local community or the wider society or nation to which an individual, family or group belongs." [417] Deprivation may have a material basis, for example inadequate food or shelter, or a social basis, such as a lack of family ties or educational opportunities.

"The European Commission emphasizes the idea that each citizen has the right to a certain basic standard of living and the right to participate in the major social and occupational institutions of the society—employment, housing, health care, education, and so on." [415] However, in a 1992 statement, the Commission also noted the emergence of structural barriers that may displace some segments of the population to the fringes of society and prevent them from sharing in the general prosperity. Since many European states provide at least minimum living standards, the European Union adopted social exclusion rather than poverty as a construct for analyzing social problems.

Some researchers have made a distinction between poverty, or distributional deprivation due to inadequate resources, and social exclusion or relational deprivation, predicated on inadequate social ties. But the distinction is not practical. Many social questions like literacy or infant mortality are closely associated with income levels. The distribution of income affects the capacity to function in society (in the sense that Sen defined functioning). Furthermore, the distribution of wealth and income is dependent on the structure of property rights that define social relations of ownership, control, participation, and access. The rich have more power and influence on the state than the poor and therefore have better access to political rights and liberties as well as to economic resources.

Economic, social, and political dimensions of social exclusion can be identified, but these elements are not completely separate. The *economic dimension* involves income, production, employment, and the satisfaction of basic needs. The *social dimension* extends the economic analysis to discussion of relationships that mediate the distribution of income. For example, "socially enforced moral rules can constrain or expand entitlement to food and its distribution in conditions of famine." [419] The social dimension of exclusion often overlaps economic and political aspects, but it is concerned with conditions that enhance or diminish access and opportunity. The *political dimension* of social exclusion is involved with rights and participation in the political process.

Global Relevance

New efforts at social integration in Europe focus on civil society as a vehicle for "reinforcing the social ties between the individual and society." [420] Is it appropriate to apply similar policies in developing countries that do not share the same history of the welfare state? For the first time since the 1930s, the developed and developing countries share problems of unemployment and poverty. Unemployment is rising in Europe and poverty and exclusion are growing in the United States. Poverty is growing in many developing countries. Democratization is spreading among developing countries, but its effect may be offset by reduced autonomy for nations in a globally integrated, interdependent world.

The analytical concepts are similar for both developed and developing countries, but the weights attached to elements of exclusion differ. Distributional questions may be particularly important in less-developed countries where inequality is high. But developing countries generally lack formal, state supported systems to address distributional problems. "The family, kinship relationships, and religious groups therefore act as redistributive mechanisms, as well as means of promoting interpersonal relations and the social identity of individual members." [423] Structural adjustment programs further inhibit the development of public welfare programs in developing countries.

Relational issues focus on families in developing countries rather than on relationships between individuals and the state or civil society. Three kinds of social relationships are associated with different stages of development: (1) relationships within families and extended families; (2) communal relationships, found in developing and some socialist countries; (3) relationships between the individual and the state.

An Operational Framework

To track progress in fighting exclusion, a yardstick is needed; however, measurement of such a multidimensional construct is problematical. It is not easy to aggregate economic, social, and political elements into a single index—especially since they may be moving in different directions. Weighting each element is also difficult since the importance of each one varies with the stages of development. Separate indicators may be more appropriate.

- *Economic indicators*—Measuring GNP or GDP per capita is not sufficient. The lowest income groups are often left out of the benefits of growth. Specific measures of poverty and inequality, such as Sen's index or the Gini coefficient, are more useful for a full understanding of the economic foundation of exclusion.

- *Social indicators* should include access to public goods and services such as education, health care, and so on; access to good, secure jobs; and cohesion or fragmentation in society, such as membership in civic groups, crime rates, etc.

- *Political indicators*—The UNDP and other indexes of political freedom include "personal security, rule of law, freedom of expression, political participation, and equality of opportunity." [426]

Economic, social, and political indicators do not always move in the same direction, and some countries are high in one element and low in another. Well-being is not always correlated with national wealth; conversely in some countries even the poor are not deprived of basic needs. Globalization has had uneven effects across countries. Africa has become more marginalized in terms of foreign investment, and exclusion has increased within African countries. "During the 1980s, social exclusion and human insecurity also increased as is reflected in the process of de-industrialization in many countries, the withdrawal of the public sector, and drastic cuts in public expenditures as part of structural adjustment programmes." [427]

Precarious Jobs and Social Exclusion

Precarious employment reflects both distributional and relational aspects of exclusion. It may be more valuable as an indicator of exclusion than unemployment, because it captures recent shifts toward informal labor in developing

countries and atypical forms of work in developed countries. Flexible production is often incompatible with good secure jobs. Unemployment in European
welfare states indicates exclusion, but in developing countries or weak welfare
states such as the United States, unemployment may be relatively low while
many workers simply eke out a living in insecure, poorly paid, formal or informal employment. Exclusion in these cases means a lack of access to *good* jobs.

While precariousness may be a useful concept, it raises methodological difficulties because it is not well-defined. In some cases atypical work, especially
part-time work, may reflect personal choices. A prominent French research center developed a complex instrument for studying the risks of various types of exclusion, using categories for conditions of employment, income distribution,
and social vulnerability (family and associative support networks). "The CERC
results show that precariousness is at the heart of economic poverty and social
vulnerability. The risk of being excluded from the labor market has the potential of progressive disintegration of social ties." [429]

Such an elaborate survey would be difficult to undertake in many developing
countries because of the expense and lack of a sufficient data-collection infrastructure. It is particularly difficult to involve respondents in informal labor
markets, yet information on the informal sector is crucial to an understanding
of employment-related aspects of social exclusion.

Summary of

Poor Relief and the Dramaturgy of Work

by Frances Fox Piven and Richard Cloward

[Published in *Regulating the Poor: The Functions of Public Welfare*
(New York: Vintage Books, 1993), Ch. 11, 343–405.]

The chapter summarized here argues that welfare provision responds to shifting
motivations held by powerful interests. During economic crises the threat of
civil unrest must be controlled, so welfare expands, offering more benefits to
more people. Once the danger of unrest subsides an underlying problem re-
asserts itself: motivating a low-wage labor force.

In the first edition of their book, published in the wake of the urban riots and
civil rights protests of the 1960s, the authors predicted that a campaign to regulate labor would overtake the need to regulate civil disorder. That campaign
did indeed take place, intensified by changes in the nature and conditions of
work. "The problem that thus lent special urgency to work-enforcing reforms
in relief policy in the 1970s and 1980s was how to get people to accept lower
wages, fewer benefits, and less job security." [346]

Labor Regulation

Empirical research supports the proposition that mass disorder influences welfare growth and offers some evidence that welfare growth mitigates civil unrest. However, the moment of crisis is short-lived. Taxpayers resent rising welfare costs, but a deeper objection comes from employers' desire to discipline labor. Social programs protect potential workers from the need to take undesirable jobs, undermining the power of employers. Employers respond with a political agenda designed to cut benefits, restrict eligibility, and stigmatize welfare recipients.

The post–World War II economic boom, marked by rising profits, wages, and living standards, peaked by the early 1970s. The U.S. industrial sector declined under competitive pressure from both developed and developing countries. Employment shifted from heavily unionized manufacturing industries to service sectors where many jobs offered low pay, few benefits, and little job security. It is not necessary to resolve debates over causality to understand that labor regulation came to the forefront of the welfare agenda. "The salient point is that the peak of the welfare explosion in the early 1970s coincided with a growing crisis in the economy, and with the mounting of a campaign by business to solve its problems of profitability by forcing workers to take less." [348]

Other industrial countries faced similar pressures but many promoted investment, innovation, and retraining workers. For a time these strategies—enabled by strong unions, left political parties, and income support programs—upheld profits, wages, and stable class relations. In the United States, corporate and government elites preferred plant closings, speculation, leveraged buyouts, and mergers. The Reagan administration reduced taxes on corporations and the wealthy and gutted programs that protected the environment and workers' health and safety.

A major part of the campaign to restore profitability was an assault on labor costs. "The threat of plant closings accompanied by capital flight struck fear in the hearts of workers." [350] Union-busting, violations of fair labor practices, and replacement of or threats to replace striking workers diminished the power of the labor movement. Union membership fell and contracts contained many concessions and few gains. Permanent jobs were cut, real wages declined, health and pension benefits shrank, and part-time, temporary, and subcontract workers increased. Real hourly wages for nonsupervisory personnel (81 percent of the workforce) fell 15 percent between 1973 and 1992. In 1990, 18 percent of full-time year-round workers earned less than a poverty level income for a family of four, compared to 12 percent in 1979. The purchasing power of the minimum wage was 40 percent less in 1990 than in 1978.

Business interests objected to the redistribution of income through expansion of welfare in the 1960s. "However, we think the more fundamental reason for the attack on these programs is that social benefits strengthen workers in labor market bargaining." [354] This position follows from Marxist insights about the reserve army of labor: Unemployed workers compete for work against the employed. Although unemployment rose in the 1960s and 1970s, wages did not fall. Many analysts concluded that expanding social programs insulated wages from the effects of rising unemployment. Broader coverage under Social Security, disability, AFDC, and food stamp programs enabled many people to withdraw from the labor force, while generous unemployment insurance allowed unemployed workers to hold out for better jobs.

Popular support protected some programs like Social Security, but many faced drastic changes. Unemployment benefits were taxed for the first time and eligibility was curtailed. Cuts in job training programs threw 400,000 people into the labor market. Changes in eligibility rules and/or benefit schedules cut disability and food stamp programs. The expanding service sector, with many low-wage jobs held mostly by women and minorities, benefited. "The resulting cut-backs in social programs . . . made this new service proletariat all the more vulnerable to onerous working conditions. And restricted access to unemployment benefits or disability benefits or AFDC benefits intensified the fear of being fired which underlies employer power." [362]

The Reordered Class Structure

Altogether these changes in the structure of labor markets, taxes, and social programs produced a massive redistribution of income from poorer to wealthier segments of U.S. society. Inequality increased as both poverty and wealth grew. "Between 1977 and 1992, the poorest tenth lost 20 percent of its post-tax income. The top tenth gained 41 percent, the top 5 percent gained 60 percent, and the top 1 percent gained 136 percent." [363] The wealthiest 1 percent of families went from a 31 percent share of net private wealth to 37 percent. Poverty, after falling from 22 percent of the population in 1959 to 12 percent in 1977, rose again to 14 percent in 1991. But the official statistics underestimate actual poverty because the definition has not changed with changes in the expenditure share of necessities like food or housing. A more realistic poverty line would fall at 155 percent of the current one—$21,700 for a family of four rather than $13,360. By this measure, 62.8 million people, or 26 percent of the population, would have been in poverty in 1989—twice as many people as shown by official count.

Justifying Labor Regulation

Along with restrictions on benefits and eligibility, welfare recipients were subjected to a relentless campaign of stigmatization. Politicians shifted attention on inequality away from deteriorating wages onto the nonworking poor. Mothers on AFDC, the majority of whom were black and Hispanic, were convenient scapegoats for white resentment of deteriorating economic conditions. In line with historical precedent, social commentators alleged that welfare fosters dependency, prolonging poverty rather than alleviating it. They failed to acknowledge that welfare expansion usually follows economic dislocation.

"At the same time . . . economic dislocations also produce widespread disorganization. They wipe out the resources on which social life is constructed. . . . The costs of these market developments for people at the bottom thus go beyond material hardship to the rupture of ties to place, kin, and community, and to the fraying of cultural patterns which make coherent social and personal life possible." [369] Relief programs may mitigate hardship, but cannot by themselves repair the social ruptures or halt disorganizing processes. Welfare critics, however, equate social disorganization with welfare rather than with the underlying economic dislocation.

In the early 1970s welfare benefits became competitive with falling real wages; but soon AFDC payments eroded as well. The purchasing power of AFDC benefits fell 42 percent from 1970 to 1990 (27 percent from 1972 to 1990 when combined with food stamps, which maintained their value). Eligibility rules, which had become more inclusive during the 1960s, were rewritten in the Nixon era; state-level administrative procedures became more complicated—increasing the risk that benefits would be denied due to incomplete applications.

Welfare to Work

Programs to encourage welfare recipients to enter the workforce date to the 1960s; however, they were often expensive to administer rather than cost-saving. Work incentive programs supplemented wages (rather than deducting earnings from welfare grants). Workfare programs placed recipients in government or nonprofit agencies to gain experience and earn their welfare grants. Other programs required recipients to look for work or acquire training.

Welfare-to-work programs have not been successful. High unemployment rates during the 1970s and 1980s meant there were not enough jobs for unskilled workers. Available jobs often did not pay enough to support a family. Many women lacked skills needed in the labor market. Welfare supplements were designed as a bridge to self-sufficiency, but poor working women combined welfare and earnings to support their families.

Irrational claims have been made that "work would transform family structure, community life, and the so-called 'culture of poverty.'" [392] Yet welfare reform alone could not alter the underlying conditions that reduced work opportunities for men, nor could it provide adequate socialization for poor children. Welfare mothers struggle to protect their children from the dangerous environment of urban poverty. One observer stated, "In many poor communities they are the only signatures on the social contract, the glue that keeps our communities from spinning out of control." [393–394]

Both liberal and conservative politicians have taken up the campaign against dependency. Early in his presidency Bill Clinton proposed to limit welfare to two years. This focus on self-sufficiency has a hidden agenda. The degraded status of the welfare mother serves as a warning to others of a fate worse than even the most miserable job.

Summary of

Not Markets Alone: Enriching the Discussion of Income Distribution

by Chris Tilly and Randy Albelda

[Published in *Political Economy for the 21st Century: Contemporary Views on the Trend of Economics,* ed. Charles J. Whalen (New York: M.E. Sharpe Co., 1996), Ch. 10, 195–210.]

The resurgence of inequality in the industrialized world, particularly in the United States, over the last quarter of the twentieth century has revived old debates in economics about the relationship between inequality and growth. The article summarized below argues that the realities of income distribution gets short shrift in this discussion—that growth is prioritized and only market-based factors are given serious consideration. Yet there are good reasons for concern about income distribution in its own right and good reasons to examine income distribution in the context of the political and social institutions that shape and constrain it.

A richer understanding of income distribution can be found in several economic theories outside the mainstream, particularly within the Marxist and Keynesian traditions. But for a comprehensive investigation, economics must seek insight from related disciplines in the social sciences.

Growth and Distribution

Since the 1930s social movements in the developed and developing worlds have struggled for equality on many fronts—for women, for minorities, for nations—with some measure of success. However, in the last two decades the trend has reversed: "Categorical disparities grew by race, educational level, occupation, industry—virtually every criterion except gender. Inequality also rose *within* groups defined by those criteria. Meanwhile, inequality among countries worsened as well." [196] Rather than joining the fight to stem the resurgence of inequality, many economists have rushed to defend it, claiming that inequality resulting from the operation of free markets must be tolerated in the interests of efficiency and growth. But markets are not free—they exist within an institutional framework that is neglected in much economic analysis.

Two theories frame much of the discussion of income distribution. Simon Kuznets proposed in 1955 that during the process of development, the composition of a country's economy changes from an agricultural to an industrial basis. At first incomes are generally low but relatively equal. As some people move into industry their incomes rise, introducing inequality between industrial and agricultural sectors. As more and more people move into industry, incomes become more equal, but at a higher level. As long as economic growth proceeds without obstruction, inequality will be transitory.

In 1975 Arthur Okun proposed that there is a trade-off between growth and equity. Attempts to redistribute income in the direction of more equality constitute disincentives to work and investment. Conversely, inequality introduces efficiencies that foster growth. Okun's own values led him to assert that societies should accept a modicum of economic inefficiency in the interest of equity. Later, neoclassical economists took up Okun's technical argument with a vengeance, but abandoned his humane conclusion. If there is a trade-off between equity and growth, then society must live with inequality in the interest of growth. Furthermore, growth *requires* inequality because needed investments depend on savings, which depend on wealth.

Three Challenges to Neoclassical Theory

The subordination of income distribution to growth can be challenged on moral, theoretical, and empirical grounds. Quite simply, it is morally right to care about who prospers and who doesn't and about the social instability that results from inequality. Theoretically, there are conflicting theories hidden beneath apparent economic consensus. Even within the three best known schools of economic analysis—neoclassical, Marxian, and Keynesian—there are differing views.

Most theorists consider only the relative distribution of income between capital and labor: the average profit rate and wages. For neoclassicals, labor markets are efficient (i.e., there is no involuntary unemployment or shortfall of labor), the rate of growth of the employed work force determines the rate of economic growth and, together with savings (investment), determines the profit rate. What's left goes to workers' wages. Any attempt to redistribute income reduces the efficiency of the labor market and therefore reduces growth.

In standard Marxian theory wages are set by customs and class struggle.

What's left goes to capitalists as profit. Profits are the source of reinvestment capital for a new round of growth, so wage levels have an inverse relationship with the rate of economic growth: higher wages mean less growth. This resonates with Okun's theory of a trade-off between equity and growth.

Some Marxians are more like some Keynesians, but Keynesians are split. Some uphold neoclassical views that equality is detrimental to long-run growth. Others hold that intended savings and investment are a function of the profit rate and wages are a residual. Stagnation theorists propose that large corporations simply set profits at a fixed markup and consumption drives growth. Institutions like minimum wages or unions that increases the workers' share of income will stimulate growth.

Some of these models describe real situations, but none captures all capitalist societies at all times and none investigates inequalities *among* workers. Many empirical studies focus on the short-run business cycle trade-offs between inflation and unemployment described by the Phillips Curve, which shows the inverse relationship between the rate of change in wage rates and the unemployment rate. Unemployment hurts the poorest most; but when growth is rapid, inflation may be more of a burden on the wealthy who have fixed-rate assets while the poor benefit from rising employment. Tight labor markets also benefit low income workers most because that is where the most slack in the labor market occurs. These arguments worked from the 1950s until the 1980s, when economic growth and inequality both increased. Further investigation reveals that historically, the equality-growth confluence depends on the institutional environment.

The Labor Market in Context

"The dominant, neoclassical theory of labor markets is institutionally naked." [199] The model we are left with depends solely on supply and demand factors: individual preferences, marginal revenue product, and prices of goods and of labor (wages). In the long run human capital investment influences worker productivity.

"What does this omit? Among other things: the family, race, ethnicity, gender, community, employer strategy, non-Walrasian power, unions, culture, customary wage patterns, and level of worker effort." [199] Some neoclassical economists derived certain wage-setting institutions, for example efficiency wages, or wages set above market wages to induce greater effort and loyalty from employees, from neoclassical principles. But they still neglect factors like power or culture.

Labor market segmentation theories have a historical and institutional bent, finding that "jobs cluster in segments that differ systematically by the skill and training involved, job security and attachment, opportunities for advancement, breadth of job definition, level of worker participation in decisions, and compensation." [200] Much of our understanding about these issues comes from sociologists and historians. Economists must be humble enough to learn from these related disciplines.

Income in Context

Other forms of income and income distribution are also important to understand as well as the simple reality that humans have physical, emotional, and social needs. These needs can be met in three ways: make, share, or buy. Under capitalism more and more need fulfillment is commodified, requiring money to buy things. But there are still sectors of the economy outside of market exchange where making and sharing occur, notably households and government transfer programs. Many economists assume that Walrasian power, the power to buy and sell freely, is the only power that matters, but firms may have monopoly power, or there may be more buyers than sellers or vice versa in the market for particular commodities. Concepts of class, the family, and the state are key to understanding extra-market mechanisms of income distribution.

- *Class*—Marx defined class in relation to the means of production (capital): One either owned capital or one worked for someone who did. However, rather than generating two polarized classes, "modern capitalism . . . has led to a proliferation of classes and subclasses" [202] with varying characteristics and economic outcomes. Many economists use class to identify groups with similar size incomes: rich or poor or in between. This shift is partly due to the fact that many people, in the United States at least, own some stock in corporations. Neoclassicals focus on endowments (like education) that influence productivity. Participants in the economy receive rewards based on the marginal productivity of their contributions to production.

- *Family*—Families have been troublesome for researchers for many reasons. It is necessary to define the relevant unit and adjust measurements for the number and ages of members. Other reasons go deeper than measurement problems. First, the usual accounts of income distribution neglect unpaid labor and the making and sharing of goods and services that occur in the home. Second, family structure affects income distribution within the family. Extended families have different patterns of allocating work and consumption than nuclear families. The number of working adults or whether there are young children to care for profoundly influence a families economic constraints and opportunities. It is not surprising, therefore, to discover that poverty rates for single mothers are nearly four times as high as for the average family. Third, income opportunities affect family structure as women are drawn more and more into market-based work. Fourth, mainstream economic theory considers the family to be a black box, a single unit whose internal decision-making processes are invisible and irrelevant. Feminist economists have broken open the black box, revealing that exploitation may exist within the family and resources are often distributed asymmetrically.

- *State*—The state is the usual agent of redistributive activity. For neoclassical economists, this means that the state should provide incentives for growth, encouraging saving and work rather than consumption and leisure. In the United States, redistribution has gone to the extreme in recent years of transferring income from the poor to the rich. Even some economists with less-extreme views believe that higher welfare benefits encourage dependency, but this is not borne out by empirical research in the United States. Sweden, with generous welfare benefits, also has a 93 percent labor force participation rate among single mothers. Redistributive transfer policies should take into account the lower wages and greater child care responsibilities that women face, expand opportunities for the poor to control their own lives, and include universal benefits to build widespread political support.

PART VI

Intrahousehold Dynamics and Changing Household Composition

Overview Essay

by Laurie Dougherty

The household is an important, yet largely opaque, unit of economic analysis. According to economic theory, the household provides resources to the economy and acts as the agent of consumption of production. Empirical economists often base their research on households, and statisticians routinely collect data on household variables. Yet, for many mainstream economists the internal operations and diverse composition of households are of little concern. Perhaps this simply reflects the conventional belief that the workings of the household are private matters, carried out through the medium of personal, often intimate, relationships. Perhaps mainstream economists are simply honoring the old maxim: "A man's home is his castle," along with the implied corollary—to do with as he will. For feminists, however, the veiled character of the home is not the end of the matter, but rather the beginning. Feminist economists clearly understand that the household is the site of complex, age-old patterns of interaction between men and women (and their children) and that these relationships often entail economic inequalities and asymmetries in power that affect economic decision processes and outcomes.

This essay and the summaries in this part are largely concerned with two themes that involve the social and economic ramifications of domestic relationships: intrahousehold dynamics and changing household composition. The discussion of intrahousehold dynamics brings to the foreground processes through which households arrive at decisions about their resources and consumption. These decisions shape the well-being of family members and determine the role each one will play in the larger economy. Rather than viewing the household as the domain of a benevolent dictator making decisions for the family unit as a whole as proposed by neoclassical economists, less-orthodox economists perceive the household as an arena in which family members negotiate for fulfillment of their needs and preferences. Customs, norms, and circumstances in the larger society play an enormous role in determining the relative strengths of men and women participating in these transactions. In turn, the relative strengths of men and women and the economic roles they play in the family are of interest to policy makers. Programs and benefits that are targeted either to men or to women or geared toward changing the balance of power in the home may be better able to achieve particular policy goals than a less-focused agenda.

The topic of changing household composition reflects the increasing diversity of models of household formation, with particular attention to the economic difficulties faced by single-mother families in the United States. Single parents and their children form a growing share of all families for a number of reasons, some positive, some troubling. Divorce and unwed motherhood are more common and more widely accepted than in earlier periods of time. Women have achieved a greater measure of economic independence and are participating in the labor market in increasing numbers, both as a result of the women's liberation movement and in response to the fact that most men's wages have been stagnant or dropping for two decades.

Families with two working parents are also increasing as a result, but they face disorienting stresses as roles and expectations change. In some cases men who are unable to fulfill the breadwinner role or unwilling to share power within the family simply drop out of the picture, leaving women to raise children alone. And, as we discuss in more detail in Part VIII, women, particularly women with children, are still at a disadvantage in the labor market; and female-headed families all too often fall into poverty. This is not a universal fate, however, since many other countries are more successful than the United States at relieving economic strain on single mothers and their children. Sweden presents an interesting and important contrast to the U.S. experience, as we will discuss in more detail later. In Sweden, both social welfare policy and labor market interventions offer a supportive environment to all families—and single-parent families benefit enormously from this regime.

Intrahousehold Dynamics

Gary Becker's theoretical formulation known as the New Household Economics presents the generally accepted statement of neoclassical economic theory with respect to the household (Becker 1981).[1] Becker argues that households have a unified utility function that governs decisions about the internal allocation of resources. This theory claims that resources are acquired through an efficient division of labor under which, in the usual case, men work for wages in the labor market and women perform nonwaged work in the home. The head of the household makes decisions about allocation of family labor and distribution of resources, acting in an altruistic manner so as to maximize the welfare of the family.

Even if one or more family members are selfish—Becker uses the example of a Rotten Kid—all will act in such a way as to maximize family welfare. Becker reasons that if a Rotten Kid acts to increase his or her own income at the family's expense, the benevolent head of the household will balance the outcome by taking family income away from the Rotten Kid and distributing to other family members. However all—including the Rotten Kid—will now be worse off because the Rotten Kid's behavior has diminished the family's total income. So all members will find it in their interests to maximize total family outcomes and abide by the dictates of the benevolent head[2] (Becker 1981).

The New Household Economics has been challenged by feminists who claim that family members have different, often conflicting interests and preferences, but that they often differ in their abilities to realize these goals. Distributional outcomes reflect the balance of power among family members. In her study of relationships between gender and development, Naila Kabeer offers a thoughtful critique of Becker's theory along with an outline of its origins and a review of other feminists' criticisms (Kabeer 1994).

Kabeer argues that neoclassical economic theory is inadequate for dealing with collective phenomena. "A major obstacle to incorporating the collective nature of households was that economic modeling had been developed to deal with individual preferences and behavior" (Kabeer 1994, 98). She traces the use of altruism to characterize intrafamily relationships to Paul Samuelson who, in 1956, posed the problem of reconciling the preferences of individual family members with the need to establish an aggregate family utility function for the convenience of economic analysts. Samuelson assumed that a natural altruism among family members would resolve this dilemma, forging what he called a social welfare function.

Becker went on to elaborate the theory of the household, complete with benevolent dictators at the head, Rotten Kids, and "tied movers" and "tied stayers." The latter two categories contain working spouses who either move to a locale with less desirable job prospects or stay in one because the partner's job prospects are superior. Without explanation or apology for furthering the stereotype of the male head of household, Becker states in a footnote: "To distinguish the altruist from the beneficiary, I use the masculine pronoun for the altruist and the feminine pronoun for the beneficiary" (Becker 1981, 13, reprinted in Folbre 1996, 109). Kabeer points out that John Kenneth Galbraith and Amartya Sen were among early critics of Becker. Both Galbraith and Sen took note of the fact that the subordination of women within the family was ignored by this development in neoclassical theory.

Elaine McCrate also offers a critique of Becker, discussing his theory as one of three metaphors for marriage. Two of the analogies she examines—trade and merger—emerged from neoclassical models of economic activity; the third is based on Marxist ideas about employment. These analogies focus on the allocation of household labor either to external (market-based) production of goods and services for cash income, or to internal (home-based) production of goods and services for the family's own consumption.

Becker developed the trade motif, describing marriage as involving exchanges between partners with differing productive capacities. Women are presumed to be most productive when working in the home; therefore, the greatest returns to the family's allocation of her labor will come from her work in the home. Men, as a rule, work outside the home, bringing in income. Husbands and wives exchange the fruits of their efforts, with husbands receiving domestically produced goods and services from their wives in return for a share of their income. The assumption of a benevolent head acting in the interests of the whole family offers a framework for decision making. Family members are disciplined to the principle of maximization of total family welfare by the operation of the Rotten Kid Theorem—whoever acts selfishly against the family's interest will be prevented from benefiting from that act by the benevolent head and forced to share in the family's reduced fortunes.

The second metaphor discussed by McCrate comes from Robert Pollak. Pollak introduced the concept of a merger, describing marriage as a process that created a single entity out of two individuals. He proposed this model to resolve the problem of transaction costs embedded in a contractual relationship, the terms of which are not fully knowable in advance. The effort required to negotiate every last detail of daily life in an intimate relationship would be extreme. In marriage, as in merger, two entities become one, with legal standing and specified rights and responsibilities.

As McCrate points out, both the trade and merger models obscure inequalities among family members. The Rotten Kid, who, as Becker himself points out, represents any member of the household other than the head, will only bow to the dictates of the altruist if their relationship is unequal. The position of the head is inherently one of greater power, but power goes unacknowledged by the theory. In Pollak's merger framework, no decision process for resolving internal conflict is obvious. The model offers no clear principle of operation for internal market transactions within marriage.

McCrate's own metaphor compares marriage to employment as it is understood in the Marxist tradition—because Marxism admits the existence of asymmetries of power, particularly as those asymmetries are expressed in the context of dependency. Just as workers are dependent on capitalists for work and income, women traditionally have been dependent on men for income.

Kabeer notes that discussions about the allocation of women's labor have a circular quality. Some analysts propose that families invest less in women's human capital (i.e., skills valued in labor markets) because women's prospective earnings are less than men's. Others propose that women's labor market prospects are poor because their human capital is underdeveloped (Kabeer 1994, 135, 1). This vicious circle still propels many women along a frustrating path of underdeveloped human potential, but it is beginning to break up. Although women's labor market earnings have not caught up to men's earnings, the gap is shrinking. More women than men in the United States are enrolled in college and 55 percent of bachelor's degrees in 1995 went to women (Bell 1999). As more and more women enter the labor market, their economic independence rises. Many women choose to delay marriage or remain unmarried; and married women achieve better bargaining positions within their households (McCrate 1987).

Bargaining in the Household

Many feminist are interested in the dynamics of collective behavior within the household and have applied new theories from microeconomics to the analysis of family decision processes. Marjorie McElroy spelled out the process of Nash bargaining and its implications both for household formation and intrahousehold allocation[3] (McElroy 1996 and 1997). Nash bargaining can be used for a simultaneous analysis of household formation and intrahousehold allocation because the strength of each party's bargaining position within the family depends on his or her threat point—that is, the point at which he or she would be indifferent between entering or refusing to enter a marriage. This is also the point of decision for remaining in or leaving an existing marriage.

The relative strength of each party influences how resources are allocated within the relationship. The threat point is determined by what McElroy calls extrahousehold environmental parameters. These parameters include factors such as those affecting the possibility of forming other relationships and those related to the potential for economic independence of each party (for example, employability or wealth of the family of origin). Because the threat point pivots on the existence or nonexistence of the marriage, its use is credible only for major decisions with long-run consequences. Pierre-Andre Chiappori proposes that bargaining positions evolve into stable "sharing rules," which households use to allocate resources (Chiappori 1997).

McElroy also develops an analysis of marriage markets that match husbands and wives. The process is related to bargaining in that external resources influence each party's strength within the relationship and his or her command over the resources shared within the relationship (McElroy 1997). Both bargaining and marriage market models have implications for economic and social policy. If resources that men and women bring into a marriage are not completely pooled, as is assumed by the Becker model, then policies targeted to men or to women will influence bargaining positions within households. To give one example, welfare benefits for which only unmarried women are eligible may still improve the position of married women because they need only stay in a marriage if their access to resources within it is greater than they would have on welfare (McElroy 1997).

Nancy Folbre takes up the argument that Nash bargaining depends heavily on threats of withdrawal from the relationship. Bargaining power depends on the strength of the fallback position. If one person (usually the woman) is economically dependent on the other and unable to survive outside the relationship, that person will be less able to achieve goals within the relationship. Folbre argues that marriage cannot survive under constant threat of dissolution, that marriages mingle self-interest and altruism, and that there must be institutions and norms supporting the relationship and influencing the family decision process. It is in women's interest to form coalitions to participate in shaping these institutions and norms.

Pooled and Non-Pooled Income

Although she does not couch her discussion in terms of a fallback bargaining position, **Martha Roldan** presents the results of a qualitative study of women workers in Mexico City that shows that their ability to achieve their own goals vis à vis their husbands improves as their access to income improves. Her research also points to another question that is exposed once the black box of the household is opened up—the extent to which husbands and wives pool their income.

The Becker model assumes that income is fully pooled and available as a common resource for all family members. However, research into actual behavior indicates that this is not always the case. Eleanor Fapohunda argues that income-pooling patterns actually form a continuum. At one end is the complete pooling implied in Becker's theory. At the other end, "pooling may entail merging limited economic resources for specific expenditures within a limited time frame" (Fapohunda 1988, 145).

Roldan's research further illuminates some of the diversity in pooling arrangements. Most of the husbands in her sample had control over their own income and retained at least some of it for spending on their own needs (clothing, transportation to work, and so on) and social and recreational activities. In some cases, generally among poorer families, husbands and wives pooled income to cover expenses like rent, food, utilities, and children's school and clothing expenses. Women in this group contributed all their earnings to the household pool. In other, generally better off, families, husbands were considered the main breadwinners. They controlled their own income and gave their wives allowances to cover basic expenses like food and rent. The women's earnings went for extras to improve family living standards. However, differences of opinion over what constituted necessities meant that women often bought household and children's items that their husbands would not pay for.

Fapohunda's own research in Nigeria among Yoruba families in Lagos found less evidence of income pooling. Her interviews with wives from three different types of Yoruba families found that men and women tended to divide responsibility for household expenses, with women paying for clothes and personal items for themselves and their children while men paid for rent, consumer durables, and children's school and medical expenses. Few women knew what their husband's earnings were. It is interesting to note that her research included traditional Yoruba families, low-income migrants to the city, and well-to-do families in the modern sector, yet similar patterns were found in all three groups. The implication is that increasing the income of husband or wife will enhance his or her own domain of responsibility, rather than improving family welfare in general (Fapohunda 1988).

Development analysts are interested in these issues because they want to understand how best to target development initiatives. If the family does have a unitary utility function, then it will not matter who in the family receives income from new job opportunities or benefit programs; the whole family will gain. If, however, as the empirical research record seems to indicate, men and women have different preferences, different degrees of altruism, and different levels of strength, then resources will be allocated differently depending on who in the family acquires the income. Using data from a large-scale survey of Brazilian households, **Duncan Thomas** developed an empirical test of the unitary preferences theory. His report is summarized here in Part VI. He rejected the unitary model based on findings that increases in income generated different consumption patterns between men and women. Income that went to women resulted in far larger increases in household expenditures for human capital and leisure, improved nutritional content of food intakes, and better health for children in the family.

Changing Household Composition

More and more, the poor in the United States are women and children. The increase in single-mother families plays a large role in this, but it is not taking place in isolation from other social and economic processes. Women, particularly women with children as Jane Waldfogel points out, are disadvantaged in the labor market (Waldfogel 1997). They earn less than men, to some degree because responsibility for children limits their ability to make an intense commitment to a career. Not only do single mothers earn less because they are women and mothers, they also often bear full financial and parental responsibility for their children. Nancy Folbre and others have called this the pauperization of motherhood (Folbre 1984).

Randy Albelda and Chris Tilly present detailed documentation of the intensification and concentration of poverty among single mothers (Albelda and

Tilly 1997). In 1993 single mothers comprised 4 percent of all adults but 16 percent of poor adults in the United States. As Figure VI.1 shows, a little more than 50 percent of single mothers were poor, compared to just over 10 percent of other women and 10 percent of men. Figure VI.2 shows trends in poverty rates for all children and for children in families headed by women. Poverty rates for children fell steadily from around 27 percent in 1959 to below 15 percent in 1969. After remaining fairly steady in the 1970s, they rose sharply to about 23 percent in 1983 and have stayed over 20 percent for most years since. According to the U.S. Census Bureau, children under 18 in single-mother families were 23 percent of all children in 1997, but 59 percent of poor children.

As shown in Figure VI.3, poverty is an even greater problem among single-mother families who are black or Latino. In 1997, 35 percent of all people living in female-headed families were poor. For whites the proportion was 31 percent and it has been close to 30 percent since 1980. Among Latinos, the proportion is 51 percent and has ranged from 50 to 60 percent since 1973. Although the share of black people in female-headed families who were poor is 42 percent, it has been dropping steadily from 70 percent in 1959.

High and increasing rates of female-headed families among black people are related to worsening economic conditions for black men, particularly young black men. **William Darity and Samuel Myers** link the increasing marginalization of black men to an inability to form stable family units. Young black men were particularly hard hit by deindustrialization in the 1980s, suffering from loss of manufacturing jobs, falling wages, and deteriorating conditions in inner cities. This downward economic spiral has spawned an environment of

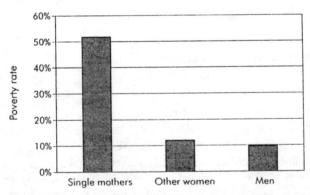

Figure VI.1. The Pauperization of Motherhood: Poverty Rates for Single Mothers, Other Women, and Men, 1993.

Source: Reprint of Figure 2.6, page 29 in Randy Albelda and Chris Tilly, *Glass Ceilings and Bottomless Pits: Women's Work, Women's Poverty.* Boston: South End Press, 1997. Reprinted with permission.

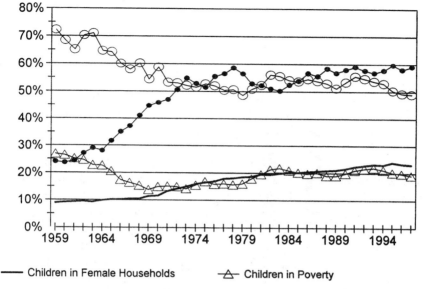

— Children in Female Households   —△— Children in Poverty

—●— Poor Children in Female Households   —⊖— Female-Household Children in Poverty

Figure VI.2. Children in Poverty, 1959–1997

Source: Excerpted from Table 10 in March Current Population Survey, U.S. Bureau of the Census.

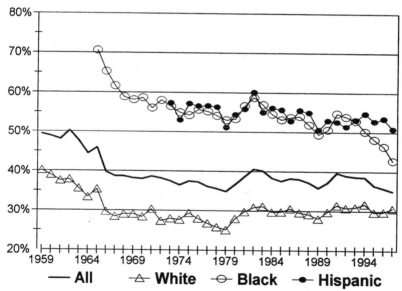

— **All**   —△— **White**   —⊖— **Black**   —●— **Hispanic**

Figure VI.3. Female Headed Families in Poverty by Race and Hispanic Origin, 1959–1997

Source: Excerpted from Table 2 of the Historical Poverty Tables, U.S. Bureau of the Census.

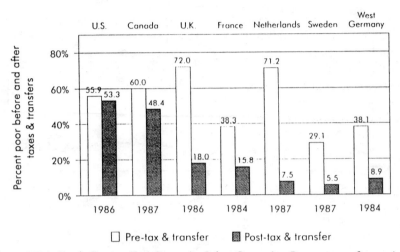

Figure VI.4. Single Parents Fare Better in Other Countries: Percentage of poor single-parent families before and after tax and transfer policies in seven industrialized countries, various years. Poverty line is defined as the median income of nonelder families. *Source:* Reprint of Figure 6.3, page 84 in Randy Albelda and Chris Tilly, *Glass Ceilings and Bottomless Pits: Women's Work, Women's Poverty.* Boston: South End Press, 1997. Reprinted with permission.

violence and involvement with criminal activity that reduces the pool of young black men able to marry and support children.

Urban decay is just one of several signs that the United States is particularly reluctant to come to grips with effective social policy. The tightening labor market of the late 1990s has improved the employment situation for young African-Americans; however, passage of a sweeping welfare reform bill in 1996 weakened the safety net for families. The dynamics of the present economic boom are not well understood. Should it falter, young adults from the inner cities will be among the first to feel the effects.

With respect to the situation of single-mother families, the policy regime in the United States lags far behind many other industrialized countries. Figure VI.4 shows graphically that few poor single-mother families in the United States are brought out of poverty by social welfare policies.[4] The United Kingdom and the Netherlands, which would have much higher rates of poverty among single-mother families than the United States in the absence of policy measures, have much lower poverty rates when the effect of tax and transfer policies are included.

Sweden presents an interesting case. It has the lowest rate of poverty among single-parent families of the seven countries in this graph both before and after welfare policies are accounted for. This is due in part to the high rate of employment among Swedish single mothers. Yet, as **Siv Gustafsson** points out, Sweden has very high rates of unwed motherhood. Her article presents a detailed examination of the Swedish policies that support single mothers. Not only does Sweden provide financial support and child care for mothers and children, but the social and economic climate is more conducive to involvement on the part of the fathers in their children's upbringing. Many of Sweden's social policies do not exclusively apply to single mothers. They are part of a much broader agenda to provide security for families with children and to encourage women to participate in the labor force.

Conclusion

Reducing household inequality requires both internal and external initiatives. It is necessary to redress the power imbalances within the family that are the legacy of a long history of patriarchal social structures. The larger community must recognize, value, and support the dual role of the family as the agent of reproduction of society and as the nurturer of human development.

For decades most discussion around household issues has concerned family and child welfare policy on one hand and the movement of women into the workforce on the other. The context within which these issues are debated is often strident and polarized. Conservatives view any deviation from monogamous heterosexual marriage with a homemaker wife and breadwinner husband as an attack on sacrosanct family values. On the policy front, progressives are fighting a rear guard action against the destruction of the social welfare infrastructure built up in the New Deal of the 1930s and the Great Society of the 1960s.

It may be useful to conclude by looking back to the late nineteenth century, which was also a period of economic ferment. Decades of rapid industrialization and burgeoning immigration put tremendous strains on the traditional family structures of people from many cultures who met in the cauldron of the U.S. melting pot. Feminists of the day were very much engaged in rethinking the nature and role of the family. One of the most outspoken and visionary was Charlotte Perkins Gilman—novelist, essayist, activist, and economic and political thinker.

Gilman's concept of the family was as an institution shaped by men to benefit men and oppressive and stifling for women. "What man has done to the family, speaking broadly, is to change it from an institution for the best service of the child to one modified to his own service, the vehicle of his comfort, power, and pride" (Gilman 1911). As one of her biographers put it, Gilman's mission was to build domestic liberty for women (Allen 1988). Gilman felt very keenly the isolation and drudgery of women in the home. Her goal was to reinvent the way in which domestic work was done, to make it social and capable of generating economic independence for women. She envisioned not only new economic vehicles, but also a new architecture with commercial or communal facilities for house cleaning, cooking, laundry, and child care. Women would share the work in collectives or small businesses in a process that would break down their isolation and confer on them and their work visibility and economic standing.

Gilman was not alone in her ideas. She was part of a vibrant community of intellectuals and activists who hoped to reshape society in a more socially conscious way. Unlike today, when conservatives seem to have captured the field of family values and liberals are on the defensive, in Gilman's day, the family was prominent on the progressive agenda and was a topic that engaged creative and innovative minds. Of course, we can no more recoup the milieu of the turn of the last century than we can reconstruct the New Deal or the Great Society. But in trying to develop institutions that support both economic independence for women and economic security for families of all kinds, we need to look not only at social and economic policy, but also at new vehicles for carrying out household activities.

Notes

1. This theory was developed over several years starting in the 1960s. Becker (1981) is a succinct presentation of the main points of the theory.
2. A distinction is often made between households and families. Households are generally considered to be made up of persons who share living quarters, whether they are related or not. Families are made up of persons related by blood or marriage whether they live together or not. The present discussion is concerned with relationships among people who share economic resources, usually including, but not limited to, housing; and who also share bonds of kinship or marriage (including common-law marriage). So the terms household and family will be used interchangeably.
3. Nash bargaining is a two-party process in which equilibrium occurs when each party reaches its maximum position, given what the other party is doing. The strength of each party is a factor in determining the equilibrium position (Pindyck and Rubinfield 1992).
4. Poverty rates in this graph differ from rates based on U.S. Census official poverty thresholds. The figures here are based on median incomes to ensure comparability across countries. The U.S. Census has developed experimental poverty thresholds more in line with international reporting methods (Garner et al. 1998).

Summary of

Trade, Merger, and Employment: Economic Theory on Marriage

by Elaine McCrate

[Published in *Review of Radical Political Economics* 19, 1 (Spring 1987), 73–89.]

Gary Becker set the stage for analysis of the family as an economic unit with his application of the metaphor of free trade to interactions within the family. In

Becker's view husbands and wives are free and equal parties to marital transactions while the family head makes decisions on behalf of all members. Robert Pollak later introduced the idea of merger to the discussion of what has been termed the New Home Economics. Pollak sees marriage as akin to the unstable form of a bilateral monopoly with no clear framework for resolving disagreements.

The article summarized here critically examines the trade and merger models of the family and proposes a third metaphor—employment as it is understood in Marxian analysis—as an image for the family decision-making process. This framework is more compatible with the efforts of feminist economists to grapple with power and inequality between men and women within the family as well as in the larger society.

Introduction

In recent years the percentage of female-headed households has been growing as a result of an increase in divorce and postponement of marriage. Women's economic independence has been growing as well. To better understand these changes economists have taken an interest in modeling family behavior. Recent models take the form of metaphors, using the economic decision-making behavior of firms as the analytical framework for understanding the economics of the family.

Trade

Becker's trade model has become the standard neoclassical theory of the family. Marriage is a free-trade agreement between two parties who bring different productive capabilities to the table. Because women earn a lower wage in the labor market, marriage is a rational choice that frees men for market work "with women trading household services for a share of men's money incomes." [156] Once the marriage contract is established, the family is assumed to function as a unit with the head acting altruistically to distribute family income among all its members. Unlike contracts in the business world, however, most terms of the marriage contract are unspecified and, in fact, unknowable in advance. To protect the interests of children, Becker asserts, the state imposes a lifelong contract. Yet many couples have no children at present and many never have children at all.

"Consequently, the first problem with the trade metaphor is its lack of correspondence with the institutional structure governing trade between men and women. The second problem . . . is that Becker's attempt to dismiss power relations from the picture founders precisely where he tries to theorize family conflict resolution, in the Rotten Kid Theorem." [157] This theorem holds that a selfish family member (Rotten Kid) may want to increase his or her own income even at the expense of the family's total income, but the selfish one would be foolish to do this because the altruist will reduce the transfer of family income to the Rotten Kid.

The Rotten Kid scenario can be interpreted as a dynamic of inequality and control as well as one of altruism. The Rotten Kid would only respond as the theorem predicts if his or her initial situation were one of inequality vis à vis the altruist; otherwise the transfer would not be sufficient inducement to prevent the selfish behavior. The transfer would also have to be the best alternative, that is the Rotten Kid's options are restricted. Another critic of the theorem notes that the transfer must take place over time or else the Rotten Kid would be able to take the transfer and then do as he or she pleases. The implication is that nonselfish behavior on the part of the Rotten Kid is enforced by delayed gratification.

The analysis can be extended to the relationship between husband and wife. Under the trade motif, the wife depends on transfers from her husband in return for household services, and this transfer is her best option. So, for example, she would not be free to take a distant job that would cause her husband to lose his own more lucrative one. Because men's earnings generally rise for a good part of their work lives while women's are generally flat, women receive the largest transfers late in life. The implication is that compliant behavior will be enforced over a lifetime because women lack access to subsistence on a par with men.

Merger

Pollak's metaphor of merger was developed to overcome the problem of transaction costs inherent in a situation where full information about the terms of the relationship is unknowable and thus unnegotiable in advance. Without the ability to specify transactions precisely in advance, spouses must engage in a bilateral bargaining process, the outcome of which is unknown and which may put their relationship in jeopardy. Merger gives both parties the same legal identity. "Each one internalizes the costs and benefits accruing to the other, motivating each one to establish an internal governance structure for the marriage." [159] The merger model acknowledges the possibility of chaotic states with unresolved conflicts, because the invisible hand of the market is inoperative within the merged environment.

Here again the state or church assumes a role in establishing and enforcing the terms of the marriage arrangement, not only on behalf of children, but also in recognition that marriages produce goods other than children. Although this transaction cost approach is better than Becker's thesis, it fails to acknowledge the unequal terms of interaction between husband and wife. Yet history bears witness to innumerable asymmetries in the marriage relationship. For example, under British common law a woman's property and wages belonged to her husband; women until very recently were punished more severely by law and custom for adultery than men were.

Employment: A Marxist-Feminist Approach

Although neoclassical theory does not admit to asymmetries in power within the employment relationship, Marxian theory does. Ownership of the means of production confers to capitalists control over working class access to subsistence. The traditional situation of men and women in marriage is similar: Through their market-based work men gain access to income, but women are dependent on men for their subsistence. "If we focus on the economic dimension of feminine dependence, we quickly observe that 'getting a husband' occupies a position in feminist theory on women's oppression, which is analogous to 'getting a job' in the Marxian theory of capitalism." [160] Two corollaries to women's dependence are the power of men to extract economic benefits from marriage and the undemocratic nature of family decision-making processes.

Common law proclaimed the suspension of a woman's existence and its consolidation with that of her husband for the term of marriage, a status known as coverture. This suspension of existence played out through myriad detailed prohibitions governing women's sexuality, rights to income or property, custody of children, and so forth.

The most extreme aspects of coverture were overturned in the nineteenth century, but just as class relations persist under "free market" conditions, men continued to have privileged access to the means of subsistence. As late as 1958, according to one study of women in U.S. labor markets, only 34 percent of white women and 32 percent of black women worked in capitalist or government work settings (that is, outside of paid or unpaid domestic work). "Twenty-five years later, in contrast, women's personal economic dependence on men had been substantially reduced, contributing to unprecedented instability and contingency of marriage." [162] Women entered the labor force in increasing numbers. Although occupational segregation was high, women began entering some male-dominated jobs. Government transfers to female-headed families increased until the 1970s. Family size fell after the late 1960s, easing the strain on single mothers' income. At the same time, declines in male-dominated sectors in manufacturing reduced the control of men over the means of subsistence. With growing economic independence, "the relative economic attractiveness of marriage to women had diminished, and with it the incentive for women to endure physical, emotional, or economic oppression as wives." Married women also benefited as the option of independence increased their power to bargain within their marriages over the distribution of resources and responsibilities or over exchanges of support and intimacy.

Frederick Engels predicted that such an alteration in the balance of power in families would reduce the need for women to exit or postpone marriage, transforming rather than ending the institution. That women increasingly choose nonmarriage indicates that the transformation is not complete. Some analysts argue that men, not women, are rejecting marriage, and rejecting responsibilities for children as well. It may be that men are exhibiting a refusal to adjust to women's demands.

Summary of

Gender Coalitions: Extrafamily Influences on Intrafamily Inequality

by Nancy Folbre

[Published in *Intrahousehold Resource Allocation in Developing Countries—Models, Methods, and Policy,* eds. Lawrence Haddad, John Hoddinott, and Harold Alderman (Baltimore and London: Johns Hopkins University Press for the International Food Policy Research Institute, 1997), Ch. 16, 263–274.]

Economic analysis has shifted in recent years from treatment of the household as an undifferentiated unit with a single decision-making head, to models that incorporate power, inequality, and bargaining processes between members. However, "there has been remarkably little discussion of *why* certain policies have been biased not only against women but against equality in the household." [263]

Laws, customs, and other institutions of the larger society can support varying degrees of equality in relationships between men and women within the family. These extrafamily institutions are beyond the reach of economic analysis as it is currently conducted. The author recommends an interdisciplinary approach to better comprehend the dimensions of intrafamily allocation. Here she argues that collective action to influence public policy and social norms can play an important part in altering the environment within which family-based decision processes occur.

The focus is on the family rather than the household because legal and cultural rules bind families. In turn, family bonds have economic consequences beyond the situation of shared living quarters (e.g., noncustodial parents providing child support, or adult children contributing to the care of elderly parents).

Fallback Positions and Social Norms

Bargaining models of family decision making do not negate the existence of altruism. However, they introduce the idea that, while family members are concerned about each others' well-being, there are inequalities in the degree to which each member is able to fulfill his or her own interests. "[T]here is likely to be a positive relationship among an individual's power, his or her influence on family decision making, and his or her share of family resources (including leisure). [264]

In Nash bargaining, a well-known economic model for family decision making, power is a matter of "fallback position," that is, the set of options available to a person who decides to leave the family. This fallback position is based on the wealth and/or income a person would derive from the resources and human capital he or she is able to command. While these factors are easily quantifiable, the full dimensions of a person's fallback position are generally neglected in economic models or empirical research.

The strength of the fallback position depends on the circumstances under which the break from the family occurs. For example: "the distribution of the responsibilities and costs of caring for children, the extent of public transfers, and the probability of enjoying a share of another person's income stream through remarriage." [265] These circumstances are shaped by laws, policies, and other institutional factors whose effect depends in large measure on the gender identity of the person in question. One example of "gender-specific environmental parameters" is the practice of awarding custody of children to mothers after divorce coupled with poor enforcement of child support payments from fathers. Gender-specific effects encourage gender coalitions formed to influence laws, policies, and mores.

Nash bargaining implies frequent reference to the fallback position—that is, repeated threats of divorce. Few marriages could survive Nash bargaining for long. "Thus it seems quite reasonable to suggest that social norms play an important role in family allocation, specifying a set of mutual obligations among kin. A number of economists argue that norms are 'gendered' in the sense that they rely on a social construction of masculinity and femininity." [266]

Norms and bargaining position interactively influence negotiated decisions within the family. Traditional norms assign responsibility for children to women and for paid work to men. A man and a woman who want to switch these responsibilities may choose to violate the norms to please themselves. However, if the woman wants to engage in paid work but the man does not want to stay home with the children, the woman may offer concessions in order to be able to take a job. In this case the norm reinforces the bargaining position of the man and undermines the woman. Women may engage in collective action to change the norm while men may try to defend it collectively.

Endogenous Preferences

Neoclassical economic theory claims that preferences are exogenous and makes no attempt to explain how they come about. If the traditional division of labor between men and women is the result of a rational pursuit of preferences, it must be concluded that women prefer work in the home, perhaps having more affection for children than men have or gaining pleasure from children that offsets the cost of caring for them. The theory holds that the head of the family (usually a man) is the most altruistic, making decisions to benefit all.

A number of analysts have begun to reconsider the role of preferences and suggest they are not predetermined. Some women may realize that acceptance of traditional preferences puts them at a disadvantage, so they may raise their daughters to be less altruistic. Another explanation holds that childrearing fosters altruism as a kind of addiction. An addicted person may want to change but finds it difficult. Parents may teach their children to care in hopes that the children will care for them in old age. Men benefit from social norms that promote caring behavior in women. Women would benefit from caring behavior from men. "But if men exercise more power than women over the design of social institutions, they will win the caring game." [268]

Gender Coalitions

Economists generally assume that collective activity suffers from free rider problems and that self-interest is the better foundation for analyzing economic choices. Recently, however, there has been a lot of attention to rent-seeking behavior—that is, attempts to gain unearned revenues. Interest groups may propose a real or metaphorical tax on other groups, obstructing their performance in the marketplace. Men might try to prevent women from competing with them in the labor market. Affirmative action could be considered a form of rent seeking undertaken by women in retaliation.

Other forms of collective action, however, involve nonmarket institutions. The family is one such institution. The state regulates the family to ensure the welfare of dependents. "Historically state governance of family life has provided a powerful excuse for imposing limits on women's participation in markets. However, women have engaged in collective efforts to redefine family rights and responsibilities." [269] In developing countries feminists often struggle over the institution of property rights to enlarge women's rights to own land, control their own earnings, take custody of children, and win child support from their children's fathers.

These efforts impact the distribution of income and the relative balance of power in the family, but they do not affect output or the efficiency of markets. Consequently they hold little interest for most economists. "The design of family and social policy . . . poses the types of ethical and political questions from which most economists fled when they chose their discipline." [270]

The behavior of interest groups may serve some instrumental purpose that is amenable to rational choice economic analysis. But there is no choice about membership in categories like race, gender, or nationality. These categories may produce organizations that act to further the interests of category members, such as the National Organization of Women, but solidarity and informal collective action extend beyond the boundaries of the formal interest group and challenge social norms as well as specific laws and policies. In some cases groups that exist for other purposes, such as religious organizations, develop a gender-related agenda. Fundamentalist factions associated with several religions espouse traditional gender roles, claiming they were ordained by God; yet these roles have a very material impact on intrahousehold allocation.

Ironically, the economics profession ignores the impact of interest groups on economics itself. Intellectual priorities are influenced by the identities, including gender, of those in a position to make decisions over research funds or data collection. "Many well-established economists currently enforce strong taboos against interdisciplinary research, nonquantitative methods, and divergence from traditional neoclassical assumptions, making it difficult to develop alternative approaches to intrafamily inequalities." [270]

Institutionalized Forms of Gender Bias

Institutions that restrict women's role and limit their bargaining position have a long history. For 150 years women have been challenging these institutions with important but uneven results. Struggles over property rights provide examples with economic impacts. Rights to inherit, own, and co-own land are particularly important where wage labor is not common. Rights to custody of children vary. When children contribute to family income, custody is generally awarded to fathers, but when children are costly, mothers get custody. Protection against domestic violence, reproductive rights, education, employment, and control over earnings have all been the focus of women's collective action.

Other public policies—antidiscrimination laws, tax and welfare structure, maternity and child care policies—create incentives or disincentives for employers to hire women. The full gender-specific implications of many laws, policies, social norms, and other institutions are not well understood and deserve further research attention from economists.

Summary of

Renogiating the Marital Contract: Intrahousehold Patterns of Money Allocation and Women's Subordination Among Domestic Outworkers in Mexico City

by Martha Roldan

[Published in *A Home Divided: Women and Income in the Third World*, eds. Daisy Hilse Dwyer, Judith Bruce, and Mead Cain (Stanford, Calif.: Stanford University Press for the Population Council, 1988), 229–247.]

Economic theory treats the household as a unit, subsuming the interests of its members into one decision process in which the household head allocates resources altruistically for the benefit of all. In contrast, feminist theory treats the household as a site of differing, often conflicting, interests with an imbalance of power between men and women.

For the research summarized here fifty-three married women, a subsample of a study of women who do industrial piecework in their homes in Mexico City, were interviewed in detail about their roles as earners and as wives and mothers. Where women were able to contribute a significant share of the household's income, their ability to renegotiate their position in the family improved.

Domestic Outwork

The working-class family faces contradictory pressures. The earning and allocation of money takes place within the context of other processes: production of goods and services for the family's own consumption, emotional and sexual relationships, and in some cases violence or other forms of coercion. Domestic outworkers are invariably women, working at home, caring for children at the same time, and fitting the job around household duties. Many outworkers in this study also worked part-time as maids or took in sewing, laundry, or ironing for additional income.

Outwork is monotonous, insecure labor, requiring few skills and offering poor pay, usually on a piecework basis. "[T]he work is industrial, not artisan, and results from the division of labor associated with the very fragmented labor process that typifies modern production . . . tools, raw materials, and components are provided by 'jobbers' or subcontractors." Local jobbers are often linked through subcontracting chains to supplier networks for multinational firms.

Patterns of Intrahousehold Allocation

Although the earnings of the women interviewed were low, their husbands often held low-waged jobs as well. A woman's income often made a critical difference in meeting her family's needs. Where the husband's income was higher, the wife's earnings allowed the family to enjoy some comforts. These circumstances governed two broad patterns of allocation, the *pool pattern* and the *housekeeping allowance,* among the families in this sample.

Under both allocation patterns, men controlled their own incomes, often withholding information from their wives about weekly earnings, overtime, bonuses, or tips. Men controlled their spending money, on average holding back nearly a fourth of their income for transportation, meals at work, clothing, drinking, and other social activities. Wives accepted their husbands' right to money for personal expenditures; however, they often contested the amount. In a few cases, the amount was decided jointly or set by the wives.

Pooled Income Pattern

In the thirty-three families that used the pool pattern, or common fund, the husband's income was low (minimum wage or less) or his contribution to the household inadequate. Husbands and wives pooled their earnings to cover basic household expenses: rent, food, gas, light, water, children's schooling, and clothes. In some cases, the men put in enough each week to cover their share. In most cases, the men put in part of their share.

Most women preferred to receive the men's share all at once. This reduced begging or quarreling over each expense and ensured that household money would not be spent on drinking, gambling, or other women. However, it also meant that women bore the brunt of making ends meet out of the common pool. "This requires a great deal of ingenuity and is itself a major cause of psychological stress." [234] By the end of the month families often reduced food consumption or borrowed money to meet rent payments.

The women contributed 100 percent of their earnings to the household pool, keeping none for personal expenses. They did this voluntarily, but the "ideology of maternal altruism" exerted a strong pressure for them to consider family needs before their own. Although women managed the household budget, they had little discretion because the pooled income barely covered necessities. Husbands made decisions about occasional large-scale purchases like land, furniture, or appliances.

Housekeeping Allowance Pattern

The twenty families with the housekeeping allowance pattern were better off than families that pooled income. Most men in this group earned two to three times the minimum wage. The husband was the breadwinner, providing for basic needs, while the wife's earnings went for extras—to improve the standard of living or obtain special treats. However, men and women often had different ideas about what constituted a necessity, or its appropriate quality or urgency. Men's opinions usually prevailed, so that women often paid for clothing, linens, utensils, and other things that men did not consider necessary.

Renegotiating Marital Contracts and Income Allocation

Along with factors like age and experience, the contribution made by husband or wife to the family's economic well-being plays an important role in the "process of continuous renegotiation of the terms of interaction and exchange." [238] Most women approached marriage with the expectation that husbands would provide for the family's basic needs while granting a husband's right to keep money for personal spending. Women felt that men should help with household chores (but with little expectation that they would). A few newly married women hoped for affection and companionship, but most women wanted respect, sensitivity, and recognition from their husbands. In return, women expected "that they should provide unpaid domestic service, child care, and sexual faithfulness. . . . Men expect and usually get obedience and deference. But they usually do not feel obligated to attend to their wives' similar demands for respect whether by recognizing and appreciating their contributions as housewives and mothers or through companionship and affection." [239]

Women did outwork to alleviate financial need; most women in the pool group also wanted a measure of autonomy to offset their husbands' dominance. Some husbands objected to their wives working, fearing they might lose face as breadwinners, or that the women would take less care of home and children, or would stop respecting them. Domestic outwork was less of a threat to these men because it was less visible, earnings were low, and the women remained close to their duties at home. Even when low, independent income did enable women to renegotiate some aspects of their marriages, especially if their earnings constituted a large share of the household's income. Three patterns emerged for the pool group and a fourth for the housekeeping allowance families.

When women contributed less than 40 percent to the household pool (nineteen cases), they gained little leverage over the allocation of income or over their husbands' personal spending and disbursement habits. As a rule, husbands also controlled whether their wives could work outside the home, or visit friends or relatives, and decided when to have sex. Husbands generally made decisions about disciplining children, although other issues concerning children—contraception, how many children to have, and how long they stayed in school—were made jointly. Although they might quarrel over specific expenditures, wives respected their husbands as reliable providers and behaved deferentially to encourage continued support for themselves and their children.

A second group of women contributed more than 40 percent to the pool (eleven cases), and their husbands also met their obligations. These women played a significant economic role within the family, which increased their influence over some kinds of decisions, particularly those involving children and whether to work or socialize outside the home. Husbands still decided when to have sex in most cases, controlled their own earnings, and decided how much to contribute to the household pool and how to deliver it. Women respected their husbands, but behaved less submissively and openly expressed opinions. Quarrels over women's assertiveness were common.

Three families established a third pattern. Women earned more than 40 percent of family income, but the men made little or no contribution to the pool. These women lost respect for their husbands and took control over the family budget and other decisions concerning themselves and their children. They quit cooking and doing laundry for their husbands and responded in kind to abuse or violent behavior.

In the higher-income housekeeping allowance group, women had to struggle for permission to work and to retain some control over their earnings. Men felt their breadwinner role was threatened and demanded that their wives uphold their duties in the home if allowed to work. Because wives' earnings went for extras, not necessities, gender asymmetries remained. However, women could make some discretionary purchases without begging their husbands for money.

Conclusion

The trend toward an increase in domestic outwork means an increase in poorly paid, isolated, insecure employment for many women. On the other hand, even though outwork increases their total hours of work, women can remain at home and care for children, reducing conflict over their responsibilities. Men often resist women's struggle for economic autonomy; and quarreling and abuse are frequent. "But no matter what allocational category a woman belongs to, her small yet independent income constitutes a lever to secure a measure of autonomous control and ameliorates the damage to her self-esteem done by economic dependence." [247]

Summary of

Incomes, Expenditures, and Health Outcomes: Evidence on Intrahousehold Resource Allocation

by Duncan Thomas

[Published in *Resource Allocation in Developing Countries: Models, Methods and Policy,* eds. Lawrence Haddad, John Hoddinott, and Harold Alderman (Baltimore and London: Johns Hopkins University Press, 1997, for the International Food Policy Research Institute), Ch. 9, 142–164.]

The author of this article is particularly interested in whether development policies that increase income for families would have different impacts if targeted to male or female heads of households. Traditional economic theory holds that resources are distributed within households in such a way as to maximize the utility of the entire household. According to this theory, it would not matter which household member controlled and allocated resources because each one would operate according to the same principle of maximization.

Critics of this theory suggest that different household members have different preferences, and they engage in various strategies to arrive at decisions about household resources. The article presents an empirical test of the traditional theory using data from a large-scale, detailed survey of households in Brazil. If the allocation of the household budget is sensitive to whether the male or female head of household receives an increase in income, then the traditional model of unitary household decision making should be rejected.

Modeling and Measuring Welfare in the Household

The welfare of a household depends on the satisfaction (utility) each member gains from his or her share of the goods, services, and leisure consumed or produced by the household. Household demand for these things is constrained by the household budget, composed of members' labor and nonlabor income. Demand is likely to depend on such characteristics as age, gender, or education of household members.

The traditional theory of intrahousehold allocation views the household as a black box with a unitary set of preferences. This theory does not attempt to explain how those preferences are determined; rather it assumes that some mechanism exists that aggregates the preferences of individual family members. It may be that all members share the same utility function, that all are perfectly altruistic (i.e., each prefers to fulfill the preferences of others), or that one member makes all economic decisions. A more general model of economic decision making in the household would allow for the possibility that preferences, degree of altruism, and power within the family differ, and that intrahousehold allocation is determined by a collective decision-making process.

One of the difficulties of testing intrahousehold allocation is that earned income (or household production of goods and services) is not an exogenous factor that can be viewed as independent of household demand for goods and services. Income from labor depends on the willingness of household members to reduce their leisure, which is an element of utility. "Intuitively, household members are likely to negotiate over the allocation of resources to goods . . . , home production . . . , *and leisure* . . . , *simultaneously.*" [145] To address this problem, the analysis examines the effects of nonlabor income (from physical and financial assets, pensions, social security, workers compensation, gifts, etc.), and total income (which is instrumented with nonlabor income). Slightly over half of all households report some nonlabor income; it accounts for a quarter of total income.

Data for this analysis came from an urban subset of the *Estudio Nacional da Despesa Familiar* (ENDEF), a survey of household budgets conducted in Brazil in 1974–1975. The urban sample contained 38,799 households. For each household a male and/or female head were identified. Eighteen percent of households were headed by single women and 6 percent by single men. The rest had both male and female heads. Virtually all male heads reported some income, averaging Cr$28,000 per month. Slightly less than half the female heads had some income, averaging Cr$8,700 per month. The survey gathered information on incomes and their sources, and on consumption at a very detailed level. Expenditures on 300 different goods were reported. Interviewers weighed and measured food prepared in the home for a week to determine levels of specific nutrients and measured the height and weight of all household members.

Differences in Consumption

The analysis tested for differences in the impact of income attributed to either the male or female head of household on the share of the budget allocated to specific goods and services. Because income from wage labor is not necessarily independent of the household's decisions about leisure and consumption, the main thrust of the analysis concerned the effect of nonlabor income on household demand.

Additional nonlabor income, whether received by a woman or a man, changes budget shares in the same direction—the percentage spent on food, adult clothing, alcohol, and tobacco goes down, and everything else goes up. But all these effects are larger—often three to five times larger—when the income is received by a woman. The share of the budget spent on investments associated with human capital accumulation (health, education, and household services) increases when both a man's and a woman's income increases, but the increase is well over four times greater for a woman. Similarly, the share of the budget spent on leisure (an aggregate of recreation and ceremonial expenditures for birthdays, weddings, etc.) increases over three times as much when a woman's income increases relative to the income of a man. The budget share of food declines, as would be expected with a rise in income, but to a much greater extent when a woman's income increases. Yet, as discussed below, the nutritional value of food intake improves when a woman's income increases. In only one category, "adult" goods (tobacco, alcohol, and adult clothing) is there little difference between men and women in the effect of income on the budget share. Essentially the same results emerged when the effect of total income (treated as endogenous) was examined.

Differences in Nutrients and Child Anthropometrics

The ENDEF survey reports consumption of particular nutrients and anthropometric measures. The study examines the effect of income on these outcomes. Although the budget share of food declines as income increases for both men and women, expenditures on food increase in absolute terms, and per capita consumption of calories and protein increase. Again, the increase in nutrients is much higher as a woman's income increases in relation to a man's income. In Brazil higher intakes are associated with improved health, so an increase in a woman's income appears to result in better health for members of her household. Two measures of the health of children under eight, height-for-age (a longer-term measure) and weight-for-height (a shorter-term measure), show a similar pattern. Both measures increase more as mother's income rises relative to the effects of father's income.

The study directly addresses the fact that it is difficult to measure income, particularly at the individual level. In an attempt to address this issue, part of the analysis examines differences in the effects of parental income on siblings. In this case, measurement error in parental income would affect siblings in the same way and thus differential effects on sons and daughters will not be biased. If an increase in income to either a mother or a father produces different outcomes for sons or daughters, the unitary allocation model would be rejected.

The results show that an increase in a mother's income improves height-for-age and weight-for-height of both sons and daughters, but the effect on daughters is much greater. An increase in a father's income has a much smaller effect on the health measures for both sons and daughters; in this case the effect is larger for sons. (In fact, the estimated effect of fathers' incomes on daughters' health is not significantly different from zero at conventional significance levels.) The difference-indifference between the effect of maternal-paternal income on sons and daughters is significant. This indicates the unitary model of the household should be rejected. The test is robust to correlations between parental incomes and unobservables that affect child outcomes (including measurement error in income) as long as those correlations are not gender-specific.

To complete the analysis, tests based on the consumption, nutrition, and child anthropometric data were carried out on two subsets of the sample: one containing only intact couples with both male and female heads (75 percent of the total sample); and one in which both male and female heads reported some income (29 percent of the total). The results for intact couples generally reflect the same pattern as the tests described earlier, although the male/female differences are now smaller for many variables. For households where both male and female heads report some income, differences in income effects for men and women tend to be even smaller and most are not statistically significant. That is, only in the case of two-parent, two-income families is the data consistent with the unitary or common preference model of household decisions. However, this test suffers from the problem of endogeneity—the decision to be a two-income household is not independent of other family choices concerning resources.

The study indicates that the unitary model of household decision making proposed by traditional economic theory is not supported by the ENDEF data. Male and female heads of households do not share common preferences in all cases. Increases in women's income are associated with a higher share of the household budget for expenditures on human capital and leisure. The share going to food expenditures declines, but "food composition also changes, with nutrient intakes rising faster as women's income increases." [164] Moreover, indicators of children's health are more responsive to maternal income relative to paternal income.

Summary of

The Marginalization of Black Men: Impact on Family Structure

by William A. Darity, Jr., and Samuel L. Myers, Jr.

[Published in *The Black Underclass: Critical Essays in Race and Unwantedness* (New York and London: Garland Publishing, Inc., 1994), Ch. 7, 143–185.]

The book chapter summarized here jointly analyzes two trends of great concern to analysts of inequality: the marginalization, or unwantedness to society, of black men, and the growth in black female-headed families. The authors compare competing explanations for the increase in female-headed families. A structural explanation incorporates changing socioeconomic circumstances for black men that are likely to have a bearing on the formation of black families. Behavioral models claim that welfare policy offers incentives to single mothers to remain unmarried. The evidence discussed below favors a structural explanation.

The authors develop a chain of association between deteriorating economic circumstances for young black men, increased participation in illegal and violent activity, involvement in the criminal justice system, increased mortality, and a reduction in the numbers of young black men capable of forming and supporting families. They then examine the sensitivity (elasticity) of the incidence of female-headed families to changes in structural and behavioral variables.

Marginalization of Young Black Men

Young black men in the United States are in crisis. "Black males are withdrawing from many productive spheres of the economy: Arrests, increasingly for drug-related crimes, serve to drain off large pools of black males unwanted in the industrial era." [143] High rates of homicide, often by other young black men, further reduce their numbers.

Since the late 1970s, the economic position of young black men has declined rapidly. In 1979, median weekly earnings for black men aged 16 to 24 working year-round full-time were $167, which came to 57 percent of the comparable $291 median for all men. By 1987 the ratio dropped to 49 percent: $214 per week for young black men, compared to $433 for all men. Earnings for young black men with less than a high school education fell off drastically in comparison to white men of similar age and education. In 1970, poorly educated young black men earned $1.11 for every dollar earned by comparable white men. By 1988, these black men earned only 35 cents for every dollar earned by similar white men.

"With legitimate work becoming less and less a viable option for economic survival, crime and illegal entrepreneurial pursuits have become more and more viable alternatives." [146] Falling drug prices and easy access to crack cocaine in the 1980s also drew many young black men into illegal behavior. Drug-related activity led to an upsurge in violence, homicide rates, and imprisonment.

The prison population quadrupled between 1970 and the late 1980s. At the same time, the proportion of blacks in the prison population grew. Arrests for drug-related offenses among blacks rose from 100,000 in 1980 to 350,000 in 1988; from under 6 percent of all arrests in 1980 to over 11 percent in 1988. In comparison, among whites, drug arrests rose from under 6 percent to just over 7 percent.

Homicide rates for young black men remained nearly stable from the 1950s through the early 1980s at around 60 per 100,000 in the 15 to 25 age group.

By 1988, homicides rose to 102 per 100,000 black men aged 15 to 24, accounting for 46 percent of all mortality for this age group. Compared to childhood years (5 to 14), adolescence and young adulthood are dangerous times for young black men, and they became even more dangerous in the late 1980s. From 1970 to 1980, mortality rates for 15- to 24-year olds were about 4.5 times the rate for the younger group. In 1988, the rate for the 15 to 24 age group was 5.3 times the rate for black male children. In general, the age-adjusted death rate for black women is lower and has been dropping much faster than the comparable rate for black men. This trend implies a decrease in the relative supply of men.

Impact on Family Structure

In 1967, 27 percent of black families were headed by a woman; by 1991, the proportion had grown to 46 percent. Structural theorists attribute this to the marginalization of young black men and the increasing gap between mortality rates for black men and black women, trends that diminish black women's prospects for marriage. Behavioral theorists claim that the increase in female-headed families results from perverse incentives furnished by the welfare system, which encourage black women to have children out of wedlock.

It is not easy to compare and evaluate these two explanations. Complex relationships and feedback effects between structural elements are difficult to disentangle. For example, as other researchers have pointed out, the ratio of unmarried men to unmarried women may not be useful for understanding family structure because unemployed men may not be desirable candidates for marriage. (For this reason the authors include only those unmarried men who are employed, looking for work, or in school in the marriageable pool.) Illegal or violent activity may involve men who are not marriageable to begin with. Education has ambiguous effects on marriage prospects because higher education increases the probability that a man will be in the labor force but decreases the probability that he will remain unmarried. However, higher education increases the probability that a black woman will be unmarried.

Despite these difficulties, it is possible to analyze the effect of changes in the condition of marginality, specifically the probability of being murdered or imprisoned, on the ratio of marriageable black men to unmarried black women. The effect of changes in this sex ratio on the structure of the black family can then be evaluated and compared to the effect of changes in welfare benefits.

Elasticity Analyses

Using data from the Current Population Survey (CPS) for March 1976 and March 1985, the authors calculate the Darity-Myers sex ratios of marriageable men to unmarried women. The ratios are generally well below 1.0; the lower the ratio, the worse the prospects for women finding husbands. Overall, changes in the ratio of mortality rates for black men to black women have negligible effects on the Darity-Myers sex ratio; however, for young, less educated, urban blacks, increases in the mortality ratio lead to a sharp drop in the sex ratio.

In earlier research, the authors demonstrated that "Black males are considerably more likely to be out of school, out of the labor force, and not married when imprisonment and homicide rates are high." [164] Their estimate is that the proportion of black men who fall into this "unmarriageable" category rises by 1.4 percent for a 1 percent increase in homicide, and by 0.5 percent for a 1 percent increase in incarceration. Education and age also influence the marginalization process, but this may reflect cohort rather than maturation effects. Older cohorts passed through adolescence and young adulthood in years when homicide and incarceration rates were lower. Less educated black men in today's younger generation "may never survive to become the fathers and heads of families tomorrow." [165]

Behavioral Explanations

Changes in the supply of marriageable men do not translate directly into changes in the proportion of female-headed families. For blacks in 1985, a 1 percent drop in the Darity-Myers sex ratio was associated with a 0.16 percent increase in female-headed families among 20-year-olds; the same effect was only 0.05 percent among 30-year-olds. As a result of a complex series of calculations like these, the estimated aggregate effect of a 1 percent increase in the homicide rate is a 0.09 percent increase in female-headed families; the corresponding effect for incarceration is 0.03 percent.

These estimates, arising from the structural theory, may finally be compared to the effects of welfare on family structure, the foundation of the behavioral theory. There is a positive relationship between welfare payments and female-headed families, as hypothesized by the behavioralists. In various specifications of this relationship, a 1 percent increase in welfare payments causes an increase in female-headed families of 0.10 percent or less (again for blacks in 1985)—coincidentally similar to the effect of homicides.

Unlike the structural factors, however, the effect of welfare payments points in the wrong direction. From 1976 to 1985, the real value of welfare payments to a typical black family fell by 25 percent; this should have caused a drop in female-headed households of more than 2 percent, according to the behavioral theory. In fact, the proportion of black families that were female-headed rose by more than 20 percent (from 36 percent to 44 percent).

Clearly other circumstances overwhelmed the welfare effect. By raising the probability that a black man will be a poor marriage prospect, higher homicide and incarceration rates influence the incidence of female-headed families. The overall impacts are small, but become much larger when young black families— "the source of future parenting in the black community" [171]—are considered. There is grave possibility of devastating consequences for the black community.

Summary of

Single Mothers in Sweden: Why Is Poverty Less Severe?

by Siv Gustafsson

[Published in *Poverty, Inequality and the Future of Social Policy: Western States in the New World Order,* eds. Katherine McFate, Roger Lawson, and William Julius Wilson (New York: Russell Sage Foundation, 1996), Ch. 8, 291–323.]

In the United States poverty is increasingly concentrated among single-mother families. In 1986, 53 percent of families with only one parent present were poor. Yet in Sweden less than 6 percent of single-parent families were in poverty. This striking difference results from state policies that promote equality between men and women and support their endeavors in the workplace and in the home. The Swedish model emphasizes labor force participation, but rather than generating American-style forced workfare, Swedish policy promotes full employment, reduces inequality, and supplements earnings with services and benefits. Policies directed specifically at single mothers are less important than policies that extend to all families and support women's labor force participation under diverse family circumstances.

Swedish family policy has evolved over decades and continues to evolve in response to changes in social values, the political balance of power, and the macroeconomic environment. Much of the framework was established during the Depression when low birthrates were a concern. It reflects pro-natalist policies proposed by the great Swedish economists and sociologists Alva and Gunnar Myrdal.

Trends in Family Composition

Sweden has long been relatively tolerant of women who became pregnant before marriage. But even for Sweden the recent rise in births to unwed mothers from 12.6 percent of all births in 1963 to 48 percent in 1986 is startling. This phenomenon does not indicate similarly high levels of single parenting, but rather reflects the fact that Swedish couples frequently cohabit without or before marrying. It is not unusual to get married after having had a child, a fact reflected in statistically higher median age at first marriage than at first birth. Tax law changes in the last few decades have removed economic incentives for marriage. Illegitimacy is not stigmatized and has no legal bearing on inheritance. Joint custody of children is now the default outcome of divorce and separation. The incidence of teenage pregnancy is low due to extensive use of contraceptives.

Most Swedish children live with both parents, but the percentage dropped from 88.6 percent in 1975 to 85.9 percent in 1985. Of these, 14.4 percent lived with unmarried cohabiting parents in 1985, up from 7.6 percent in 1975. The proportion of children living with single parents grew slightly over the same decade: from 1.3 percent to 1.9 percent with single fathers; 10.1 percent to 12.2 percent with single mothers. (In the United States the percentage of children living with single mothers rose from 11 percent in 1970 to 21 percent in 1988.)

Labor Market and Workplace Policies

Earnings are important for most women in Sweden, including single mothers. Although many women work part-time, single mothers are more likely to work longer hours than married mothers; 48 percent of single mothers work full-time. Occupational segregation remains high, with women concentrated in lower paying jobs; but the gender wage gap in Sweden is not as great as in other industrialized countries. Nearly 60 percent of women work in the public sector where wage inequality is less than in the private sector. In the 1960s and 1970s, wage differences across occupations narrowed. They have widened since then, but wages for men and women still remain more equal in Sweden than elsewhere.

At present, conflicting trends mean that women's prospects in the labor market are uncertain. Global economic pressures are eroding the solidaristic political values that tended to reduce wage differences throughout Swedish society. Since women are concentrated at the low end of the wage structure, they will be disadvantaged if wages are set solely in response to market pressure without intervention from government or other institutions. On the other hand, women are increasing their education levels and moving into the ranks of higher paying jobs.

Generous paid and unpaid family leave policies for both men and women enable parents in Sweden to enjoy job security, income stability, and time with young children. The amount of time allowed for family leave stood at 15 months in 1992—12 months at approximately 90 percent of full pay plus 3 months at a daily rate. (Nonworkers receive a lower rate.) Family leave can be used by either parent until a child is eight years old and can be configured so that a parent saves blocks of time for children's medical emergencies or works shorter hours while young children are in school.

Tax and Transfer Policies

Government support for single mothers and their children is based on benefits available to all families, or to all low-income families. All parents receive an allowance for each child aged 16 or younger. Many also receive means-tested benefits, the most common being housing subsidies. Single mothers, and in recent years single fathers, also receive assistance from the government in collecting child support from noncustodial parents. The system is very complex and subject to frequent revision. It involves formulas for determining each parent's fair share of the child's expenses based on parents' incomes, how much time the child spends with each parent, stepfamily arrangements, and so forth. If necessary, the government will advance child support money due from a nonpaying parent and attempt to collect the money later.

The tax structure contains no deduction for dependents. The tax structure once taxed husbands and wives jointly and penalized working wives. Today's system taxes men and women separately at a rate nearly proportional to their income. Recently progressivity of taxation has been increasing.

Child Care

The Swedish government subsidizes child care heavily. Nearly half of all children under six were either enrolled in state-funded child care centers or in the care of host mothers who are paid by the local governments. Fees from parents cover only 10 percent of total day care costs. Private child care is expensive and not tax deductible, so most families, including 84 percent of single mothers, who use child care place their children in publicly supported situations. Forty-two percent of children under six have one parent at home on family leave (some attend part-day kindergarten).

Rated on a continuum of public to private responsibility, "Great Britain and the United States come closest to 'maximum private responsibility for children,' and Sweden comes closest to maximum public responsibility." [312] To some extent this commitment to children on the part of the state traces its origins to discussions of family policy in the 1930s. The Myrdals promoted the idea that children would be better off in the care of professionally trained caregivers than with untrained mothers. Child care under this regime was seen as a kind of poverty relief. The expansion of the publicly subsidized child care system came about only in the 1970s and 1980s in response to the demands of working mothers.

School hours in Sweden are also compatible with working mothers' hours, particularly if one parent takes advantage of the opportunity to use family leave to shorten the work day. Children remain in school until late in the afternoon, eating lunch there and performing most of their work at school. In comparison, German children get out of school around one o'clock in the afternoon, eat lunch at home, and require help with a heavy load of homework.

Conclusion

During the 1980s and 1990s, economic insecurity in the global economy has increased. Although Sweden has not been immune to these pressures, welfare policies and institutions buffered the Swedish people from the worst global trends and protected single mothers and their children from the poverty that too often faces single mothers in the United States. It is not clear if and to what extent these publicly furnished supports will persist; however, the fact that most benefits extend to all families improves the chances for widespread political support.

In the 1990s Sweden has experienced the worst economic recession since the 1930s with, in some years, double-digit unemployment figures. The family support system, under heavy attack because of its heavy load on public finances, has survived with modification. The 12 months paid parental leaves are now compensated at 75 percent of foregone income rather than the previous 90 percent.

PART VII

Technology, Skills, and Education

Overview Essay

by Laurie Dougherty

One aspect of inequality that has received a great deal of attention is the large gap in wages between people with higher education and those with a high school diploma or less. Neoclassical economists attribute this to the dynamics of human capital, claiming that better educated workers are more productive and, therefore, better rewarded in the labor market. In trying to understand the upsurge of inequality in wages in the 1980s, many analysts turned to the burgeoning use of computer technology in the workplace as a contributing factor. An argument widely accepted among labor economists claims that technological change is skill-biased—that is, it raises the demand for workers with sophisticated skills and/or reduces the demand for less-skilled workers.

Other analysts challenge the idea that the relationship between technology and inequality is quite so straightforward. However, it is clear that new technologies raise skill levels in some occupations and reduce them in others; reconfigure the distribution of tasks; create new occupations and render others obsolete. The increasing complexity of living and working at the end of the twentieth century means that access to quality education is ever more important, for reasons that go beyond the returns to education that come in the form of higher wages (see Table VII.1).

In Volume 4 of this series, *The Changing Nature of Work,* we examined these changes and their implications for the work experience itself. In this part and essay we will review the arguments for and against skill-biased technical change and its implications for wage inequality (the trade and institutional theories are discussed in detail in other parts of this volume). We will also examine inequality in the education system itself.

Technology and Wage Inequality

A major problem for economists with respect to the wage trends of the past two decades is that the premium paid for skills in the labor market has grown at the same time that the supply of more highly skilled workers has grown. This pattern

Table VII.1. Table Educational Attainment by Median Earnings and Gender, 1997

	Male		Female	
	No. with Earnings (000s)	Median Annual Earnings	No. with Earnings (000s)	Median Annual Earnings
Total				
Less than 9th grade	50,802	$35,715	34,611	$25,823
9th to 12th grade (no diploma)	1,914	$18,551	791	$13,447
High school graduate (includes GED)	3,548	$24,241	1,761	$15,907
Some college, no degree	16,220	$30,655	11,470	$21,291
Associate Degree	9,169	$35,087	6,628	$25,035
Bachelor's degree or more	15,864	$51,198	10,425	$36,346
—Bachelor's degree	10,349	$46,255	7,712	$33,432
—Master's degree	3,228	$57,553	2,447	$41,856
—Professional degree	1,321	$78,290	488	$54,528
—Doctorate degree	966	$70,706	318	$50,758

Source: Excerpted from Historical Income Tables, p. 21 in March Current Population Survey, U.S. Bureau of Census.

emerges regardless of the empirical measure of skill that is used. Some analysts use education levels as a proxy for skills, while others use the broad occupation categories of production versus nonproduction (or blue-collar versus white-collar workers). By any of these measures, the share of highly skilled workers in employment and in the total wage bill has increased (Berman, Bound, and Griliches 1994). Given this apparent anomaly, many researchers infer that the demand for higher-skilled workers must have grown enough to offset the difference in cost between high- and low-skilled workers (Acemoglu 1998).

Economic logic predicts that, in the absence of intervening factors, an increase in the supply of something should reduce its price: In this case more skilled workers should lead to a lower wage or salary paid to those with skills. Alternatively, faced with a high-priced workforce, employers would be likely to substitute lower-priced (i.e., lower-skilled) workers to reduce labor costs (Berman, Bound, and Griliches 1994; Mishel and Bernstein 1999). In line with this prediction, a surge in college-educated workers in the 1970s was in fact accompanied by a reduction in the premium paid to college graduates. The experience of the 1980s, when both the supply and the wage premium of college graduates increased at the same time, is not as easy to explain. It is the events of the 1980s that gave rise to the hypothesis of a shift in demand for skilled labor.

Looking inside the pay gap between higher- and lower-skilled workers we find that real wages for poorly educated workers have fallen sharply since the 1970s, while real wages for most other workers have fallen somewhat or remained stagnant. Only women with a college degree or better and men with advanced degrees have experienced real-wage gains. Overall, only the top 10 percent of the wage distribution experienced substantial real-wage gains from 1979 to 1997 (Mishel and Bernstein 1999). While mainstream economists generally focus on the relatively higher demand for higher-skilled workers to explain increased inequality, their critics emphasize the deterioration of wages for the less-skilled. The former approach leads to investigation of labor demand factors such as technological change or international trade as likely explanations for inequality; the latter leads to analysis of the collapse of wage-setting institutions.

The Mainstream Argument for Skill-Biased Technical Change

Anne Bartel and Frank Lichtenberg claim that highly skilled workers are best able to use new technologies; therefore workplaces with high proportions of such workers will readily adopt new tools and methods (Bartel and Lichtenberg 1987). Making a similar argument but taking the question of causality one step further, Daron Acemoglu argues that the increase in supply of college-educated workers after World War II, which accelerated after 1970, induced technological change in a manner that is complementary to highly skilled workers. Technological change need not always be compatible with the skills of the workforce. In fact, as Acemoglu points out, technological change has often replaced rather than complemented workers' skills. He describes the relationship between skills and technology in the postwar era as the "directed technology effect."

Eli Berman, John Bound, and Zvi Griliches demonstrate that the share of nonproduction workers in manufacturing employment has increased over time, and this increase accelerated in the 1980s. "Between 1979 and 1989 the employment of production workers in U.S. manufacturing dropped by *15 percent* from 14.5 million to 12.3 million, while nonproduction employment rose 3 percent, from 6.5 to 6.7 million." (Berman, Bound, and Griliches 1994, 368) Over two-thirds of this shift in employment occurred within finely defined manufacturing industries. Between-industry changes can be attributed largely to the effects of trade and government procurement for defense purposes, but these factors cannot account for within-industry changes in employment share. The authors attribute the residual within-industry shifts to technological change that reduces the need for production (versus nonproduction) labor. They find this change to be correlated with changes in technology inputs, specifically investment in computers and research and development (R&D) expenditures. They corroborated their econometric results with reference to case studies of a number of industries undertaken by the Bureau of Labor Statistics (BLS). These case studies indicate widespread displacement of production workers by new technologies.

David Autor, Lawrence Katz, and Alan Krueger extended the scope of this analysis to a broader set of industries, using data that cover both use of computers by individual workers and industry-level investment and technology adoption. They also extended the time frame of their study back to the 1940s to capture the full range of experience with computers in business applications.

Their findings (summarized in *The Changing Nature of Work*) indicate that relative demand for college-educated workers has increased over the past five decades, accelerating in the 1980s, and slowing somewhat in the early 1990s. "[W]ithin-industry skill upgrading increased from the 1960s to the 1970s throughout the economy, accelerated further in manufacturing from the 1970s to the 1980s, and remained high from 1990 to 1996." (Autor, Katz, and Krueger 1998, 1203) Autor et al. included several measures of technology, such as Current Population Survey (CPS) data on use of a keyboard at work; National Income and Product Accounts (NIPA) data on overall capital investment and high-tech capital intensity; and National Science Foundation data on R&D. They conclude that skill upgrading is greatest in those industries where computer use is heaviest (Autor, Katz, and Kreuger 1998, 1997; Kreuger 1993).[1]

Challenges to Mainstream Theory: The Role of Wage-Setting Institutions

Trade and labor economists use different methodologies, and in earlier rounds of analysis often came to mutually exclusive conclusions, that either trade or technology or institutions account for a significant portion of the polarization of wages. Analysts who favor trade or technology arguments tended to eliminate the alternate theory as a viable explanation, even though both theories leave most of the increase in inequality unexplained. However, this dichotomy may be softening as researchers realize that their favored methods can only account for some part of the recent increase in inequality. Autor, Katz, and Krueger point out that their findings of skill-biased technological change leave room for fluctuations in labor supply, globalization, and institutional arrangements (Autor, Katz, and Krueger 1998). Berman, Bound, and Griliches point out that the share of manufacturing employment fell in the economy as a whole. This would tend to reduce the share of production workers overall, since they are overrepresented in manufacturing. This effect is more susceptible to influence from international trade than the changes within manufacturing that they studied in detail.

Stephen Machin, Annette Ryan, and John Van Reenan find evidence for skill-biased technological change in a shift toward higher proportions of skilled workers within similar industries in four countries (U.S., U.K., Denmark, Sweden). However, they also find that wages polarized most in the United Kingdom and the United States, where institutional protections for workers are weak. Machin and Van Reenan confirmed these conclusions in a 1998 study of seven OECD countries and offer evidence for skepticism about trade as an explanation. Although they do not investigate labor market institutions, Machin and Van Reenan suggest that such an investigation would provide useful insights into the phenomenon they have described: similar within-industry indications of skill-biased technological change across several developed countries, but dissimilar wage patterns.

David Howell did undertake an analysis of changes in wage-setting institutions in the United States. He argues that the changing institutional environment in the 1970s and 1980s led to the collapse of wages for the low-wage labor market. While he gives some credence to the role of globalization (trade and immigration) in increasing competitive pressure on low-wage workers, he is critical of the skill-biased technological change hypothesis. Among other things he points out that the major shift in composition from low- to high-skilled labor occurred in the early 1980s before the upsurge in computer investment.[2]

Howell also points out that in several highly unionized industries with high-paid but low-skilled labor, from the mid-1970s to 1990, the share in employment of less-skilled workers did fall somewhat, but the share of low-wage workers rose dramatically. One among several examples he presents is the automobile industry in which the share of *low-skilled* employment went from 76 percent to 71 percent, but the share of *low-wage* employment went from 17 percent to 40 percent. Both Howell and Machin et al. conclude that trade or technology may exert pressure on labor markets, but the distribution of wages depends on the institutional structure.

Technology in Context

Pinning down the effect of technology on labor markets is difficult because the definition and measurement of relevant variables are not precise. Technology plays a complex role in the economy. For example, the availability of labor-saving technology may make the institutions that protect wages and working conditions either more or less effective. On the other hand, when technology raises productivity, wages can also rise without raising prices for goods and services. But here too, institutional factors determine the distribution of productivity gains.

The role of technology is also complicated by the pervasiveness of recent innovations in transportation and in information and communications technology. On the one hand, this allows multinational corporations to move production to low-wage locations. On the other hand it leads to what Adrian Wood calls defensive innovation—using labor-saving technology in high-wage locations in order to compete with low-wage imports.

Autor et al. have been criticized for concluding that use of computers raises wages, when it may be that computer use is picking up on the influence of other characteristics associated with education or occupation. John DiNardo and Jorn Steffen-Pischke, using a detailed data set of German workers, found that other variables, such as use of pencils or sitting at a desk, also had statistically significant and positive effects on wages. Since they do not believe that use of pencils and chairs lead directly to higher pay, they concluded that a similar analysis does not prove the existence of a causal link between computers and wages. It is equally possible that computers are associated with some as-yet-unobserved skills or that computers were first used in jobs that paid more in the first place. DiNardo and Steffen-Pischke do not deny that computer technology has an impact on the workplace, but claim that the mechanism may be complex and indirect. This debate has been carried out over several years in working papers and in *The Quarterly Journal of Economics*. Two major articles, one from each side of the discussion, were summarized in *The Changing Nature of Work*.

While sticking with their conclusion that computers are implicated in recent increases in wage inequality, Autor et al. also point to research on changes in work organization and a heightened emphasis on customer service as factors raising demand for cognitive skills. Computers play a role in a general restructuring of tools and techniques. "We do not view the spread of computers as simply increasing the demand for computer users and technicians, but more broadly as a part of a technological change that has altered the organization of work and thereby more generally affected the demand for workers with various skills" (Autor, Katz, and Kreuger 1998, 1186). They cite work by other researchers who found information technology associated with higher levels of education and training, greater responsibility, and decentralized decision making.

In *The Changing Nature of Work* we also found much research that emphasized new configurations of skills. Team-based work organization requires that workers learn to perform multiple tasks, participate in decision processes, and negotiate tasks and responsibilities among groups of coworkers. Productivity and quality increases expected with the introduction of new technologies in manufacturing were usually realized only when compatible changes in work organization were undertaken (MacDuffie and Krafcik 1992; Ichniowski, Shaw, and Prennushi 1997). Other researchers have noted an increase in the need for "soft" skills. Soft skills encompass a variety of attributes and attitudes including communications, teamwork, networking, entrepreneurship and managerial potential, motivation, and the ability to learn and to adapt to changing technology and forms of work organization. The demand for these kinds of skills is particularly noticeable in situations where the workers are in contact with, or performing a direct service for, a firm's customers, but is also apparent in factory or office situations in which teamwork is prized and initiative is rewarded (Moss and Tilly 1996).

Education and Inequality

Despite the difficulty in determining exactly the impact of technology on wages, and particularly on our concern in this volume with wage polarization, there is no doubt that new technologies themselves require new skills, or that the diffusion of information and communication technology is changing the way work is done. However, technology is not the only influence on the workplace.

David Howell points out in a summarized article that in many U.S. industries both the share of high-skilled employment and the share of low-waged employment have increased concurrently. This indicates a "hollowing out" of employers who had been in the middle region of skills and wages. At the same time as there has been a proliferation of low-wage, low-skilled jobs, there has also been a clear trend toward a greater share in employment for better-educated workers over the postwar period. This happens when jobs in unionized industries are moved to nonunion plants, or when work is contracted to low-wage suppliers or assigned to lower-wage workers within the parent firm through two-tiered pay schedules or use of part-time or temporary workers.

Many of the problems of low-wage employment can only be addressed through the use of wage-setting institutions such as labor unions, a minimum wage adequate for a decent standard of living, and vehicles to bring wages and benefits for part-time or contingent workers in line (on a prorated basis) with full-time permanent workers. Social welfare benefits provided by the state, such as health care or pensions, can also ease the burden of inequality faced by low-wage workers. However, even if such institutional programs were securely and generously in place, inequalities in the education system would still relegate some workers to more tedious, less rewarding jobs while offering others opportunities for prestige and fulfillment.

In developing countries, education nurtures the skills necessary for using and managing the new technologies that are required for growth (Behrman, Birdsall, and Kaplan 1996). One of the debates surrounding education in the development context concerns the distribution of educational resources. **Ajit Bhalla** cites World Bank research that concludes that widespread basic education is necessary for economic growth. Behrman et al., on the other hand, argue that a highly educated elite is necessary for economic growth. While Bhalla's argument is egalitarian, it is focused on growth and engagement with market-dominated economic forces. A broader discussion would place education in the context, articulated by Amartya Sen, of enlarging the ability of individuals to participate fully in community life as well as achieve economic well-being.

In developed countries, education has been seen as the vehicle for upward mobility. As the skill-biased technological change debate discussed above indicates, that is not always the case. The supply of educated individuals can overshoot market demand, or technology can make certain jobs obsolete, among the well-educated as well as among the less well-educated. Still, there is a high correlation between wages and educational attainment in industrialized countries, and justice requires that the opportunities afforded by higher education be distributed fairly.

Michael Hout, Adrian E. Raftery, and Eleanor O. Bell found, in studies of three countries (Ireland, U.K., and U.S.) that educational stratification tends to persist over long periods of time. Even while more people are achieving each level of attainment, relative positions will be maintained as long as some members of the upper class have not attained the highest educational levels. Among socioeconomic strata, all but the exceptional few will have to wait their turn. While the analysis put forward by Hout et al. was directed toward the persistence of stratification, they also found evidence of an emerging underclass in the United States. Although high school graduation had become almost universal, in recent years there has been an increase in the proportion of high school dropouts, particularly males, among the children of parents who did not themselves graduate from high school. This reverses the trend for later generations to graduate at higher rates than previous generations.

Henry Levin supports the view promulgated by John Dewey that education ought to be the leveling agent that eliminates the effects of disadvantage. To that end, fairness demands that educational resources be distributed according to need. He goes so far as to argue that where discrimination persists in society, those discriminated against will need superior education in order to compete adequately. Levin also argues that inequality in education has social costs in health, welfare, correctional institutions, and lost productivity that far outweigh the costs of providing quality education to all.[3]

Recently several state-level challenges have been made regarding inequalities in the U.S. public school funding. Since public schools in most states (California has been an exception) are operated by local districts and funded mainly from local sources—usually property taxes—funding is highly unequal. These cases, often in the form of lawsuits claiming that local funding is unconstitutional, seek state-level funding to equalize resources across districts. Several have been successful and reform efforts are under way in several states. David Card and Alan Krueger have also investigated questions related to the school funding equity debate. While some critics of funding reform object outright to the redistribution of resources from richer to poorer districts, others question whether increasing resources to school districts can actually improve student performance. Card and Kreuger found evidence that increased resources improve both educational attainment and earnings (Card and Krueger 1996).

These issues concern equity in education for children and have important consequences for their ability to meet the twenty-first century on a level playing field. At the same time rapid changes in technology and work organization mean that many adults are also faced with the need for education and training.

Birgit Mahnkopf addresses this need in a critique of the German system of apprenticeship and training. This system is widely praised for its capacity to train young Germans, particularly young men, with appropriate skills and to integrate them into employment. However, as Mahnkopf points out, the programs are less successful at bringing women into desirable jobs and have not been able to address fully the need for retraining adults with obsolete skills.

Martin Carnoy and Manuel Castells, in an article summarized in *The Changing Nature of Work,* call for a new outlook on employment that incorporates the need for periodic retraining and shifts of career emphasis at various stages of the life cycle. They envision a collaborative effort among businesses, governments, communities, and families to ensure that innovation and flexibility can be accommodated, that skills are available when and where they are needed by the economy, and that people are supported in their efforts to upgrade their skills and during periods of transition.

Conclusion

Equality in access to education and the application of educational resources is an important justice issue in a society where education is heavily rewarded. However, attention needs to be directed toward the context in which those rewards are determined. Many roles in society do not require advanced education. People who fulfill these roles should not be excluded from the benefits of technological progress. There also needs to be more attention to aspects of education that are not solely productivity oriented, such as individual fulfillment and citizenship.

Notes

1. Berman, Bound, and Griliches pointed out, without further analysis, that computerization is more extensive in service industries than in manufacturing (Berman, Bound, and Griliches 1994). Autor, Katz, and Kreuger indicate that, historically, computers affected skill demands in services earlier than in manufacturing.

2. William Greider makes the point in *Secrets of the Temple,* his account of the role of the Federal Reserve Bank in the U.S. economy, that recessions generate employment changes; but following the recession investment does not simply reproduce the old situation but uses new, often labor-saving, technologies. Therefore, technology preserves the drop in demand for less-skilled labor first created by recession. I have seen this at first hand, and also have been told the same thing by the personnel manager of a large company whom I interviewed in conjunction with previous research.

3. In a critique of *The Bell Curve* by Hernstein and Murray, a group of sociologists from the University of California/Berkeley claim that inequalities in education, not deficiencies in intelligence, are responsible for the relatively poorer performance of blacks and other disadvantaged groups on standardized tests (Fischer, Hout, Jankowski, Lucas,

Swidler, and Voss 1996). Their critique is addressed in more depth in Part VIII, but it has relevance here.

Summary of

Institutional Failure and the American Worker: The Collapse of Low-Skill Wages

by David R. Howell

[Published as *Jerome Levy Public Policy Brief* No. 29 (Annandale-on-Hudson, N.Y.: Bard College, 1997).]

One of the most troubling aspects of the surge of inequality since the mid-1970s is the sharp decline in real earnings for less-skilled workers, particularly for men with a high school education or less. Most economists and policy makers attribute the problem to a decline in the demand for low-skill workers, which is seen as a result of technological change and/or international trade. This essay challenges the conventional interpretation. Based on a careful analysis of the timing of labor market changes and the particular groups that were affected, the author argues that changes in management practices and government policies provide a better explanation of the collapse of low-skill wages..

The Collapse and the Standard Explanations

The collapse in the real value of workers' paychecks is a well-known and troubling development in the U.S. labor market. Average real weekly earnings for production and nonsupervisory workers rose steadily after World War II until the 1970s, then fell steadily from 1973 to 1990. The gap between more and less educated workers widened rapidly, particularly among men. In the 1980s, real earnings rose 5 percent for men with college degrees while falling 11 percent for male high school graduates and 20 percent for high school dropouts.

The collapse at the bottom of the earnings ladder is almost universally attributed to downward shifts in the demand for low-skill workers; there is said to be a mismatch between the skills employers demanded and those that workers could supply. The most popular explanation for the skill mismatch is technological change in the workplace, perhaps augmented by growing import competition from low-wage developing countries. Technology and trade are thought to have reduced the demand for low-skill American workers, a pattern apparently consistent with the empirical evidence of skill upgrading, introduction of computer-based workplace technologies, and the growth of imports in the 1980s. The technology-trade explanation is also consistent with simple supply and demand models of the labor market—and it leads directly to the policy conclusion that education and retraining are the only appropriate responses to the wage collapse.

Computerization and the Demand for Skills

Two major empirical studies are often cited to support the "fact" that skill-biased technological change caused a collapse in the demand for low-skill workers (Berman, Bound, and Griliches 1994, and Katz and Murphy 1992). These studies demonstrate that both substantial skill upgrading and computerization of workplaces occurred in the 1980s; they infer that there is a causal connection.

Yet on closer examination, the two great changes of the 1980s were not simultaneous. Investment in computers and related equipment took off only after 1983, increasing from less than $200 per full-time worker in 1982 to more than $600 in 1989 and more than $1000 in manufacturing by 1992. However, these studies present annual employment figures that show that virtually all of the observed skill upgrading had taken place by 1982. For lack of better data, skilled work in manufacturing is often identified with the category of nonproduction workers; the nonproduction worker share of manufacturing employment climbed rapidly in the early 1980s, but was the same in 1983 as in 1989. And it has remained essentially unchanged in the 1990s.

Further analysis by the author confirms the stability of the skill mix in manufacturing after 1983. The ratio of skilled craft workers to unskilled laborers in manufacturing actually dropped slightly from 1983 to 1988, while the ratio of craft workers to semi-skilled workers remained constant. In contrast, in the service sector there was a modest decline in the employment share of low-skill white-collar workers, such as clerical workers, that occurred simultaneously with computerization in the late 1980s. However, the change in shares was not large, and service-sector employment as a whole continued to expand.

Joblessness and Low-Wage Employment Trends

If the 1980s were characterized by a strong "twist" in labor demand toward higher skills, the simple supply and demand model predicts that we should observe growing joblessness among low-skill workers and a declining share of employment in low-skill jobs. Again, the timing is wrong. For the 1970s and 1980s as a whole, there was an increase in unemployment, but the upward trend is visible only through 1982, before computerization became significant. Many measures confirm this pattern: For example, the proportion of black males aged 20 to 24 who were employed fell from 73 percent in 1973 to 54 percent in 1982, but then rose steadily to 64 percent by 1988. If the problem was a skill mismatch, why did joblessness increase so sharply in the decade before new computer technologies were introduced in the workplace, but shows little or no increase when those technologies arrived?

The skill mismatch theory also predicts a decline in the employment share of low-skill and low-wage workers. The author's calculations show that for workers under 40, there was steady decline from 1975 to 1990 in the proportion with a high school degree or less as predicted by the theory. However, the proportion of young workers earning no more than 1.5 times the poverty level actually increased, with the largest jump again occurring in the early 1980s. The same is true for many individual industries. For example, in the auto industry the low-skill employment share declined from 76 percent to 71 percent between 1975 and 1990, but the low-wage share grew from 17 percent to 40 percent.

Further evidence that skill mismatch does not explain the actual patterns of low wages can be found in the much-discussed contraction of the middle of the earnings structure, as corporate downsizing during the 1980s drove many workers into lower-paid jobs, even in boom years. Throughout the 1980s about 20 percent of college graduates were working at jobs that don't normally require a college degree, and that proportion is expected to increase. The proportion of black and Hispanic college graduates with poverty-level wages rose from about 9 percent to 15 percent during the 1980s, casting doubt on the efficacy of education alone as a cure for low earnings.

Other problems have been found with the skill-biased technological change argument. Although some researchers found a statistical link between earnings and computer use at work, others found similar results from using pencils.[1] It is likely that computer users have unobserved, valuable skills or that computers were first introduced in higher paid occupations. Another study found that research and development (a proxy for technological change) is associated with higher wages for college graduates but is unrelated to wages for other groups. Finally, some computer technologies, such as scanning devices used by cashiers, can reduce skill requirements and expand job opportunities for the least skilled.

The Political Economy of the Wage Collapse

An institutionalist framework is needed for an adequate explanation of wage trends in the 1980s. In such a framework, "[d]emand and supply matter, but so do management strategies, worker militance and organization, and perceptions of fairness and community values." [28] Workers and employers bargain over wages, individually or collectively, and the outcome reflects their relative strengths as well as factors like productivity, incentives, and morale.

In the late 1970s, faced with growing competition from the recovering economies in Europe and Japan and from newly industrializing countries, employers became more confrontational in their approach to workers. Some firms took the "high road," investing in the technology and training necessary to create high-performance workplaces. Most, however, appear to have taken the low road, making reduction of labor costs their top priority. They undertook what Douglas Fraser, then president of the United Auto Workers, called a "one-sided class war": downsizing, demanding concessions in wages and benefits, out-sourcing or relocating production to low-wage regions or countries, and increasing part-time and contingent employment.

Political and ideological shifts in the direction of a laissez-faire approach to management strategy and economic policy led to reductions in regulation and a freer hand for market-based economic activity. The financial sector reinforced the focus on cost-cutting and profit-maximizing, putting the short-run interests of stockholders first and workers last. Unions came under attack as management demanded (and usually got) reopening of contracts to freeze or reduce wages, hired permanent replacements for striking workers, and relocated work to nonunion facilities. The real value of the minimum wage fell sharply.

"The consequence of low-road employment policies . . . has been declining real wages for those with the least skills and . . . a job structure that is being transformed from one with a diamond shape (lots of good, relatively low-skilled jobs) to one with an hourglass shape (only the best and worst jobs are expanding)." [36] Since the skill mismatch alone does not explain the wage collapse, education alone cannot solve the problem. Few would, or should, oppose efforts to raise skill levels, but there is a need for public policies that will create better jobs as well as "better" workers. Tax or benefit policies should be designed to raise the after-tax incomes of low-wage workers. All of America's leading international competitors in the developed world have stronger labor market institutions and more active government intervention, suggesting that the declining position of American workers cannot be blamed solely on competition.

Note

1. Studies on both sides of this debate are summarized in our previous volume, *The Changing Nature of Work.*

Summary of

Technology and Changes in Skill Structure: Evidence from an International Panel of Industries

by Stephen Machin, Annette Ryan, and John Van Reenan

[Published in Centre for Economic Policy Research Discussion Paper No. 1434 (London: Centre for Economic Policy Research, 1996), 1–42.]

The growth of inequality in wages in recent years is to some extent associated with changes in the structure of skills. Whether defined by occupation or education, or measured by their share of employment or their share of the total wage, workers with higher skills have become a larger proportion of the economies of industrialized countries. The difference in wages between higher-skilled and lower-skilled workers increased in the United States and even more so in the United Kingdom. In several European countries, unemployment rose, accompanied by employment shifts that adversely affected less-skilled workers. There is a great deal of debate about whether these changes result from the spread of new computer technologies, global trade patterns, or changes in labor market institutions.

This article examines four countries where comparable data are available over a number of years from the 1970s and 1980s: the United States, the United Kingdom, Denmark, and Sweden. The authors find evidence that technological change shifted demand toward higher-skilled workers in each of these countries. However, labor market institutions had an important influence on the extent to which less-skilled workers suffered wage declines or increasing unemployment.

Changes in the Skill Structure of Industries

Several influential studies have claimed that technological change in the United States is a major factor in the polarization of wages. According to this argument, new technologies are skill-biased—that is, operating and managing these technologies requires high levels of skill. Demand for skilled workers increases and their wages rise. Low-skilled workers, on the other hand, are left behind by new technologies. Demand for their labor decreases and their wages fall.

To test the skill-biased technological change argument, this article compares data on changing skill structure in the United States with comparable data from the United Kingdom, Denmark, and Sweden. The data, drawn from merged OECD and UN sources, contain information over a seventeen-year period on wages, production and nonproduction employment, R&D expenditures, value-added investment, and trade for sixteen manufacturing industries in these four countries. (Nonproduction employment is often interpreted as a proxy for skilled labor.) As a check on results from this data set, surveys in the United States and the United Kingdom contain information on education as a measure of skill. The alternate U.S. and U.K. data also allow analysis of all industries, not just manufacturing, and of computer use to substitute for R&D as a measure of technology.

Between 1973 and 1989 the nonproduction shares of both the wage bill and employment in manufacturing rose in all four countries that form the basis of this study. Decomposition of the change in shares between production and nonproduction workers indicates that by far the greatest part of the change in all four countries—for both employment and the wage bill—occurred within rather than between industries. In the United Kingdom, almost 90 percent of the increases in the nonproduction worker share in both employment and the wage bill happened within industries; in the United States and Denmark, over 80 percent of these changes were within industries. In Sweden 73 percent of the change in the wage bill share and 68 percent of the change in the employment share was within industries. A number of researchers highlight within-industry change in skill structure as an indicator of a possible technological cause.

Before incorporating direct measures of technology, however, some methodological problems with the four-country analysis should be noted. First, some analysts consider education to be a more appropriate measure of skill. Second, the large and growing service sector is not included. Third, the industries are highly aggregated, which may account to some extent for the large amount of within-industry change.

The four-country data set was not comprehensive enough to address these issues, however, suitable data for the 1980s from the United States and the United Kingdom produced similar results: The share in employment of workers with low educational attainment (high school or less) fell in all industries as well as in manufacturing. The share of workers with medium (some college) and high education (college graduate) rose. For both aggregated and disaggregated industries, the changes overwhelmingly occurred within rather than between industries. The largest changes occurred in the same industries across all four countries, further indicating the presence of structural change.

Changes in Skill Structure and Technology

A time series model was developed for the four-country data using the ratio of R&D to value added as a measure of technology and production versus nonproduction worker shares as a measure of skill. The results make it clear that higher skills are associated with new technology in all four countries. Similar, but somewhat less decisive results were obtained with the alternate U.S. and U.K. data using education as a measure of skill. Research and development generally has negative effects on the wage and employment shares of the least educated group and positive effects on the most educated; however, in the United Kingdom the effect for the highly educated is not statistically significant.

The United States and the United Kingdom also allow examination of computer use as a technology variable. Neither R&D nor computer use is a perfect measure of technology, but the two measures are highly correlated. Substituting computer use for R&D in the regression analysis also produces evidence of skill-biased technical change.

Implications of Cross-Country Variation

Despite the similarities in the patterns of change in the skill structure of the four countries analyzed earlier, the amount of change in each country that can be explained by the change in technology varies. In Sweden, 83 percent of the increase in the share of the wage bill for higher-skilled workers can be attributed to the R&D effect; in Denmark 39 percent, in the United States 27 percent, and in the United Kingdom 19 percent. "It is interesting that, in the country with the least institutional change (Sweden), technology appears to do a good job at accounting for shifts in the skill structure. By contrast, in the country which has (arguably) experienced the most institutional change (the U.K.) technical change makes the smallest contribution." [22]

The inability of the skill-biased technological change hypothesis to offer a complete explanation for changes in the skill structure raises questions about other possible explanations. Foreign competition is another explanation favored by several researchers who argue that low-skilled workers in industries with increasing trade deficits are at a competitive disadvantage. However, when added to the regression analyses performed for this study, trade effects were insignificant in three countries. There is weak evidence that import intensive industries in Sweden suffered a faster shakeout of low-skilled workers, consistent with evidence that between-industry change was somewhat larger in Sweden than the other three countries. Still, the R&D effects were strong in all countries, even with the addition of trade-related variables.

The other explanation for changes in skill structure, hinted at in the comparison of Sweden and the United Kingdom mentioned above, is institutional change—specifically, changes in union membership. From 1973 to 1989 union density in the United States fell steadily to 15 percent, in the United Kingdom it rose through the late 1970s then fell to 42 percent, and in Denmark it rose through the late 1970s then leveled off at 80 percent; but in Sweden it rose to over 90 percent. Because union coverage in Sweden is almost universal, distinctions across industries cannot be made. For the other three countries, however, analysis of manufacturing industries indicates that "the degree of change in the skill structure is relatively slower where unions have greater influence in wage setting." [26]

It may be that unions are able to achieve a higher skilled/unskilled labor mix than employers prefer, or unionized industries may have better opportunities for training than other industries. Rather than simply serving as a proxy for wage rigidity, unionization seems able to mitigate the effects of skill restructuring for low-skilled workers.

Summary of

The "Skill-oriented" Strategies of German Trade Unions: Their Impact on Efficiency and Equality Objectives

by Birgit Mahnkopf

[Published in *British Journal of Industrial Relations* 30, 1 (March 1992), 61–81.]

Rapid economic changes in industrialized nations have generated rising wage and income inequality in the United States and Great Britain and high unemployment in Western Europe. The exact causes are a matter of much theoretical debate and empirical research. The article summarized here does not attempt to resolve this debate, but rather points to three of the suggested elements—changing skill needs, increased demand for flexible labor, and the declining relevance of unions—which can be linked in the German context. The author proposes that German unions could overcome their "dinosaur" image by adopting a positive strategy toward training and retraining their members for emerging skills. By encouraging adaptation rather than resistance to change, unions could hope to stabilize employment for their members by offering a functionally flexible workforce in response to employer attempts to hire for particular skills on an as-needed basis. Some German unions have begun to develop such a skill-based strategy. This project meshes well with Germany's existing vocational training program for youth. But to be effective it will need to extend to underserved groups of workers and to the retraining needs of older workers.

Industrial Restructuring

"Without a doubt, the flexibilization of labor organization, labor time, labor contracts, wages, etc., stands at the center of efforts to achieve new industrial relations in most of the OECD countries." [62] However, the uncertainty that accompanies such a regime may prove as counterproductive for employers as it is unsettling for their employees. Some firms and unions are coming to the conclusion that upgrading the skills of the workforce is a better strategy. The changing global economy presents unions with two choices. A conservative response would entail vigorous defense of the early postwar industrial regime—its legal protections, division of labor, skill structure, and employment opportunities—and resistance to technological and institutional change. An alternative approach would involve an active modernization policy, which, in turn, presents unions with two options: price orientation or skill orientation.

A union adopting a price orientation would respond to market competition by supporting employers' efficiency goals either by maintaining wage increases below the rate of productivity growth or by agreeing to flexibility in the number of workers employed. This strategy allows firms to pursue short-term profitability at the expense of developing a skilled, stable workforce. The experience of the United Kingdom is instructive. "[D]espite the decisive improvement in the bargaining position of the employers (due to concession bargaining), the increase in labor productivity is far from being overwhelming. . . . Productivity growth based entirely on cuts in labor costs, workers' fears for their jobs, and a decentralization of collective bargaining to firm and enterprise level may well prove to be a transitory phenomenon." [64] British firms view training as an expendable overhead item rather than an investment. As a result Britain lacks skilled workers in such modern occupations as software programming and engineering and even in more traditional occupations like sales and marketing. Britain is a low-quality producer, and its profitable electrical and electronics industries are likely to lose ground as the European marketplace restructures.

A union that adopts a skill orientation will focus on functional flexibility so that its members are in a position to acquire new skills and use them singly or in combination in response to changes in production technology or product demand. Such a union should proactively encourage a post-Taylorist regime that is able to employ a highly skilled workforce while at the same time discouraging price flexibility on the part of employers. The German auto industry offers a case in point. The institutional structure governing employment relations prevented the industry from reducing wages or displacing labor in response to competitive pressures. Instead firms were forced to generate internal flexibility grounded in stable employment and "oriented to a diversified output of quality goods based on skilled but expensive labor." [66]

The German environment is conducive to a skill-based employment strategy. The nation's competitive position relies heavily on high-value-added exports in technology-intensive industries like auto and chemicals. Heavy investment in technology reduces the share of labor costs in total costs while increasing the need for a knowledgeable, reliable workforce. German unions support a skills orientation on the part of employers and have a long tradition of demands for training.

Training Issues in Germany

While the general climate in Germany favors a skill-based employment strategy, most efforts have been focused on the initial training required for all students who do not pursue a university degree. Students spend two-thirds of their time with an employer and one-third at a vocational school. Examinations and certifications are the responsibility of quasi-public organizations. Germany's well-trained youth, once considered by some to be "overtrained," are proving to be an asset in the competitive global economy.

While policies exist to promote training for adult workers, particularly when their jobs are threatened, programs are fragmented and poorly planned. Private sector training programs are unregulated and vary widely in scope and quality, often providing narrow, sector- or firm-specific skills rather than general skill upgrading. Beneficiaries of private training are likely to be male, young, relatively well-educated, and employed by large firms. Women, older workers, and employees of small and medium-sized firms, groups most in need of skills upgrading, are likely to be left out of existing programs.

Unions are beginning to recognize a need to bargain over further training issues to protect older members from the risk of obsolescence. Two cases, one involving a multiemployer agreement in the metal industry, the other a major chemical firm, provide illustrations of steps taken by German unions to bring further training under collective bargaining agreements. The metal industry union, IG Metal, negotiated a multiemployer agreement that requires the companies to consult the works council on training needs. The works council is empowered to represent workers' interests and to furnish alternatives to company proposals when appropriate. Employers bear all costs of training, which takes place on company time. Employees who are not reassigned based on upgraded skills are paid a bonus for several months. Disadvantaged groups are to receive particular attention. The incentive in this agreement is for employers to reorient production to use employees' existing skills. This agreement has not been extended to other regions, possibly because companies "are concerned that unions and works councils could use plant-level training measures to gain access to firms' decision-making processes concerning investment and technology above and beyond their existing legal rights to information and co-determination under German law." [73]

A very different type of agreement was signed between Shell and several large unions. This contract, effective in 1988, "treats *voluntary further training time as an alternative to a reduction of working time* and as opposed to the training programmes [described above]. . . . it helps no employee to a claim for a higher position and higher wages." [73] This agreement has received favorable attention from employer groups throughout the chemical industry. This approach to training favors white-collar and highly skilled technical workers who prefer flexible schedules and advanced training with hopes of promotion. These workers are an increasing share of employment in the industry. The agreement is less compatible with the needs and interests of blue-collar workers who work fixed shifts and would derive no increase in pay from increases in training. Training under this regime takes place outside of work hours.

Employment in Germany is very segregated by gender. Even where men and women do the same work, women may make less. Women in the metal industry, for example, make one-third less than men for doing the same work. A few training programs in stable or expanding sectors have targeted women, but firms that employ large numbers of low-skilled women have not made any effort to upgrade women's skills. Collective agreements, generally negotiated in Germany at a multiemployer level, are needed to extend training to unskilled women. However, discussions of discrimination and the status of women are just beginning within German unions.

Although firms play an active role, the youth training system in Germany is administered on a public basis where it is appropriate to evaluate programs in light of social justice concerns. The question of further training for adult workers, however, is becoming more and more a matter defined by companies. "Thus private firms can determine, on the basis of profitability considerations, which groups of employees will receive additional qualifications and who must obtain them during or outside working hours by way of a 'voluntary' commitment." [77]

The demand for training is likely to be concentrated among a worker elite who pursue educational endeavors to better position themselves economically. This stance, with its expectation of an individual payoff to learning, conflicts with the labor movement's traditional basis in solidarity among workers. Unless there is public intervention on behalf of the unskilled and those whose skills become obsolete, large numbers of workers face exclusion from the formal labor market.

Summary of

Access to Education

by Ajit S. Bhalla

[Published in *Uneven Development in the Third World—A Study of China and India* (New York: St. Martin's Press, Inc., 1995), Ch. 10, 255–290.]

The chapter summarized here compares educational policies and practices in China and India to highlight several contexts in which inequalities manifest themselves in developing countries. Inequalities may be matters of access in that different social or economic classes may have different opportunities to attain or to utilize education. Inequalities may inhere between different school systems in investment made or quality of schooling. Inequalities in education may exist between social or economic classes or between urban and rural areas. Human capital theory holds that education improves skills and labor productivity, potentially reducing inequality. But when access to education or the quality of education differs by class or location, existing inequalities can be reinforced.

Educational Policies

In China educational policy since the Communist Revolution of 1949 has shifted in response to changing objectives of the government. In the first years after the revolution economic development had a high priority. However, political and ideological goals took precedence during the later periods of the Great Leap Forward and the Cultural Revolution. Quality considerations and higher education, looked on as favoring elites and urban residents, took a back seat to the objective of expanding literacy and vocational training in rural areas and developing practical scientific knowledge and methods in agriculture.

After the death of Mao the new leadership emphasized modernization and set out to rebuild the higher education system. The system was in disrepute following the anti-intellectual campaigns during the Cultural Revolution. Both secondary and university-level schools were expanded and improved, and Key Schools were established to prepare students for higher education. At the same time, the government was moving toward a more market-based economy and shifted some education expenditures from the state to students and their families. In the future, some privatization may occur, and foreign universities are exploring the possibility of setting up branches or contracting to offer educational services. These developments may reintroduce Èlitism and urban bias into the system.

In India, in contrast, primary and secondary education lags far behind. Until recently, the country had no concerted effort to address work-oriented primary or secondary education in rural areas. In 1986 a new policy was formulated to improve adult education, to promote equal opportunity for women and for "scheduled" (traditionally low-status) castes and tribes, and to improve both vocational and higher education. Unfortunately this program has yet to make a significant dent in India's education backlog. India has one of the world's highest illiteracy rates, and primary education is not compulsory. "While nearly 40 percent of Indian children fail to learn to read and write, the corresponding figure for China is only 5 percent." [259]

Some elements of India's 1986 plan, such as the model school program, will perpetuate inequalities in the existing system by concentrating resources in a few schools. In 1992, revisions to the National Policy on Education decentralized education planning to improve service delivery and relevance to local conditions. One major goal was to achieve universal primary schooling by 2000. However, proposed privatization of higher education, while releasing more public funds for lower schools, will make higher education less affordable for the poor, especially the backward and scheduled castes/tribes.

Economic Inequalities

Economic inequalities may come from differing abilities to pay for education or from uneven investment in different levels of education or in different regions.

International comparisons show a positive correlation between per capita income and education. Rising incomes lead to more demand for education, and a higher level of educational attainment leads to higher earnings. However, simple correlations of educational attainment with per capita income by province showed a significant effect only for secondary school and college graduates in China and for higher secondary school graduates in India. In India earnings differentials are large and attributed in part to differences in education. In socialist China, earnings differences are much smaller.

Investment in education as a percentage of GNP at 3.4 percent in India and slightly less in China (in the late 1980s), is below the 4 to 5 percent average for developing countries and the over 6 percent average for developed countries. In China, the national government supports urban schools at all levels; however, rural primary schools are supported jointly by the national government and local townships. In poor regions school quality is low. Even in prosperous areas, investment in education may be low if investments in agriculture and industry produce greater returns (although cultural and status considerations also influence demand for education).

World Bank cross-country research as well as research specific to India shows that returns to primary education are much greater than returns to investment in higher education, yet the share of India's educational resources allocated to the primary level declined from the 1950s through the early 1980s. The most recent economic plan (1992–1997) did include a dramatic increase for primary education. Per unit costs for higher education are higher than for primary schooling. But even taking this into account, university enrollments in India are too large in comparison to what the labor market will bear. Education is a status symbol among higher classes. The rural poor, however, are less willing to spend money on education because it offers them little upward mobility and the opportunity cost of foregone wages may be higher than the expected return to education. Education does not offer work skills suitable for rural life and may encourage young people to leave the countryside. A shortage of female teachers may inhibit the education of young girls.

Spatial Inequalities

In rural areas of both China and India schools, especially secondary schools, may be inaccessible to many people. In China tens of thousands of lower quality primary and secondary schools have been closed, aggravating the problem of physical accessibility. In both countries Èlite secondary schools divert resources from more egalitarian initiatives and favor urban rather than rural students. University students in China come mainly from Key Schools rather than ordinary public schools. In India Èlite urban public schools follow the British model and serve wealthy children, while a second tier of government and municipal schools exists for the poor.

India's school enrollment rates rose during the early 1980s. Enrollment rates are lower for scheduled castes and tribes, higher for urban than rural areas, and higher for girls than boys (except among scheduled groups). In China enrollment rates have shown puzzling trends, declining in the early 1980s for primary and lower secondary schools in rural areas and for primary schools in urban areas. It may be that there are greater incentives to keep children home to work in agriculture than to send them to school, since there are few jobs outside agriculture in the countryside and movement to the cities was until recently restricted by the state. Still, urban and rural enrollment rates are more equal in China than in India, reflecting the influence of egalitarian movements under Mao. This equality has eroded somewhat in secondary enrollments. In China enrollment in higher education is very low—less than 5 percent in 1985. The government prefers to send promising students to foreign universities, leaving its own higher educational system undeveloped.

Discrimination

Gender biases with respect to schooling exist in both China and India, particularly among poorer families and lower caste groups in India. Girls are more likely to be kept at home to help with domestic chores. They face fewer opportunities in the labor market, reducing the payoff to their education. When they marry they are attached to their husband's families, so their own parents lose the benefit of educating them.

In China class discrimination is based on distinctions between cadres—that is, communist party members and government officials and bureaucrats—and noncadres. Although cadres, army officers, and their families were only 5 percent of the overall population, students from these families comprised 39 percent of the entering class of Beijing University in 1979. The examination system for entrance into higher education favors students from urban Èlite schools.

During the Maoist regime, efforts to equalize education for minorities in China involved informal schooling and nationalities institutes. Now efforts are directed toward increasing formal educational opportunities for minority groups; however, illiteracy among these groups is still higher than among the Han majority. Quotas and differential admissions standards have been adopted to increase minority enrollment in higher education.

In India similar preferential programs have been instituted for scheduled groups, which were 16 percent of the population in the 1981 census. However, enrollment rates for these groups remain much lower than for other groups. Few go on to higher education because they have little hope for social or economic advancement. The low priority afforded to universal primary education by the Indian government may reflect the continuing influence of the caste system. The disproportionate allocation of resources to Èlite schools and to higher education benefits the upper castes, who may fear that better education of the rural poor might disrupt existing social arrangements. "Thus, inequality in education is a reflection of income inequalities between economic and social classes and between rural and urban people. These two types of inequalities are interdependent and cannot be discussed in isolation." [287]

Summary of

The Economics of Justice in Education

by Henry M. Levin

[Published in *Spheres of Justice in Education (The 1990 American Education Yearbook)*, eds. Deborah A. Verstegen and James Gordon Ward, Ch. 5, 129–147.]

Many economists accept that there is a trade-off between productivity and equity. This trade-off extends to public policy debates about funding for education. The issue is whether or not it is productive to devote society's resources to improving human capital (and therefore life chances) for the disadvantaged. The author of the article summarized here argues that proponents of the productivity-equity trade-off ignore the social costs of inequality. This article develops a model for optimizing educational resources that factors in the costs of inequality.

Introduction

Education has two major roles. On one hand, education prepares the young for productive roles in society, imparting skills, attitudes, and values essential for participating in economic activity. "On the other hand, schools are the major societal institution for addressing inequality, especially among persons born into different social circumstances. We expect schools to play an equalizing role so that differences in the social origins of children are not reproduced in adulthood." [11] One could argue that economic growth is served by investing more in schooling the most advantaged groups, because they will generate the largest return in productivity improvements. This will increase the total wealth of society by a larger amount than a more equitable allocation.

However, equity requires attention to the initial unfairness visited on children in poverty. They often suffer disadvantages in the education provided at home, as well as poor medical care, shelter, and nutrition. Earlier in the twentieth century John Dewey proclaimed the objective of a progressive education to be the correction, not perpetuation, of unfair privilege and unfair deprivation. "The most complete application of this principle is to create an educational system that intervenes in the social system so that there is no systematic relation between a person's social origins or gender and his or her ultimate social attainments." [12] The next section develops a model that represents the tension between maximizing productivity and redressing inequality.

Modeling Economic Justice

Both developing a more productive economy and equalizing access to productive positions within it are essential purposes of education. Schooling should compensate for any deficiencies in human capital of children from disadvantaged socioeconomic circumstances. (Within both advantaged and compensated groups, however, individual differences will exist based on talent, ability, and effort.)

For the purposes of simplicity, the following model is based on two subpopulations, one advantaged and one disadvantaged. For each group, human capital represents investment in nutrition, health, shelter, education, and so on. Initial human capital is, on average, less for the disadvantaged group than for the advantaged group. A condition of equality would seem to exist when the average human capital endowment of the disadvantaged group is the same as that of the advantaged group. However, discrimination may also reduce the rate of return on human capital for the disadvantaged. To achieve real equality of opportunity, compensating for initial human capital deficits will not be enough—the effect of discrimination will need to be offset as well.

Social welfare can be defined as a utility function based on national income and the degree of equality in society. This utility function is defined in such a way that the society strives for equality, but the final outcome depends on the trade-off between income and equality, and the relative costs of increasing income or increasing equality. The production function for national output (income) is a function of the human capital endowment of each group and the stock of physical capital. Government intervenes through its budget allocations, represented in the model by per capita expenditures directed to each group. These expenditures will vary depending on the extent to which the society chooses to equalize human capital endowments for the disadvantaged subpopulation.

With parameter estimates for the variables in this model, potential combinations of income and equality can be determined. In one hypothetical illustration of this model, a clear income-equity trade-off is assumed. Along the production possibilities frontier, a marginal increase in equality involves a decrease in income. This is so because additional human capital resources directed toward the disadvantaged group will increase income less than the same addition to the ad-vantaged group—because the disadvantaged start from a lower base level of human capital. However, the effect of additional resources for either group will be positive, and overall income in society will increase.

Although the social welfare function cannot be measured directly, the existing pattern of investment in education can be used as a guide to society's priorities. Three possible combinations are presented to illustrate different policy choices. A laissez-faire society is based on the market, and the principle role of government is to ensure efficiency. The marginal utility of additional equality is zero. An *egalitarian* society is assumed by many analysts and observers to be the preference in the United States. The marginal utility of additional equality is positive. An *elite* society is one that prefers to enhance the position of the privileged. The marginal utility of additional equality is negative.

Even an egalitarian society may only tend toward reducing inequality by small increments. While there is a positive preference for equality, it may be weak compared to the preference for growth. Depending on the exact specification of the budget and utility functions, the benefits of human capital increases directed toward the disadvantaged may or may not be offset by the utility losses from a reduction in total income. It is counterintuitive, but entirely consistent with this model, that even in an egalitarian society, less per capita will be spent on a disadvantaged group—for example, the black population—than on an advantaged group like the white population. "The answer would seem to be that the preference for greater equality may be great . . . enough to motivate us to try to move toward equality by investing more equitably than in the past, but not strong enough to invest more in absolute terms in the disadvantaged than in the advantaged." [23]

A More Complete Model

The model presented above is compatible with even very slow progress toward equality because it lacks a quality of urgency. The following discussion will bring to bear a final element that can make the model more complete and also impart the necessary urgency to encourage effective policy changes. Redefine national income from a gross to a net income concept by subtracting the costs to society of inequality. Those costs include the criminal justice system, public assistance, health care, and remedial education at higher levels. That is, part of national income is diverted to repair damage done by inadequate investment in education.

When such costs are factored into the model detailed above, they can be reduced by greater investment in human capital. Studies of educational programs targeted at at-risk youth indicate large social benefits, in the range of $6 to $9 for every dollar spent. These educational interventions both contributed to greater national income by enhancing these individuals' productivity and by reduced social costs.

The problem is that the message of these benefits has not been effectively communicated to policy makers. It should be made clear that many segments of society would benefit from educational programs that compensate for disadvantages: businesses, taxpayers, parents, teachers, families. Cities would become more attractive places to live. These constituencies are influential in shaping public policy. They should join forces in a social movement to improve the status of at-risk children and forge a truly egalitarian society.

Summary of

Making the Grade: Educational Stratification in the United States, 1925–1989

by Michael Hout, Adrian E. Raftery, and Eleanor O. Bell

[Published in *Persistent Inequality: Changing Educational Attainment in Thirteen Countries,* eds. Yossi Shavit and Hans-Peter Blossfield (Boulder, Colo.: Westview Press, 1993), Ch. 2, 25–49.]

Education and social stratification are closely linked, but the pattern of the relationship differs from one society and time period to another. In the United States, education is presumed to be integral to the American Dream of upward mobility. Secondary and higher education have expanded much faster than the school-age population, creating more equality in educational attainment by many measures. Yet it is widely believed that educational stratification remains important, perhaps in new forms that escape detection in standard analyses.

The authors of this essay introduce, and apply to U.S. data, a framework that they call "maximally maintained inequality," first developed in their studies of educational stratification in Ireland and Britain. This framework focuses attention on the long-term changes in the patterns of inequality in education, highlighting trends that do not show up in static analyses of experience at a single point in time.

The underlying idea is that existing patterns of inequality will tend to be preserved, regardless of whether educational opportunities are static or expanding. In the former case, the status quo in education will be maintained; in the latter case, higher-status groups will gain preferential access to new levels of education, and lower-status groups will follow only after everyone above them has had the opportunity to move up. This pattern might emerge from the rational choices of parents and students, if privileged groups are primarily interested in maximizing their own families' education, not in the derivative goal of maintaining class differentials.

Trends in American Education

Compared to other developed countries, education in the United States is quite decentralized, with a minimal federal role; most policy decisions are made at the local or state level. Public school districts are typically dependent on local funding sources, which vary widely from one community to the next. About 10 percent of primary and secondary school students attend private schools; the largest subgroup are those operated by the Catholic Church. Higher education is even more varied, spanning the range from two-year community colleges, technical and trade schools to liberal arts colleges and major universities. Despite this institutional diversity, education is compulsory from the ages of 6 to 16, and there are well-established patterns of tracking or ability grouping that establish an educational hierarchy in most schools.

Enrollments increased rapidly in the first half of the twentieth century. Half the male population aged 5 to 19 was in school in 1900; by 1970 the figure had risen to 90 percent. Female enrollment rose at a similar rate. Thus average levels of schooling were rising rapidly as well. The authors' analysis of levels of schooling focuses on transition rates: the probability of finishing a stage of education (primary, secondary, or higher) once it has been started, and the probability of entering the next stage once a lower stage has been completed. They use data on the education of a large sample of working adults over age 25, collected in several years from 1972 to 1989. As in their studies of Ireland and Britain, they distinguish the experience of successive birth cohorts in order to study changes over time. The U.S. data include seven cohorts, those born before 1905 and in each decade from 1905–1914 through 1955–1964—that is, from the end of the baby boom back through their grandparents.

Studies of educational mobility have often relied on data for men only. This study includes data on women as well as men, generally finding that pronounced gender differences in the older cohorts (at any level of social status, men used to go further in school) have been vanishing in the younger groups. In the youngest cohort, born in 1955–1964, men are more likely to have dropped out of high school (that cohort's gender differences are much smaller for other transitions), and women averaged a quarter of a year more education than men.

A simple analysis of the data suggests that, as average educational levels have risen, the apparent effects of social origins have declined. Influences such as mother's education, father's occupational prestige, and farm versus nonfarm origins have a much smaller effect on educational attainment in the most recent cohorts; in contrast, the effect of father's education does not show a clear trend over time. However, a subtler analysis is required to test the authors' hypothesis.

Growth and Inequality: Analysis of Transition Rates

As more and more students advanced to higher educational levels, the earliest transitions became saturated: Across the seven cohorts in the study, the proportion completing primary education grew from 68 percent to 98 percent, while the probability of starting secondary education after finishing the primary grades grew in tandem from 72 percent to 99 percent. The upgrading of students' origins may have contributed to this change: Years of school completed by the average worker's mother rose from 7.7 in the oldest cohort to 12.0 in the youngest.

The "maximally maintained inequality" hypothesis says, roughly speaking, that socioeconomic groups will pass through successive educational transitions in order of their social status. A careful formulation of this model turns out to imply that the influence of socioeconomic background on education is variable over time. When the probability for the whole society of any one transition is close to zero or close to 100 percent, then the measured influence of social class and family background on that transition will be minimal. At intermediate transition levels, in theory reaching a peak at 50 percent transition probability, the measured influence of background should be much greater. Over a long enough interval of time, the influence of any given background variable on a particular transition should therefore rise as the transition becomes moderately common, and then fall again as the transition becomes nearly universal.

The principal empirical result of the study, a regression analysis that estimates the cohort-by-cohort effect of measures of social background on each educational transition, is consistent with the expected pattern in many but not all cases. Other factors have also shaped educational mobility, including the Depression-era decline in educational attainment and the pronounced drop in high school completion rates for those from low-status backgrounds in the latest cohort (who were in high school in the 1970s).

The latter trend is evidence of an emerging educational underclass: "For men whose parents did not attend secondary school (8 percent of the 1955–1964 cohort) [high school] graduation rates are actually below the rates for men from comparable backgrounds born earlier in the century." [43] High school graduation rates also dropped for low-status women, though not as sharply as for men. The rise in high school dropouts could represent educational retrenchment and increased competition for resources, but it seems more likely to be a result of growing urban disorganization. (It is not a reflection of the rise of single-parent families, in this study at least, because the sample is restricted to people who know both of their parents' education—ruling out most of those raised by a single parent.)

Conclusion

The expansion of secondary schools and institutions of higher learning in the United States throughout most of the twentieth century narrowed the gaps between the educational achievements of Americans from different social origins. Nonetheless, the underlying structure of inequality was to a significant extent preserved, in the manner described by the "maximally maintained inequality" hypothesis. Expanding educational resources meant that increasing numbers of students from less-advantaged backgrounds could be accommodated at higher levels of education without directly competing for resources with more advantaged students—who remained at the head of the queue even as everyone moved up. Gender inequality in education, in contrast, appears to have declined markedly; if anything, women are now slightly ahead by some measures.

One surprising result, not predicted by the authors' theoretical framework, was the emergence of an educational underclass, most dramatically among men but affecting women too. Failure to complete high school was transmitted from one generation to the next more strongly than in the past, even in the face of expanding educational opportunities.

PART VIII

Categorical Inequality

Overview Essay

by Laurie Dougherty

Differences between groups of people, such as gender, race, or ethnicity, all too often serve as lines of demarcation for economic inequalities. Part VIII explores a number of issues that these divisions raise for economic theorists, empirical researchers, policy makers, and analysts. A central question across all these domains concerns the extent to which unequal outcomes result from discrimination or from productivity considerations. There is a great deal of evidence, some of which is presented herein, that categorical inequalities persist, but their origins are complex. Both theoretical economists and empiricists attempt to examine the effect of productivity-related characteristics. Even with very careful specifications, unexplained differences remain, and even to the extent that productivity issues can explain outcomes with respect to employment and wages, deeper questions remain about how and why people acquire appropriate skills and experiences in the first place.

These deeper questions are bound up with cultural and historical legacies, two of which we will explore in this essay and in articles summarized in this section: lingering residential segregation by race and occupational segregation by gender. In the case of racial and ethnic minorities, segregation recurs in various guises. Legal segregation in the South and de facto segregation in northern cities were the focus of civil rights movements in the past. Today, residential segregation persists, but it is more and more an economic phenomenon as poor minorities are isolated in decaying inner-city neighborhoods. The spatial dimensions of racial inequality have implications for access to education and jobs as well as for the general quality of urban life.

Women must contend with the legacy of a patriarchal society. The family values so often touted in the mainstream culture of the late twentieth century hold up as a model the nuclear family with a male breadwinner going out to work and a wife at home, keeping house and taking care of husband and children. This image is very much at odds with the experience of many women who are working outside the home. Many women and more and more men are raising children alone. For women, a major source of unequal economic outcomes is occupational segregation rather than residential segregation. Although much progress has been made, the patriarchal legacy has left women as a whole at a disadvantage in the labor market. Traditionally, women were not encouraged to prepare for or enter many lucrative occupations, and even today many fields of endeavor remain strongly populated by and identified with either men or women.

Inequality: Rational Choice or Social Construction?

As the title of Charles Tilly's 1998 book *Durable Inequality* indicates, inequality can be a stubborn phenomenon. In Tilly's view, durable inequalities emerge when people are categorized according to some group-related characteristic, such as race or gender, and one or more of these groups establishes dominance over others. Dominance takes on an economic dimension when those in power control resources, hoarding for themselves and their allies the most desirable assets, occupations, and neighborhoods, as well as benefits and rewards like education, health care, and recreation. Dominance becomes exploitation when the powerful not only possess a disproportionate share of resources and privileges, but also command the work effort of members of less-advantaged groups and the distribution of the value added by their labor (Tilly 1998).

Mainstream economic theory simply wishes away the questions of power, discrimination, and exploitation that concern a historian of liberal bent like Charles Tilly. According to economic orthodoxy, choices that are not based solely on productivity factors lead to failure in a competitive marketplace. An employer, for example, who wishes to hire only from certain racial groups will not always choose the best qualified employees and will eventually fall behind competitors who hire based on qualifications alone. Discrimination should, therefore, diminish under the pressure of economic forces.

Yet there are durable inequalities associated with race, ethnicity, and gender that cannot be wished away. They are the stuff of headlines and policy debates and the day-in and day-out experiences of women and minorities all over the world. A wealth of empirical research testifies to the difficulties the disadvantaged face in catching up to the advantaged. Equality is not an equilibrium state reached by the ineluctable dynamic of clearing markets, but rather a continuous struggle marked by progress, setbacks, and the valiant endeavors of countless people remembered and unremembered by the historical record.

It is striking that Martin Luther King Jr. was not assassinated when he led civil rights marches into the Klan-infested cities of the Deep South, nor when he preached against U.S. involvement in the Vietnam War, but rather when he went to the aid of striking sanitation workers in Memphis. This was to be an opening salvo in his organization's Poor People's Campaign. The image of Martin Luther King Jr. struck down on the balcony of a Memphis hotel—with poor working people at the forefront of his agenda—remains a powerful, tragic symbol of the long, hard struggle for economic equality.

Do inequalities arise or persist because powerful groups discriminate? Trying to answer this question is like peeling an onion, revealing more questions with each layer. Some economists claim that human capital differences—which have widely accepted impacts on productivity—are legitimate determinants of differential outcomes. An educated person, according to this view, brings more and better skills to the labor market and, therefore, will reap greater economic rewards. People who do not choose to further their education face inferior labor market opportunities.

However, human capital choices do not always simply reflect the rational exercise of personal preferences about how to spend one's time. Such choices may themselves be the outcome of durable inequalities in residence, social networks, or socioeconomic status. Those who live in impoverished circumstances often don't know the right people, or can't afford the right schools. What happens, as William Julius Wilson asks, when work disappears with the shifting shocks of economic supply and demand? Do people, who may in fact have invested heavily in their own human capital (education or experience), freely choose their own obsolescence when new techniques or new products demand new skills?

Many women restrict their human capital and labor market choices in order to meet family responsibilities. Do they make this choice with the full and equal liberty attributed to rational Economic Man, or are they trapped by the legacy of a patriarchal ideology? Why don't more men clamor to stay at home cooking, cleaning, and carpooling the kids to soccer?

The deeper one goes into the etiology of economic choices the more it becomes clear that people do not simply and rationally opt for poor circumstances. To be sure there are different preferences; some people are ambitious while others are laid back. However, people need economic resources in order to survive and thrive, and they hope for fair opportunities to meet those needs. When those hopes are frustrated a vicious cycle emerges, in which disadvantage in one domain diminishes options in another. Perhaps peeling an apple is more apt an analogy than an onion, but with a twist—the peel resembles a Moebius strip that curls around, revealing first one aspect, then another, ending on the flip side of its own beginning.

Undeniable Differences

Many economists do recognize the persistence of different outcomes for different demographic groups—the data are widely available—and understand that these differences demand explanations. Figure VIII.1 shows median real-income differences by race, gender, and Hispanic origin in the United States over several decades.[1] Figure VIII.2 presents mean real-income differences. Both income measures show clear and persistent patterns of stratification, with substantial differences between white men and white women and between white men and African-American and Latino men and women. Although the

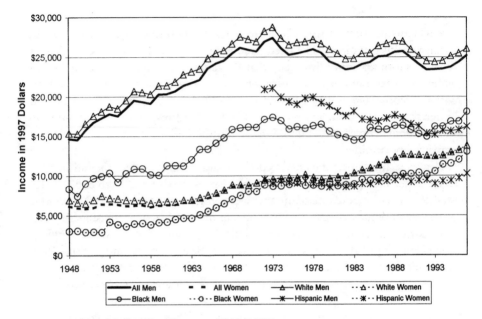

Figure VIII.1. Median Real Income, 1948–1997

Source: Historical Income Tables in March Current Population Survey, U.S. Bureau of the Census

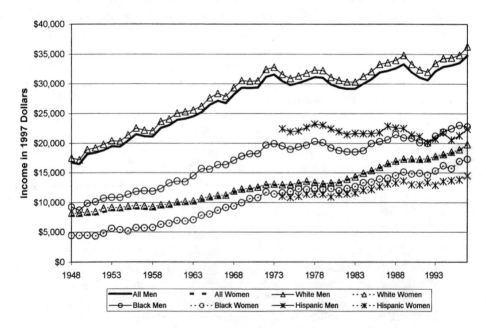

Figure VIII.2. Mean Real Income, 1948–1997

median income of white men has been fairly stagnant since the mid-1970s after rising steadily since World War II, their mean income continues to rise, although more slowly. Only men in the Asian and Pacific Islander category (not shown on the graph because historical data are not available) currently have incomes comparable to white men.

Black men's median incomes dropped between the late 1970s and late 1980s, driven largely by falling wages and high unemployment for black men, particularly young black men, with low education (Bound and Freeman 1992). Black men's incomes have only recently begun to recover. Income for Hispanic men has fallen sharply since the early 1970s.

Although women of all demographic groups have both mean and median incomes below those of men in any group, women have experienced rising mean income since World War II. All women suffered from the general stagnation of the late 1970s, but white women's real median incomes began rising in 1980, well before any other group. Black women's median incomes began rising again in the early 1990s, while the median incomes of Hispanic women have been essentially flat.

Income comes from many sources: wages and salaries, pensions, Social Security, welfare and disability benefits, interest payments, rents, proprietorship, and returns on financial and property assets. However, wages and salaries make up about three-fourths of family income in the United States, more among the middle class (Mishel, Bernstein, and Schmitt 1999). And earnings tell a large part of the story of inequality among various groups of the population. Figure VIII.3 shows median annual earnings for black, white, and Hispanic men and women who worked full time in selected years since 1985. These numbers reveal a slowly diminishing, but still substantial, gap between the earnings of white men and white women, and persistent and substantial gaps between the earnings of white men and other groups.

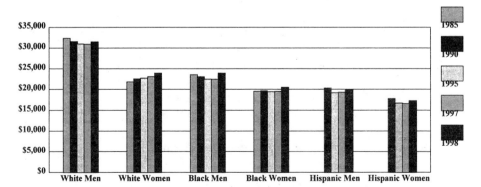

Figure VIII.3. Median Annual Earnings, 1997 Dollars
Source: Statistical Abstract of the United States 1998 and Employment and Earnings (January 1999).

Real wages were falling for most of the 1990s for all groups, except for white women and Asian men and women. Both falling real wages for men and generally rising real wages for women since the 1970s, particularly white women, contributed to the narrowing wage gap between men and women. Although women's wages are lower than men's, the earnings of working women in two-parent families made a large difference in living standards for these families. Yet, the growing numbers of single-mother families are among the most impoverished.

A larger proportion of working white, black, and Hispanic men and Hispanic women earned poverty-level wages or below in 1997 than in 1973. That is, even if working full time all year they would not earn enough on their own to raise a four-person family out of poverty. According to the official poverty measure used in the United States, this translated into an hourly wage of $7.71 in 1997 (in 1996 dollars). The proportions of working white and black women with poverty wages fell from 1973 to 1997, but still remained high. In 1997, 18 percent of white men, 32 percent of white women, 33 percent of black men, 43 percent of black women, 42 percent of Hispanic men, and 53 percent of Hispanic women earned poverty-level wages.

All of the earnings measures discussed so far refer to full-time workers, but women are three times as likely as men to work in part-time jobs. Obviously, fewer hours mean less total income, but part-time workers face a triple whammy because most part-time jobs also pay less per hour and offer fewer benefits or none at all. Women also work in other forms of nonstandard work, for example as temps, at higher rates than men, but are less likely than men to be in relatively lucrative self-employment or independent contractor positions. One-third of women and one-fourth of men work in some form of nonstandard employment. Blacks and Hispanics who work in nonstandard jobs tend to be in the less desirable types.

The *Monthly Labor Review,* published by the Bureau of Labor Statistics, has reported extensively over the last three years on the impact of part-time and contingent work, based on supplementary questions appended to the Current Population Surveys (CPS) for March of 1995 and 1997. Chris Tilly, in *Half a Job: Bad and Good Part-Time Jobs in a Changing Labor Market,* pinpoints the characteristics that make part-time work desirable for some and undesirable for others. When part-time work is offered as an inducement to highly skilled people who have other commitments or preferences for leisure, it is accompanied by good wages, benefits, and working conditions. Some women prefer part-time work in order to make time for family responsibilities; but unless they have highly marketable skills *and* an accommodating employer, they will have to work full time involuntarily, or take an undesirable part-time job, or not work at all (Tilly 1996). This is one of those instances when the economics of rational choice meets the social construction of choice. In most cases, part-time work is engineered to meet employers' demands for flexible scheduling and desires to cut costs, rather than to meet employees' needs. In many cases, women must shape their work life around family obligations because it is less acceptable for men to do so.

These are only a few of the economic inequalities associated with demographic categories. Some others are discussed in other parts of this book; for example, women are more apt to receive welfare payments as a portion of their income, while white households are more likely than black to receive some income from property and financial assets. The evidence is sufficient to indicate that there is much for economics to explain that cannot be wished away.

Race and Space

Given that earnings from work are such an important part of income, earnings and their determinants are a useful starting point for examining categorical inequalities. Neoclassical economists tend to believe that all variation in earnings can be explained by differences in human capital and that human capital differences result from rational choices made by individuals concerning their best options. They attribute unexplained residual differences to random effects or as-yet unmeasured productivity-related elements. Much recent statistical analysis has been devoted to the correct specification of the human capital model. However, even in very carefully specified models, variation remains that is correlated with group characteristics.

Catherine Weinberger undertook an analysis of a unique data set that contained detailed information about college graduates, including the college they attended, their choice of major, and postgraduate work experience. Her study is summarized below. According to human capital theory, men and women, or minorities compared with whites, who had similar educations (e.g., school attended and choice of major) and similar work experience (e.g., occupation and years of experience) would have similar earnings. However, even given the extensive statistical controls available in her data, earnings of black and white women and black men were less than those of white men by 9 percent to 16 percent.

As well as education and experience—the most obvious human capital variables—some studies have pointed to intelligence and culture as candidates for reducing unexplained variation. *The Bell Curve,* by Richard Herrnstein and Charles Murray, stirred up controversy, not only in academic circles, but also in more popular media and policy debates with its claim that innate, inherited intelligence—as measured by standard IQ tests—is the most important determinant of economic destiny. Because African-Americans generally score below whites on standardized tests, *The Bell Curve* led readers to the conclusion "that blacks are not as smart as whites, most likely because the two groups' genes differ . . . and that this distribution explains the inequality among Americans" (Fischer et al. 1996, 11).

Inequality by Design, a compendium of articles by members of the Sociology Department at the University of California, Berkeley, takes on *The Bell Curve* on methodological and factual grounds (Fischer et al. 1996). Their critique argues that Herrnstein and Murray misused their own centerpiece, the Armed Forces Qualifying Test (AFQT), a test that was also administered to respondents in a large longitudinal study—the National Longitudinal Study of Youth (NLSY). Herrnstein and Murray claim the AFQT is a test of general intelligence; however the Berkeley study, drawing on the same longitudinal data, refutes this claim. The AFQT, like many standardized tests, measures acquired knowledge. Scores are influenced by the length and quality of schooling and environmental variables such as parents' socioeconomic standing. William Darity and Samuel Myers, in a summarized article, also take on *The Bell Curve* in an analysis of their own, as well as presenting a review of the critical literature in sociology and economics. Among the critiques found in that literature is the argument by William Rodgers and William Spriggs that the AFQT is a racially biased measure of job-related skills. Scores on different components of the test (such as verbal or math) have different effects on wages for different demographic groups (Rodgers and Spriggs 1996).

Darity and Myers also discuss the cultural explanations of inequality, which hold that some national groups are more successful because of cultural supports—a form of social capital—for successful choices and behaviors. George Borjas is a prominent researcher into such cultural influences. He identifies certain "human capital externalities" that spill over to influence the behavior of members of concentrated ethnic communities. Both positive externalities (such as work ethic) and negative externalities (such as welfare dependency) may intensify within particular groups through proximity and social interaction (Borjas and Sueyoshi 1997, Borjas 1995). The effect of these externalities is a persistence of group-based inequality.

William Darity reviews several studies of cultural or social capital factors and concludes that successful immigrant groups came from relatively higher socioeconomic status origins. Because they tended to be more highly educated and to bring at least some economic resources with them, they were more able to take advantage of opportunities to enter the economic mainstream in the United States. Their mobility was more lateral than upward.

While human capital is an important determinant of earnings, the acquisition of human capital is itself embedded in historical relationships influenced by power, discrimination, and exploitation—and the struggle against them. For African-Americans, both education and work experience are influenced by the history of racial segregation and the recent trend toward spatial concentration of the poor. Sociologist Douglas Massey, in an article summarized in Part V of this volume, discusses the tendency of income groups to concentrate spatially. The current trend is for the poor to become more and more isolated in derelict inner cities while the middle class moves to comfortable suburbs with a prosperous tax base and the wealthy reside in luxurious enclaves with expensive private services to pamper and protect their lifestyle. In other articles, Massey develops in detail the implications of spatial segregation when compounded by de facto racial segregation (Massey 1990, Massey and Eggers 1990).

John Kasarda is another sociologist who has written extensively on the relationship of race and space, particularly with respect to the movement of jobs out of older industrial cities to suburban areas distant from poor neighborhoods and poorly served by public transportation. Kasarda points out that women are even more dependent on public transportation than men, yet in order to work women face formidable transportation challenges. Women's household and family responsibilities require both that they be able to get to and from home quickly and that they be able to undertake "complex journeys to nonwork destinations" to accommodate child care arrangements and household errands (Kasarda 1996, 407).

Spatial concentration of poor and minority communities has also resulted in their greater exposure to sources of pollution, because the urban poor cannot afford to move to the cleaner environment of the suburbs. Thomas Lambert and Christopher Boerner reviewed several studies that lead to the conclusion that polluting private-sector industries and public-sector facilities, like landfills and waste transfer stations, are more likely to be found in poor and/or minority neighborhoods (Lambert and Boerner 1997). Advocates for environmental justice claim that this is evidence of discrimination—that the decision to situate an undesirable facility is motivated by a willingness to cater to privileged members of society at the expense of the disadvantaged.

However, Lambert and Boerner claim that the origin of the problem may be more complex than it appears. They cite research undertaken by Vicki Been in Houston and results of their own research in St. Louis that examine historical patterns of demographic change in neighborhoods containing polluting facilities. These studies found a tendency for such neighborhoods to become poorer after the facilities were built and for the proportion of minorities in these neighborhoods to grow faster than in the general population of the cities in question. In the St. Louis case, the concentration of minorities in a given census tract increased by 29 percent on average from 1970 to 1990, and the poverty rate increased by 10 percent. In census tracts containing the pollution sources included in the study, the concentration of minorities grew by 67 percent and the poverty rate increased 53 percent over the same period. (Lambert and Boerner 1997).

Lambert and Boerner favor an economic solution to what they claim is an economic problem. They advocate compensating victims of pollution through payments to individuals; fees or grants to communities that would lower taxes or provide for offsetting health and social services; or the provision of public amenities like parks. Compensation programs would mean that polluters would bear the costs of their negative impact on the community. **Vicki Been,** on the other hand, raises a number of objections to compensation schemes. Such proposals are morally repugnant to many people because they do not relieve the health risks from proximity to pollution sources while they do provide an escape mechanism for those who can afford to pay for it. Many people object to the commodification of human life, health, and dignity. Been methodically looks at several theories of fairness underlying proposals for improving environmental justice, detailing the pros and cons of each. Relief of the unfair burden of what she calls Locally Undesirable Land Uses (LULUs) in disadvantaged communities requires both a careful development of a conceptual framework of fairness and a thorough understanding of the impact of undesirable facilities on particular communities.

The implications of the spatial segregation of the poor, particularly the concentration of poor African-Americans in the inner city, are at the heart of another highly charged topic: the urban underclass. William Julius Wilson has made the underclass a major theme of several books since the late 1970s, taking particular note of the difference in economic outcomes between the black middle class and the urban poor.

While the proportion of African-Americans in poverty has been declining, the condition of blacks who are poor has deteriorated. Falling unemployment in the latter half of the 1990s has improved the situation somewhat, but inner-city blacks, particularly young black men, have been in crisis for two decades. Deindustrialization in the North and Midwest threw many men with little education and few skills out of unionized jobs. Black men were particularly hard hit since they were overrepresented in the affected industries. Wilson contends that the loss of well-paid industrial employment has had far-reaching effects. Young people were left not only without jobs, but also without positive role models or stable home and community environments.

One of the clearest manifestations of the crisis among young blacks is reflected in rates of incarceration. **Jerome Miller** presents compelling evidence that the heavy involvement of black men with the criminal justice system results in great measure from an accumulation of discriminatory practices. At every stage of the process—arrest, indictment, adjudication, sentencing, parole—black men face more serious consequences than white men with similar criminal behavior. One frequently cited example corroborates Miller's view that the "War on Drugs" has had a discriminatory and devastating impact on black communities. Mandatory prison sentences are set for much smaller amounts of crack cocaine, used more commonly by African-Americans, than for powder cocaine, preferred by whites. In an article summarized in Part VI, William Darity describes the debilitating consequences that incarceration and violent crime have on black family life, leaving fewer young men available to marry and support children.

Gender and Jobs

Rather than spatial segregation, women face occupational segregation. Although women are entering, or increasing their share of, many fields traditionally dominated by men, women are still over or underrepresented in many occupations. Table VIII.1 shows several dozen occupations in which women hold 75 percent or more, or 25 percent or less, of the jobs in the occupation. The table also compares wages for men and women when such information was available. Occupations held largely by women tend to be poorly paid, and women frequently earn less than men even in the same occupation.

Although Table VIII.1 is based on U.S. data, similar patterns exist worldwide. The International Labor Office undertook a detailed and extensive cross-national study that found occupational segregation by gender virtually everywhere in the world (Anker 1998). This report also found that occupations with high concentrations of women tended to be poorly paid. However, in many cases occupations that have been growing rapidly are those that have high concentrations of women, offering women greater opportunities to enter the labor force. Patterns of segregation differ, for example in the Middle East and North Africa, women were concentrated in professional positions (primarily teaching and health care), but cultural restrictions meant that few women were in clerical or service positions. Men in these countries do what is considered "women's work" in other parts of the world.

In Scandinavian countries, known for their progressive social policy, higher proportions of workers were in female-dominated occupations than in other OECD countries. Sweden in particular provides many supportive programs for working women, and many women, in turn, work in public-sector occupations such as health care and teaching. Richard Anker points out that wage-setting institutions in Scandinavian countries reduce the gap between men's and women's wages, so that occupational segregation is not as burdensome for women as in other countries.

Francine Blau analyzes the effect of wage-setting practices in Sweden on the gender gap. She found that wages in general are more equal in Sweden so that workers at the lower percentile of the wage distribution are closer to the median wage than in many other countries (particularly, in this comparison, the U.S.). Women are at a similar percentile position in the overall wage distribution in both countries—and therefore much closer to men's wages in Sweden. Even though women are concentrated in relatively lower-paying jobs, the wage structure and other social welfare supports reduce the negative impact. This still does not address the point made by Anker in the ILO report that occupational segregation reduces women's choices and shunts workers into jobs that may not be the best match for their interests and abilities.

Jobs with a high proportion of women often tend to mimic the kind of care-

Table VIII.1. Share of Women in Selected Occupations/Median Weekly Earnings by Occupation

	Median Weekly Earnings		Women in Occ.
	Men	Women	(% Share)
Total, 16 years and over	598	456	43
Secretaries, stenographers, and typists	484	436	98
Child care workers (private household)	208	97	
Cleaners and servants	227	95	
Finanical records processing	466	426	91
Information clerks	453	363	89
Health service occupations	342	315	87
Health assessment and treating occupations	791	730	83
Librarians, archivists, and curators	640	82	
Miscellaneous administrative support occupations	482	389	82
Records processing, except financial	419	416	80
Communications equipment operators	368	79	
Managers, medicine, and health	869	679	79
Health technologists and technicians	588	486	78
Sales representatives, commodities, except retail	765	603	25
Guards	378	330	20
Freight, stock, and material handlers	350	312	20
Laborers, except construction	384	331	19
Engineering and related techns	668	529	19
Supervisors (precision production)	686	478	17
Police and detectives	662	583	16
Related agricultural occupations	314	274	15
Farm managers	486	14	
Farm occupations, except managerial	288	264	14
Precision woodworking occupations	507	13	
Vehicle washers and equipment cleaners	322	11	
Engineers, architects, and surveyors	1,007	827	11
Motor vehicle operators	514	362	9
Supervisors (protective services)	786	8	
Garage and service station related occupations	297	7	
Transportation occupations, except motor vehicles	862	7	
Precision metalworking occupations	621	444	7
Supervisors (mechanics and repairers)	748	6	
Material moving equipment operators	510	397	6
Mechanics and repairers, except supervisors	592	516	4
Construction laborers	393	3	
Plant and system operators	703	3	
Firefighting and fire prevention	731	3	
Construction trades, except supervisors	522	403	2
Helpers, construction and extractive occupations	340	1	
Supervisors (construction trades)	709	1	

Source: Excerpted from Household Data for 1998 from *Employment and Earnings,* January 1999.

taking labor women have traditionally performed in the home. Some feminist economists would say that this caring work, like nursing or education, done by women is undervalued by society. Barbara Bergmann developed a model (Bergmann 1974), further elaborated by Elaine Sorenson (1989), which explains lower pay in jobs held primarily by women by virtue of the high concentration of women. Her theory holds that discrimination excludes many women from male-dominated occupations. Women must crowd into a set of occupations where demand is smaller than supply, so wages in those jobs are reduced.

While equal pay for equal work amounts to the simplest form of justice, the extent of occupational segregation makes it difficult to upgrade women's pay based solely on that criterion, since men's and women's jobs are often not exactly the same. However, it is possible to rate jobs on the basis of particular characteristics such as supervisory responsibility or customer contact and to develop compensation equity on the basis of comparable characteristics. In fact such rating systems are widely used by large companies to establish pay schedules, and their scales influence other firms that may not be able to undertake a large study. With the use of rating systems, it is possible to evaluate the "comparable worth" of various jobs based on underlying skills and demands. **Ronnie Steinberg,** in a summarized article, calls for such a process, but she also calls for careful evaluation of the construction of rating instruments themselves. She offers a critique of several well-known and widely used systems because they tend to undervalue occupations predominantly held by women. In one egregious example, one system rated dog pound attendant as a more complex position than child care worker.

Comparable worth is a remedy targeted to a specific kind of gender-based inequality—occupational segregation. Affirmative action is broadly applicable to women and minorities in a variety of settings: education, employment, political, civic, and social life. Affirmative action programs have always faced criticism and resistance for their alleged implementation of "reverse discrimination." Barbara Bergmann has developed a straightforward, clearly written defense of affirmative action as a necessary antidote to a socioeconomic regime that privileges some and deprives others of opportunity and advantage (Bergmann 1996). William Bowen, former president of Princeton University and Derek Bok, former president of Harvard University, present results of a study of minority graduates of several colleges and universities of high academic quality. They extend the research to postbaccalaureate experience and conclude that affirmative action improved outcomes for many minority students and served to promote leadership among minorities and to increase diversity in professional, business, and civic spheres (Bowen and Bok 1998).

Susan Sturm and Lani Guinier again bring up the issue of inordinate reliance on test scores as measures of merit. Opponents of affirmative action often claim that in specific instances female or minority applicants were chosen even though male or white applicants had higher scores on a standardized test administered in conjunction with the candidacy. Sturm and Guinier argue that such tests measure a very limited range of qualifications and are incapable of evaluating many valuable traits such as leadership, motivation, or integrity. Furthermore, the differences in scores that have become the basis for litigation are often extremely slight and well within the margins of error of the test instruments themselves. Sturm and Guinier propose a more holistic approach to making decisions among applicants for schools and jobs, taking account of a broader array of instruments and relying on observation of actual performance when possible.

William Julius Wilson expresses deep concern about the effects of the backlash to affirmative action. He fears it is divisive and may intensify prejudice and hostility toward minorities. He also argues that affirmative action, as it has been implemented to date, tends to favor relatively privileged members of targeted groups. Entry into higher education or desirable employment can only be achieved by individuals with at least some socioeconomic resources. The "truly disadvantaged," to use Wilson's own phrase, fall farther and farther behind. Wilson proposes a class-based system of preferences that would take economic circumstances as the basis for affirmative action. Poor women and minorities would benefit, but so would poor whites.

Conclusion

The evidence for persistent categorical inequalities is undeniable, but there are also undeniable signs of progress. A recent study by Richard Freeman and William Rodgers confirms what many have suspected: The economic boom of the late 1990s has made a definite improvement in the employment and wages of young non-college-educated workers, particularly the young African-American men who have taken the brunt of recent economic turmoil (Freeman and Rodgers 1999). Young women going to work in the wake of welfare reform have also benefited from the tightening labor market. The problem is that booms are known to go bust and the last to be hired are usually the first to be let go in an economic downturn. A further finding in the Freeman and Rodgers study is that: "Youths do particularly well in areas that started the boom at lower jobless rates, suggesting that minimizing the impact of recessions allows youths to make real gains instead of making up ground lost during the recession."

This result hints at a role for public policy to mitigate the harsh cycles of free-market economies in order to maintain the momentum gained in this recovery. Policy interventions will be particularly necessary to balance the positive effects of growth against its negative environmental effects. A truly sustainable society cannot tolerate runaway growth and rampant consumerism, but neither can it place the burden of restraining growth on those who are already disadvantaged.

Women have also made great strides in recent years by many measures: increasing participation in the labor force, the shrinking of the wage gap, moving into more occupations. The greatest hurdle here is also one of balance: how to engage in the social, public, productive life of the larger economy while providing care and nurturance for families. This is not just a question for women, but one with which society as a whole must grapple.

Note

1. Statistics based on the Current Population Survey administered by the U.S. Census Bureau and the Bureau of Labor Statistics contain findings for both men and women in white, black, and Asian and Pacific Islander racial groups, and for men and women in Hispanic and non-Hispanic white groups. Other groups are not reported due to small sample size. Persons of Hispanic origin may be of any race.

Summary of

Race and Gender Wage Gaps in the Market for Recent College Graduates

by Catherine J. Weinberger

[Published in *Industrial Relations* 37, 1 (January 1998), 67–83.]

The persistence of racial and gender gaps in wages is a controversial and perplexing problem for economists. The gap between men and women has been closing but remains large. The gap between white and black men is even more problematic because it began to grow in the 1980s after diminishing for several years. Where some see evidence of discrimination, others see differences in productive characteristics, which remain to be measured. School quality and occupational preference are two characteristics cited as having a probable effect on wages, but which are difficult to measure with generally accessible labor market data. This article makes use of a unique data set to examine the influence on wages of the college attended and choice of major (as a proxy for occupational preference and skills acquired in college) for a sample of recent college graduates. Even with careful accounting for these and other productivity characteristics, evidence of discrimination persists.

Measurement Issues

Differences in wages between racial, ethnic, and gender groups are easy to document but difficult to explain. Some of the difference is due to differences on average in well-understood productivity characteristics such as educational attainment and experience. Other, more subtle productivity issues may also play a role. One obvious candidate is occupation. "If we believe that labor markets allocate individuals to the jobs for which they are best suited, then occupation is a good proxy for an individual's productivity and preferences. . . . The limitation of this method is that occupation is a labor market outcome. Occupational assignments may themselves be affected by labor market discrimination." [68]

Choice of college major is arguably a better indicator of individual preference. This study uses the *1985 Survey of Recent College Graduates* (a large sample of students who received degrees between July 1983 and July 1984), which includes information on college attended, college grades, and college major. It also includes earnings in April 1985, which was on average about a year after graduation. The data captures type and quality of education for this sample with a high level of detail. "Because college attended, major, and grade are all correlated with race, gender, and ethnicity, failure to control completely for these factors results in apparent wage differentials between groups even in the absence of labor market discrimination." [76] This data set is limited, however, to a sample of people who completed college and is not able to capture effects of previous discrimination—which might have influenced the decision to attend college, the ability to complete college, or the choice of college or majors.

Respondents were chosen who were employed, no older than 30, and not in school full time in April 1985. Full-time graduate students, who had higher college grades, more educated parents, and less work experience while in college, were not included; 246 out of a possible 300 college majors were represented in the sample. For some purposes of analysis, these were collapsed into 12 broad categories: business, communications, computer science, economics, education, engineering, humanities, mathematics, nursing, science, social sciences, and other.

Results

The most salient finding of this analysis is that, although statistically controlling for college major and college attended often has large effects, these controls do not explain away the wage disadvantage faced by any racial/ethnic or gender group. The model using demographic variables, college grade point average, and little else, explains only 6 percent of the individual variation in wages. When controls are added for the choice of a college and major, the model explains 40 percent of the individual variation—and estimates smaller demographic effects.

Different majors generally lead to more or less remunerative occupations. Controlling for major is intended here to account for the effect of personal occupational choices. The quality of education depends in part on the college attended, and the quality of education should influence productivity and earnings. An assessment of the quality of the individual school is not attempted here; the analysis merely assumes that each school represents a consistent indicator of educational quality for each of its graduates.

The effects of controlling for choice of college and major can be expressed in terms of the change in the average wage gap between each demographic group and white men. The effects are as follows:

- *White women*—Controlling for the 12 aggregate college major categories explains almost half the wage gap, reducing it from -17 percent to -9 percent; there is little effect from using controls for college attended. That is, half of the wage gap can be traced to the choice of lower-paid majors; the quality of colleges attended by white men and women appears to be comparable.

- *Black men*—Controlling for college major and college attended has no effect; the wage gap is consistently about 9 percent, regardless of controls.

- *Black women*—Controlling for college major and college attended reduces the wage gap from -25 percent to -16 percent.

(Removing graduates of historically black colleges from the sample has virtually no effect on these results for either black men or black women.)

- *Hispanic men*—College-educated Hispanic men earn more than white men, but their wage advantage drops from +8 percent to +1 percent when college major and college attended are controlled. That is, Hispanic men earned a little more than white men because they chose more remunerative colleges and majors.

- *Hispanic women*—Controlling for college major and choice of college reduces the wage gap from -11 percent to -6 percent.

- *Asian men and women*—Average incomes for this group often reflect the choice of colleges and majors that lead to highly compensated jobs. But when college major and college attended are controlled, Asian men drop from a wage advantage of +8 percent to a wage gap of -14 percent relative to white men, the largest shift for any group in this study. Asian women fall from a wage gap of -6 percent to -15 percent.

There is a striking similarity in the wage gaps, after controlling for college and major, of most of the groups examined here. White women, black men and women, and Asian men and women all have wage gaps of roughly -10 percent to -15 percent relative to white men. Only the small number of Hispanic college graduates do better.

The wage gap, after controls, is an estimate of the differential treatment of individuals with the same, or equivalent, human capital. "If labor market discrimination is defined as a mechanism that causes individuals with the same productive characteristics but different ascriptive characteristics to be valued differently by the labor market, then this is very strong evidence that discrimination operates in the market for recent college graduates." [82]

Summary of

Intergroup Disparity: Economic Theory and Social Science Evidence

by William A. Darity, Jr.

[Published in *Southern Economic Journal* 64, 4 (April 1998), 805–826.]

Neoclassical economic theory proposes that employment discrimination is inefficient. An employer who chooses employees on the basis of some trait, such as skin color, that is unrelated to productivity will be less successful than competitors who hire solely on the basis of productivity characteristics. Eventually, employers with a "taste for discrimination," as economist Gary Becker put it, will fail in the marketplace. Inequalities must therefore be associated with productivity-enhancing human capital attributes such as educational attainment or experience.

A corollary to this argument is that affirmative action and other initiatives to address labor-market discrimination are at best unnecessary and at worst counterproductive. The article summarized below challenges this orthodox conclusion, points to extensive evidence of discrimination, and argues that "neoclassical economics cannot be manipulated to produce a convincing story of why groups or individuals who differ ascriptively but who share similar productivity-linked attributes experience differential treatment in markets over time." [807]

Statistical Analysis of Discrimination

Basic evidence of labor market discrimination comes from two types of indirect statistical tests applied to labor market outcomes (i.e., the distribution of wages). The first—a race coefficients approach—uses regression analysis with a dummy variable for race while controlling for human capital variables. A negative, statistically significant coefficient on the race variable is evidence for discrimination—that is, inequality unexplained by standard human capital factors. Using this method, in a 1997 study Peter Gottschalk found that being black reduced earnings by 11.5 percent in 1980 and 11.9 percent in 1990.

The second indirect statistical test is the "Blinder-Oaxaca decomposition," which distinguishes between two components of inequality. Outcomes for different demographic groups may vary because of average differences in relevant characteristics, or because of different returns to average characteristics; the latter is interpreted as a sign of discrimination. The author and colleagues analyzed 1980 and 1990 census data, dividing the U.S. population into fifty racial/ethnic groups. (Note: This study analyzed men and women separately, examining inequality within each gender. It did not compare women to men.)

The decomposition "found no systematic evidence of in-market discrimination on the basis of race or ethnicity among women." [809] Among men, some groups (those of Cuban, Mexican, Puerto Rican, and Native American ancestry) had losses compared to average American men stemming both from human capital differences and from discrimination. The human capital deficits accounted for a greater part of the overall difference, but for most of these groups, the gap due to discrimination actually grew between 1980 and 1990.

Black and Vietnamese men also had gaps due both to differences in human capital and returns to human capital, but here differential returns had the greater weight. Both in 1980 and 1990 black men lost 10 percent compared to the overall average due to productivity characteristics (such as lower education) and 15 percent due to discriminatory returns to those characteristics. In 1990 Chinese, Filipino, Japanese, and Korean men had better than average returns to their characteristics; for men of Indian ancestry better than average characteristics were offset by discrimination. "Virtually all of the white male ethnic groups experienced advantageous treatment of their characteristics (or racial nepotism)." [809]

Cognitive Skills and Culture

In the face of this evidence orthodox economists claim that there must be unobserved characteristics related to productivity and correlated with race/ethnicity. Two candidates are cognitive skills and culture. To evaluate cognitive skills, researchers examined results of the Armed Forces Qualifying Test (AFQT) given to 1980 respondents in the National Longitudinal Survey of Youth (NLSY). For both men and women, AFQT scores explained most of the black-white wage gap and the Hispanic non-Hispanic white gap.

This appears to support the human capital argument. However the AFQT is problematic and several researchers have explored its implications further. The AFQT is not a test of general intelligence. Rather, AFQT scores can be "treated as outcomes of a structural process generated by the influences of family background, school quality, and psychological motivation. . . ." [810] When a test that *was* intended to measure general intelligence was included in a wage regression, the effect of race remained negative and statistically significant. Some researchers found a fundamental bias in the AFQT itself, which yielded different scores for blacks and whites when variables in the NLSY like family background, schooling, and motivation were treated as determinants of AFQT re-

sults. Psychological variables from the NLSY suggest that blacks are more motivated than whites on average, an unobserved productivity factor that should
improve outcomes for blacks.

It is sometimes claimed that the returns to cognitive skills have risen over time,
so that the human capital cap now explains a greater income gap than in the past.
It may be that returns to cognitive skills have risen, but this does not eliminate the
evidence of discrimination. One influential study that found rising returns to math,
reading, and vocabulary skills in two longitudinal data sets also found a negative
and statistically significant effect from race that worsened for 1980 black high
school graduates tested in 1986 compared to 1972 graduates tested in 1978.

Two different decompositions performed by the author analyzed the effect of
culture. One looked at blacks from different backgrounds: West Indian, Hispanic,
European, and other blacks—primarily descendants of U.S. slaves. The other compared black and white Hispanics. Most black women had less-than-average human
capital, but slightly better than average returns to their human capital. Black Hispanic women earned more than white women because they had more human capital, but the payoff to their human capital was less than that for all American
women. For white Hispanic women the payoff was higher given their human capital than that for all women. For men, results of both analyses clearly showed that
discrimination on the basis of color outweighed the effects of culture.

While not specifically examining the unobserved human capital thesis, a number
of other studies have examined the effect of skin shade (in India, Japan, the United
States, the Caribbean, and among Chicanos) on socioeconomic outcomes and
found that darker skin was associated with poorer outcomes. One study also analyzed the level of African ancestry (as determined by genetic tests, not appearance)
and "found no correlation between degree of African ancestry and performance
on IQ tests, but they did find a correlation between skin shade and IQ scores. This
suggests that it is the social perception and treatment of darker-skinned persons
that dictates their weaker social outcomes, not their biological inheritance." [821]

Audit Studies

Audit studies provide a more direct test of discrimination and have been used
with employers, Realtors, and lenders. In audit studies black and white applicants are carefully matched, either by training actors to present a similar de-
meanor and/or constructing similar documentation of qualifications. An
Urban Institute audit of employment in three U.S. cities found that

> black males are three times as likely to be rejected for jobs as white males, and
> Hispanic white males also are three times as likely to be rejected for jobs as
> non-Hispanic white males. . . . Another study . . . found evidence of discrimi-
> nation against blacks at all stages of the employment process: lower likelihood

of invitation to interview, considerably lower likelihood of receipt of job offer, lower wage offers when job offers were made, and less consideration for unadvertised positions at higher levels than jobs originally advertised. The same study also detected systematic evidence of discrimination against black women when compared with white women, unlike the typical finding in the indirect statistical tests of the types described above. [815]

Discrimination and Its Effects Over Time

The Gottschalk study mentioned earlier shows a negative effect on earnings from being black in each year from 1964 to 1995. But in the years immediately following the 1964 Civil Rights Act the earnings gap narrowed sharply, from –0.426 in 1964 to –0.126 in 1976. Then it stabilized, actually increasing slightly to –0.140 in 1995. This pattern of falling discrimination in the 1970s with little change since then was also evident in a decomposition of census microdata performed by the author and colleagues using an index of occupational prestige as the outcome variable.

Inequalities among racial/ethnic groups (whether from human capital differences or discrimination) persist over long periods of time. A two-stage statistical analysis of occupational status among almost forty racial and ethnic groups of men concludes that disparities found in census data from 1880, 1900, and 1910 continue to influence occupational status reported in census data from 1980 and 1990.

When policies such as affirmative action have been proposed, opponents often claim that such measures cannot achieve a raceless society. "But is a raceless society one in which race merely is omitted from official or legal categories or one in which race is not a factor in influencing life chances? . . . If we are collectively to agree to ignore race, then we should be in a world where race truly does not matter." [822]

Summary of

What's Fairness Got To Do With It? Environmental Justice and the Siting of Locally Undesirable Land Uses

by Vicki Been

[Published in *Cornell Law Review* 78, 6 (September 1993), 1001–1084.]

Certain kinds of facilities are often unwelcome as neighbors. Locally undesirable land uses (LULUs), including waste disposal sites, pollution generating factories, or nuclear power facilities, are often characterized by environmentally harmful effects. Prisons and even social service agencies such as drug and alcohol treatment centers or homeless shelters may also be considered undesirable. This is well known as NIMBY—"not in my backyard"—phenomenon. Many environmental impacts are concentrated in the immediate neighborhood yet the benefits of a particular facility are shared by society as a whole. This creates a real dilemma about the fairness of locating a particular facility in a particular community. Using protests, lawsuits, and lobbying efforts, advocates for environmental justice have called attention to the disproportionate presence of undesirable land uses in poor and minority communities.

The article summarized here argues that siting issues are difficult to resolve unless the decision is grounded in a particular theory of fairness. A number of theories may have resonance with a given situation, each one presenting a particular set of opportunities for solution; yet each theory also presents problems of a philosophical or pragmatic nature. The author surveys several theories of fairness as they apply to LULUs, working through the complex options and obstacles associated with each.

Environmental Justice

Evidence from a number of studies conducted on a national, regional, or local basis suggests that a disproportionate number of undesirable facilities are located in poor or minority communities. However, the related claim that this is the result of discrimination in the decision where to site these operations has not, in most cases, been studied directly. If the neighbors of undesirable facilities are disproportionately minority, it may be that these demographics played a role in the choice of sites. But it is also possible that these neighbors "moved to the nuisance." Once an undesirable facility is sited, wealthier people may have moved away from undesirable locations, the presence of LULUs may have reduced property values, and the neighborhoods may therefore have become affordable for poorer and minority residents.

Whether the facilities were imposed on a minority neighborhood or minorities moved near the facility, it is appropriate for these communities to seek legislative redress of the unfair burden that LULUs now place on their neighborhoods. Although the ethical, legal, political, and practical problems involved in finding a fair and workable solution are formidable, "[t]he government must find a satisfactory answer, or else society will find itself in the stalemate that planners refer to as the 'build absolutely nothing anywhere near anybody' (BANANA) dilemma." [1015]

Objections to Fair Siting Proposals

There are four general objections to the consideration of fairness in response to siting issues. One claims that proximity to undesirable facilities results from the dynamics of the housing market. Older factories and waste sites were located in central cities near transportation, markets, and workers. As workers moved out of inner cities, poor people, often members of minority groups, moved in. Related to this is the mobility issue that claims that in a free market, some people will be better able to distance themselves from LULUs than others, and therefore actions to promote fairness in the siting of facilities are fruitless. However, relocation costs and evidence that many LULUs do not dramatically lower property values, as is often feared, mean that neighborhoods may change slowly. Further, the government has an obligation to foster fairness even if the market may undo these effects.

The aggregation objection holds that LULUs need to be considered within the context of all the benefits and burdens regularly allocated by society. A fourth objection is made by those who believe that the free market should distribute environmental quality in the same way it distributes amenities like proximity to a mountain stream. Many aspects of life are allocated to some extent by government—education, health care, military service, jury duty; advocated for "fair" siting, the allocation of LULUs are analogous to these situations.

The Meaning of Fairness

Although environmental justice activists have not made explicit the underlying theories of fairness on which they base their claims, these theories must come into play in formulating resolutions to specific cases. Several of these theories will be discussed under three overarching categories: (1) fairness in the pattern of distribution; (2) fairness as internalization of costs; and (3) fairness as process.

Fairness in the pattern of distribution might impose a proportional distribution of the burdens of LULUs throughout the population so that each neighborhood has the same number as every other one. However, this will still leave some individuals in closer proximity to the facilities than others. Suitable sites are not likely to be distributed evenhandedly, so proportional distribution might compromise other siting criteria. Because different facilities have different effects, it is difficult to balance burdens. Neighborhoods are difficult to define and the effects of many LULUs are not confined to neighborhood boundaries.

Many academics favor compensation schemes, but others criticize them as immoral. Such schemes place the less fortunate at risk while those who can afford to escape do so. Compensation commodifies life, health, safety, and human dignity. When a community already suffers from inequality, it is questionable if it can truly make a voluntary decision about compensation. There are also pragmatic obstacles to translating risk into monetary terms, among them problems of measurement and achieving consensus. There are also problems in determining who should receive compensation, who receives offsetting benefits (e.g., employment), and how to compensate future residents.

Progressive siting would allocate more of the burden of LULUs to advantaged neighborhoods either by physically siting facilities there or by requiring wealthy communities to bear a larger share of compensation costs. Progressive siting would redress both past and present disadvantages. Poor communities are likely to be poorer than others in health as well as wealth and, therefore, more at risk from the effects of environmental toxins. Putting LULUs in wealthier communities may create incentives for society to reduce its need for such facilities.

Internalizing the costs of LULUs puts the burden on those who benefit from them and also encourages greater efficiencies. Unfortunately, it is not always possible to match benefit and burden precisely. Cost internalization is also more compatible with compensation schemes than with physical siting schemes, yet proponents of internalization often oppose compensation on moral grounds.

Fairness as process demands that the decisions about siting be free of discrimination and that they treat all people involved as equals. Seemingly neutral procedures like cost-benefit analysis can contain hidden biases. For example, the cost effectiveness of siting a particular facility may depend on land values, which are higher in more privileged communities.

Legislative Strategies

State and local governments and legislative proposals at the federal level have adopted five strategies for fostering fairness in siting: dispersion, impact statement, fair share, hybrid impact statement/fair share, and suspect class.

The dispersion approach has been applied mainly to the siting of group homes in the wake of deinstitutionalization of mental hospitals, but also to environmental hazards. It prohibits concentration of LULUs in any one neighborhood; however, it does not specify any particular consideration between white and minority communities.

Impact statements mandate that local authorities either monitor the status of LULUs in the area or develop analysis of the impact of proposed sites on socioeconomic factors in the area. Impact statements take into account the existing burden and potential impact of undesirable facilities on the community. However, there is lack of consistency in measurement and lack of clear definition of impacts in these mandates.

The fair-share approach was developed with respect to low- and moderate-income housing to ensure that communities receive a fair share of such housing on one hand, and a fair distribution of costs on the other. Determining costs and benefits and weighting factors such as need or suitability make this a very complex process, subject to bias and resistance.

New York City incorporated a hybrid fair-share/impact statement approach in its 1989 city charter. This has become an acclaimed model in urban planning circles. It requires notification to communities well in advance of changes to city facilities and establishes vehicles for feedback and participation on the part of city residents and community leaders. The fair-share criteria mandate that the city consider compatibility with existing programs and facilities, potential adverse effects on neighborhood character, cost-effectiveness, and consistency with the mayor's annual Statement of Needs. There are shortcomings to this approach. For instance, the compatibility criterion may tend to funnel LULUs into neighborhoods where they are already concentrated; and while impact statements must be drawn up, there is no mandate that they be followed. Still, this is an innovative and promising program.

The suspect class approach is embodied in proposals to Congress similar to civil rights legislation in specifying certain classes of people for protection. One such proposal is narrowly confined to prevention of racial discrimination in the siting of LULUs. Another would prohibit facilities that threaten the health or environmental quality of poor or minority communities.

Abstract calls for fair siting in the absence of a theory of fairness offer no guidance about "what fair siting will look like in practice or . . . how effective proposals to ensure fair siting will be." [1085] Working through all the conceptual and pragmatic problems attendant on each particular approach to fairness is difficult, but in the end it will lead to sounder solutions.

Summary of

Tracking Racial Bias

by Jerome G. Miller

[Published in *Search and Destroy: African-American Males in the Criminal Justice System* (Cambridge: Cambridge University Press, 1996), Ch. 2, 48–88.]

The situation of young African-American men in the United States is one of crisis. They suffer unemployment rates about double those of white men, in good economic times and bad, and are far more likely to be involved with the criminal justice system. Often they are perceived to be violent and sociopathic. Law and order advocates are satisfied to lock them up and throw away the key without questioning the fairness of the system. The consequences for these men, their families, and communities are deeply disturbing.

The book chapter summarized here exposes the pervasive racial bias that threatens an entire generation of young men. The author draws on an extensive review of social science literature as well as his own experience as an administrator of and high-level advisor to state and local corrections systems.

Historical Perspective

"While those who are confined in a country's jails or prisons are a rough measure of the types of criminal activity at a given time, they provide a sharper picture of who is at the bottom of the socioeconomic heap or on the political outs at that given time." [48] In the late nineteenth and early twentieth centuries prison populations reflected the waves of immigration from European countries. One study of Chicago's ethnic neighborhoods reported that 28 percent of 17- to 21-year-old men in the Back of the Yards neighborhood were arrested for serious crimes between 1924 and 1926. The researcher blamed this high rate of criminal involvement on the social disorganization and moral confusion resulting from the rapidly shifting ethnic composition of the neighborhood.

As white ethnic groups assimilated to U.S. society, crime rates dropped. For African-Americans, however, assimilation proved elusive. They remained on the bottom rung of the economic ladder. A 1918 Census Bureau report on the history and status of blacks noted that blacks were 11 percent of the general population but 22 percent of the population of correctional institutions. The report went on to ask whether this was due to greater "criminality" among blacks or the result of discriminatory treatment. The report failed to mention the brutal history of lynching of black men with the support of white citizens and law enforcement officials. For decades black men were subjected to a reign of terror. Lynchings were often attended by huge crowds in a spectacle meant to intimidate and torment as well as punish. "Castration, lynching, and other vigilante-type actions were characteristically reserved for citizens of color and provided the backdrop and collective memory against which the formal criminal justice system functioned when it came to blacks." [53]

Progress in civil rights since the 1960s has been undermined by surging rates of imprisonment, particularly during the federal government's war on drugs. By 1993, 55 percent of admissions to state and federal prisons were black, although blacks were still only about 13 percent of the total population. "In 1991 . . . the national incarceration rate in state and federal prisons was 310 per 100,000. For white males it was 352 per 100,000. For black males ages 25 to 29 it stood at an incredible 6301." [54]

Racial Bias Research

Through the 1970s criminologists generally accepted that racial bias was present in the criminal justice system. In the 1980s and 1990s "a sea change in the national mood as well as in the methodologies that came to characterize American criminological research" [56] was accompanied by a shift in the tone of research. A number of researchers reached the conclusion that more blacks were in prisons simply because they committed most of the crimes. Some revived genetic explanations for criminal behavior.

Criminal justice records are problematic as data because they reflect the results of a series of actions and decisions on the part of the alleged criminal, attorneys, judges, police, probation, and correctional officers. Yet the record is devoid of the personal histories, attitudes, and motivations that influence choices and behaviors at each step in the process. Another problem with analysis of criminal justice records occurs when stages of the process are taken in isolation. For example, one influential study found that the demographics of arrest for serious crimes corresponded well with commission of these crimes. However, a related study noted that over the period 1976 to 1992 arrest rates for violent crimes were relatively stable: in the range of 50 to 54 percent were whites; 44 to 47 percent were blacks. The black share of serious crime arrests was nearly 3 percent *lower* in 1992 than in 1976, but the black share of admissions to federal and state prisons increased from 35 percent to 55 percent from the 1970s to the 1990s.

Other studies present conflicting results with a number of researchers claiming to find no bias. However, 98 percent of judges and court managers surveyed by the New Jersey State Supreme Court perceived racial bias in the courts. One study of imprisonment by race in 1982 found that only two-thirds of black imprisonment nationwide could be explained by the arrests of blacks for serious crimes; moreover, this proportion varied widely from state to state. Often black men are disadvantaged when their cases fall into gray areas where judges and attorneys exercise discretion over the specification of charges and determination of sentences.

Ironically, some measures designed to remove sentencing discretion from individual judges, such as habitual offender or mandatory sentencing laws, simply displaced the source of bias. Although judges hands were now tied, prosecutors were more apt to charge blacks than whites with crimes associated with lengthy legislated sentences.

Racial Bias Affecting Juveniles

Young black people are most likely to face racial biases in early and late stages of the criminal justice process. "Black teenagers were more likely to be detained, to be handled formally, to be waived to adult court, and to be adjudicated delinquent. If removed from their homes by the court, they were less likely to be placed in the better-staffed and better-run private-group home facilities and more likely to be sent into state reform schools." [72] In the middle phases of the process, black youth were more likely to have charges dismissed, but this may simply reflect the fact that they were excessively charged in the first place. A sample of 11- to 17-year-olds from the National Youth Survey was chosen for in-depth confidential interviews about their involvement in criminal activity. Their self-reports were checked against actual police records and found to be relatively accurate, often revealing more delinquent acts than official records showed. Few differences were found in rates of criminal activity along racial lines, but blacks were more likely to be apprehended than whites for similar behavior. Furthermore, blacks were apt to be charged with more serious crimes for comparable activity.

Arrest rates for serious crimes remained stable among white and black youths from 1978 to 1989. Whites accounted for 67 percent of arrests, but minorities were 60 percent of institutionalized youth. The involvement of black youth with the criminal justice system is entangled with stereotypes that label them as criminal and sociopathic. White youths, particularly middle-class youths, are more apt to be considered troubled and channeled into private psychiatric clinics and substance-abuse programs.

In the war on drugs, disparities in the treatment of white and black young people are clearly evident. In 1992 the U.S. Public Health Service estimated 76 percent of drug users were white, 14 percent black, and 8 percent Hispanic. Yet African-Americans and Hispanics made up the bulk of those being arrested, convicted, and sentenced to prison for drug offenses. Possession of crack cocaine, used primarily by minorities, was penalized far more severely than possession of powder cocaine, used primarily by whites. Such discrepancies pervaded the antidrug campaign. Whites were far more likely to be sent to a drug treatment program; blacks were more likely to be sent to prison. In California 70 percent of drug-related sentences went to blacks, while whites got two-thirds of the treatment slots. By 1990 in Baltimore, young black people were arrested at 100 times the rate for whites on drug charges.

Unfortunately, prospects for young black men appear bleak. Racism is deeply embedded in the criminal justice system. Some individuals in positions of power are overtly racist, others quietly so, and many others are indifferent.

Summary of

The Impact of Economic Change on Minorities and Migrants in Western Europe

by Ian Gordon

[Published in *Poverty, Inequality and the Future of Social Policy: Western States and the New World Order,* eds. Katherine McFate, Roger Lawson, and William Julius Wilson (New York: Russell Sage Foundation, 1995), Ch. 16, 521–541.]

Waves of animosity in Western Europe against immigrants from Asia, Africa, the Caribbean, and Islamic countries made headlines during the mid-1990s. Earlier waves of migration involved people of similar ethnic and cultural background to residents of the host country. Shortly after World War II and again in the 1990s, the movement of Eastern Europeans to the West dominated immigration flows. However, for most of the postwar period migrants came from the eastern Mediterranean and from countries with colonial ties to Europe.

The article summarized here links the marginalization of immigrants in Western Europe to two interacting factors—difference and changing economic conditions—that funneled them into particular economic niches. The cultural and ethnic qualities, and often darker skin, of these groups made them easy to distinguish and, therefore, easy to relegate to positions of economic, political, and social inferiority. The desire of employers for cheaper labor encouraged this process. "Continuing price advantage for this labor depended on its remaining in some respects 'distinct' from the host population." [522]

Minorities in Europe

Migration from southern Europe and former colonies peaked in the early seventies then faced restrictions when the oil crisis of the mid-seventies threw the west into recession. Immigrants could no longer come and go from the host country. Many chose settlement, inducing a new round of immigration of dependents. On the part of host countries generally, "acceptance of the reality of settlement has led toward a policy set combining strict control with efforts at improved integration." [523]

These common trends and policies notwithstanding, the actual experience of immigrants has been diverse and all too often accompanied by unemployment, poverty, and second-class status. Ethnic groups exist in different concentrations in different places, with strong networks of government agencies, recruiters, and migrants themselves reinforcing these concentrations. Different measures—"referring variously to place of birth, nationality, residence status, and family origins" [523] not only make cross-country comparisons difficult, they also reflect different concerns about the social position and legal status of minorities. Illegal immigration also makes measurement difficult, particularly in Italy.

Perspectives

Analyses of immigration trends and the situation of minorities in Europe generally stem from three different perspectives: market economics, ethnic discrimination, and labor market restructuring.

Market Economics

Both neoclassical and Keynesian economists have argued in favor of immigration. One particularly influential view held that immigrants could provide fresh sources of labor to growing economies, fitting into the labor market wherever their skills and abilities were in demand. Those with good skills would prosper; those with poor skills would enter low-wage employment. Normal labor market processes would leave immigrants neither more nor less vulnerable to poverty and unemployment than domestic workers. In times of downturn, repatriation might be desirable. However, if unemployment is induced as a matter of fighting inflation (rather than resulting from a shortfall in demand), the repatriation of immigrants would simply lead to higher unemployment among indigenous workers. Mainstream economic theory would therefore view the legal impediments to immigration introduced in the mid-seventies (and earlier in Britain) as a mistake.

Ethnic Discrimination

Other analysts proceed from the premise that postwar migrants "are not only much poorer than the receiving economies but ethnically and culturally quite distinct from the majority of the home populations . . . distinctively cheap (whatever their level of human capital), subject to prejudices about their abilities or suitability, and perceived as 'outsiders' by incumbents with established interests to protect." [525] Employers faced with the problem of finding the most productive workers in a heterogeneous labor pool may rely on stereotypes, recruitment networks, or internal labor markets when hiring. In these circumstances individual outcomes will depend on group processes.

Immigrants are perceived as outsiders, as rivals, and as less entitled to the rights and benefits belonging to citizens in European welfare states. Immigrants may be crowded into the bottom of the labor market, further reducing wages and job security in that segment. "Poverty among migrant groups is then the expected outcome of processes of exclusion and marginalization, from which the protected majority of workers benefit, through a stabilization of their employment opportunities." [526] Legal restrictions on immigration were politically rather than economically motivated, a position supported by the fact that controls were enacted in Britain and France well before the recession induced by the oil crisis.

Labor Market Restructuring

According to this approach, employers played an active role in influencing immigration policy and in recruiting cheap immigrant labor, often to replace indigenous workers who abandoned less desirable jobs as they became more educated. Later in the postwar era, labor markets changed. It became technologically feasible to move production to low-wage countries and politically feasible to sustain less-than-full employment among indigenous workers. This put pressure on indigenous workers to improve productivity. Internal labor markets gave way to flexible labor markets, and employers became less likely to pursue costly recruitment strategies, especially in unstable low-wage sectors.

Manufacturing, transport, and distribution industries all lost manual labor jobs while the growing service sector polarized between highly skilled business and professional services and consumer services mainly carried out by low-wage workers in small businesses. Demand for immigrants increased in the low end of the service sector, but neither recruitment nor political pressure on immigration law was well organized. From this perspective, mid-seventies legal restrictions on immigration occurred when primary-sector employers lost interest in immigrant labor.

Changing Labor Market Roles and Experiences

Immigrant workers primarily functioned as replacement workers in jobs abandoned by native workers, but these niches varied by country and tended to change over time. The general trend has been from manufacturing to low-wage services. Evidence on the mobility of first generation immigrants is sketchy, but some groups have done better than others. For example, Afro-Caribbeans in Britain moved from manufacturing into the public sector, Indians showed less convergence with native British workers, and Pakistanis and Bangladeshi none at all.

Contrary to expectations, the second generation of immigrant families has not improved its position. Their educational attainments are uneven, the outcome of "environmental disadvantages, institutional racism, and doubts about the likely rewards for qualifications." [530] Along with the most recent migrants they have been seeking work during a period of economic restructuring, but they have no country of origin to which to return during hard times. Informal networks reduce mobility since job seekers go where members of their community are already employed. Many young people reject the undesirable jobs once performed by their elders and end up in unstable work or in the underground economy.

Unemployment statistics are easier to track than mobility, but they differ from country to country according to the legal situation of immigrants. For example, in Austria, immigrants are not eligible for unemployment benefits and so less likely to be recorded in official statistics. "In general, however, it is evident that since the first oil price crisis . . . foreign workers have been much more likely to experience unemployment than their domestic counterparts." [531] Differences in human capital play a role and immigrants are often employed in declining industries, but there is evidence of discrimination as well. Studies in Britain confirm that certain immigrant groups are more likely to be unemployed even when human capital, occupation, and industry characteristics are controlled. Non-European groups tend to face the worst unemployment levels (with some exceptions, such as high unemployment rates among Italians in Germany and Belgium).

Governments often encourage ethnic entrepreneurship as a response to unemployment because it is consonant with free-market ideology and requires less extension of government services than other job-creating policies. The proportion of minorities in self-employment has been increasing. Entrepreneurship can provide opportunities for particular individuals, but it is not adequate for raising the entire community out of poverty. Not everyone has entrepreneurial skills, access to capital, or an ability to take risks; and small ethnic businesses are unlikely to provide sufficient jobs of good quality to improve substantially the lot of large numbers of immigrants.

Marginalization

The citizenship status of immigrants varies across countries and can bear on issues of residence, employment, welfare entitlements, social position, and relationships within the larger society. Uncertain or secondary status weakens the immigrant's position in each of these domains. France, the Netherlands, and Britain once extended significant rights to migrants from former colonies. Where colonial ties were weak or nonexistent, as in Germany, Austria, or Switzerland, most immigrants were guest workers "originally with strictly temporary rights to residence and employment, no right to political participation, and extremely limited rights to naturalization." [534] Recently, however, these positions have tended to converge: Britain became less open, France encouraged repatriation, while Germany and Switzerland moved toward greater integration of migrants.

Hostile attitudes toward minorities are evident to some extent in all host countries. In some cases, violence is a real threat, but here again, both the incidence and intensity of xenophobic reactions varies across countries. Of the main host countries, the Netherlands tends to show the most tolerance, while Belgians are most apt to be "'disturbed' by the presence of people from another race." [535]

The Political Economy of Gender *and* Economic Progress and Gender Equality

[Claudia Goldin, *Understanding the Gender Gap: An Economic History of American Women* (New York: Oxford University Press, 1990), Chs. 7 and 8, 185–217.]

Summary by Laurie Dougherty

Although occupational segregation and the wage gap between men and women have been decreasing, they persist, and progress remains vulnerable to shifts in cultural, political, and economic realities. Historically, workplace discrimination and a gendered division of labor were rationalized by social norms defining activities appropriate for men or women. The rebirth of the women's movement in the 1960s exposed these norms to critical examination and produced an ideology of equality capable of giving voice to women's aspirations and frustrations. Ironically, some of the most stubbornly persistent obstacles to workplace equality were regulations put in place to protect women from oppressive working conditions.

The first of the two chapters summarized here examines the historical relationship between economic policy and the position of women in the workplace. The second chapter sums up the record of economic progress as it influences the economic position of women.

Historical Dimensions of Public Policy

Politics and public policy play an important part in defining women's status in the workplace. Even before women were a significant part of the paid labor force, working women received attention from policy makers. However, women themselves only became a major political force in shaping the rules of the workplace long after they gained the vote. Alexander Hamilton and other eighteenth-century economic leaders encouraged women to take jobs in manufacturing, hoping to tap this underutilized labor force to build the industrial strength of the nation.

By the late nineteenth century policies regarding women and work tended to protect women against exploitation. Two groups of working women received particular attention. Young women from small towns and rural areas moved to the cities to work, living on their own without parental guidance or support. Many other young women did live with their parents, turning over their earnings to the family, gaining little from their own labor, and suffering a loss of leisure and schooling. In either case the vulnerability of their youth and their exposure to exploitation drew efforts by reformers to regulate their working conditions.

Working Hours

Reform efforts were complicated by motivations aligned with the interests of men rather than women. Some men felt threatened by competition from women, particularly during times of high unemployment, and supported regulation to restrict where and when women could work. In other cases men wanted reforms of their own working conditions, particularly reduced working hours, but were thwarted by the courts. They hoped that instituting protective legislation for women and children, to which the courts were more sympathetic, would force employers to apply the same reduced hours over the whole workforce. Research indicates little or no reduction in women's employment from restrictions on working hours, and then mainly in industries where women were rarely employed. In manufacturing and sales, the effect may even have been positive, possibly because work became "more pleasant, convenient, and compatible with household duties." [197]

Protection versus Equality

After World War I the Women's Bureau of the Department of Labor developed policies concerning women's work and began to draw attention to the needs of women with families. The Women's Bureau promoted the legitimacy of women workers based on their need to support families and defended them against charges that they took jobs from men. The bureau also advocated protective legislation regulating maximum hours, night work, minimum wages, and workplace safety. But by the 1920s, the goals of protection and equality for women began to diverge. "A woman's right to a job, equality in pay, and occupational opportunity were all antithetical to her being singled out for protection." [189] However, protective legislation was firmly entrenched. Until the 1960s, "[l]iberals continued to define the female labor force . . . as young, poor, transient, and unorganizable women workers who needed protection more than they needed equality." [199] Support for protective legislation delayed the fight against discrimination by defining women as marginal workers and opposing real equality.

Women's role within the family, particularly with respect to the care of children, also seemed to justify differences in the workplace for women and men. Until the middle of the twentieth century women who sought higher education usually forfeited marriage, and women who did marry were barred from many firms. Powerful social forces discouraged deviance from accepted gender roles and gendered occupations. But discontent among women became more evident, particularly as larger numbers of women gained a college education only to confront limited opportunities for employment and advancement.

Movement for Equality

By the 1960s the struggle for equality was at the forefront of a renewed feminist movement, and a number of remedies for inequality emerged—affirmative action, comparable worth, civil rights, and equal employment opportunity legislation. In 1963 the report of the President's Commission on the Status of Women presented clear evidence of discrimination against women in public- and private-sector employment. It found that restrictions on hours of work hindered women in professional and managerial careers, and laws prohibiting night work affected others. Also in 1963 the Equal Pay Act required equal pay for equal work. A year later Title VII of the Civil Rights Act prohibited "discrimination on the basis of race, color, religion, sex, or national origin in hiring, promotion, and other conditions of employment." [201]

Because of the extent of occupational segregation by sex, the Equal Pay Act was not sufficient to address wage inequalities. Men and women rarely performed exactly the same work. Women began to demand equal pay for jobs of *comparable worth* as measured by characteristics of jobs such as the level of skill required or responsibility exercised. Although the courts have not been sympathetic to the extension of Title VII of the 1964 Civil Rights Act to cover comparable worth, several local and state governments have enacted comparable worth provisions for their own employees. The increased power of women in the labor market and increased presence of unions in the public sector played an important role.

Economic Progress and Gender Equality

Although many observers believe that economic progress has not resulted in fully equal treatment for women and that the progress that has been made is vulnerable to reversals, there is reason for optimism. The ratio of women's earnings to men's has been narrowing since 1981 after remaining stable from 1950 to 1980. Occupational segregation is also diminishing.

However, there is concern that women are losing ground in the home. Women still bear the primary responsibility for the care of home and children. The time women spend in unpaid work in the home has not dropped enough to offset the increase in hours of paid work. Increasing divorce and paternal default on child support combined with lower earnings for women mean that women are 1.5 times as likely as men to be in poverty.

Economic progress is often ambiguous. When white-collar employment expanded, women's labor force participation rose. "Office work, teaching, and other white-collar employment offered women better working conditions, shorter hours, and higher pay than manual labor." [214] But formal barriers to women's employment, such as prohibitions against working after marriage arose in office work rather than in manufacturing. Progress may be hidden under seemingly regressive trends. For example, when women who had left the workforce to marry and have children returned to work in the 1950s and 1960s after their children were grown, their lack of skills and experience reduced the attainment of women in the aggregate. However, they contributed to the rise in women's labor force participation.

Although reversals of fortune are unpredictable, signals for the future can be read in the situation of young women today. "The young initially receive the fruits of economic progress through, for example, advances in education, training, revised expectations, and greater control over fertility." [214] The wage gap between men and women is smaller among younger cohorts. Women are also closing gaps in college graduation and postgraduate education, choice of major, and entrance into professions. Women with children are increasing their rates of labor force participation, continuity of employment, and full-time employment. And younger women are developing more realistic assessments of the skills needed for employment. All these trends imply greater equality between men and women in the future.

Summary of

The Gender Pay Gap

by Francine D. Blau

[Published in *Women's Work and Wages,* eds. Inga Persson and Christina Jonung (London, New York: Routledge, 1998), Ch. 1, 15–35.]

The gap in wages between men and women has been the subject of intense scrutiny in recent years, accompanying the increase in women's labor force participation. Understanding what determines this difference is no easy matter, since wages themselves are the outcome of a number of factors, each of which may differ for men and women. Most analyses of the gender gap focus on gender-specific issues such as differences in human capital or labor market discrimination. The article summarized here adds another dimension: wage structure—the prices offered by the labor market and the institutions that influence them. Wage structure contributes to our understanding of the wage gap, while bringing gender (and race) into the equation increases our understanding of the wage structure itself.

Gender-Specific Determinants of the Wage Gap

Human capital and discrimination dominate the discussion of gender wage differentials. "Human capital explanations . . . explain gender differences in economic outcomes on the basis of productivity differences between the sexes." [16] These productivity differences arose from the division of labor in the family. Women traditionally took most responsibility for the home and family, so women acquired less education than men, particularly in fields valued by the market. Women's experience in market-based work was episodic, interrupted by marriage and child raising. Lower experience and less market-oriented education led to lower earnings for women, and also led women to choose occupations that required less investment in human capital. Employers preferred not to hire women for jobs that involved lengthy development of firm-specific skills because they might not remain with the firm long enough to warrant the training. Career-oriented women who would, in fact, make a long-term commitment to a job, often suffered "statistical discrimination" from employers unwilling to risk hiring any women. To the extent that human capital differences do explain the gender gap, the gap should diminish as women gain more and more consistent labor market experience and more market-oriented education.

To the extent that human capital differences do not explain the gender gap, discrimination is a likely cause. Discrimination may reflect outright prejudice against a group of people or take the statistical form described above in which individuals are excluded based on employers' perception of typical characteristics of the group. When women are excluded from male-dominated jobs they are "crowded" into female jobs, creating an oversupply of labor that lowers wages in those jobs. In both the human capital and discrimination models, occupational segregation potentially plays a role.

Human capital differences between men and women and discrimination may coexist and can be difficult to distinguish empirically. In statistical analysis discrimination is not directly observed, but is inferred from the residual unexplained by measured characteristics. (It could also be the case that the residual, in whole or in part, captures the effect of unmeasured productivity-related characteristics.) On the other hand, employer discrimination may discourage women from making human capital investments, reinforcing their choices to stay at home. "Even small initial discriminatory differences in wages may cumulate to large ones as men and women make human capital investment and time allocations on the basis of them." [18]

Wage Structure and the Wage Gap

Over the last two decades labor markets in industrialized countries have undergone many changes, including a rise in wage inequality, especially in the United States. This turmoil focused attention on the determinants of wages, particularly changes in skills and the rewards to skills. The precise causes of increasing inequality are matters of debate among economists, but technological change, international trade, and institutional factors are likely candidates.

In other work the author, with Lawrence Kahn, investigated wage-setting institutions like unions and minimum wage laws. The findings indicate "that systems of centrally determined pay are likely to entail less wage inequality and smaller gender wage differentials. . . ." [20] In the decentralized system in the United States, where wages are generally set on a firm by firm basis, "a significant portion of the male-female pay gap has been found to be associated with inter-industry or inter-firm differentials." [20] In many other industrialized countries union wage scales have a strong influence (in some cases legally enforceable) on wages of all workers. Such centralized systems tend to reduce variation across industries and firms and thus lower the gender gap. In addition, since the distribution of women's wages lies below that of men, minimum wage laws will also reduce the gender gap by raising the relative position of those at the bottom of the scale.

International comparisons raise a puzzling question. Women in the United States have high qualifications and the United States has a long-standing legal commitment to eliminate discrimination, yet the United States has one of the largest gender pay gaps. The solution comes in looking at "the fairly large penalty that the U.S. wage structure imposes on groups that have below average skills (measured or unmeasured) or are located in less favored sectors." [21] Sweden and the United States provide a useful comparison because Sweden has one of the highest female-to-male wage ratios and the United States has one of the lowest. (However, the U.S. gap has been narrowing and the Swedish gap widening since the data used here were collected in 1984.)

In 1984 the unadjusted female-to-male wage ratio for the United States was 66.9 and for Sweden 82.7. (All ratios are expressed as percentages.) Adjusted for human capital and industry and occupation variables, the U.S. ratio was 82.2 and the Swedish ratio 90.9. One could infer that Swedish women suffer less discrimination or have better unmeasured characteristics than women in the United States, but this conclusion would be wrong. "Differences in women's qualifications or labor market treatment are not responsible for the larger U.S. gender gap, rather it is differences in overall labor market prices in the two countries." [23]

The analysis assigns each woman the percentile ranking she would hold in the *male* wage distribution. Qualifications and discrimination determine the position of women on this scale, while the male wage structure assigns a particular reward or penalty to each position. The mean percentile rank for women is at the 29.6 percentile level in the United States and 29.9 in Sweden—almost exactly the same, the 30th percentile in round numbers. In other words, 70 percent of the men in each country earn more than the average woman. The average female-to-male wage ratio in each country is equal to the ratio of the 30th to 50th percentile male wage—which is a much larger gap in the United States than in Sweden.

Repeating the analysis with controls for job-related characteristics—education, experience, occupation, and industry—finds that the average woman would be at the 36.6 percentile of the male wage distribution in the United States and the 37.4 percentile in Sweden—again, almost identical. The first comparison shows that in both countries the average woman earns more than 30 percent of men in general; the second shows that in both countries the average woman earns more than 37 percent of men with the same job-related characteristics. Even though the average woman's wage in each country falls in the low end of the male wage range, the low end is better off compared to other workers in Sweden than in the United States.

The gender gap in job characteristics is similar in both countries. A slight difference in experience and occupation favoring Swedish women is offset by differences in the gender gaps in education and industry favoring U.S. women. However, the wage differentials for these characteristics are quite different in the two countries. For example, the wage differentials between industries are much smaller in Sweden; this is the most important, though not the only difference in wage structures.

A final analysis compares the wages of all women in each country to all men. The U.S. and Swedish situations are very similar throughout the distribution and almost identical in the middle ranges. At the bottom, more women are in the lowest male decile in Sweden than in the United States (29 percent versus 20 percent). Labor market institutions that bring up the bottom of the wage distribution are therefore of particular importance in reducing the gender gap in Sweden.

Swimming Against the Tide

With inequality growing in the United States and the wage structure shaped by rising returns to skills, "women's relative skills and treatment have to improve merely for the pay gap to remain constant. Still larger gains are necessary for it to be reduced. Yet the gender gap has actually been falling in the USA since the late 1970s." [28] Women's qualifications improved in the 1970s and 1980s, particularly through improvements in experience and reduction of occupational segregation. Declines in unionization hit men harder than women. The unexplained portion of the gender gap fell, reflecting reduction in discrimination or gaps in unmeasured characteristics. As women increased labor market attachment, statistical discrimination may have declined. Although enforcement of antidiscrimination statutes fell in the 1980s from initial levels, earlier enforcement may have encouraged women to undertake greater levels of human capital investment. It may also be the case that shifts in prices for skills have affected men and women differently, favoring women over men among low- and medium-skilled workers.

On an international basis, wage structure explains why the U.S. gender gap is high relative to other countries; gender-specific factors do not appear to play a role. In contrast, within the United States gender-specific factors such as improvement in women's qualifications and declines in discrimination are very important causes of the narrowing of the gender gap over time. As a practical matter it seems easier to attack gender or other differentials directly. Without such differentials, men and women would be similarly affected by the wage structure and changes in it.

Summary of

Social Construction of Skill: Gender, Power, and Comparable Worth

by Ronnie J. Steinberg

[Published in *Work and Occupations* 17, 4 (November 1990), 449–482.]

Pay equity is an important part of the movement for gender equality in the workplace. Early demands for equal pay for equal work proved insufficient to deal with the reality that men and women rarely perform exactly the same job. Achieving pay equity on the basis of comparable worth is a popular alternative; however, comparable worth presents its own set of problems because it requires a precise, ordered, and easily understood measure of skills that often occur in fluid, complex combinations. The article summarized here argues that existing instruments for evaluating skills are themselves biased toward male-dominated occupations and reflect gendered power relationships in the labor market. Rather than objectively based criteria, skill definitions are social constructions developed under particular historical conditions. The movement for compensation based on comparable worth both brought these biases to light and developed strategies to overcome them when conducting job evaluations.

Skills in Context

Discussions of skill among sociologists and political economists take two basic paths, situating skill within either the historical trajectory of industrial capitalism or within a framework of "stratification and the distribution of job rewards." [451] The first path focuses on the effect of mechanization and automation on skills, particularly artisan's skills. Some analysts, epitomized by Harry Braverman in his 1974 book *Labor and Monopoly Capital,* make the further claim that technological change enhances control of the employer over the employee. Others view the progress of industry as a neutral process accompanied by compatible changes in the skill content of jobs. The second path views skill as a "major variable in explaining labor market outcomes." [451] Functionalism related skill differences to unequal economic rewards based on differences in the functional values of jobs within firms, while human capital theory focused on skill as one of the determinants of differential rewards to individuals.

Most studies of wage determination accept simple indicators of skill with the implication that these are objective measures capable of distinguishing between occupations with accuracy and reliability. However, some feminist analysts have begun to question whether generally accepted conceptualizations of skill are truly unbiased. This is particularly important because a great part of the gap in wages between men and women has been attributed to human capital differences or lower skill levels for jobs traditionally held by women. The women's movement in the 1960s targeted economic equality as one of its major goals and quickly confronted the fact that the demand for "equal pay for equal work" was ineffective in a labor market heavily segregated by gender. Women and men rarely performed the same work; however, the level and complexity of skills required for different jobs was often comparable. This insight gave rise to the movement for compensation based on comparable worth.

Comparable worth proponents hold that the "femaleness" of a job lowers the wage rate of the job net of other characteristics. Characteristics of jobs are measured by employees using job evaluation systems. Evaluation procedures vary in their degree of rigor, and the most sophisticated systems assign points to such factors as education, responsibility, effort, working conditions, and skill; make an overall assessment of complexity; and attach wage rates. However, advocates and researchers found that existing evaluation systems were often based on assumptions derived from male-dominated manufacturing, craft, administrative, and managerial occupations. In some women's occupations, job descriptions were lacking in sufficient detail to capture all compensable qualities.

Exposing Bias

Investigation of the assumptions underlying definitions of skill and the construction of systems of compensation revealed pervasive sex bias in the design and application of job evaluation systems. Such systems tend to undervalue the work women do in the marketplace either by ignoring the skills required for women's jobs or underrating them. The skill content in the work that women do is often not recognized. Even when detailed descriptive information from the *Dictionary of Occupational Titles* (DOT) was used to control for skill differences, some studies found that "the percentage of females in an occupation accounts for a significant portion of wage differentials by gender." [453] In some cases the DOT itself evidenced biased ratings. For example, a 1974 review of the DOT "found that dog pound attendant, parking lot attendant, and zookeeper were rated as more complex than nursery school teacher and child care worker." [456]

Underlying Ideology

During the nineteenth century few women worked outside the home after marriage. Men were expected to be the breadwinners and jobs were developed with this principle in mind. When women did work, their opportunities were limited, and their wages were premised on the idea that men in their families furnished their main support. Over time this assumption became institutionalized both in the job structure and in the evaluation systems set up as metrics for determining compensation. The National Research Council found an extremely high level of correlation among evaluation systems, so that flaws are widespread.

Invisibility

Certain characteristics are well defined in the context of male jobs, yet may remain unrecognized—and therefore uncompensated—when associated with female jobs. Firefighters are clearly understood to be dealing with emergencies. Flight attendants also must deal with emergencies (in fact the job came about as a result of Federal Aviation Administration regulations), but this aspect of the job is not recognized for compensation purposes. In each of the major evaluation areas—skill, effort, responsibility, working conditions—characteristics that come with women's jobs are often overlooked or vaguely described in contrast to very detailed descriptions of men's jobs. A few examples of often overlooked characteristics from each area are communication and coordination, lifting people or performing multiple tasks, caring for patients or representing an organization to the public, exposure to disease or to difficult clients or patients.

Undervaluation of Complexity

In some cases a job characteristic is noted but rated as less complex when attached to a woman's job. Communication is ranked hierarchically so that communication with "higher-status persons is defined as inherently more complex" [463] than communication with the general public. Men are more likely to interact with higher levels of an organization while women are in direct contact with clients or patients. Fiscal responsibility is generally rated higher than the responsibility of caring for the lives of patients. Clerical workers' knowledge of grammar and composition are not rated as highly as the technical skills of entry-level craft workers. In some cases an evaluation system developed in one context is a poor fit with another situation, for example a system set up for a bureaucratic organization will not adequately address the teamwork needed among professional and technical personnel in a hospital.

Factor Weighting

Evaluation systems generally assign weights to various job characteristics. One frequently used scheme, the Hay Guide-Chart system assigns managerial know-how five times and technical know-how seven times the weight of human relations know-how. Yet human relations includes supervision of other employees, so that managers get points under both managerial and human relations subcategories while a nurse supervisor receives points only under human relations. "[T]he New York State Comparable Pay Study concluded that working with difficult clients and dying patients, repetitious work, and undesirable working conditions received negative weights, net of other job characteristics." [466] Presence of these characteristics actually reduced compensation.

Inconsistency

Job evaluations are often conducted by employee committees trained to use a particular evaluation system. In one case reviewed by outside experts, the point scores of the Hay system, a well-known evaluation model, were applied in such a way that women's jobs received low-end scores and men's jobs received high-end scores. The evaluators themselves were unaware of this pattern. In another case employees brought substantial knowledge of the jobs to bear on the evaluation, supplementing formal job descriptions with information about the actual duties of the job. An observer noted that when women reported that a job in question was more complex than the specification, their comments were rejected by men on the committee, while men's reports were accepted by women evaluators.

The Politics of Skill Reconstruction

The movement for comparable worth has taken place largely in the public sector; by 1989 all but four states had enacted some kind of pay equity measure. Yet resistance and political maneuvering caused delays or compromised results. During the first phase, in the early 1970s, most efforts used existing job evaluation systems. By the second phase, in the early 1980s, the gender biases of these systems were becoming known and advocates of comparable worth began to struggle over the evaluation process itself as well as the outcome. Personnel administrators used various strategies to retain control over the evaluation process; however, even within existing systems of evaluation women made gains as pay equity became an acceptable goal. During the third phase advocates of comparable worth have become more adept at gaining control of the entire job evaluation process, choosing consultants and technical advisors, and forming their own review teams to monitor the evaluation process.

Summary of

Racial Antagonisms and Race-Based Social Policy

by William Julius Wilson

[Published in *When Work Disappears: The World of the New Urban Poor* (New York: Alfred A. Knopf, Inc., 1997), Ch. 7, 183–206.]

Race in America is intricately tied up with social, political, and economic processes that have made cities their most recent battleground. Poor African-Americans are concentrated in deteriorating inner-city neighborhoods from which whites and middle-class blacks have fled, taking business and financial resources with them. Public services suffer as the urban tax base falls and cities lose clout in state and federal politics.

In this chapter Wilson examines policies that have exacerbated the poverty and isolation of inner-city ghettos. He argues that race-based policies may ignite a conservative backlash rather than improve conditions for poor African-Americans. Policies that apply to all low-income people would be more politically acceptable while still helping disadvantaged African-Americans who meet their need-based criteria.

Racial Conflict

Race-related incidents receive a great deal of media attention, which contributes to an atmosphere of fear and heightened racial tension in U.S. cities. In such an atmosphere it is easy to overlook the political, economic, and social context of racial conflict. "In 1960, the nation's population was evenly divided between cities, suburbs, and rural areas. By 1990 . . . suburbs contained nearly half of the nation's population. . . . As cities lost population they became poorer and darker in their racial and ethnic composition." [184] The city of Chicago, for example was 63 percent minority in 1990, while its suburbs were 83 percent white.

With declining population, cities also lost political influence. Suburbs represented 36 percent of the vote in the 1968 presidential election and a majority of the vote by the 1992 election. By 1980 the emerging policy agenda, New Federalism, favored suburban areas at the expense of the cities. Urban initiatives were cut back. On top of this, economic recession reduced tax revenues. Many cities faced fiscal crises, which led to further service cutbacks. Taxes increased to alleviate budget deficits. As a result, cities became even less desirable places to live and the flight to the suburbs continued.

Job opportunities also moved out of the city and property values fell in older city neighborhoods. Working-class whites could not sell their homes in these neighborhoods at a price that would allow them to buy new homes in the suburbs. Trapped in the cities, minorities and low-income whites struggled for control of shrinking political and economic resources. Mayoral elections in several cities have been notable for racial animosity, while battles over housing integration on Chicago's South Side and busing children to integrate public schools in Boston have become icons of America's racial malaise.

Racial–Ethnic Conflicts

Tensions between African-Americans and whites are complicated by large immigrant populations in many cities. Latinos, who may soon overtake African-Americans as the largest minority group in the United States, are competing with blacks in several cities over legislative redistricting, political power, and the distribution of jobs, government contracts, and social services. Latinos interviewed in a large Chicago study expressed fear of and animosity toward African-Americans, claiming that black neighborhoods are unsafe. One respondent made a clear distinction between working and nonworking blacks: "The ones who work are very nice and respectable, but the ones who don't work, well, you have to hide yourselves from them." [188] Racial attitudes among Latinos are not a simple matter, however. In Miami, for example, black and white Latinos mingle freely and live in mixed neighborhoods with Haitians and other Caribbeans blacks, while native-born, English-speaking African-Americans remain segregated "in neighborhoods characterized by high levels of joblessness and marred by pockets of poverty." [189]

Relationships between African-Americans and Koreans are also strained. Facing poor employment prospects, many Korean immigrants opened small businesses, often in poverty-stricken black neighborhoods. Many Koreans have negative views of black people. Conflicts over quality or service and fears that Korean businesses threatened black economic prospects bred hostility. In New York, boycotts of Korean businesses were the result. During the Los Angeles riots in 1992, Korean businesses suffered heavy damage.

These tensions emerged against the background of "declining real wages, increasing job displacement, and job insecurity in the highly integrated and highly technological global economy." [192] Economic insecurity encourages demagogic political leadership that incites people to blame each other rather than confront the roots of economic problems. The social consequences of joblessness are filtered through the lens of individual failure. An ideology that blames the victim justifies diminished support for programs to alleviate urban poverty and joblessness. Many white people have turned against programs they believe would benefit only minorities. Race-based strategies such as affirmative action benefit the more advantaged minority individuals without remedying the problems of disadvantaged inner-city blacks. New policies are needed that can attract a wider constituency and affect a broader population.

Rising Inequality

Until the early 1970s the effects of race far outweighed any effects of class among African-Americans. With the success of the civil rights movement, black presence increased dramatically in higher education; in professional, technical, managerial, and administrative occupations; and among homeowners. Successful black people were finally able to pass the fruits of their success along to their children, constituting a new upwardly mobile black middle class. At the same time, the condition of disadvantaged black people deteriorated and "many dire problems—joblessness, concentrated poverty, family breakup, and the receipt of welfare—were getting even worse between 1973 and 1980." [194] This pattern continued into the 1990s. Since the mid-1970s inequality in the United States has risen generally; however, income inequality increased among blacks even more dramatically than among whites. Average income for the lowest three quintiles of black families fell between 1975 and 1992 (-33 percent for the bottom fifth), while average income for the highest two quintiles rose (+23 percent for the top fifth). Among blacks in 1992, the top fifth of families received 48.8 percent of family income; among whites the corresponding figure was 43.8 percent.

The dynamics of inequality within the black population must be understood if policies for alleviating ghetto poverty are to be effective. The civil rights movement focused on individual advancement through the elimination of discrimination and improvement of access to education, employment, voting, and public accommodations. However, "the most disadvantaged minority individuals, crippled by the cumulative effects of both race and class subjugation, disproportionately lack the resources to compete effectively in a free and open market." [196]

Black leaders began to advocate programs like affirmative action that would counteract the effects of the past. Here again, however, more-advantaged African-Americans were better prepared for new opportunities—college, better jobs, promotions. Many affirmative action efforts were directed at blue collar jobs like law enforcement or craft and construction occupations; some low-income students were able to enter professional schools. But the masses of disadvantaged black people were unaffected by these initiatives. At the same time they were negatively affected by structural changes in the economy "such as the shift from goods-producing to service-producing industries, the increasing polarization of the labor market into low-wage and high-wage sectors, destabilizing innovations in technology, and the relocation of manufacturing industries outside the central city." [198]

Feasible Policy Options

Calls for an end to affirmative action have been met with efforts to develop affirmative action programs based on need. These efforts stem from a realization that disadvantages in income, education, family stability, and the like are not solely the result of racial discrimination. "Minorities would benefit disproportionately from affirmative opportunity programs . . . because they suffer disproportionately from the effects of such environments, *but the problems of disadvantaged whites would be addressed as well.*" [198, italics in original]

Need-based affirmative action may miss some of the more subtle consequences of a history of discrimination. If need is the sole criteria for affirmative action, many middle-class blacks will be excluded. They may suffer from accumulated effects of racial discrimination that operate irrespective of class, but these effects would not be addressed by a need-based affirmative action agenda. A more flexible approach combining need and race would offer the most comprehensive set of remedies.

Reducing residential segregation is one race-based program that could improve the lives of poor African-Americans. This would bring them closer to better job and educational opportunities. However, there are serious political and practical obstacles to large-scale desegregation. When blacks move into a neighborhood, whites move out, with neighborhood composition often changing quite rapidly. Restrictions on movement are undesirable in a democratic society; a more promising approach involves efforts to eliminate exclusionary zoning and to enforce the Fair Housing Act.

There is less support among white people for overtly discriminatory policies now than in the past. However, many white people associate a general disapproval of welfare recipients with a belief that blacks benefit more from state-provided welfare than white people do. While whites tend to oppose programs designed to guarantee equal outcomes (e.g., preferential college admissions or employment quotas), survey research indicates that most white people support compensatory programs like targeted recruiting that improve opportunities for disadvantaged blacks. Racially neutral proposals like national health care or job training would have widespread benefits and could form the basis for a new social agenda with widespread support.

Summary of

The Future of Affirmative Action: Reclaiming the Innovative Ideal

by Susan Sturm and Lani Guinier

[Published in *California Law Review* 84 (July 1996), 953–1036.]

This article reframes the discussion of affirmative action to focus on the underlying question of how to allocate high stakes opportunities in an increasingly diverse and changing environment. Along with its critics, many proponents of affirmative action leave unchallenged embedded assumptions that conventional processes of selecting workers and students are functional and fair, and that affirmative action programs serve as limited exceptions to these normally adequate and unbiased processes. In fact there are significant flaws in the way institutions select among applicants, and the debate over affirmative action can serve as an opportunity for institutions to evaluate and reform conventional selection processes in general.

This article shows that the current "meritocracy" is neither fair nor functional. This purported "meritocracy" is actually a "testocracy" founded on the use of standardized tests to predict future accomplishment in work and study. These tests fail to predict future performance for the majority of test takers and do not equip employers and educational institutions to respond to the demands of an unpredictable, rapidly changing economy. The authors argue that there is a need for a new paradigm for recruitment, selection, and promotion. They offer as one alternative a framework for selection that shifts the focus from prediction to experience based on structured, participatory, and accountable assessment.

The Stock Affirmative Action Narratives

The critics of affirmative action offer a stock narrative that revolves around the themes of merit and fairness. In this narrative, a white male applicant is denied employment or school admission in favor of a woman or person of color whose test scores are a few points lower. Underlying this stock story there are two important assumptions: that standardized tests such as the SAT, LSAT, and civil service examinations accurately and neutrally measure merit, and that fairness is the allocation of opportunity according to this objective measurement of worth. The stock story frames the affirmative action debate in terms of racial preferences that depart from the normal, universal for determining merit that are purportedly functional and fair. These stock stories thus mask more fundamental concerns about the adequacy of current selection processes. The ensuing debate over the legitimacy of current affirmative action programs takes on a static, win-lose character. By examining the assumptions that shape the stock narrative, the prospect of constructing effective and fair approaches to selection can emerge.

Unpacking Merit, Fairness, and the "Testocracy"

Among its various possible meanings, merit is most widely embraced as a functional concept related to the capacity to perform effectively. While the stock affirmative action narratives equate merit with performance on standardized tests, numerous studies show that employment and educational test scores correlate poorly with later performance levels and that these tests do not accurately predict achievement. Attributes such as discipline, emotional intelligence, commitment, drive to succeed, reliability, creativity, and interpersonal and leadership skills—attributes shown to be important to successful work and school performance—are not measured by any paper-and-pencil test. When institutions rely heavily on standardized test scores in their selection processes, they end up excluding successful performers and potential leaders whose skills are not easily quantifiable. Not only do standardized tests fail to "measure merit," they arbitrarily rank-order candidates for selection who are indistinguishable in their predicted future performance.

The stock narratives of affirmative action assume that a process is fair that treats everyone the same. But studies show that standardized tests advantage candidates from higher socioeconomic levels and disproportionately screen out women, people of color, and those in lower-income brackets. These tests therefore do not provide a fair ranking of candidates. They arbitrarily employ a method of selection that favors a particular group, when there are other methods that are equally or more reliable that can avoid these exclusionary effects. The stock affirmative action narratives therefore normalize and legitimate selection processes that closer inspection reveals to be neither functional nor fair.

The Need for a New Paradigm of Selection and Inclusion

Judicial opinions about affirmative action rarely scrutinize the general selection processes themselves, and many critics concerned about racial and gender justice continue to treat affirmative action programs as add-ons to existing, admittedly dysfunctional selection standards. There are several reasons why it is important to move from affirmative action as an add-on to affirmative action as an occasion to rethink the organizing framework for selection generally.

One reason for refocusing the affirmative action debate is that affirmative action as add-on is often counter-productive. While relying on race and gender plus factors to reach numerical hiring goals may at times make short-term sense by providing quick and visible results, race- or gender-based departures from prevailing standards are not perceived, treated, or responded to in the same ways as other departures from these standards. These departures are more highly visible than those benefiting dominant groups, and they therefore frequently arouse suspicion or resentment among coworkers and students toward perceived beneficiaries of affirmative action and play into existing stereotypes about gender and race. Affirmative action-based departures can also appear to pit diversity concerns against concerns about merit and institutional efficiency and too often divert attention from the role of diversity in enhancing the productivity and efficiency of organizations.

Another reason for refocusing the affirmative action debate on overall selection processes is that such a debate can reveal the inaccuracy of these processes' underlying assumptions about workers and jobs. Current selection standards treat the capacity to perform as though it exists in people apart from their opportunity to work on the job—and standardized tests as though they can measure this capacity in applicants. Experience shows, however, that the capacity to

do a job is typically gained by having the opportunity to do it and that performance correlates best with on-the-job training.

Conventional selection processes also presume that institutions know what
they are looking for and value in workers and students, yet research shows that
many institutions have no clear definition of successful performance. Standardized selection focuses on the decontextualized individual, even though team performance and the capacity to interact effectively is increasingly essential in today's
workplace. Prediction as the model of selection has created an illusion of precision
and validity that disables institutions from developing more dynamic and functional ways of choosing qualified candidates. Assessment through opportunity to
perform works better for a variety of reasons than tests for performance.

Reclaiming Merit and Fairness: Opportunity and Accountability

The current debate over affirmative action could potentially become a dialogue
about how to reconceive approaches to selection that will benefit everyone.
This reconceptualization of selection is a critical step in the pursuit of racial and
gender justice. As part of an effort to spark this dialogue, the authors propose a
framework to selection that attempts to meet the dual challenge of inclusiveness
and economic revitalization.

The proposed model of selection starts by moving from prediction-based assessment to performance-based assessment. The first step in this move is to
change how test scores are used in selection. At the very least, decision makers
should only take into consideration bands or zones of scores that are reliably
different from one another instead of unreliable, numerical scores; and test
scores should not be used to rank candidates or as independent screens that
function as prerequisites for further consideration.

To compensate for a reduced reliance on test scores, this model proposes
that institutions employ a variety of other means to distinguish between candidates. In the employment context, decision makers would assume responsibility for constructing a dynamic and interactive process of selection that is integrated into the day-to-day functions of the organization. This process might,
for example, rely on assessment done by those who would work with particular
candidates on a day-to-day basis. A significant challenge posed by relying on individual assessments is to develop systems of accountable decision making that
minimize the expression of bias. One way of doing this is to require decision
makers to articulate criteria of successful performance, document activities and
tasks relevant to the judgment, assess candidates in relation to those criteria,
and offer sufficient information about the candidates' performance to enable
others to exercise independent judgment.

In the educational context, too, there are various ways in which schools could develop opportunities for selecting students based on their performance rather than on standardized test scores. Schools, for example, can make admission decisions based on students' performance in preparatory programs, and universities can emphasize transfers from community colleges as a significant part of admissions.

The role of race, gender, and other categories of exclusion in this proposed model of decision making changes significantly from what it is currently. Rather than operating as an add-on, after-the-fact response to the failure of the overall selection process, race and gender would serve as a signal of organizational failure and as a catalyst of organization innovation. The proposed model embraces a functional conception of diversity that builds on both instrumental and normative goals.

The proposed model seeks to integrate selection and productivity. Perhaps the most broadly persuasive instrumental argument for this model is that it has the potential to improve institutional efficiency and productivity in a variety of ways. By reducing decision makers' reliance on ineffective standardized testing, a performance-based model would allow institutions to develop means to select better-qualified candidates. At the same time, a more dynamic, interactive approach to selection would require institutions to assess and monitor their needs in order to continually reformulate and update standards for recruitment.

Although the proposed model may appear more expensive to implement than traditional standardized selection processes, an investment of resources up front has the potential to enhance the overall productivity of the organization, both by identifying more productive individuals and by enabling the institution to adapt better to its changing environment.

This model builds on a functional theory of diversity. Research has shown that organizations that incorporate diverse groups of people with their various vantage points, skills, and values promote creativity, problem-solving, and innovation, among other qualities valuable to successful institutions. At the same time, diversity concerns that highlight race and gender discrimination within the organization can treat such discrimination as a signifier of systematic breakdowns within the organization's decision-making structure. By monitoring for race and gender discrimination, institutions can also discover and address more general management problems, such as poor organization or arbitrary treatment of workers. Finally, appealing to race and gender concerns remains an important way of bringing marginalized groups into the general dialogue about creating a new progressive agenda.

The proposed model attempts to develop a truly fair selection processes in contrast to the failed meritocracy currently in place. Performance-based selection is less likely to exclude people who can actually perform in a position and has the potential to create a participatory and accountable selection process, which can enhance individuals' autonomy and institutions' legitimacy.

Finally, there is normative basis for the proposed model based on the democratic imperative. Work and education are becoming basic components of citizenship in today's world, and selection processes serve as screens to participation. These screens must be drawn in the least exclusive manner consistent with an institution's mission. The current testocracy, however, screens out candidates unfairly, while performance-based selection would increase democratic decision making and broaden opportunities for participation.

In conclusion, our institutions do not currently function as fair and functional meritocracies. Only by rethinking our assumptions about the current system and future possibilities can we move toward the ideals about opportunity based on merit that so many Americans share. This enterprise offers the possibility of bringing together many who are adversaries in the current affirmative action debate and reconnects affirmative action to the innovative ideal.

PART IX

World Income Inequality and the Poverty of Nations

Overview Essay

by Kevin Gallagher

Diverging levels of national income are among dominant features of the contemporary world. While global income and real GDP have risen sevenfold since the end of World War II, and threefold in per capita terms, the gap in incomes between the developed and developing nations continues to widen. Large income disparities can also be seen within both the developed and developing nations.

Conventional economic wisdom has suggested that such trends need not cause alarm. It has been argued that long-term economic growth fueled by globalization in the form of trade booms, mass migrations, and huge capital flows, will solve each of these problems. Across nations, growth will eventually cause a convergence in world incomes. Within nations, economic growth will decrease inequality in the long term. Thus, the world's policy makers have had a justification to largely ignore questions concerning inequality in their decision making.

This essay reviews the current trends in income distribution both across and within the nations of the world, then discusses an emerging literature that offers critiques and alternatives of the conventional view. On both theoretical and empirical grounds, the literature reveals that economic growth and equity concerns need not be separated. In fact, it is shown that economic policies that incorporate equity concerns from the outset can be the most successful.

International Income Distribution Across Nations

Several years ago, the United Nations Development Program (UNDP) published a much publicized graph of the world's income distribution: in 1989, with world population on the X-axis and GNP per capita on the Y-axis. The graph was striking. It showed that the richest fifth of the world's population received roughly 85 percent of global income, world trade, domestic savings, and domestic investment. Conversely, the poorest fifth of the world's population received 1.4 percent of global income, 0.9 percent of world trade, 0.7 percent of domestic savings, and 0.9 percent of domestic investment (UNDP 1992). When combined with a mirror image of itself, this information appeared to be presented as a champagne glass of world income distribution. Later, UNDP put together a similar graph with 1991 data—little changed.

Is the glass half empty or half full? As Figure IX.1 illustrates, using 1997 data the graph (with its reflection) continues to look broad on the top, narrow on the bottom. The nations closest to the bottom are all in Africa. India is the first long straight section of the stem, and China is the second. The glass abruptly widens—that is, incomes get higher—within the top fifth of the world, a region inhabited by the developed industrial countries, oil producing nations, a few of the East Asian "tigers," and Argentina. Taking the metaphor a bit further, it seems that about one-sixth of the world's people actually get to enjoy the champagne, while the rest of the world gets to hold it up!

Others would still contend that all this gloom need not be coupled with doom. **Jeffrey Williamson** argues that the late nineteenth and late twentieth centuries are similar in many respects. During the late nineteenth century there was a relatively large opening in world trade and an increase in mass migration. Such occurrences narrowed the economic distance between rich and poor countries, as seen in Figure IX.2.

Contrasting "New World" with "Old World" nations, Williamson used the ratio of unskilled wages to farm rents, and the ratio of the unskilled wage to GDP per worker hour to explain wage changes in the wage distribution from 1854 to 1913. The result of the convergence was the result of both a trade boom and mass migrations. Williamson argues that the trade expansion ac-

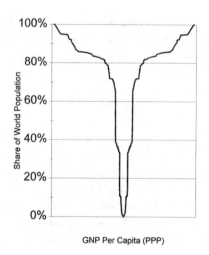

Figure IX.1. World Income Distribution, 1997. On the right half of the X-axis, GNP per capita ranges from 0 to $30,000. The left half of the graph is a mirror image added solely for the sake of appearances. *Source:* UNDP, 1997.

Coefficient of variation

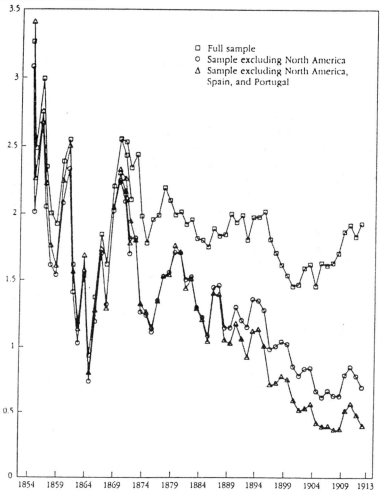

Figure IX.2. Real Wage Dispersion, 1854–1913. Note: Wage data are urban, male, adjusted for purchasing-power parity.
Source: Reprint of Figure 1, page 122 in Jeffrey Williamson, "Globalization and Inequality." *The World Bank Research Observer* 12, 2 (August 1997), 117–135.

counted for 10 to 20 percent of the convergence in GDP per worker hour and in the real wage. This is also the explanation given for the fact that wages for unskilled labor rose relative to land rents and skilled wages in poor countries and in rich countries.

In the years from 1913 until 1945, a period of protectionism and immigration quotas, the gap between rich and poor nations began to widen again. Because we are now entering another era of trade expansion and mass migration,

Williamson's analysis raises the question: Will the current era of globalization and growth bring about a similar convergence to that of the late nineteenth century?

Charles Jones (1997) and Paul Krugman and Anthony Venables (1995) argue that under certain conditions the answer to Williamson's question is yes. Assuming that the economic policies of the 1980s prevail, Jones predicts that world income distribution across countries is likely to be more compact in the future as a result of the general upward movement (Jones 1997). Krugman and Venables come to similar conclusions by employing a complex model under what one may consider unrealistic assumptions. The authors predict an inverted U-shaped pattern of global economic change, with divergence in the short term followed by convergence in the long term (Krugman and Venables 1995).

While the last 150 years have been characterized by eras of lower and higher inequality, the dominant overall trend for the past century has been dramatic divergence. **Lant Pritchett** argues that the income of the richest seventeen nations massively diverged from the incomes of all other nations during the period from 1870 to 1990. As illustrated in Figure IX.3, Pritchett demonstrates that the ratio of income of the seventeen richest nations to all other nations almost doubled from 2.4 to 4.6 during that period.

In Pritchett's view, overcoming the disadvantages of being at the bottom is one of the most serious challenges to economics. This conclusion differs con-

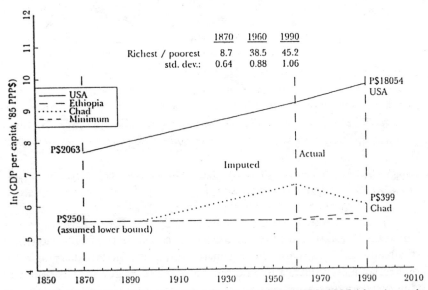

Figure IX.3. Simulation of Divergence of Per Capita GDP, 1870–1985 (showing only selected countries)

Source: Reprint of Figure 1, page 10 in Lant Pritchett, "Divergence, Big Time." *Journal of Economic Perspectives* 11, 3 (Summer 1997), 3–17.

siderably from the business as usual approach that would follow from the analysis of Jones and others.

Income Distribution Within Nations

More recently, large income disparities have emerged within developed and developing economies as well. Similar to the previous discussion, it has been argued that this may only be a short-term phenomenon; inequality might increase in the early stages of growth but decrease in the later stages. This relationship between distribution and growth has not held up empirically, however. Moreover, the development policies pursued by those nations who were led to believe in this relationship have at times exacerbated existing inequalities.

Kwan Kim discusses the different experiences of income distribution in developed and developing countries in recent decades. As discussed in Part I of this volume, inequality in the industrial democracies of Western Europe and North America have begun to widen since the 1970s. Inequality is on the rise in other countries as well. Here is a brief canvas of recent trends around the globe.

- In Central and Eastern Europe, inequality and poverty have risen during their period of economic restructuring—the situation being most severe in Russia and Bulgaria. Russia experienced a 0.14 to 0.24 rise in its Gini coefficient from 1987 to 1993, and Bulgaria experienced a 0.11 increase.

- The Latin American economies are more unequal than other developing regions. Peru, Mexico, Venezuela, and Colombia all have Gini ratios above 0.50, and Brazil leads the list at 0.605.

- Sub-Saharan Africa remains the poorest region in the world, where the most grave concern remains the fundamental issue of human survival.

- Developing countries in the Asia-Pacific region have, on the whole, done better in alleviating both relative and absolute inequalities. Malaysia, Indonesia, and Singapore stand out as nations that made progress in reducing inequality while China and Thailand did not.

Explanations for these variations are discussed later in this essay.

The picture is even worse for women. The 1995 UN Human Development Report (HDP) surveyed the condition of women across the globe. Problems of measurement and vast differences between countries (often driven by traditional cultural norms about appropriate roles for women) make cross-country comparisons difficult and render averages almost meaningless. However, common themes emerged from this UN undertaking: women lag behind men in both developed and developing countries along many economic and political dimensions.

A large majority of the world's poor are female, and the feminization of poverty is becoming worse. For many women, access to independent income through employment, land ownership, or credit is out of reach or falls short of self-sufficiency. In all countries reported on in the 1995 HDP, women's labor force participation rates and shares of earned income were less than men's. The UN cites a number of reasons for these disparities: women's concentration in low-skilled jobs; lack of bargaining power through unions; lack of access to maternity leave; and strongly held cultural norms that specify which jobs are suitable for women and/or discourage mixing men and women in the workplace (United Nations 1995).

Interpretations of the Kuznets Curve

In a pioneering 1955 paper, Simon Kuznets hypothesized, on the basis of cross-sectional data, that inequality tends to increase in the early stages of economic growth and decrease in the later stages. For decades afterwards, development theorists vehemently advised policy makers to ignore questions of inequality in the short term.

Today, there are more extensive cross-sectional and time-series data available to test these ideas. Empirical tests of these hypotheses establish that there is no consistent tendency in the inequality-development relationship.

A look at the time-series data reveals that a good Kuznets curve is hard to find as well (see Figure IX.4). In his look at this data, Fields concludes that "there is no empirical tendency whatsoever in the inequality development relationship." In his sample, inequality increased in half the countries growth experiences and decreased in the other half. This result held when looking at fast-growing developing economies as well. Inequality rose with the same frequency in the fast-growing developing economies as in the slow-growing ones.

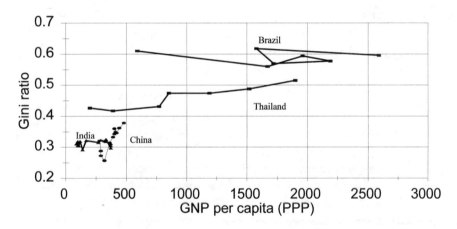

Figure IX.4. A Good Kuznets Curve Is Hard to Find
Source: The World Bank, *World Development Indicators,* 1998.

Irma Adelman and Nobuhiko Fuwa assert that the share of the poorest quintiles follows a path shaped more like a Nike "swoosh" than a U. Looking at all the less developed countries for which income distribution data could be found—forty-five countries for the 1970s and thirty-eight countries for the 1980s—they found that, on average, very little movement toward equality accompanies the process of growth. This is the case in all but the richest quintile; for the top group, the U is inverted. However, the right-hand side of the U is extraordinarily flat. The share of the poorest quintiles drops rapidly, at very low levels, and then rises very slowly thereafter. This becomes vivid in Adelman and Fuwa's graph, reproduced in Figure IX.5.

The share of the poorest quintiles drops rapidly, at very low levels, and rises very slowly thereafter. The poorest quintile does not recover the income share it had at a per capita income of $100 until the country reaches the income level of a developed nation. The flatness of these curves shows that the poorest, for all practical purposes, stay that way.

Although the empirical evidence to support the Kuznets curve has faded, a parallel idea has come to life in another literature. A 1995 paper by Gene Grossman and Alan Krueger found, for a number of environmental variables, that the relationship between per capita income and environmental degradation is an inverted U form (Grossman and Krueger 1995). In simpler terms, environmental quality first worsens but then improves with rising income. Unfortunately,

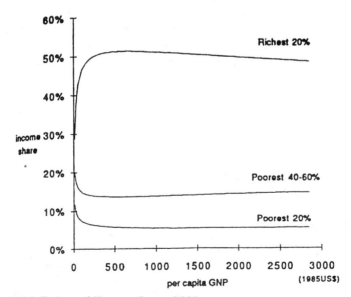

Figure IX.5. Estimated Kuznets Curve, 1980s
Source: Reprint of Figure 2, page 21 in Irma Adelman and Nobuhiko Fuma, "Income Inequality and Development: The 1970s and 1980s Compared." *Economie Appliqué* XLVI (January 1994), 7–29.

the same misguided policy prescriptions that came with the original Kuznets argument are being advocated in the environmental arena—grow now, clean up the environment later (to be addressed at length in the next Frontiers volume, *Sustainable Human and Economic Development*). This body of work has become known as the Environmental Kuznets Curve (EKC) literature. Like the debates over the original Kuznets work, the EKC is under empirical and policy attack.

An article by Mariano Torras and James Boyce in the EKC literature is of particular relevance to this volume. They look at the relationship between income, inequality, power, and levels of pollution (Torras and Boyce 1998). What is unique about the Torras and Boyce approach is that they attempt to see if inequality and the level of power in a nation are the key links between pollution and per capita income. Their theoretical inspiration for this approach comes from none other than Kuznets himself. They refer to Kuznet's "unsung" hypothesis as the base of their analysis:

> One may argue that not only the welfare equivalents but also the power equivalents of the same relative income spread show a much wider range when the underlying average income is low than when it is high. (Kuznets 1963, 49)

The authors plausibly hypothesize that greater inequality of power will be associated with higher levels of pollution. Those who benefit from pollution will be better able to prevail against those who bear the costs of pollution. The devil here, however, is in the details. To test for power inequality the authors include the literacy rate, Gini ratios, and a set of measures reported to represent political rights and civil liberties. The latter set of variables are what makes their analysis problematic. Based on a ranking system deployed by an organization called Freedom House, the authors create a 0 to 12 scale that has higher values representing greater freedom. This is a prime example of the oversimplification of political science that Atkinson refers to in Part I of this volume—creating an arbitrary and obscure quantitative summation of characteristics of complex societies for the sole purposes of quantitative analysis. A critique of such methodologies is discussed later in this essay. This being said, the Torras and Boyce article is a pioneering first attempt to introduce power and inequality into the EKC debates.

The Consequences of the Growth First Paradigm

Relying on the early appearance of supporting evidence for the Kuznets curve, development economists sternly advised developing nations to grow first and worry about inequality later. A consensus emerged that growth could best be attained in developing countries by making the following "adjustments": liberalizing trade, privatization, public sector reforms, and currency devaluation. In many cases, these policies took the form of formal structural adjustment programs administered by the World Bank and the International Monetary Fund.

Trade liberalization has been the pillar of the "growth first" agenda. The last *Frontiers* volume, *The Changing Nature of Work*, discussed opposing views on the effects of trade liberalization on inequality in the developed nations.

George Borjas and Valerie Ramey, looking at the United States, bolsters the minority view by arguing that trade is a major cause of wage inequality. They demonstrate empirically that the trend in wage inequality parallels the U.S. trade deficit in durable goods, and suggest that in theoretical terms, import competition would be expected to have a particularly strong effect on wages in concentrated industries such as durable manufacturing. They show that evidence on wage trends in selected industries lends support to the theory.

The "growth first" paradigm also has problematic implications for developing countries. Economic theory suggests that greater openness to world trade in developing countries would reduce wage inequality because liberalization raises the relative demand for unskilled workers and therefore reduces the wage gap between the skilled and the unskilled. In some cases this has been the case, in others it has not. **Adrian Wood** shows that the evidence from East Asia during the 1960s and 1970s supports the theory but the Latin American experience since the mid-1980s has not.

During periods of trade liberalization in Latin America, skill differentials in wages widened. Many of these changes are attributed to changes in labor market institutions in those countries and to overall changes in the world economy—specifically the entry of large low-income Asian countries into world markets. Earlier, when the East Asian "tigers" entered the world market they were relatively low-wage producers, with a comparative advantage in labor-intensive manufacturing. But by the 1980s, Latin American countries were middle-income range, and their unskilled workers in labor-intensive export industries could not compete with their East Asian counterparts.

Another pillar of growth-first schemes has been privatization. Since the late 1980s, privatization efforts have surged in the developing countries. During this period, revenues increased from $2.6 billion in 1988 to $23.1 billion in 1992. Privatization occurred most in Latin America and the Caribbean—accounting for 70 percent of all the privatization in the developing world. Infrastructure was the leading sector for privatization; the second most important was industrial production.

Who have been the purchasers of privatized enterprises? Increasingly the answer is foreign investors. From 1988 to 1992, privatizations accounted for close to 10 percent of all foreign direct investment flows to the developing world. This trend presents developing country governments with a distributional dilemma. The developing countries desperately need funds from their privatization schemes, but they also want some amount of control over who receives the benefits. However, the exertion of control over the process may scare away foreign investors.

Balance-of-payments shortages and other macroeconomic disequilibria make it hard to turn away foreign investors. At the same time, the World Bank and related institutions have actively encouraged privatization in developing countries. Close to 70 percent of all structural adjustment loans and 40 percent of sectoral adjustment loans during the 1980s had a privatization component.

Paul Cook and Colin Kirkpatrick argue against the tendency of economists to evaluate privatization programs on efficiency grounds alone, leaving distributional concerns to political scientists. This approach, in their view, is one of the primary reasons so many economists cannot adequately explain the development process. Cook and Kirkpatrick develop a political economy approach to examine the distributional impact of privatization in developing countries. Their analysis reveals that privatization has occurred to promote specific groups' economic interests, rather than the advancement of welfare in the entire nation. Privatization usually benefited the same interests and groups that were favored before the schemes were utilized.

Adelman and Fuwa show that for the 1980s, structural adjustment policies appeared to have become the more important influence causing inequality in developing countries. While this is the overall case, structural adjustment seems to have had varying degrees of success and failure worldwide. There is an enormous literature that consists of case studies of structural adjustment programs on specific countries, but they all seem to have a similar and relatively unsatisfying conclusion—the effects of adjustment are varied, complex, and locally specific. (See, for example, Bourguignon et al. 1991.)

Nevertheless, structural adjustment policies are said to affect individuals and households in developing countries in three ways: changes in employment and income, changes in the price of goods and services, and changes in the provision of public services. One survey suggests that the groups that are least linked to the market, the rural poor and informal sectors in urban cities, are the least exposed to price changes. The formal sectors in cities are seen to be the hardest hit because they are exposed to changes in consumer prices (Nelson 1992).

There is an emerging consensus that the equity effects of structural adjustment in Africa have been largely negative. In 1995 the Ministry of Foreign Affairs in Denmark published a comprehensive study of the effects of structural adjustment in five African countries: Burkino Faso, Ghana, Tanzania, Uganda, and Zimbabwe. The report shows that rural areas in these countries experienced an increased differentiation as a result of adjustment-induced changes in agricultural pricing and marketing. Conversely (and contrasting the broad conclusions of researchers such as Nelson), urban areas seemed to benefit from the increase in aid flows and imported goods. The developments in the urban areas brought about a surge in the construction sector and in the demand for informally provided services. The two trends taken together imply that the rural/urban wage gap greatly increased during the course of adjustment in these African countries.

Concluding an assessment of the developing experience during the heyday of structural adjustment policies, noted development economist Lance Taylor concludes: "There is no single answer to the fundamental question of why nations grow at different rates, with diverse distributions of income and wealth. It is clear that policy must be tailored to the local situation and even to the particular conditions prevailing at the time" (Taylor 1996, 262). He goes on to show how sharply this view contrasts with the "Washington Consensus" about how a relatively uniform policy package can be applied to developing countries with beneficial results almost everywhere.

Learning Without Curves

If the Kuznets curve estimates and actual development experiences show us that growth-only policies do not ensure equality, what does? An empirical literature is slowly emerging that challenges the studies that support and advocate the growth-first agenda outlined earlier. An empirical literature arguing that unequal societies tend to have weaker economic performance than egalitarian societies is beginning to break into the more mainstream economic journals. While intuition and idealism would cause many, including the editors of this volume, to applaud the intent of such studies, a look at their methodology reveals that this literature is still in its infancy.

Alberto Alesina and coauthors looked at seventy-one countries during the period 1960–1985. They argue that the evidence in these studies implies that the more egalitarianism from the onset is correlated with a positive growth path. Their theory however, is based on the "median voter" theorem: The tax rate or other economic policy selected by the government is the one preferred by the median voter. That theorem is relevant because the more equitable the income distribution, the better endowed is the median voter with capital—and hence the more reluctant is the median voter to favor taxation of capital. It is also assumed that the lower the level of capital taxation, the more the economy will grow. A related argument is that inequality will fuel political instability and reduce investment, and therefore reduce growth. As a result, inequality and investment should be inversely related (Alesina and Rodrik 1994, Alesina and Perotti 1996, Persson and Tabellini 1992).

While these studies seem consistent with intuition, if somewhat constricted in their view of both politics and economics, they have been shown to have serious methodological flaws. Because the authors rely heavily on cross-sectional analyses using the median voter theorem, the designation of what is a democracy is a crucial part of the analysis. One study listed South Korea (in the 1960s and 1970s), El Salvador, and Panama as democracies! In an article that makes a number of other important critiques of the data and methodology in these studies, another author wrote "coding South Korea as a democracy in the 1960–1985 period is fairly outrageous: grabbing power by military coup and persecuting opposition leaders is simply incompatible with elementary democratic procedures" (Weede 1997). A.B. Atkinson, in an article summarized in Part I, has added "In my view, this understates what economists can usefully learn from political scientists. . . . The median voter theory is far from being 'standard'" (Atkinson 1997).

Like the article by Adrian Wood discussed earlier, **Gary Fields** points to the successes of the East Asian countries to show how an equality-first approach can work. Inspired by the work of philosopher John Rawls, Fields hopes that development would focus on maximizing the well-being of the worst-off person. Thus, an approach of broad-based growth—growth that is targeted on raising the living standards of the poor but that also raises the living standards of all socioeconomic levels—is most effective.

Based on the success of the East Asian nations, Fields provides the following list of parameters that can help nations achieve broad-based growth:

- Policy makers have to strike a balance between not raising the returns to labor prematurely (if wages are excessive, employment and output could be reduced) and not repressing wages permanently (which would exclude the poor from the benefits of growth). Because labor is so abundant in the developing world, labor intensive growth can be more beneficial for the poor than capital intensive growth.

- Just as important as the quantity of labor demanded is the quality or skills that workers bring to the labor market. There may be no trade-off between equity and efficiency when it comes to education. Spending additional educational dollars on primary education rather than higher education may add more to the productive capacity of workers and spread the benefits of growth in a more broad-based manner.

- As with resource allocation for education, there may not be an equity-efficiency trade-off when it comes to land. In the early post–World War II period there were significant land reforms in many of the East Asian countries, laying a relatively egalitarian foundation. There are three advantages to having such an initially egalitarian distribution. First, the asset of land generates income and hence spreads the benefits of growth to the poor. Second, since it is well known that small farms have higher yields per acre, a more equal distribution of land would raise total agricultural productivity. Finally, those with land hold a great deal of political power. Keeping power out of the hands of a landed oligarchy can be beneficial to the poor.

- Key to a successful development approach is sound trade and industrialization strategies. The East Asian economies were able to maintain full employment and rapidly rising real wages. Much of this is attributed to export-led growth. These nations chose their trade policies carefully, adapting their policies as their comparative advantage shifted more to lower-wage countries, as they moved into higher-wage sectors.

Summary

The articles included in Part IX and the other literature cited here cover a lot of ground. An enormous amount of theoretical, econometric, and case study work has aimed at documenting and understanding the extent of inequality and poverty around the world. To summarize the major themes in this essay:

- Income distribution across nations has remained dramatically unequal since the late 1980s.

- Over the past 200 years the overall trend has been a divergence of income across nations, but during that time there have been relatively more equal periods than others, particularly from 1854 to 1913.

- The Kuznets hypothesis, that inequality tends to increase in the early stages of economic growth and decrease in the later stages, no longer holds up to empirical and theoretical tests.

- The "growth first" development policies of recent decades, including trade liberalization, privatization, and structural adjustment, have had varied results on income distribution within nations. Standing in stark contrast are the East Asian and Latin American experiences.

- "Broad-based growth," growth that is targeted on raising the living standards of the poor but also raises the living standards of all socioeconomic levels, can be most effective.

Summary of

Divergence, Big Time

by Lant Pritchett

[Published in *Journal of Economic Perspectives* V11, 3 (Summer 1997), 3–17.]

"Divergence in relative productivity levels and living standards is the dominant feature of modern economic history." [3] In particular, this article documents that, between 1870 and 1990, incomes in the developing world fell far behind those of the developed world in both relative and absolute terms. This finding emerges from an examination of each group of countries separately, then together. However, the larger group of less developed countries is far from homogeneous; marked divergences in income growth can be found within it as well as in comparison to those that have "arrived."

Convergence in Growth Rates of Developed Countries

Looking at the seventeen "advanced capitalist countries (twelve in Western Europe plus the United States, Canada, Australia, New Zealand, and Japan) as a group, we can make three strong generalizations about their economic performance during the period under consideration. First, these countries experienced strong convergence in per capita incomes during this period. Second, while the poorer countries in this group grew faster than the richer, it is striking how narrow the range of growth rates were from 1870 to 1960. Finally, since 1870, there has been no acceleration of overall growth over time.

Evidence of convergence can be seen in the fact that the poorest six of the now-developed countries had five of the six fastest national growth rates from 1870 to 1960. Moreover, the richest five now-developed that were richest in 1870 experienced the five slowest growth rates during the same period. Nevertheless, the range of growth rates was very narrow: only from 0.9 (Australia) to 1.9 (Switzerland and Finland). During this period the standard deviation of average annual growth rates was only 0.33. The spread became much wider from 1960 to 1980, from New Zealand's 1.4 to Japan's impressive 6.3 annual per capita GDP growth. When the developed countries' average growth rate for 1980–1994 returned to the pre-1960 level of 1.5, the variance again narrowed.

We should not be surprised to find convergence among the now-developed countries; indeed, it could be viewed as almost tautological. Countries that are now rich either started rich and grew slowly or started poor and grew rapidly. The result is that those who have arrived at similar endpoints must have converged (at least not diverged) over time.

Comparing the Two Groups

A very different picture emerges from a comparison between the group of seventeen just mentioned and all the other countries. Since historical data are harder to come by for the less developed nations, in order to make the comparison the author started by establishing, as a lower bound, the lowest GDP per capita that could have prevailed for a significant length of time in any of the places under consideration. Logic and available data are used to conclude that a 1985 purchasing power equivalent of $250 is the lowest that GDP per capita could have been in any country in 1870.

This figure can be defended on three grounds: first, no one has ever observed consistently lower living standards at any time or place in history; second, this level is well below extreme poverty levels of nutritional intake; and third, at a lower standard of living the population would be too unhealthy to expand. [7]

Starting with this assumption, along with the estimates of historical growth of developed nations and the current cross-national comparisons of income, it is easy to see that the two groups of countries, defined in terms of income, pulled apart over the period 1870–1990. One way to illustrate this claim is to examine the ratio of the income of the seventeen richest nations to all other nations. From 1870 to 1990 this ratio almost doubled, from 2.4 to 4.6.

It is also illuminating to compare the United States, the world's richest country, with the rest of the world. Per capita income in the United States grew about fourfold from 1870 to 1960. So any nation whose income was not four times higher in 1960 than in 1870 must have grown slower than the United States. One-third of the nations of the world that offer data for 1960 had per capita incomes below $1,000. Therefore, if their incomes were at least $250 in 1870, they must have grown less than fourfold, or more slowly than the United States. A more dramatic point emerges if we compare GDP per capita of the United States to the average GDP per capita of all other countries. Over the twelve decades in question this absolute income gap grew by an order of magnitude, from $1,286 to $12,662.

Poverty Traps, Takeoffs, and Convergence

The countries lumped together as "other than" the seventeen industrialized nations are a highly diverse group, in terms of both historical performance and current economic situations. While some countries have begun to experience strong and sustained growth rates, some continue to have slower growth rates than the richest nations, and some have even experienced negative growth.

A standard can be set for "explosive growth" as the rate that would have taken a country from the lower bound in 1870 to the U.S. level of per capita GDP in 1960. Such an achievement would require a 4.2 percent annual growth in per capita GDP. Among the advanced capitalist countries, even during their period of most rapid growth, only Japan exceeded this. From 1960 to 1990 growth was faster than this standard in eleven "developing" nations, many in East Asia. However, sixteen developing countries had negative growth over the same period, and forty countries (more than a third of the sample) had growth rates of less than 1 percent per year.

In the 1960s Alexander Gerschenkron popularized the optimistic view that backwardness presented an opportunity for rapid catch-up in technology and productivity. "However, the prevalence of absolute divergence implies that while there may be a potential advantage to backwardness, the cases in which backward countries, and especially the most backward of countries, actually gain significantly on the ladder are historically rare." [15] A variety of forces appear to be present, under a variety of circumstances. Some countries have been able to realize explosive growth, but there are also forces for stagnation and for drastic social and economic decline. Overall, it appears that "[b]ackwardness seems to carry severe disadvantages." [15] One of the most serious challenges to economics is that of overcoming the disadvantages of "being at the bottom." Rather than deriving a single growth model, a unified theory of economic growth and development must address the questions:

> What accounts for continued per capita growth and technological progress of those leading countries at the frontier? What accounts for the few countries that are able to initiate and sustain periods of rapid growth in which they gain significantly on the leaders? What accounts for some countries fading and losing the momentum of rapid growth? What accounts for some countries remaining in low growth for very long periods? [15]

Judging from the varieties of experience shown in this study, it seems that the appropriate growth policy will differ according to the situation. We cannot gain much from theories or policies for promoting growth that are insensitive to the distinctions between mature versus booming economies, or between these and the countries that are still in the poverty trap.

Conclusion

This article clearly documents the divergence in relative productivity levels and living standards in the modern era. Economists of the more optimistic variety have pointed to divergence as a source of hope. They claim that the poorer nations can leapfrog many of the richer ones and experience periods of rapid growth. However, the fact that there has been an absolute divergence shows that there have been very few examples of such rapid growth—especially among countries on the lower end of the income ladder. There is equally the possibility that rapid decline could incur instead. How to overcome the disadvantages of "being at the bottom" is one of the most serious challenges to economics.

More than revising conventional growth theory, for such a challenge to be met, four questions must be addressed: "What accounts for continued per capita growth and technological progress of those leading countries at the frontier? What accounts for the few countries that are able to initiate and sustain periods of rapid growth in which they gain significantly on the leaders?

What accounts for some countries fading and losing the momentum of rapid growth? What accounts for some countries remaining in low growth for very long periods?" [15]

Judging from the variations in experience shown in this study, rather than a universal approach, most policies should differ according to their respective situations. This would be a marked "divergence" from current notions of growth theory.

Summary of

Globalization and Inequality, Past and Present

by Jeffrey G. Williamson

[Published in *World Bank Research Observer* 12, 2 (August 1997), 117–135.]

The late nineteenth and late twentieth centuries are similar in many respects. Each era has been characterized by increased economic growth, economic convergence, and globalization. From 1914 to 1950, however, the world economy experienced lower rates of growth, a retreat from globalization, and economic divergence. Will the world economy reverse its surge toward globalization as it did a century ago? This article examines the historical debate about the nineteenth-century globalization boom and links it with the globalization and inequality debates of the late twentieth century.

Globalization and Inequality in the Late Twentieth Century

Much of the scholarly literature on the relationship between globalization and inequality has focused on the case of the United States, but a number of recent studies have examined globalization's effects on developing countries as well. During the period from 1973 through the 1980s, inequality rose in the North, in part due to globalization forces. Economic theory and a few studies argue that such rises in inequality would be coupled with a more egalitarian South.

The recent widening of wage inequalities in the United States occurred simultaneously with a trend toward rising trade liberalization and the increased immigration of unskilled workers from developing countries. George Borjas has estimated that these forces have contributed to 15 to 20 percent of the relative decrease in the wages of high school graduates compared with college graduates: trade accounting for one-third, immigration two-thirds. Have these patterns resulted in stimulating the relative demand for unskilled labor in the developing countries and thus made developing countries more egalitarian?

In a comprehensive study, Adrian Wood also contends that the fall in relative wages of less-skilled northern workers is caused by the reduction in trade barriers and by an increasing number of southern workers with a basic education. His detailed empirical analysis concludes that the ratio of the unskilled to the skilled wage should then rise in the South and fall in the North, producing rising inequality in the North and falling inequality in the South. While Wood's assertions are consistent with economic theory, recent studies show that a number of countries in Latin America and East Asia have experienced increases, not declines, in wage inequality after trade liberalization.

Globalization and Inequality in the Late Nineteenth Century

From 1854 to 1913 there was a convergence in the economic distance between rich and poor countries. Much of this convergence is the result of both a trade boom and mass migrations. The trade boom has been attributed to 10 to 20 percent of the convergence in GDP per worker hour and in the real wage. In addition, it meant rising wages for the unskilled relative to land rents and skilled wages in poor countries, and that unskilled wages fell relative to land rents and skilled wages in rich countries.

The correlation between real wages or GDP per worker hour and migration is also positive and very significant. The poorest Old World nations experienced very high emigration rates while rich New World nations tended to have low ones. Because the migrant populations consisted of largely unskilled workers, receiving countries' labor markets became flooded at the bottom of skill ladders. The immigration-related trends imply increased inequality in rich countries, and the emigration-induced trends reduced inequality in the Old World.

Two kinds of evidence can be used to investigate trends in inequality during the late nineteenth century: the ratio of unskilled wages to farm rents per acre, and the ratio of unskilled wages to GDP per worker hour. In previous work with his colleagues, the author constructed a panel database documenting the convergence of the ratio of unskilled wages to farm rents among late nineteenth century countries. This database reveals that from 1870 to 1913 farmland was plentiful and cheap in the New World, while scarce and expensive in the Old World Therefore, the ratio of wage rates to farm rents was high in the New World, low in the Old. When looking at the wage-rental ratios in the fourteen countries sampled, because landowners were near the top of the income pyramid inequality rose in the rich, labor-scarce New World and fell in the poor, labor-abundant Old World. Examinations of the ratio of unskilled workers' wages to GDP per worker hour, or computing the annual percentage change in the index, reveal similar results.

The Impact of Globalization on Inequality Trends, 1870–1913

Economic theory argues that in eras of unregulated international migration, poor nations will have the highest emigration rates and rich nations will have the highest immigration rates. In addition, under liberal trade policy, poor nations should export labor-intensive products and rich countries should import them.

As far as the impact of mass migration, where immigration increased the receiving country's labor supply inequality rose. Conversely, when emigration reduced the sending country's labor supply, inequality declined. Some nations in Europe began to back away from trade liberalism after 1880. Before that period the correlation between rising inequality and initial labor scarcity was better than from the period 1890 to 1913, the era of rising protectionism. While it is impossible to separate globalization effects into trade and migration with these regressions, an effort was made by creating a trade-globalization-impact variable as the interaction of initial labor scarcity and openness. The results maintain under these conditions. Overall then, there is strong support for the impact of migration on income distribution and weak support for the role of trade. Another study found that globalization was responsible for more than half of the rising inequality in rich nations and for more then a quarter of the falling inequality in poor nations. Technological change, here too a culprit, accounted for 40 percent of the rising inequality in rich countries prior to World War I and for close to 50 percent of the decline in inequality in poor ones.

A great reversal in these trends occurred during the period 1921 to 1938. First, there was a divergence in wage differentials between rich and poor nations. Second, in a complete reversal, inequality rose more sharply in poorer countries than in richer ones, where in some cases it actually declined.

Some Things Never Change

While there are striking similarities between the late nineteenth and late twentieth centuries with respect to globalization and inequality, some differences should be noted. First, the more egalitarian outcomes of poor countries as a result of globalization in the first period has not in large part been echoed in the second. As far as migration, it seems to have more of an impact on inequality than trade did in the late nineteenth century. One thing is true—that globalization and convergence ceased between 1913 and 1950. Rising inequality in rich nations came to a halt when immigration was kept away by quotas and when a more protectionist era arose. Will such a retreat occur again?

Summary of

Income Distribution and Poverty:
An Interregional Comparison

by Kwan S. Kim

[Published in *World Development* 25, 11 (1997), 1909–1924.]

While low inequality is most likely to be consistent with sustained growth, positive growth is neither a sufficient nor necessary condition for low inequality or poverty incidence. This article reviews the different experiences of developed and developing countries through their integration into the world economy, economic growth, and income distribution. Drawing from these experiences, the article reassesses the nature of the linkage between growth and distribution.

Trends in Distribution and Poverty

Global income and real GDP have risen sevenfold since the end of World War II and threefold in per capita terms; but during that time, the gap in incomes between developed and developing nations continued to widen. In addition, large disparities emerged among developing countries.

The industrial democracies of Western Europe and North America are known to be relatively more equal than the rest of the world, but since the early 1980s inequality had begun to widen. There is variation among this group, however, with the United States and Japan at two extremes. The United States has become the most unequal of the industrial democracies. From 1980 to 1990 the Gini distribution rose from 0.36 to 0.43. During that period only the top quintile of families gained, in real-income terms, while the rest experienced a decline. On the other hand, throughout Japan's high growth period of the 1970s its Gini index stayed at around 0.34. During the 1980s the income share of the lowest quintile in Japan exceeded that of the Nordic welfare states and Western Europe and was about twice that of the United States.

In Central and Eastern Europe both inequality and poverty rose over their period of economic restructuring. These trends vary between countries. Income distribution and poverty has become more severe in Russia and Bulgaria. According to various estimates, Russia experienced a 0.14 to 0.24 rise in its Gini coefficient from 1987 to 1993, while Bulgaria had a 0.11 increase. Conversely, economies like those of the Czech Republic, Hungary, and Poland that benefited from stabilized and faster growth, fared better with more modest increases in inequality. These nations chose to proceed with reforms more cautiously and gradually to minimize abrupt impacts on unemployment and inequality.

Sub-Sahel Africa is the poorest region in the world, where the fundamental issue of human survival remains a grave concern. Malnutrition and disease are more widespread than they were 30 years ago, even though most African nations have undergone drastic market-oriented adjustment policies. In most African nations real incomes fell or remained stagnant from 1987 to 1994.

The Latin American economies are more unequal relative to other developing regions. For instance, the Gini ratio is 0.605 in Brazil, 0.618 in Colombia, 0.500 in both Mexico and Venezuela, and 0.568 in Peru. Across the whole continent the working poor were not necessarily worse off, but growth reached them very slowly, causing the relative distribution to worsen. Increases in inequality in the region were coupled with rising poverty. Almost 40 million people were added to the officially defined poor in the region, and the region's incidence of poverty rose to 43 percent by the end of the 1980s. While economic recovery in the early 1990s boosted the region's growth rates, the real income of the bottom 40 percent remained below the poverty line in most Latin American countries. The rise in poverty is correlated with a decline in real wages. For the entire region, real wages from 1980 to 1987 fell 15 percent in the formal private sector and 30 percent in the public sector.

Developing countries in the Asia-Pacific region are an exception—although there are wide disparities in this region, on the whole they have done better in alleviating relative and absolute inequality. Malaysia, Indonesia, and Singapore stand out as nations who made progress in reducing inequality, while Thailand and China are examples of areas where inequality rose. In regard to poverty, the Asia-Pacific region has made progress as well.

Causes Behind Interregional Disparities

There is no overarching explanation for worldwide income inequality. In the industrialized world inequality is associated with changing labor and capital markets within the domestic economy, which are linked to the global economy in technology, trade, and capital movement. The consequences of globalization are rising profits relative to wage income and growing concentration of employment in higher-wage professional occupations and lower-wage service industries. In addition, the adoption of labor-saving technologies and the shift in consumer demands toward technology-intensive products away from standardized products have caused a polarization of the wage gap between skilled and unskilled workers. Increased capital outflow and outsourcing of production to developing countries are added sources of the decline in demand for less-skilled workers.

The developing country experience is more varied. Large disparities in inequality and poverty can be attributed to differences in the role of government. In general, the most successful East Asian nations placed an emphasis on poverty alleviation rather than on reduction of inequality. Their strategy focused on human capital development targeted toward the rural poor and small industry. More specifically, these nations packaged a unique blend of community-based basic health and education, rural credit subsidies, and infrastructure development, combined with growth-oriented market interventions and the stabilization of prices and foreign exchange rates.

In addition to government intervention, social and labor movements played a critical role in the Asia-Pacific region. In South Korea, for example, throughout the 1980s until 1992 grassroots movements (that were sometimes violent) prevailed in achieving many concessions. In China, however, the story is different. China experienced double-digit growth rates since 1976, but its development strategy, based on expanding urban areas along selected coastal areas, has widened the income gap among regions as well as between cities and farming villages.

Inequality in Africa and Latin America has been due in part to structural reforms. In Africa, where the majority of the poor are in rural areas, poverty is exacerbated by a lack of political commitment to land reform or public sector support for rural development. The rural poor experience very little access to credit, land, and extension services. In Latin America, inequality and poverty reflect the legacy of import substitution strategies. This caused Latin American countries to embrace austerity measures in the 1980s, which quickly increased the numbers of critically poor, low-paid underemployed low-wage workers. In addition, repeated currency devaluations hit wage-earners, self-employed workers, and others who had less capacity to protect themselves against price increases.

Distribution and Growth: The Search for a New Link

Market-oriented growth does not automatically reduce inequality and poverty. Postwar discussion of the distribution/growth relationship has centered around the concept of the Kuznets hypothesis: that inequality rises in the early stages of development and falls at its later stages. This hypothesis is not supported empirically, whether the studies are cross-sectional or time-series. That positive growth is not a sufficient condition for reductions in poverty or inequality has been seen in many countries. As described earlier, the supply-side policies of the United Kingdom and the United States during the 1980s shows that growth does not automatically reduce poverty. Likewise, in China and Thailand, impressive economic growth has not reached the poor.

In the cases where growth has been associated with reduced poverty or inequality, the state has been involved. Examples are Japan and the East Asian countries. In postwar Japan, land reform and subsequent improvement in the terms of agricultural trade gradually eliminated rural poverty. Japanese governments initiated a universal education system at the basic and secondary levels, at the same time implementing comprehensive social security and national health programs. In other Asian situations, it took spontaneous and often violent social movements to bring about redistribution. In the Philippines innovative grassroots movements and labor's efforts for collective bargaining had positive effects on the incomes of the working poor.

Inequality is often rationalized by supply-side economists who say that by enduring inequality now nations can have more opportunities for equality later. There is no empirical evidence supporting these claims either. Indeed, a number of recent studies point to a strong relationship between equality and growth. Japan, Finland, Germany, the Netherlands, Belgium, and Sweden, which were more equal in distribution in the 1980s, were associated with faster productivity growth, whereas less equal countries, such as New Zealand, Australia, Switzerland, and the United States, tended to be correlated with slower growth.

Conclusion

This article has shown that the relationship between distribution and growth is affected by the country's development strategy as well as by its sociocultural environment. It further argues that the alleviation of poverty calls for a strategy to target specifically the disadvantaged population for social adjustments so that they can share in the benefits of growth. The state should provide better health care, education and training, and other social adjustments to help broaden the participation of those left behind. Such a strategy has been shown to have long-term payoffs, since equitable distribution appears to be compatible with sustained economic growth.

Summary of

Income Inequality and Development: The 1970s and 1980s Compared

by Irma Adelman and Nobuhiko Fuwa

[Published in *Economie Appliqué* 46, 1 (January 1994), 7–29.]

Is there a trade-off between inequality and economic growth? This article uses data from the 1970s and 1980s to estimate the relationship between the stages of economic growth and the income shares of rich and poor. It finds that on average, very little movement toward equality accompanies the process of growth.

Moreover, in the 1980s structural adjustment policies gave many countries an additional push toward inequality.

Previous Studies of Equality and Growth

In his path-breaking 1955 article, Simon Kuznets formulated the hypothesis that early economic growth increases inequality while later economic development narrows it. A graph of the share of the poor in national income would therefore be shaped like a U. In the climate of optimism about development that followed World War II, Kuznets' hypothesis was initially ignored; it was reconsidered only in the late 1960s, as problems of unemployment and poverty emerged even in fast-growing countries.

Statistical research into income distribution and development began in the 1970s, although it was hampered by the lack of adequate distributional data. Studies published in the 1970s and 1980s differed in many details, but generally confirmed the existence of the U-shaped Kuznets curve; some studies, however, found the curve to be quite flat. None of these studies is entirely satisfactory, and none had access to today's more ample sources of data.

Theory Guiding Variable Selection

An empirical study of income distribution in developing countries must take account of the factors that explain the Kuznets curve, as well as many other long- and short-run influences on distribution. The discussion of these factors here includes previews of the findings of the international comparative analysis described below.

Most models that generate the Kuznets U rely on intersectoral movements of population and income. For example, industrialization transfers labor and resources from the low-productivity, relatively egalitarian, traditional agricultural sector to the high-productivity, inegalitarian industrial sector. This initially increases inequality; but once more than half the labor force is employed in the modern sector, continued industrialization will decrease inequality. Yet surprisingly, the relative sizes of the agricultural and industrial sectors have no consistent relationship to the distribution of income in developing countries.

Productivity differentials between agriculture and industry, or between modern and traditional agriculture, are another source of inequality. Kuznets and some subsequent writers suggested that there would be a U-shaped movement in the intersectoral productivity gap, first widening as industry pulls ahead and then narrowing in a later stage of balanced growth. A measure of the intersectoral gap—the ratio of productivity in agriculture to productivity in industry—proves quite significant in explaining income inequality.

More rapid growth requires higher investment, which, in a closed economy, must come from savings. Greater inequality puts more income in the hands of the rich, who are more likely to save; in this sense, inequality might be thought to promote growth. In an open economy, other sources of investment financing are available. Measures of savings or other financing availability—the rate of inflation, the ratio of foreign debt to GDP, and the ratio of foreign capital investment to GDP—had a significant relationship to inequality, particularly in the 1980s.

The distribution of wealth—including land, physical capital, and human capital—should have a major effect on the distribution of income. Major redistributions of land and physical capital are rare; however, many people advocate broadening education as a route to equality and growth. A key measure of the distribution of wealth, the Gini ratio for land ownership, is significantly related to the distribution of income in the 1970s.

Political and institutional factors shape the distribution of income. Governments invest in infrastructure and education, set and collect taxes, and establish the policies and legal frameworks within which economic activity takes place. Elite-oriented governments carry out these functions in ways that promote the interests of the rich; populist or socialist governments seek to promote the interests of the poor. Dummy variables describing the extent of socialist influence on government policy had a significant relationship to inequality in the 1970s.

Finally, the initial physical and demographic conditions affect a country's options for development, and hence its income distribution. Countries with abundant natural resources tend to specialize in primary product industries, which create relatively few jobs while often involving dependence on foreign economic interests. Therefore, natural resource abundance is often associated with inequality; the present analysis confirms that conclusion for the 1970s. Greater population density implies less arable land per agricultural worker, which often means that there are many small, uneconomic holdings engaged in low-productivity agriculture. These may coexist with high-productivity commercial agriculture, implying a high degree of inequality. We would thus expect less arable land per agricultural worker to be associated with more income inequality, which is again empirically valid for the 1970s.

The Statistical Analysis

The sample encompasses all less developed countries for which income distribution data could be found: forty-five countries for the 1970s and thirty-eight countries for the 1980s. The analysis seeks to explain the shares of income of population quintiles (i.e., the poorest fifth, the second fifth, and so on). It uses the explanatory variables discussed above, and the log of per capita GNP and its square. The presence of the square of the income variable allows the estimation of a Kuznets U.

The U-hypothesis is confirmed for both periods. A graph of the share of the poorest quintile first declines with growing incomes and then rises again at higher income levels. In fact, a similar shape is traced by all but the richest quintile; for the top group, the U is inverted. However, the right-hand side of the U is extraordinarily flat. The share of the poorest quintiles drops rapidly, at very low levels, and then rises very slowly thereafter. "The major declines occur at income levels corresponding to those of South Asia, where the bulk of the world's poor are. . . . The income share of the poorest quintile is within 3 percent of the minimum at income levels ranging from $485 to $1000 for the 1970s and $1689 to $5000 for the 1980s." [19] The poorest quintile does not recover the income share it had at a per capita income of $100 until the country reaches the income level of a developed nation.

Results for the 1970s and 1980s

Aside from per capita GNP, there are a wide range of variables that are significantly related to income distribution in the two decades, as suggested above. Macroeconomic variables play essentially no role in the results for the 1970s; instead, structural and institutional factors and initial conditions appear more important. Factors associated with greater inequality in the 1970s include the productivity differential between sectors, the inequality of land ownership, the abundance of natural resources, and population density. The degree of socialist influence on the government is correlated with greater equality, suggesting that more market-oriented policies promote inequality. Also, foreign investment is associated with inequality: the greater the size of foreign direct investment relative to the economy, the lower the share of the poorest four quintiles, and the higher that of the richest.

For the 1980s, macroeconomic adjustment policies appear to have become more important, replacing several of the influences seen in the 1970s. The intersectoral productivity differential and the extent of foreign investment remain correlated with inequality, as in the earlier decade. For many reasons, foreign investment may be associated with political and economic inequality, which applied equally in the 1970s and 1980s. An additional reason, specific to the 1980s, is that foreign investment was more likely to flow to countries that followed IMF adjustment policies more closely—and those policies were a force for inequality.

Inflation becomes a major influence on income distribution in the 1980s; at the average rate of inflation for the sample, inflation reduces the income share of the poorest by about one-sixth. In times of rapid inflation, wage increases usually lag behind prices, while the returns to the assets of the rich (land, foreign exchange, and physical capital) keep pace with price increases. Moreover, inflation in the 1980s was more likely to lead to IMF-inspired adjustment policies, relying heavily on wage repression and cuts in government subsidies to mass consumption. The literature on the adjustment to the debt crisis points out that the poor have borne the brunt of the costs of IMF adjustment policies; the statistical research described here confirms this observation.

In conclusion, there is a Kuznets curve, but its right-hand side is so flat that it cannot be relied on to cause a noticeable increase in the income share of the poor. Other readily understandable factors also affect the distribution of income in developing countries, such as the distribution of land and other wealth, the nature of government intervention, the role of foreign investment, and the impact of structural adjustment policies. "[I]n the lowest income countries, the primary hope of the poor lies not in raising their countries' growth rates, but rather in changing the structure of assets of the poor and the nature of macroeconomic adjustment policies." [25]

Summary of

The Relationship Between Wage Inequality and International Trade

by George J. Borjas and Valerie A. Ramey

[Published in *The Changing Distribution of Income in an Open U.S. Economy,* eds. J.H. Bergstrand et al. (New York: Elsevier Science, 1994), Ch. 7, 217–241.]

Wage inequality in the United States, by virtually any measure, began an unprecedented rise in the late 1970s. The change is primarily due to the deterioration of the real wages of less educated and experienced workers, not to gains by those at higher levels. Many explanations for increasing wage inequality have been proposed, including the shift away from manufacturing toward service industries, the effects of international trade or immigration, the decline in unionization and the fall in the real value of the minimum wage, and a decline in the level of skills supplied by the American educational system. The residual inequality that cannot be accounted for by these factors is often attributed to "skill-biased technological change."

This article presents a version of the argument that trade is a major cause of wage inequality. It demonstrates empirically that the trend in wage inequality parallels the U.S. trade deficit in durable goods, and suggests that in theoretical terms, import competition would be expected to have a particularly strong effect on wages in concentrated industries such as those found in many branches

of durable manufacturing. Finally, it shows that evidence on wage trends in selected industries lends additional support to the theory.

Trends in Trade and Inequality

The empirical analysis of wage inequality is based on annual Current Population
Survey data for 1963 to 1988, for samples of adult men who worked full-time
year-round and were not self-employed or unpaid. In each year, average wages
were estimated for each of four groups—high school dropouts, high school
graduates, those with some college, and college graduates. Inequality is then
measured by the wage ratios between groups—for example, the ratio of average
wages for college graduates versus high school graduates, or college graduates
versus high school dropouts. Both of these measures display similar patterns,
rising slightly in the 1960s, remaining roughly constant for most of the 1970s,
and then rising rapidly in the 1980s.

The goal of this section of the article is to identify trade-related data series
that move in parallel with the measures of inequality. Because the analysis involves time series with nonzero trends, there is a danger of being misled by spurious correlations between actually unrelated series. Recent developments in
econometrics, involving the analysis of "cointegration," address this problem;
the article contains an accessible summary of these developments and references to more detailed texts.

For readers who are not interested in pursuing the cointegration problem,
the authors' argument can be seen in a series of three graphs. The graphs compare the college graduate versus high school dropout wage ratio to the U.S.
trade deficit in services, nondurable goods, and durable goods (as a percentage
of GDP). The wage premium for education has essentially no relationship to
trade in services, and only a weak or inconsistent relationship to trade in non-
durables. In contrast, there is a close relationship between the wage premium
and the net imports of durable goods.

Statistical analysis confirms and elaborates the impression created by these
graphs. Only the relationship of the wage premium to trade in durable goods
passes the test of cointegration (i.e., avoids the problem of spurious time-series
correlations). Separate examination of durables exports and imports shows that
the increase in inequality caused by imports is greater than the decrease in inequality due to the same amount of exports.

Changes in durables imports and exports precede and appear to cause (in
technical jargon, "Granger-cause") changes in the wage premium; the reverse
relationship does not hold. Finally, the relationship between trade in durables
and the wage premium was similar before and after 1980. That is, the relationship estimated on the basis of data for 1963–1979, if applied to the actual trade

figures for the 1980s, predicts the pattern of inequality in the 1980s quite accurately.

A Model of Wages and Employment Rents

The differential effect of trade in durables on wage inequality is difficult to explain in terms of standard trade theory. Durable goods industries use skilled labor *more* intensively than other goods-producing industries, so one might expect that import competition in durables should weaken the relative position of more highly skilled workers. Yet in fact, the exact opposite occurs.

Why does an increase in net imports of durable goods weaken the relative position of low-skilled workers? Two distinguishing characteristics of durable goods industries are relevant to this question. First, industries producing durables tend to be more concentrated than other industries. Second, workers in more concentrated industries tend to earn higher wages, for any given level of skills. This is in part because more concentrated industries are more likely to be unionized, but there is an effect independent of unions as well. There is an industry rent in concentrated industries, a portion of which is received by workers.

These facts provide the basis for a plausible explanation of the statistical results discussed above. Most workers in manufacturing are either high school dropouts or graduates. Those in more concentrated industries, where there are higher rents, earn higher wage premiums relative to the average for their skill levels. When foreign firms enter the market, they capture a portion of the industry rents and reduce the wage premium formerly enjoyed by American manufacturing workers. The reduction occurs both because import competition leads to wage reductions for those who remain in the industry, and because it drives some workers into other, lower-paid industries. Foreign competition in low-wage industries, in comparison, matters less for overall inequality trends, because the workers there have less to lose. A mathematical model in the article offers a rigorous demonstration of these arguments.

Trends in Labor Compensation in Key Industries

The theoretical model discussed in the previous section implies that when import competition affects durable goods industries, their wage bill, or total employee compensation, should decline—at least as a percentage of aggregate employee compensation in the economy as a whole. If this model correctly describes the mechanism by which import competition causes wage inequality, then the trend in employee compensation in durable manufacturing should parallel the measures of inequality, such as the college versus high school dropout wage premium. At first glance, this relationship does not hold. The wage bill in durable manufacturing parallels the college versus high school dropout wage premium only very approximately—the two series fail the cointegration test for a meaningful relationship.

In reality, however, only a few durable goods industries account for most of the volume of trade. Three industries—motor vehicles and parts, capital goods (largely nonelectric machinery), and primary metals—account for a significant fraction of all durable imports and exports. Metal mining, though not part of manufacturing, is similarly affected by trade in durables because so much of the demand for its output comes from the same three industries. The trend in employee compensation in the four industries—three manufacturing sectors plus metal mining—is quite similar to the trend in the college versus high school dropout wage premium. The cointegration test confirms the existence of a meaningful relationship in this case; the same is true, somewhat more weakly, when using the four industries and the college versus high school graduate premium.

These final statistical tests suggest that import competition in just four industries could be responsible for trends in the educational wage premiums. It may be hard to believe that such a small set of industries could have such a tremendous impact; however, the industries involved are not small ones. The trade deficit in motor vehicles and parts alone amounts to 1 percent of GDP, and the automobile industry is one with substantial rents. A large part of the trade deficit, then, represents oligopoly rents shifted to foreign producers. Moreover, there may be important spillover effects, through both income effects and upstream linkages from the affected industries, that magnify the effect on wage inequality.

Summary of

Openness and Wage Inequality in Developing Countries: The Latin American Challenge to East Asian Conventional Wisdom

by Adrian Wood

[Published in *World Bank Economic Review* 11, 1 (January 1997), 33–57.]

Economic theory suggests that greater openness to world trade in developing countries will reduce wage inequality. Trade liberalization raises the relative demand for unskilled workers and therefore reduces the wage gap between the skilled and the unskilled. The evidence for East Asia during the 1960s and

1970s supports this theory, but the Latin American experience since the mid-1980s does not. This article examines this conflict of evidence. It asks whether these findings reflect a difference between the time periods.

Heckscher-Ohlin Theory

The dominant theory in the neo-classical economics of international trade is referred to as the Heckscher-Ohlin theory. This theory says that nations will choose to export goods that maximize the use of factors of production that are abundant within their borders. These exports will be exchanged for goods that use factors of production that are relatively scarce at home. The expansion of exports will raise the demand for abundant factors, while the growth of imports will reduce the demand for scarce ones. Thus, in the developing world where unskilled labor is a majority and skilled labor is scarce, increased trade tends to increase unskilled wages, lower skilled wages, and therefore reduce the gap between them.

The Heckscher-Ohlin theory holds both in simple situations that include only two goods, two factors, and two nations, and in more complex cases where there are many goods and many countries. However, when considering multiple goods, countries, and factors, the inclusion of nontraded goods or factors such as transportation and infrastructure can change the results, allowing trade to induce substitution between traded and nontraded goods as well as shifts within the realm of traded goods.

Overview of the Empirical Evidence

Some of empirical literature regarding the relationship between greater openness and relative wages in developing countries supports the conventional wisdom, as in the case of East Asia; some of it does not.

Almost all of the factor content studies in developing countries show that exports are less skill intensive than imports, thus supporting the view that greater openness benefits the unskilled. Factor content of trade studies calculate the amounts of skilled and unskilled labor used to produce a nation's exports and then compares these with the amounts of skilled and unskilled labor that would be used to produce at home the goods that the nation imports. When the ratio of skilled to unskilled labor is lower for exports than for imports, then increased openness to trade should raise the demand for unskilled workers.

Time-series studies tell a more varied story. They look at the changes in the relative supply of skilled and unskilled labor, and to changes in labor market institutions that increase or reduce wage flexibility. In this literature there is a conflict: In some countries and periods increased openness has caused a narrowing of the skill gap, but in others the opposite has occurred.

A good deal of the evidence for East Asia supports the conventional view that openness raises the demand for unskilled relative to skilled workers. During the decades in question, this was the case in the Republic of Korea, Singapore, and Taiwan. In Hong Kong the wage gap widened, but this could be due to a large increase in the supply of unskilled labor. Another possible reason for the narrowing of the wage gap in these nations is the expansion of post-basic education. Following export-oriented industrialization in these nations, the expansion of higher education compressed wage differentials. However, in all three of the cases where differentials narrowed, the change in trade regime was at least partly responsible. For other countries in East Asia, such as Malaysia, the evidence is not as clear.

Contrary to conventional wisdom, during periods of trade liberalization in Latin America, skill differentials in wages widened. In Argentina and Chile this occurred from the mid-1970s to the early 1980s; in Mexico after the mid-1980s; and between the mid-1980s and the mid-1990s in Colombia, Costa Rica, and Uruguay. In all of these cases, the number of skilled workers was rising.

In some of these cases changes in labor market institutions may help explain the widening of skill differentials. In Chile the widening of wage differentials in the late 1970s during the rise of the authoritarian Pinochet regime coincided with severe curtailment of union activity. Similarly, wage differentials widened in Argentina after a military coup and parallel declines in union activity during the late 1970s.

Differences Between East Asia and Latin America

Is the conflict of evidence due to regional differences between East Asia and Latin America in resource availability or choice of trade liberalization policies?

East Asian and Latin American natural resources differ in several respects, but it is difficult to draw a causal connection between these differences and the difference in the impact of trade liberalization on wage inequality. Where Latin America is resource-rich and enjoys a comparative advantage in primary products, East Asia has few natural resources but is better endowed with manufactures such as footwear and clothing. However, primary exports tend to employ even more unskilled workers than manufactured exports. So one would expect the conventional effect to be stronger in Latin America than in East Asia.

Perhaps the combination of nontraded sectors as well as natural resources could explain these differences in Latin America. If trade liberalization caused both nontraded and export sectors to expand the net effect might be an increase in the relative demand for skilled labor. While this may seem farfetched, it warrants further research. The policy mechanisms used in opening to trade in each region were also different. In East Asia, liberalization was achieve by increasing incentives for exporters and protecting selected sectors against imports. Latin America, however, opened trade by reducing barriers to imports. Because neither subsidies nor barriers are the same across sectors, their effects on the skill composition of the demand for labor could be different. However, as in the case of natural resource endowments, the explanation of the widening gap in wages in Latin America cannot be explained by the nuances of its changing trade regime.

Differences Between the 1960s–1970s and the 1980s–1990s

Changes in the makeup of the world economy during the periods examined are the most convincing explanations of the Latin American challenge to conventional wisdom. Specifically, the entry of large low-income countries into world markets in the 1980s and the shift in the skill content of technology are the most plausible explanations.

The entry of nations such as China and Indonesia into the world market for labor intensive manufactures in the 1980s shifted the comparative advantage of middle-income nations into goods of more medium-skill intensity. Thus, trade liberalization in middle-income countries reduced the demand for unskilled workers by causing sectors of low-skill intensity to contract. The world economy of the 1960s and 1970s consisted primarily of developed and middle-income countries so that middle-income East Asian countries, liberalizing at that time, had a comparative advantage in unskilled labor. In contrast, trade liberalization in Latin America in the 1980s coincided with expanding exports. During this period, the world price of unskilled labor dropped relative to that of skilled labor.

Perhaps trade liberalization had different effects on wage inequality in the 1980s than in the 1960s because of the content of technological change. Imports of new technology into Latin American countries could have been what raised the relative demand for skilled labor. This "skill-enhancing trade" explanation has considerable support in the literature, but certain doubts about it have been raised.

Conclusions

The conventional wisdom would postulate that increased trade liberalization in developing countries would increase the demand for unskilled relative to skilled labor and thus reduce wage inequality. The Latin American experience in the mid-1980s and 1990s challenges this wisdom. The Latin American exception is due to the entry of low-income nations into the world economy and to skill-biased technological change.

Summary of

The Distributional Impact of Privatization in Developing Countries

by Paul Cook and Colin Kirkpatrick

[Published in *Privatization and Equity* (London: Routledge, 1995), Ch. 2, 35–48.]

Privatization, the change in ownership of an enterprise from the public to the private sector, has been a centerpiece of the market-oriented development strategies employed in developing countries over the past two decades. Most economists have evaluated privatization schemes on efficiency grounds alone, leaving distributional concerns to the political process. This article argues that the distributional impact of policy changes are of major concern to economists, and develops a political economy approach to examine the distributional impact of privatization in developing countries.

A Political Economy Approach

How does privatization affect economic welfare? Who gains and who loses from this policy change? Such questions present a paradox to conventional thinking about the political decisions of state actors.

The changes in welfare associated with privatization can be simplified by considering the following equation:

$$\Delta W = \Delta S + \Delta I + \Delta P$$

Here, welfare changes (W) are separated into a change in consumer surplus (S), a change in rents (I) received by the providers of inputs (labor), and a change in firm profits (P). If greater efficiency reduces profits, then consumer surplus will be positive. The change in factor rents would probably be negative (publicly owned enterprises often have above-market wages), and if the privatized firm's financial performance improves, then the change in profits will also be positive. This article focuses on the latter variable. The distribution of the change in profits between the seller (the state) and the buyer (a private firm) is determined by the negotiated price at which the enterprise is sold.

The act of privatization poses a dilemma for conventional economic theories about state actors. This literature sees the policy maker as a rational self-interested actor dependent on social and state forces that seek to advance their own interests by influencing the policy process. In such a framework, the state is an agent of various interest groups that negotiates the transfer of income and wealth among different factions.

In this light, the economic crises of the developing countries are seen as a re-sult of self-interested state actors' over-subsidization of those who influenced economic policy. A shift to privatization by these actors would thus seem irra-tional. Why would it be in the state's interest to sell off the friends that it bought off?

This paradox can be partly resolved in three ways. First, it is perfectly consis-tent with the new political economy literature that state policy makers will rep-resent private sector interests. Privatization would then represent a change in the means of distribution rather than the ends. Second, state actors can be seen as "enlightened" technocrats who gamble the state's interests but receive ex-post validation for their good economic policy. Some point to the success of the East Asian economies as an example. Bureaucrats in these countries are said to have acted independently of interest-group pressure to pursue economically ef-ficient policies. The rapid growth associated with these efforts led to great gains for many of the key interest groups associated with the state.

Third, and perhaps most important in the context of developing countries, is the influence of other economic factors on the privatization process. The fact that so many developing countries were facing balance of payments shortfalls and other macro-disequilibria forced many of them to change their ways. By opening the sale of private enterprises to multiple bidders, governments were able to in-crease potential revenue yields—revenues that they needed very quickly.

The form of privatization affects the state's ability to control its distributional impact. In general, the more transparent and "open" the privatization process, the less control the state will have over distribution, leaving it less able to serve its constituents' interests. For example, stock market flotation may give a state a lot of revenue, but allows almost no state control over who purchases the sales. On the other hand, closed sales allow governments to influence who will benefit from privatization. The next two sections outline how these choices have come into being on the international stage.

The International Dimension

From 1988 to 1992 privatization efforts surged in the developing countries. During this period, revenues increased from $2.6 billion in 1988 to $23.1 bil-lion in 1992. The biggest recipients of this activity were nations in Latin Amer-ica and the Caribbean, accounting for 70 percent of all the privatization in the developing world. The leading sector for privatization was in infrastructure, and the second most important was industrial production.

Who have been the purchasers of privatized enterprises? Foreign investment is increasingly the source of funds for privatization. In 1988, foreign investors had participated in only seven developing country privatization sales, but in 1992 they participated in 191, for a total of 375 over the entire period,

1988–1992. From 1988 to 1992, privatizations accounted for close to 10 percent of all foreign direct investment flows to the developing world.

Privatization presents developing country governments with a distributional dilemma. The developing countries desperately need funds from their privatization schemes, but they also want some deal of control over who receives the benefits. However, the exertion of control over the process may scare away foreign investors.

Again, the pressure of balance of payments shortages and other macroeconomic disequilibria force nations to come up with quick funds. If the FDI is there, it is hard to turn away. Second, the international financial institutions such as The World Bank and related institutions have actively encouraged privatization in developing countries. Close to 70 percent of all structural adjustment loans and 40 percent of sectoral adjustment loans during the 1980s had a privatization component.

The Domestic Dimension

A brief examination of the Malaysian privatization experience can illustrate the political economy approach to privatization policy. (See the sources cited in the original article for greater detail and documentation.)

Malaysia was one of the earliest countries in the developing world to start a privatization program, committing to privatization in 1983. The goals of the program were to reduce the financial and administrative burden on government, to promote efficiency and competition, and to stimulate private investment. Foreign investment, however, was to be limited to 30 percent of that private investment.

The record in Malaysia suggests that privatization was often used to enhance the wealth of certain groups closely aligned with the government. In important cases there was not an open sales process. The ruling party at the time had control over a good deal of the corporate sector, and the privatization process strengthened the party's corporate interests and the party's rule in the country. The literature shows that by and large, the Malaysian government used privatization as an instrument for the distribution of privatized assets and associated rents to favored groups close to the government party. Setting aside a percentage of privatized assets for indigenous people, a much-discussed government initiative, may have been more successful in creating inequality within the indigenous population than in raising the fortunes of that group as a whole.

Summary and Conclusions

A political economy examination of privatization schemes in developing countries reveals that privatization occurs to promote specific interest groups' economic interests, rather than the advancement of communal welfare. Privatization has usually benefited the same interests and groups that were favored before such schemes were employed. The more transparent and open the privatization process, the less the state can control the distribution of the benefits. Economists' analyses of privatization have been skewed by an overemphasis on efficiency concerns, and may have overlooked the crucial dimension of distribution.

Summary of

Income Distribution in Developing Economies: Conceptual, Data, and Policy Issues in Broad-Based Growth

by Gary Fields

[Published in *Critical Issues in Asian Development,* ed. M.G. Quibria (Hong Kong: Oxford University Press, 1995), Ch. 4, 75–93.]

This article maintains that broad-based growth, growth that raises the living standards at all socioeconomic levels in a country, is the key to a successful development approach. This point is illustrated by an examination of the recent development experience in the newly industrializing East Asian nations—Taiwan, South Korea, Hong Kong, and Singapore.

Income Distribution and Broad-Based Growth

The case has been made that the poor deserve special attention in the development process. Inspired by the work of philosopher John Rawls, a school of development thinking has arisen that focuses on maximizing the well-being of the worst-off person. From a political economy perspective, however, it has been shown that such an approach must be coupled with benefits to the nonpoor in order to secure their political support. Thus, an approach of broad-based growth, growth that is targeted on raising the living standards of the poor, but also raises the living standards of all socioeconomic levels, can be the most effective.

Changing Poverty and Inequality

Development analysts have used two criteria to determine the distributional aspects of economic growth: one absolute and one relative. To look at the absolute effects of growth, one determines if incomes have risen in all strata of the income distribution. When examining the relative distributional effects of growth, one determines whether income inequality has increased, decreased, or remained unchanged. Development analysts have now pieced together good databases using available data.

When looking at absolute poverty, individuals who fall below a specified income or expenditure level are said to be poor. While poverty lines are set differently in different countries (sometimes by scientific methods, such as caloric intakes, other times using minimum wages, and so forth), by and large it has been found that more economic growth can be expected to help all income groups, including the poor. The limitation of this methodology is that it can be hard to tell whether particular target groups such as the poor benefited a lot or a little. Thus, other researchers turn to examinations of relative poverty.

Comparisons of relative inequality were pioneered by Simon Kuznets. In 1955, Kuznets hypothesized, on the basis of cross-sectional data, that inequality tends to increase in the early stages of economic growth and decrease in the later stages. Today, there is more extensive data available to test this hypothesis. In recent times, has economic growth been broad-based enough that the Gini coefficient (a common measure of inequality) has fallen? The answer is decisively indecisive.

The literature inspired by Kuznets has given rise to four hypotheses, none of which holds in current development experiences. The four hypotheses are (1) inequality tends to change systematically in developing countries; (2) inequality tends to increase in the early stages of development and to decrease in latter stages; (3) inequality is more likely to increase in fast-growing developing economies than in slow-growing ones; and (4) a more unequal distribution of income leads to a faster rate of economic growth. Empirical tests of these hypotheses establish that there is no tendency in the inequality-development relationship. "If inequality does not tend to increase before it decreases, to fall with economic growth (or rise), or to change systematically with the rate of economic growth, it must be that it is not the *rate* of economic growth, but rather the *type* of economic growth, that determines the extent to which the poor share in the growth process." [83] In addition, the empirical evidence shows that when inequality has changed, those changes have been small in magnitude. For the poor to receive a better share of the benefits of growth, reforms in development policies are needed.

Broad-Based Growth in East Asia

The most outstanding example of broad-based growth in recent decades have been the experience of the newly industrializing economies in East Asia. The

East Asian "miracle" was made possible by the full utilization of labor, land, and educational reforms, a pact between government and the business community, and countries' trade and industrialization strategies. The following are lessons learned from that experience.

Policy makers have to strike a balance—not raising the returns to labor prematurely (if wages are excessive, employment and output could be reduced) and not repressing wages. Because labor is so abundant in the developing world, labor-intensive growth can be more beneficial for the poor than capital-intensive growth.

Just as important as the quantity of labor demanded is the quality or skills that workers bring to the labor market. There may be no trade-off between equity and efficiency when it comes to education. Spending educational dollars on primary education rather than higher education may add more to the productive capacity of workers and spread the benefits of growth in a more broad-based manner.

As with resource allocation for education, there may not be an equity-efficiency trade-off when it comes to land as well. In the early post–World War II period, significant land reforms in many of the East Asian countries laid a relatively egalitarian foundation. There are three advantages to having such an initially egalitarian distribution. First, the asset of land generates income and hence spreads the benefits of growth to the poor. Second, since it is well known that small farms have higher yields per acre, a more equal distribution of land would raise total agricultural productivity. Finally, those with land hold a great deal of political power. Keeping power out of the hands of a landed oligarchy can be beneficial to the poor.

When it comes to the role of government in the private economy, governments have to learn to strike a delicate balance between the interests of workers (who want fair wages), the interests of consumers (who want relatively cheap and stable prices), and the interests of businesses (who want to earn profits). What worked in East Asia were labor market policies that pulled the poor along with economic growth. This was chosen over pushing wages up in the hope that the economy would somehow absorb these costs. This is not an argument for unregulated labor markets—they should certainly be regulated to prevent abusive practices.

Key to a successful development approach is sound trade and industrialization strategies. The East Asian economies were able to maintain full employment and rapidly rising real wages. Much of this is attributed to export-led growth. These nations chose their trade policies carefully, adapting their policies as their comparative advantage shifted more to lower-wage countries as they moved to higher-wage sectors. At first textile exports were in their favor, but then fell. The same experience held for exports in heavy machinery and consumer electronics.

Conclusions

The East Asian experience suggests certain parameters that can guide policy makers toward development strategies that will ensure broad-based growth; however, more research is needed. While the East Asian nations offer an interesting example, they are only four nations. Additional country studies are needed to identify what works and what does not under different scenarios.

This article has shown that a concern for broad-based growth must include the distributional aspects of economic development. When determining policy for distributional purposes, analysts must first decide whether they are concerned with changes in absolute or relative poverty. The evidence to date on the distributional effects of growth give an entirely different impression depending on which of these distributional approaches is adopted. We now know that there is no relationship between economic growth and changing income inequality. Income distribution does not have to get more unequal first—and it does not even tend to. A real-life example of this is the experience of East Asia, where full employment, rising real wages, falling absolute poverty, and low to moderate levels of inequality accompanied economic growth. The key factors in maintaining such broad-based growth are labor market policies, the distribution of education, the distribution of land, government regulation and private enterprise, and trade and industrialization strategies.

PART X

Responses to Inequality: The Welfare State

Overview Essay

by Frank Ackerman

The degree of inequality that would be created by an unfettered market economy is unacceptable to almost everyone. In every developed country, and many developing countries as well, the government engages in large-scale intervention in the market to promote some aspects of equality. Among the most common forms of intervention are public pensions for retirees, free or subsidized medical care, unemployment benefits, and progressive taxation. In the most ambitious cases, these measures are joined by many more government programs and initiatives aimed at increasing equality.

Is this the solution to the problems of inequality? If we dislike the distribution of resources achieved by the market, can we simply vote to have the government change it? In a more optimistic and expansive era, such as the 1960s and 1970s, the affirmative answer to these questions might have been taken for granted. The last two decades of the twentieth century, however, were a time of growing pessimism, cutbacks, and conservatism. The new conventional wisdom suggested that little could or should be done to modify the market allocation of resources. As a cynic said, referring to one of the celebrated liberal initiatives of the 1960s, "America fought a war on poverty, and poverty won."

In the short run, there was a partisan political explanation for the reversal. Poverty and inequality won the war, in the Anglo-American context, because the politicians of the Reagan and Thatcher administrations decided to surrender, if not switch sides, in the 1980s. Yet the retreat from government activism has outlasted those politicians, and has reached beyond the United States and the United Kingdom. The critique of the welfare state is often presented, not as a political choice, but as an economic necessity. In a time of greater global competition and slower growth, it is claimed that even the richest countries can no longer afford the high levels of interference with the market that they have previously indulged in. Growth and employment are said to depend on efficiency, which requires minimization of costs and elimination of market distortions. Adherence to this doctrine compels endless efforts to cut back taxes and benefits, to make national economies lean and mean enough to endure.

This point of view is sure to cause discomfort among those who are concerned about equality. In fact, if our goal is greater equality, there is no comprehensive alternative to political action. Private bargaining between unequal parties in the marketplace will inevitably lead to unequal outcomes. Organization of unions or other grassroots initiatives to gain economic power, while essential, is a slow and difficult process—and if it succeeds, it will surely rely on the government to preserve and strengthen its gains. Thus if we care about equality, we need to recreate an economics that legitimizes government intervention and activism, and critiques the pessimism of the recent past. That is, we must explain what is wrong with the new economic orthodoxy of the late twentieth century, the prescription that movement toward laissez-faire is the best medicine for so many different diseases.

This essay begins with a look at the theoretical grounds for supporting government activism. It then presents a typology of different welfare state models, followed by a more detailed examination of the polar cases of Sweden and the United States. The final section returns to the nature of the trade-offs involved in social welfare programs.

Theorizing Intervention

A good place to start in developing a theory of government intervention is the recent review article, "Does Egalitarianism Have a Future?" (Louis Putterman, John E. Roemer, and Joaquim Silvestre 1998). Putterman et al. offer a critique of the way that economic theory treats the issue of equality, on many levels (only a few of which are mentioned here). The textbook notion that maximum efficiency is always desirable depends on the implausible assumption that distribution can be handled separately in a subsequent transaction: Once the economy has reached its peak output, a hypothetical set of "lump-sum" transfers supposedly could achieve any preferred income distribution, without reducing efficiency. Since these hypothetical transfers never occur, and are in fact politically and organizationally impossible, economic theory cannot rely on them to solve (or dissolve) the question of distribution.

On a more practical level, Putterman et al. cite reviews of empirical research suggesting that the disincentive effects of welfare state benefits and taxes are relatively small. Nor is it obvious that removing all taxes and benefits would lead to a more ideal economy. There are, for example, large negative environmental externalities from many economic activities; taxing pollution and other undesirable environmental activities would lead to better, not worse, economic outcomes.

There are also institutional barriers to economic efficiency that result from extremely unequal distribution of resources, suggesting that some forms of government intervention can increase efficiency. To cite an example from more agrarian societies, land reform has frequently led to an increase in agricultural investment and output, due to the incentive effect of giving former tenant farmers an ownership stake in their farms. The same might be true for tenants in large-scale public or absentee-owned housing developments in major cities. More broadly speaking, public policies that guarantee an income floor or equalize access to credit may encourage low-income individuals to take more desirable economic initiatives—investing in their own education, or in new business ventures, for example.

The institutional and informational limitations that constrain the market are a major theme in the work of Joseph Stiglitz. In his interesting reflections on the failure of Soviet planning (Stiglitz 1994), he argues that the same limitations were even more problematical for socialism. Indeed, according to Stiglitz, if a perfectly competitive market economy were possible, then market socialism would also be possible, and might be preferable to private ownership. The private market succeeds, in his view, not because it is perfect or even perfectible, but because it deals with imperfections in a manner that is somewhat less bad than the alternatives.

However, in an economy characterized by limited information, institutional barriers, and unfortunate incentives, it is easy to see that the textbook theorems about general equilibrium fail, implying that market outcomes may be neither equitable nor efficient. Consequently, some forms of government intervention can lead to simultaneous improvement in both equity and efficiency (Stiglitz 1991). There is a vast literature on the unrealism and impossibility of general equilibrium (too vast for comprehensive citation; my own contribution is Ackerman 1999), all of which at least indirectly supports the idea that government activism could make market outcomes better rather than worse.

A similar theoretical perspective, more directly focused on the welfare state, is provided by Nicholas Barr (1992). The traditional economic justification for the welfare state, as explained by Barr, is that it arises in response to market failures in the areas of risk and insurance. The private market is incapable of providing affordable health insurance to all regardless of congenital defects or preexisting illnesses; it cannot provide insurance against income loss due to cyclical unemployment, except for narrowly defined, low-risk groups; it cannot guarantee the real value of pension payments in the face of uncertain levels of inflation. Because people want these and other guarantees and services that the private sector cannot offer, they inevitably turn to the state. That is to say, some of the things that people want are universal guarantees of well-being, which are structurally so different from commodities that there is no possible private sector supplier.

Once the fabric of market optimality begins to unravel, there are many loose threads that can be pulled on. Consider the common belief that regulation of prices or quantities always makes market outcomes worse. A counterexample to this misleading bit of conventional wisdom is found in the analysis of minimum-wage legislation by **David Card and Alan Krueger.** Economists are nearly unanimous in believing that minimum-wage laws reduce unemployment, based largely on a priori reasoning from the simplest model of labor supply and demand. In their book, Card and Krueger describe extensive empirical evidence that is inconsistent with this conclusion, repeatedly finding either no change or a slight increase in employment due to increases in the minimum wage.

The chapter summarized here offers a theoretical explanation: To oversimplify slightly, the U.S. minimum wage is so low that it provides little incentive to work hard or remain on the job. So when fast-food restaurants are forced to pay slightly more, they attract more and better motivated workers, and slow down their rapid rate of employee turnover. In an extended and somewhat critical review of Card and Krueger, John Kennan (1995) claims that their data is ambiguous and frequently mis-specified, rendering it difficult to draw any clear empirical conclusions. However, Kennan agrees that there is no large employment effect (and often no significant effect at all) of minimum-wage changes, in essence supporting a modest version of Card and Krueger's key point.

Three Varieties of the Welfare State

Turning from theory to reality, it is clear that there is a widespread perception of crisis in the modern welfare state. Pressure for cutbacks has proved irresistible in one country after another. A major comparative study, directed by Gøsta Esping-Andersen, examines the problems and responses of welfare state policies in the 1990s in seven different regions of the world (Esping-Andersen 1996). As in his earlier work (e.g., Esping-Andersen 1990), Esping-Andersen emphasizes that there is nothing inevitable about the development of public policies for health, education, and welfare. Different countries at comparable levels of economic development have quite different levels and styles of services, growing out of their distinct political histories. As shown in Table X.1, public social security and health expenditures in 1990 ranged from about one-seventh of gross domestic product (GDP) in the United States to one-third in Sweden. In many countries there was a moderate increase in these expenditures during the 1980s.

There are some common roots (as well as divergent branches) to the budgetary crises facing the social welfare programs of many countries in the 1990s or earlier. Slower economic growth has reduced tax revenues and increased the need for income supports. The aging of the population throughout the developed world—which is most acute in Japan and in southern Europe—increases the cost of pensions and medical care. Growing numbers of single mothers and other nontraditional household structures create a demand for new services and programs. Yet none of this has led to wholesale abandonment of past approaches. When faced with a budgetary crisis, most countries make only marginal adjustments in the type of social welfare they provide for their citizens.

Table X.1. Public Social Security and Health Expenditures

	Public social security and health expenditure as a percentage of gross domestic product	
	1980	1990
Canada (1982 and 1990)	17.3	18.8
Denmark	26.0	27.8
France	23.9	26.5
Germany	25.4	23.5
Netherlands	27.2	28.8
Norway	21.4	28.7
Sweden	32.4	33.1
United Kingdom	14.1	14.6

Source: Excerpted from Table 1.1, page 11 (based on OECD data), in Gøsta Esping-Anderson, ed., *Welfare States in Transition: National Adaptations in Global Economies.* London: SAGE Publications, 1996.

Drastic changes in political philosophy are largely confined to the cases of abrupt overthrow of a regime, as in the end of the Soviet era, or earlier in Chile.

Esping-Andersen's widely cited typology of the varieties of welfare states divides most developed countries into three groups:

- The Anglo-Saxon countries (Britain, U.S., Canada, Australia, New Zealand), where "neo-liberal" or "residual" programs rely largely on limited, means-tested benefits and modest social insurance plans

- Continental Europe (Germany, France, Italy, and others), where "corporativist" programs provide a high level of job security and social insurance, but do little to find jobs for the unemployed, or to provide family-oriented benefits such as child care

- Scandinavia, where the "universal" approach to social welfare combines a high level of income maintenance and wage equality with active labor market policies, social service expansion, and gender equalization.

The three varieties of welfare states have measurably different effects in reducing poverty. Table X.2 contrasts the extent of poverty both before and after government intervention in fifteen developed countries. The data for this and many other international comparisons comes from the Luxembourg Income Study, a massive compilation of comparable economic and demographic data for different countries. In Table X.2, the columns labeled "Pre" show the extent of poverty based on pre-tax, pre-transfer incomes—that is, poverty that would have occurred based on market incomes alone. The columns labeled "Post" present the corresponding poverty rates based on post-tax, post-transfer incomes—that is, actual poverty based on household incomes after government intervention. The "Change" columns are the difference between Pre and Post, or the percentage reduction in poverty rates achieved by taxes and transfers.

In addition to documenting the dismal U.S. performance, the table illuminates two aspects of Esping-Andersen's typology. First, the Anglo-Saxon coun-

Table X.2. Impact of Taxes and Transfers on Poverty Rates

	Year	All persons Pre*	Post*	Change (%)	Children Pre*	Post*	Change (%)
United States	1994	26.7	19.1	−28.5%	28.7%	24.9%	−13.2%
Australia	1989	23.2	12.9	−44.4	20.5	15.4	−24.9
Canada	1991	23.4	11.7	−50.0	22.7	15.3	−32.6
United Kingdom	1991	29.2	14.6	−50.0	28.7	18.5	−35.5
Finland	1991	15.6	6.2	−60.3	11.6	2.7	−76.7
Spain	1990	28.2	10.4	−63.1	20.7	12.8	−38.2
Ireland	1987	30.3	11.1	−63.4	30.3	13.8	−54.5
Italy	1991	18.4	6.5	−64.7	11.0	10.5	−4.5
France	1984	21.6	7.5	−65.3	27.4	7.4	−73.0
Germany (W.)	1989	22.0	7.6	−65.5	11.7	8.6	−26.5
Norway	1991	21.8	6.6	−69.6	12.7	4.9	−61.4
Netherlands	1991	22.8	6.7	−70.6	15.2	8.3	−45.4
Denmark	1992	26.9	7.5	−72.1	17.1	5.1	−70.2
Sweden	1992	34.1	6.7	−80.4	18.4	3.0	−83.7
Belgium	1992	28.4	5.5	−80.6	17.2	4.4	−74.4

*"Pre" means poverty rate based on pre-tax, pre-transfer income; "post" means poverty rate based on post-tax, post-transfer income. In both cases, poverty is defined as 50% of each country's median income, adjusted for household size.

Countires are listed in order of the change in poverty of all persons.

Source: *State of Working America*. Excerpted from Table 8.15, page 377 in Gøsta Esping-Anderson, ed., *Welfare States in Transition: National Adaptations in Global Economies*. London: SAGE Publications, 1996.

tries accomplished the least in overall poverty reduction; and second, the Scandinavian countries did far better than some (not all) other European countries in reducing child poverty.

Specifically, the welfare state achieved a mere 28 percent reduction in overall poverty in the United States, by far the worst performance in any of the fifteen countries. The other Anglo-Saxon countries, Australia, Canada, and the United Kingdom, reduced overall poverty by 44 to 50 percent, more than in the United States but less than in any of the other European nations, where 60 to 80 percent of poverty was eliminated by government intervention. Sweden would have had the highest rate of overall poverty in the absence of the welfare state, but it also had one of the highest rates of poverty reduction.

In terms of reduction in child poverty, the picture is somewhat different. The United States lifted only 13 percent of pre-tax-and-transfer poor children across the poverty line. Italy did worse in percentage terms, though it had the lowest level of pre-tax-and-transfer child poverty. In all the other countries, taxes and transfers reduced child poverty by at least one-fourth. However, Germany (and Italy) did no better than the other Anglo-Saxon countries, while the four Scandinavian countries, France, and Belgium each eliminated more than 60 percent of child poverty.

Among Esping-Andersen's three models, the continental European one is perhaps the least successful, particularly in its more rigid, southern European variants. The numerous job-related provisions keep the cost of labor quite high; indeed, the trend has been toward declining employment rates due to earlier retirement, high youth unemployment, and other factors. Yet little is done to create new employment opportunities. Social programs, influenced by strong religious traditions in several countries, assume the existence of a traditional family. Unpaid, usually female labor is still frequently required for care of children and the elderly in the home. While most European countries have achieved relatively equal distribution of income across broad population groups, they have not done so in a way that sustains employment growth, nor in a way that supports gender equality and autonomy within the household.

The other two models attract more attention, as plausible, rival responses to the economic problems of the end of the twentieth century. The Anglo-Saxon approach helps to maintain labor market flexibility, lowering the price of unskilled labor by limiting the cost of social supports. The result has been high and rising inequality, far beyond the continental European or Scandinavian levels—but also low unemployment, in Britain and particularly in the United States, in the 1990s. In contrast, the Scandinavian model offers numerous egalitarian benefits, many of them tied to employment, along with active training, information, and other programs designed to move as many people as possible into paid work. Family-oriented social programs such as extensive public child care increase both the supply of, and the demand for, paid female labor. The result is far greater equality than in the Anglo-Saxon model, but also greater public sector costs and, it seems, higher unemployment.

We will turn, therefore, to an examination of the polar cases: Sweden, the best-known and in some ways most complete example of the Scandinavian model; and the United States, the most extreme case of the Anglo-Saxon approach. The overarching question is, can Sweden's expansive egalitarianism be sustained, and even imitated elsewhere—or is it necessary to cut back to the minimal American levels of social welfare to recreate the foundations for growth? There is an obvious parallel with the discussion of the "high road" and "low road" management strategies in earlier parts of this book.

The Scandinavian Route

Much has been written about the Scandinavian welfare state in general, and about Sweden in particular (see, for example, John Stephens 1996). The article by **Anders Bjorklund and Richard Freeman,** summarized here, analyzes the economic basis for Swedish egalitarianism. According to Bjorklund and Freeman, Swedish workers are much more equal than American workers in hours of work per year, as well as in hourly wages. Wages are compressed both on the supply side, by the labor movement's long-term efforts to achieve wage equalization, and on the demand side, by government policies designed to pay many low-productivity workers more than their marginal product. This form of sub-sidy brings many handicapped and low-skilled people into the labor force, where they enjoy the same benefits that are available to all Swedish workers, rather than creating isolated, separate programs for them.

The Scandinavian model grew out of a political and economic theory that is relatively little known outside its home region. The political philosophy of the Swedish Social Democratic Party (the long-dominant political party and archi-tect of the welfare state) is explained in Timothy Tilton (1990). The core prin-ciples of Swedish social democracy include a belief that democracy should in-clude full participation in economic and social as well as political life; a view of society and the state as "the people's home," characterized by solidarity and equality; and a preference for a socially controlled economy, in which proper expansion of the public sector can extend, not threaten, freedom of choice. So-cial democracy seeks to restrict the scope of the market, not necessarily through public ownership, but through "decommodification" of human needs—that is, by making essential services available as the rights of all citizens, independent of their status in the marketplace.

The economic theory of social democracy, and the reasons for its success in its heyday, are explored in the article by **Karl Ove Moene and Michael Wallerstein.** The political basis for social democracy is the strength of the labor movement. Yet contrary to widespread fears, a strong labor movement does not always mean that industry is weak. In fact, centralized nationwide wage bargaining, with a powerful union federation that pushed for equaliza-tion of wages, turned out to be surprisingly efficient for Scandinavian industry. Newer plants and higher-productivity industries gained an advantage from the compressed wage schedule, while older plants were forced to retire, and labor and capital were driven out of lower-productivity industries. The union feder-ations recognized that their jobs depended on Scandinavian exports remaining competitive in world markets and, while working for wage compression, re-strained the growth of average wages. Industry, for its part, maintained rela-tively high and steady employment—which, as Moene and Wallerstein demon-strate, may be the profit-maximizing strategy if labor market institutions make it difficult to hire and fire workers, and the business cycle swings rapidly up and down.

The Scandinavian economic model is widely seen as being in decline, or at least in retreat. (Assar Lindbeck 1997 provides a relatively critical evaluation and literature review.) Sweden's centralized wage bargaining broke down in the 1980s, and there has been a recent trend toward less equal wages—though by comparison with any standard except Sweden's past accomplishments, the wage structure remains remarkably compressed. The breakdown occurred initially because employers faced shortages of skilled labor and wanted to offer higher pay to attract qualified employees; it has now spread to a somewhat more gen-eral differentiation in wage rates.

By the end of the 1980s Scandinavia, like the rest of Europe, faced an economic downturn, high unemployment rates, and budget deficits. Cutbacks in benefits and programs adopted at that time were often interpreted as signaling the failure of the Scandinavian model. Yet the death notices were premature. The Scandinavian economies recovered after the recession, just as other countries did.

The occasional cutbacks seemed, in some cases, justifiable by any reasonable standards. Sweden's sick pay policy, which previously guaranteed every worker 90 percent of usual earnings starting on the first day of an illness, may indeed have encouraged excessive absenteeism; Swedish workers took many more sick days than their counterparts in other countries. Cutting back to a guarantee of only 75 percent of earnings starting on the third day of an illness does not seem merciless, and apparently is leading to rates of reported illness more in line with experience elsewhere. Similarly, Sweden's active labor market policy, combined with wage compression, may have overshot the mark, making it too easy to get a job without advanced training. Despite generous educational funding, Sweden now has a less educated workforce than many developed countries. Slightly greater incentives to stay in school and acquire advanced education and skills might well be desirable.

Back in the United States

Americans do not, except in the most rhetorical flights of conservative imagination, experience the problem of excessively egalitarian social welfare programs. Many comparisons make it clear that among the developed countries, the United States is the least equal, and the least enjoyable place to live for those near the bottom of the income distribution. For example, in an analysis of Luxembourg Income Study data for the mid-1980s, Lee Rainwater (1995) finds that the percentage of families with children that fell below the poverty line (half of the country's median income, adjusted for family size) ranged from 3.5 percent in Sweden to 20.3 percent in the United States; all the European countries in the study were below 10 percent. The United States was also in the lead among the eight countries Rainwater examined for the poverty rate among two-parent families (11 percent). For the poverty rate among single mothers, the shocking U.S. rate of 58 percent was more than matched by Australia's 61 percent; in Sweden, only 6.5 percent of single mothers were poor.

Sheldon Danziger, Sandra Danziger, and Jonathan Stern examine the paradox of America's child poverty amidst affluence. A number of factors have led to deterioration in the economic position of poor children. In the 1970s and 1980s, an increasing percentage of men did not earn enough to keep a family above the poverty line; and an increasing percentage of children were raised by single parents, usually mothers. Government transfers targeted to children were steadily cut back. In particular, the program of last resort, Aid to Families with Dependent Children (AFDC) was squeezed ever tighter until its final abolition in the 1990s. Moreover, taxes on poor families increased in the 1980s, further reducing the net transfer they received from the government. These trends were only partially offset by the increase in women's earnings and the decrease in average family size. Danziger et al. emphasize the scandalous health and other consequences of America's child poverty and suggest several straightforward public policy initiatives that could raise the incomes of poor families.

It is sometimes suggested that the United States offers more opportunities than other countries for mobility out of poverty, potentially offsetting the effects of greater inequality at any time. While a greater percentage of people are poor in America, they might, on average, spend less time being poor. Unfortunately for this theory, an empirical study suggests just the opposite. In Figure X.1, the horizontal axis shows poverty rates for families with children in selected countries. The vertical axis represents the transition rate, or the probability of a poor family escaping poverty (defined as going from below 50 percent to above 60 percent of median income in one year). The negative slope of the graph shows that in the countries with the lowest poverty rates, a poor family was most likely to escape from poverty. There are proportionally far fewer Dutch and Swedish poor people, *and* they are much more likely than poor Americans to get out of poverty in any one year.

The study examines ethnic Germans and immigrants separately within Germany, and whites and blacks separately in the United States. Figure X.1 shows that in both countries the majority fares better than the minority. Note that the gap between the two is much smaller in Germany, and that white Americans are roughly comparable to immigrants in Germany in terms of poverty rates and transition rates. Black Americans are virtually off the chart of developed country data, with by far the highest poverty rate and the lowest likelihood of escaping from poverty.

The Anglo-Saxon version of the welfare state, although far less generous and expensive than the Scandinavian model, nonetheless provokes more controversy and resistance from taxpayers. The narrow, means-tested programs of the "residual" welfare state evidently generate less popular support than more expensive but universal programs. Middle-class Scandinavians do grumble about their tax burden, which is far greater than anything Americans would accept. Yet the Scandinavians, realizing that taxes pay for their parents' pension, their children's college education, their grandchildren's day care, and the whole family's health insurance, may not devote themselves to demanding tax cuts with the same fervor as their American counterparts.

The complex question of who pays for the welfare state is addressed in the ar-

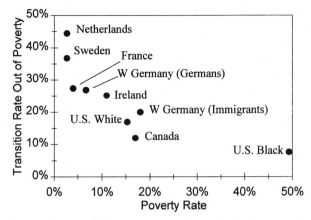

Figure X.1. Poverty Rates and Transitions: Families with Children, Mid-1980s.
Poverty rate is percent of families below 50% of country's median income. Transition
rate is percent of families who were poor one year who had more than 60% of median
income in the next year.
Source: Excerpted from Table 8.16 and Figure 8E, pages 378–379 in Gøsta Esping-Anderson, ed., *Welfare States in Transition: National Adaptations in Global Economies.* London: SAGE Publications, 1996.

ticle by **Ardeshir Sepehri and Robert Chernomas.** They divide society into
capitalists, workers, and welfare recipients, and make a number of reasonable estimates about which taxes are paid and which government benefits are received
by each group. Their awkwardly named "welfare-adjusted transfer ratio" is the
ratio of taxes paid to benefits received for workers and welfare recipients combined. When the ratio is below one, then there is a net transfer from capitalists
to the other groups; when the ratio is above one, then capitalists are net recipients of benefits funded by workers' taxes.

In both Canada and the United States, Sepehri and Chernomas find that the
ratio declined from 1955 to 1975, falling below one in the early 1970s. In the
United States the ratio began to rise steadily after 1975, shifting the financial
burden of government away from capital and onto labor. (This corresponds
closely to the discussion of the corporate offensive that began in the 1970s, discussed in earlier parts of this book.) In Canada, with a different political history,
the ratio remained below one until 1983, but then began a steady rise resem-
bling the U.S. pattern.

Targets and Trade-offs

While the universalism of the Scandinavian model is an appealing answer to inequality, it does not appear to be on the immediate agenda in most countries.
In a world of limited resources and contentious policy debates, it will continue

to be important to examine the trade-offs between the different objectives of the welfare state. In another comparative study using the Luxembourg Income Study data for the 1980s, Deborah Mitchell (1995) asks whether there is a trade-off between the *effectiveness* of income transfers in reducing poverty and income inequality and the *efficiency* of those transfers in directing their expenditures to the target groups.

A positive finding that there is a trade-off might mean, for instance, that the efficiently targeted programs are small and mean, whereas effectiveness in reducing poverty or inequality requires offering generous universal benefits that "inefficiently" spill over into the middle class. Mitchell concludes that there is a clear trade-off in relation to reducing inequality—for instance, Sweden achieves the greatest reduction in inequality through its government transfers, but with the greatest spillover. However, her findings are less clear in relation to reducing poverty. The United States, Canada, and Switzerland appear to be both less efficient and less effective at reducing poverty than the other seven countries in the study.

The last article summarized here, by **Anthony Atkinson,** offers a critical look at the practice of targeting benefits to narrowly defined, usually need-based, groups of recipients. While not rejecting targeted programs out of hand, Atkinson suggests several reasons to question the assumption that more precise targeting of expenditures is always an improvement. Some programs have objectives other than reaching the most needy, such as the promotion of social solidarity. Some forms of targeting involve significant administrative cost and potential for error. The nuisance and stigma attached to applying to a welfare bureaucracy may discourage a large part of the eligible population from claiming the benefits they are entitled to.

Perhaps most significant is the work incentive problem. Benefits that automatically fall as wages rise amount to a hidden tax on earnings, potentially discouraging work effort and creating a "poverty trap." This can be avoided either by universal benefits, or by programs that, like many European child allowances, are constant up to a high income, well above the median, and then reduced or eliminated for upper-income groups.

In conclusion, the economic crunch and budget problems that affected welfare states in the 1980s and 1990s have forced cutbacks and readjustments around the world. But these are marginal adjustments, which have not refuted the underlying arguments that support government intervention to promote equality and provide basic human welfare. Comparative analysis of the wide range of international experience underscores the effectiveness of political activism in altering distributional outcomes.

There is no reason to endorse the highly unequal distribution of resources that would be achieved by the market on its own. As we have seen, there are fundamental flaws in the argument that this process is uniquely efficient. There is no single mode of social welfare that inevitably emerges at a certain level of development: The possible outcomes range from America's relatively unequal distribution of income to Sweden's remarkably more equal pattern. While it may not be possible to jump abruptly from one end of this spectrum to the other, it is certainly possible for societies to debate and change their distribution of resources.

Summary of

Is There an Explanation? Alternative Models of the Labor Market and the Minimum Wage

by David Card and Alan B. Krueger

[Published in *Myth and Measurement: The New Economics of the Minimum Wage* (Princeton: Princeton University Press, 1995), Ch. 11, 355–386.]

Economists agree, almost unanimously, that raising the minimum wage causes increased unemployment. It is a straightforward deduction from the standard textbook model: Employers have a downward-sloping demand curve for labor; so if forced to pay more for labor, they will hire fewer workers. However, this widely held conclusion is inconsistent with the facts. As David Card and Alan Krueger demonstrate, increases in the minimum wage actually cause either no change or a small increase in employment.

The empirical evidence against the standard analysis, developed in detail in their book, is summarized briefly here. Most of this summary is based on the chapter that explores the implications of their findings for economic theory.

Six Strikes and You're Out?

Six different categories of evidence are inconsistent with the standard theory and its conclusion that higher minimum wages cause increased unemployment. First, changes in employment in the fast-food industry, a major employer of minimum-wage labor, show the opposite of the expected effect. When New Jersey raised its state minimum wage in 1992, fast-food employment in New Jersey expanded, both in absolute terms and relative to restaurants over the state line in eastern Pennsylvania, where the minimum wage remained unchanged.

Second, teenage employment in low-wage states was not hit particularly hard by the 1990–1991 increases in the federal minimum wage. Under the standard model, Mississippi, for example, where many teenage workers received the minimum wage, should have suffered relatively larger job losses than Massachusetts, where most young workers were already above the minimum. In fact, there was no meaningful difference in teenage job growth in low-wage and high-wage states.

Third, an analysis of teenage employment in the 1970s, the most widely cited evidence supporting the standard theory, becomes inconclusive when updated with data for the 1980s. Fourth, changes in minimum-wage laws lead to a number of anomalies that are inconsistent with the standard theory, including the "ripple effect" that leads to pay raises for workers who previously earned wages above the new minimum. Another anomaly is the reluctance of employers to use the subminimum-wage provisions in recent laws.

Fifth, increases in the minimum wage have reduced wage dispersion, partially offsetting the tendency toward rising wage inequality. The 1990–91 increases in the minimum wage transferred roughly $5.5 billion, or 0.2 percent of all earnings, to low-wage workers. Sixth, news about minimum-wage legislation has little or no effect on the value of stocks in companies that are major employers of low-wage workers.

These findings (documented in other chapters of the book) demonstrate the need for a new theory to explain the effects of minimum-wage laws.

Critique of the Standard Model

The standard model of the labor market rests on the fundamental assumption that employers are price takers in a competitive market. Therefore an increase or decrease in an individual firm's hiring should not affect the wage rate. Workers with the same characteristics, doing the same job, should receive the same wages regardless of where they work; there should be no variation in wage scales from one firm to another. This is a reasonable model for some purposes, and explains some important categories of labor market data. The simplest forms of the model can be extended to include distinctions between different types of labor, and between different sectors. Such extensions bring the model closer to some aspects of the evidence on minimum wages.

However, all forms of the standard model make the familiar, wrong prediction about the effects of an increase in the minimum wage on employment. Likewise, all forms of the standard model predict, incorrectly, that employers will make extensive use of subminimum wage provisions. To explain these facts, it is necessary to develop a theory in which firms are not price takers in the labor market, but have the power to set firm-specific wages.

Models in Which Firms Set Wages

> The analysis revolves around a relatively simple question: Do employers have to pay a higher wage in order to maintain and motivate a larger work force? If the answer is "yes," then a modest increase in wages induced by a minimum-wage hike can lead to an increase in employment. [369]

For a simple alternative model, consider the labor market in a one-company town. The company is a monopoly buyer, or "monopsonist," in the labor market. It cannot assume that the wage rate is independent of its hiring decisions; it faces an upward-sloping labor supply curve, since more residents of the town are willing to work if the company offers higher wages. At the profit-maximizing level of wages and employment, the monopsonist firm is paying workers less than their marginal product (just as a monopolist sells its products at more than their marginal cost). Therefore, a modest increase in the minimum wage, forcing the firm to pay more, leads to an increase in employment.

Is this model only a textbook curiosity, or is it potentially relevant to the industries that employ low-wage workers? Typically, each firm employs only a tiny fraction of the workers in its local area. If workers were perfectly informed about all job opportunities, as the standard theory implicitly assumes, then the competitive model of firms as price-takers would apply. However, in reality information about vacancies is quite imperfect, and the turnover in low-wage jobs is very high. Job openings at the going wage rate are not filled instantly, as implied by the standard model; employers spend a great deal of time and energy recruiting and training new workers. In short, imperfect labor market information makes firms more like monopsonists.

Suppose that the rate at which a firm can hire new workers is an increasing function of its wage rate, while the rate at which employees quit is a decreasing function of the wage rate. (Both of these assumptions are supported by some empirical studies.) Then to grow larger, a firm must pay higher wages. All else being equal, wage rates should be significantly related to firm size. This is true in two samples of fast-food restaurants, although the effect is small. The same model implies that moderate increases in the minimum wage will increase employment—agreeing with the data, but contradicting the standard competitive model. Furthermore, the monopsony model implies that small changes in the minimum wage should have little or no effect on the profitability of employers, just as observed.

Explaining the Dispersion of Wages

The simple monopsony model depends on ad hoc assumptions about hiring and quitting rates. More sophisticated models have provided a firmer foundation for this approach, and offer plausible explanations of the variation in wages from one firm to another. One theory assumes that each firm selects and announces its wage rate; workers slowly but continually learn about other firms' offers, and switch jobs every time they hear of an opening that pays more than their current wages. These assumptions ensure that there are more frequent hires and less frequent quits at higher-wage firms. In equilibrium there will be a variety of wage rates: Larger firms will pay higher wages and have less turnover; smaller firms will pay lower wages and have greater turnover.

A variant on this theory assumes that workers differ in productivity, in ways that firms can observe. Each firm posts its wage offer and then hires any applicant whose productivity equals or exceeds the wage. Over time, as workers learn about other job offers, the most productive employees will move to the highest-paying firms. In this theory, it is clear that most firms will reject the option of subminimum wages even if it is allowed by law—it would imply a switch to hiring workers of "subminimum productivity."

Wage dispersion models, of the types discussed in this section, provide three important insights. First, the existence of search costs gives firms some amount of monopsony power over their current employees. Second, monopsony power means that firms with different wage policies can coexist in equilibrium; some will prefer high wages and low turnover, while others will opt for the reverse. (The existence of this range of wage policies is taken for granted in personnel management textbooks.) Third, a raise in the minimum wage can lead to increased employment, by forcing low-wage firms to pay enough to reduce turnover and expand their work forces.

A similar model can be derived from "efficiency wage" theories, in which employers pay workers more than their marginal product to induce additional effort, as an alternative to direct monitoring and control. Here the theory is that employees balance their desire to shirk on the job versus the value of keeping the job; the better the pay, the harder an employee will work to avoid any risk of being fired. If management's ability to monitor individual workers declines as the firm grows larger, then larger firms have a greater need to pay "efficiency wage" premiums to obtain greater effort on the job. The implications of efficiency wage theory therefore parallel those of the monopsony model: Larger firms will pay higher wages; a small increase in the minimum wage will force low-wage firms to offer more attractive jobs, thereby leading them to expand; and subminimum wages will not be offered by most employers, since workers paid at those wages would be so likely to shirk on the job.

In conclusion, both efficiency wage theory and the theories based on the monopsony model can explain the observed facts about minimum wages and employment—unlike the standard competitive model of the labor market.

Summary of

Generating Equality and Eliminating Poverty, the Swedish Way

by Anders Bjorklund and Richard B. Freeman

[Published in *The Welfare State in Transition: Reforming the Swedish Model*, eds. Richard B. Freeman, Robert Topel, and Birgitta Swedenborg (Chicago: University of Chicago Press, 1997), 33–78.]

Sweden is often described as a model of success in reducing income inequality and virtually eliminating poverty. This article, coauthored by a Swedish and an American economist, analyzes the sources of Sweden's egalitarian achievements.

The Swedish Record

By any measure, Sweden has an unusually equal distribution of income. In the mid-1980s the ratio of disposable household income in the top decile to the bottom decile, adjusted for family size, was 2.7 in Sweden compared to 5.9 in the United States; for most European countries the ratio was between 2.7 and 4.5. The difference between Sweden and the United States is particularly pronounced in the poorer half of the distribution: hourly earnings of the tenth-percentile male worker were 76 percent of the median in Sweden in 1991, compared to 37 percent of the median in the United States in 1989.

However, the United States is the outlier in this respect. The distribution of earnings in Sweden is only slightly more egalitarian than in most OECD countries and changed very little during the 1970s and 1980s. Compared to most of Europe, Sweden stands out for its unusually high ratio of paid employment to total population (at least before the 1992/93 recession). Compared to the United States, where employment is also high, Sweden has an extremely equal distribution of hours of work among those who are working—in part a result of Sweden's generous provisions for vacation time, guaranteed by law to be at least five weeks per year for every worker. The difference in the variance of male workers' annual earnings between Sweden and the United States is due as much to the variance in annual hours as to the variance in hourly pay.

Factor incomes—pre-tax-and-transfer labor and capital incomes—are distributed far more unequally than household disposable income (after taxes and transfers). Moreover, the distribution of factor income has been growing steadily more unequal since the late 1960s, while the distribution of disposable income has, by various measures, remained roughly constant or become slightly more equal. These trends together imply that a growing share of all income is being redistributed by the Swedish system of taxes and transfers. The resulting equalization of incomes is particularly important for families with children. In the United States, child poverty rates rose from 14 percent in 1973 to 20 percent in 1990. In Sweden, child poverty, defined as an income of less than 40 percent of the median, has been eliminated.

Swedish transfer programs that affect the distribution of income include:

- Practically free health care for all
- Generous sick pay and work injury insurance
- Social assistance and housing allowances for low-income households
- Disability pensions and subsidies for jobs, training, and rehabilitation for the disabled
- Unemployment benefits and job retraining
- Heavily subsidized day care if both parents are employed or in school
- Child allowance, paid to the mother of every child
- Parental leave for childbirth, benefits to parents who stay home with sick children or visit their children's school, and an allowance paid when the noncustodial parent does not meet his obligations

These programs, excluding medical care for pensioners, total 16 percent of GNP. They are striking in terms of structure as well as size: Nearly half of the expenditures are provided only to those who are employed, thus maintaining the incentive to work, while a quarter are provided to all households regardless of income or employment status. Only a quarter have a "poverty trap" component, such as means-tested benefits that are reduced if the recipient gets a job or a raise.

System or Sweden?

It is sometimes claimed that egalitarian outcomes in Sweden reflect the homogeneity of the population or its unique culture. This claim is easily refuted. Americans of Swedish ancestry have a distribution of income quite similar to the United States as a whole, unlike that of Swedes in Sweden. On the other hand, children of immigrants in Sweden, who account for 15 percent of the adult population, have a distribution of hourly earnings comparable to other Swedes. The distribution of annual earnings is only slightly more unequal for the children of immigrants than for other Swedes, and far more equal than for Americans. In short, current country of residence, not ethnic origin, determines the distribution of income.

Other labor force characteristics might explain the Swedish distribution of earnings. There might be an egalitarian distribution of skills, due to the distribution of family incomes and/or public resources such as day care and schooling. It is true that both family and public resources are quite equally distributed, but this is not the principal factor shaping the distribution of income.

The simplest indicator of human capital created by public resources is years of schooling. The variance in years of schooling is greater in Sweden than in the United States. However, the quality of schools varies more widely in America, implying that a year of schooling has a less consistent meaning. The variation in test scores is much narrower in Sweden than in the United States. Once again, international comparisons show that the United States is the outlier. The distribution of science achievement test scores in Sweden is essentially identical to the average distribution for other developed countries. Thus the equalization of opportunity for Swedish children has not led to greater than average equalization in achievement, at least as measured by standardized tests.

The distribution of family resources in childhood also influences incomes for adults. The importance of this factor can be evaluated with data on the incomes of fathers and sons. There is a correlation between fathers' and sons' earnings in both countries, although it is much lower in Sweden than in the United States. However, this correlation does not explain most of the variation in sons' earnings in either country. Several intricate calculations show that, at most, 30 percent of the U.S.–Swedish difference in the variance of sons' earnings is attributable to differences in the contribution of family backgrounds.

Demand-Side Contributions

Since labor force characteristics cannot account for most of Sweden's greater equality, patterns in the demand for labor may play a significant role. One possibility is that public sector employment creates relatively well-paid jobs for low-skilled workers, hiring people who could not obtain comparable jobs in the private sector.

To test this hypothesis, three indirect measures of low skills and abilities were used: older workers who had only elementary school education; workers in the lowest quarter of the income distribution; and those whose self-reported health status includes limits on mobility. By these definitions, the proportion of low-skilled workers employed by the public sector rose sharply from 1968 to 1991, reaching levels similar to those for all workers by 1991. In most countries, low-skill workers are underrepresented in the public sector, so Sweden's approximately equal representation is a sign of unusually high public employment of less skilled workers. Moreover, the trend was toward increased public employment of these groups, at least through 1991.

Swedish labor market policies are designed to pay many low productivity groups of workers more than their marginal product. One important example is the employment of handicapped or disabled people. In many countries they are among the poorest workers, but in Sweden they have relatively normal incomes, thanks to government-subsidized employment. A high proportion of Swedes with reduced mobility work, with contracted annual hours, almost as long as the average; they do, however, take many more sick days than other workers.

A typical Swedish full-time worker takes five weeks of vacation, two weeks of holidays, and, in 1981, an average of three weeks of paid sick time, leaving forty-two weeks of work per year. (American workers average about one week of work time lost to illness annually, although they appear to be no healthier than Swedes and are not quite as long-lived.) Men with limited mobility, however, take roughly twelve weeks of sick time, and hence work only thirty-three weeks in a year. Yet there is almost no difference in either hourly earnings or annual earnings that is associated with mobility status. Much the same is true for women, though they are more likely to work part-time.

> In the case of the disabled, it is clear that the rest of society pays by subsidizing their employers or their sickness days. Might something similar be true of other low-skill workers? Does Sweden "pay" for its egalitarian wage policies and full employment through higher prices for the goods produced by the less skilled? [36–37]

One piece of evidence supporting this hypothesis is the relative cost of restaurant meals, a service produced by low-skilled workers. Adjusted for purchasing power parity, the prices charged by restaurants and hotels are 51 percent higher in Sweden than in the United States; in that sector labor costs are 73 percent of value added in Sweden, but only 50 percent in the United States. The difference between countries is much smaller in sectors that employ more highly skilled workers.

Finally, the reduction in hours for the most productive workers may creates a demand for less productive workers, in an implicit system of work sharing. Ranking workers by annual hours of work, the top decile of Americans work 30 percent more than the corresponding Swedes. The refusal of the most able Swedes to work American hours might indirectly allow less capable Swedish workers to take up the slack.

Much of the data discussed here ends in 1991, just before a major round of cutbacks in the Swedish welfare state. These cuts have led to some growth in inequality, but have not unraveled the fabric of Sweden's redistributive taxes and transfers. It is too early to tell whether the cutbacks of the 1990s will be a one-time change or the beginning of an ongoing trend toward increasing inequality.

Summary of

How Social Democracy Worked:
Labor-Market Institutions

by Karl Ove Moene and Michael Wallerstein

[Published in *Politics and Society* 23, 2 (June 1995), 181–211.]

Social Democracy is on the decline. According to its critics, social democracy introduces too much equality, too much security, and too much employment, thereby causing the economy to function poorly. Conversely, this article argues that social democracy consists of a set of institutions and policies that work efficiently to reduce insecurity and inequality of income without large sacrifices in economic growth and stability. By examining the experience of Norway and Sweden during the heyday of social democracy, this article shows how labor market institutions were crafted to merge equality and efficiency. This discussion can also be applied to the question of why social democracy has declined in recent years.

Corporatism and Competition

One of the most striking features of wage-setting in all four Nordic countries in the postwar period was the introduction of centralized bargaining. It is often thought that corporatism is associated with restrictive trade policies. In fact, centralized bargaining was introduced to solve problems with trade openness. In Norway and Sweden, the drive to centralize bargaining began in the 1930s as a means of forcing all workers to share the burden of reducing costs in order to maintain employment in the export sector. In the postwar period, centralized bargaining allowed workers whose wages were subject to international competition to set the pace of wage increases for the entire economy.

The Efficiency of Wage Equality

Because of the need to assure adequate profits to maintain employment and investment, unions can have a much greater influence on the distribution of wages among wage-earners than on the distribution of income between wages and profits. In the postwar period, the Scandinavian unions adopted a policy of promoting greater wage equality that was called "solidaristic bargaining." Their egalitarian wage policies were remarkably effective. Even today Norway, Sweden, and Denmark have the lowest wage differentials among OECD countries.

Many economists would assume that productivity would suffer from a wage system with a weak connection between productivity and wages. During the 1950s, however, Swedish trade union economists promoted solidaristic bargaining on the grounds that efficiency would be improved. This article models the efficiency argument. It is assumed that productivity growth is embodied in plant and equipment such that newer plants are more efficient than older ones. Employment per plant is assumed to be fixed. Thus firms have two decisions: when to build new plants and when to shut down existing plants. Total output and employment is determined by the number of new plants built each period and the age of the oldest plants in operation.

In this model, local bargaining produces a wage in each plant that is constant over time and dependent on the plant's age, with newer plants paying higher wages. With centralized bargaining, wages are independent of the plant's age and rise over time at the same rate as productivity growth. Since local bargaining allows wages to vary in proportion to the productivity of the plant, older plants remain profitable so long as their productivity exceeds workers' reservation wage. With centralized bargaining, a common wage is set for all plants that is based on average productivity. If the uniform wage exceeds workers' reservation wage, centralized bargaining forces the oldest plants to close. At the same time, centralized bargaining increases the future discounted value of profits earned by new plants as long as the uniform wage is not too far above the market-clearing wage, as was generally the case in Norway and Sweden until the late 1980s, early 1990s. If centralized bargaining is accompanied by sufficient wage restraint, the number of new plants being built can exceed the number of older plants that are forced to close, resulting in a net gain of employment and a more efficient industry.

This model can also be adapted to make a similar efficiency argument for the elimination of wage differences between industries. Centralized bargaining over a whole economy limits the ability of the most efficient industries to pay a wage premium and prevents the least efficient industries from staying in business by lowering wages. In effect, the elimination of industry wage-differentials can be seen as a subsidy for more efficient industries and a tax on less efficient ones. In contrast, strong unions with local bargaining slow the building of newer plants and the growth of new industries. Thus, in Sweden and Norway, the elimination of inter-firm and inter-industry wage differentials may have aided economic growth and increased aggregate profits.

The Maintenance of Full Employment

By today's standards, it seems miraculous that the Nordic social democracies were able to obtain wage equality and maintain full employment. Part of the explanation was the system of centralized bargaining. National-level union leaders are more sensitive to unemployment than local union leaders. Local union leaders represent workers with jobs, while national-level union leaders are more likely to consider the entire work force as their constituency. Another part of the explanation was the creation of labor-market policies that directly reduced unemployment by putting unemployed workers in labor-training programs. Yet another part of the explanation is that a full-employment environment shapes employers' employment practices in a manner that increases the scarcity of labor.

A model is presented here in which employers, facing a fixed wage and stochastic demand for their output, choose between two employment strategies. One is a flexible employment strategy in which workers are hired when production is profitable and laid off when production is unprofitable. The second is a fixed employment strategy in which labor is hoarded when demand is low in order to have a full workforce ready when demand rises.

The choice of employment policy depends on the stochastic process that determines demand, the wage, and the ease of filling vacancies. The ease of filling vacancies, in turn, depends on the employment practices of other firms. If the other firms hoard labor, there are few workers looking for work, and filling vacancies is difficult. In this case, a fixed employment strategy is likely to be optimal. If other firms lay off workers when demand for their output declines, there are more workers looking for work and filling vacancies is easier. In these circumstances, a flexible employment strategy is likely to yield higher profits. In sum, there can exist two equlibria: one where most firms follow flexible employment policies and only the most productive firms hoard labor, and another where most firms hoard labor and only the least productive firms lay off workers when demand falls. The model implies that full employment is self-perpetuating, as long as demand shocks are not too severe. In Norway and Sweden, the full-employment equilibrium lasted for four decades.

Social Democratic Decline

According to the arguments of this article, social democratic labor-market institutions worked well for a long period of time. Social democratic institutions increased the equality and security of income without disrupting the capitalist economy. Core social democratic policies received support from both employers and organized workers. That time is over, however. The previous discussion of centralized bargaining and multiple equilibria in the labor market can also be applied to the question of why social democratic institutions have declined.

The recent rise in unemployment in the Nordic countries can be explained in macroeconomic terms. The governments of Norway and Sweden (and Finland) can be faulted for allowing unsustainable boom in the mid-1980s by failing to control the expansion of credit and, later, for pursuing a restrictive monetary policy in the midst of a severe contraction in 1989/90. As the model of multiple equilibria demonstrates, a severe macroeconomic shock can have long-lasting effects on unemployment.

At the same time, central control over wage formation was weakened, especially in Sweden. Centralized bargaining was supported by employers as long as the benefits of wage restraint exceeded the costs of wage compression. Over time, however, wage compression steadily increased while wage restraint grew increasingly difficult to achieve. Centralized bargaining initially reduced wage differences between firms and between industries, but not between occupations. As the wage policy changed from one of "equal pay for equal work" to one of "more equal pay for all work," centralized bargaining created political and economic problems that split the union movement and induced some employers to push for the decentralization of wage-setting. By the 1970s, the dominance of the confederations of blue-collar unions declined as the membership of white-collar and professional union confederations grew. The professional unions, in particular, mobilized their members in defense of traditional wage differentials. In addition, the dominance of workers in the traded-goods within the blue-collar confederations declined as employment in the traded-goods sector declined as a share of total employment. The fastest growing affiliates of the blue-collar confederations in the 1970s and 1980s were the public sector unions representing relatively low-wage employees, whose wage demands were not constrained by international competition. As centralized bargaining was increasingly torn by conflicts between low-wage and high-wage workers and between private-sector and public-sector workers, wage restraint became increasingly difficult to achieve. Employers, particularly in Sweden, increasingly sought to decentralize wage-setting to the level of the industry or even, in the case of large employers, the firm.

There is no going back to the past. At the same time, the effects of social democratic labor market institutions may be long-lasting. Union membership remains high, wages continue to be commonly set in centralized negotiations in all of the Nordic countries except Sweden, and the distribution of wages and salaries continues to be very egalitarian in comparison to other societies.

Summary of

The American Paradox: High Income and High Child Poverty

by Sheldon Danziger, Sandra Danziger, and Jonathan Stern

[Published in *Child Poverty and Deprivation in the Industrialized Countries 1945–1995.* eds. Giovanni Andrea Corvica and Sheldon Danziger (Oxford: Clarendon Press, 1997), 181–209.]

High child poverty rates are a persistent feature in American life. In 1997, 21.9 percent of all America's children were living in poverty. This article discusses the economic and social factors that are contributing to this trend and outlines an antipoverty agenda that could reverse it.

Economic Factors

Between the late 1940s and the early 1970s, the economic factors that affect children's well-being moved in a direction that tended to be beneficial to the poor (and their children). Since then, the movement has generally been in the opposite direction. Median family incomes grew by about 40 percent between 1949 and 1959 and by another 40 percent between 1959 and 1969. During each of those decades, poverty for all persons declined by about 10 percentage points. Since 1973, however, mean family incomes stagnated. In 1992 the median family income was only 2 percent above the 1969 level, and poverty was higher.

Another major contributor to the rise in child poverty is the increasing percentage of men who do not earn enough to support a family of four at the poverty line ($16,400 in 1997). The percentage of men below this level fell sharply from 1949 to 1969, but climbed somewhat from 1969 to 1989. For non-Hispanic white men aged 25–54, the proportion earning below the family poverty line was 40 percent in 1949, 12 percent in 1969, and 20 percent in 1989. The levels were higher but the trends were similar for blacks and Hispanics.

Children's poverty did not decline as rapidly as a result of shrinking male earnings because of the increasing earnings of wives and declining family size. Only one-fifth of married women with children were in the labor force in 1950; in 1992 the figure was about two-thirds. In 1973 the poverty rate for children living in married couple families was 7.2 percent and rose by 1 percentage point by 1989. However, poverty would have risen by an additional 3 percentage points if wives hadn't increased their contribution to family income.

Government transfers targeted toward children are also on the decline. Between 1978 and 1987 federal funds for children declined by 4 percent. Since 1973 the average cash benefit from the government for poor families from all programs has been declining rapidly as well: from $10,000 to $7,500 in 1992 for male-headed families; from $9,000 to $5,000 in 1992 for female-headed families.

Poor families not only receive government benefits; they also pay taxes, especially state and local income and sales taxes. A four-person family with earnings equal to the poverty line paid 1.3 percent of its earnings in personal taxes in 1975, and 10.4 percent in 1986. However, the Tax Reform Act of 1986 eliminated federal income taxes for most poor families children. Subsequent expansions of the Earned Income Tax in 1990 and 1993 meant that by 1996 some poor families with children received large enough tax credits to raise their net incomes above the poverty line.

Family Structure, Family Size, Child Poverty

In addition to changes in the economy, children's well-being is also affected by changes in family structure. The most dramatic change has been the rising percentage of children living in mother-only families. The highest child poverty rates today are for children living in single-mother families; they remained as high as the rate for all children in the 1940s.

Child poverty has always been much lower in two-parent families than in single-mother families. Thus the shift in family structure was poverty-increasing. However, child poverty rates today would be much higher in the absence of two poverty-reducing trends—the decline in the number of children per woman and the increase in women's education.

The Consequences of Poverty

Child poverty is associated with both familial and economic hardship. By virtually every measure, poor children in the United States fare worse than their counterparts in other industrialized nations.

The infant mortality rate has been falling in the United States for decades but not as rapidly as in other developed nations. In the early 1950s, the United States ranked sixth among twenty developed nations, but in the late 1980s it ranked last. Within the United States there is also great variation across groups and states. African-Americans have a rate that is usually twice that of whites. Among whites, infant mortality rates are as low as 7.0 (per 1000 births) in Massachusetts and Minnesota; among blacks the rate is as high as 25.0 in Washington, D.C., Detroit, and Philadelphia.

Child health has improved for U.S. children but not relative to other industrialized nations. The United States ranks fifth to seventh among seven developed nations on child death rates due to accidents or injuries and fourth or fifth on child deaths from medical causes. Poor children are more likely to suffer from asthma and bronchitis, inadequate nutrition, physical growth retardation, mental and emotional problems, cognitive and intellectual delays, and so forth. Regarding school achievement and attainment, poor children are more apt to have low grades, poor school attendance, negative attitudes toward school, and higher dropout rates.

Adolescent child bearing is more common in the United States than in other developed nations. This is mainly due to higher U.S. poverty rates, and part of it is due to a poor family-planning system. In 1991, the U.S. adolescent birth rate, 62 per 1000, was twice that of the next highest country, the United Kingdom. Between 1970 and 1991 the birth rate to unmarried 15- to 19-year-olds in the United States doubled from 22 to 45 per 1000.

Reducing Poverty in America

A pro-child policy in the United States should be an antipoverty one. Such an agenda should be built on the assumptions that parents need to take greater responsibility for children, and the public sector must offer greater employment and educational opportunities to enable the poor to attain higher incomes. The current attack on the welfare state will only exacerbate poverty and inequality. The following efforts could raise the current incomes of poor families and the endowments that children will later bring to the labor market:

- *Income Supplements*—Policies that add to the earnings of the working poor and that provide work for the nonworking poor are sorely needed. The public sector should assure that every family has at least one full-time minimum wage earner. These families could then escape poverty via income supplements that subsidize their access to child care and medical care. Such efforts could build on or expand the Earned Income Tax Credit, the Dependent Care Credit, and the Child Support Assurance system. In addition, the minimum wage should be raised at least every five years.

- *Employment Opportunities*—The demand for low-skilled workers should be increased by establishing low-wage jobs for all poor adults. This could be achieved through a revitalized Public Service Employment program.

- *Direct Services*—Four areas of direct service programs could be expanded to improve child outcomes: prenatal care, Medicaid, and the Special Supplemental Food Program for Women, Infants, and Children (WIC); and Head Start and other school-readiness programs. Despite the proven effectiveness of these programs, in the early 1990s WIC reached less than two-thirds of those who were eligible, and Head Start and related efforts reached only about half of the eligible population, in large part due to lack of funding.

Conclusion

Spending cuts and welfare reform enacted by Congress in the mid-1990s are likely to raise the future costs associated with child poverty. The United States has lost some of the gains made in the 1950s and 1960s and is slipping behind the progress of the other developed nations. The policies advocated in this article could reduce child poverty and could be financed by modest increases in tax rates in high-income families, who have gained so much during the economic booms of the 1980s and 1990s. In contrast, the policies that reinforce the status quo will subject yet another generation to lives of unrealized potential.

Summary of

Who Paid for the Canadian Welfare State during 1955–1988?

by Ardeshir Sepehri and Robert Chernomas

[Published in *Review of Radical Political Economic* 24, 1 (1992), 71–87.]

Who bears the burden of welfare state expenditure, capital or labor? To some, the answer is capital. Some go so far as to claim that this "vertical" redistribution was responsible for the economic stagnation that occurred in the late 1970s and early 1980s. Was this really the case in Canada and the United States? This article empirically examines the distributive activities of the Canadian welfare state for period 1955–1988 and compares these findings to the United States during the same period.

State Revenues and Expenditures

Like many industrialized nations after World War II, Canada embarked on a period of extensive social service programs. Total government expenditures rose from 33 percent of GDP in 1965 to 44 percent in 1975. In addition, net transfer payments to individuals rose from 8 percent of personal income in 1955 to 14.5 percent in 1985. How are these expenditures paid for?

For the purposes of this study, tax revenues have been classified into three categories, which are assumed to be paid by different classes: (1) health and social insurance levies; (2) corporate income taxes, property taxes, and consumption taxes; and (3) personal income taxes, property taxes, and consumption taxes. Taxes under category 1 (parallel to others) are entirely allocated to labor, category 2 are paid by nonlabor. Category 3 are levied on both labor and nonlabor, with labor's share estimated as the ratio of total wages and salaries to personal income. Labor's share rose steadily in the second half of the 1960s and began to decline in the 1970s.

State expenditures can be classified into four categories: (1) social security, housing; (2) social welfare; (3) transportation and communication, health, education, and so forth; (4) general services such as protection of persons and property, foreign affairs, resource conservation, and the like. All expenditure in category 1 are allocated to labor. Welfare recipients gain from expenditures in category 2. Category 3 accrues to both labor and nonlabor according to their share in adjusted personal income. Category 4 expenditures go entirely to nonlabor when viewed as expenditures to secure the capitalist class.

The Performance of the Canadian Welfare State

How do the allocations of state taxes and expenditures balance out? This can be estimated by comparing the total taxes paid by each class with the total social benefits received by that class from state expenditures. Such estimates can be summarized by an examination of the transfer ratio (the ratio of taxes paid by workers to the social expenditures paid to them) and the welfare-adjusted transfer ratio (ratio of taxes paid to the state by workers over the income and benefits received by workers as well as families on welfare). A ratio of greater than one indicates that the benefits and income received by workers and welfare recipients falls short of taxes paid by workers.

In Canada from 1955 to 1988 the transfer ratios always exceeded 1.0. That is, taxes paid to the state by workers exceeded the benefits and income received by them. The welfare-adjusted transfer ratio fell below 1.0, indicating that workers and families on welfare received more benefits than they paid in taxes for only fifteen years out of the thirty-four examined. Within that period, however, four broad historical phases can be distinguished.

During the first phase, 1955–1969, there was a steady decline in the value of the transfer ratio. Despite rapid economic growth and expanding social programs during this era, the redistribution of income was within the working class and welfare recipients rather than from profit recipients to workers and families on welfare. In fact, there was a net transfer from labor to the state during this period.

The transfer ratio continued to decline during the second phase, 1970–1975. The welfare-adjusted transfer ratio actually dipped below 1.0 for the first time, and the transfer ratio came to as low as 1.17. Thus there was a small net payment by workers to the state as well as a net transfer from the state to families on welfare. All this was accompanied by a rise in the unemployment rate and the consolidation of social programs.

Workers and welfare recipients together continued to receive net transfers during the third phase, 1976–1983, Canada's worst postwar economic years. This economic slowdown was coupled with a squeeze on social expenditure, leaving the transfer ratio constant from 1975 to 1979, followed by a dip that was accompanied by transfers from nonlabor to welfare recipients that set the stage for large-scale cutbacks in the 1980s.

During the fourth phase, 1984–1988, both transfer ratios rose sharply, coupled with a decline in unemployment and a state "attack" on social programs. This suggests that workers and welfare recipients lost the ground they gained in the 1960s and 1970s.

Canada versus the United States

Comparison of the United States and Canada is used to isolate the effects of cyclical changes in economic activities from other forces that influence the distributive activities of the state. The post–World War II period in both countries reveal some general similarities. In the 1950s and 1960s, social programs were established and expanded in the two countries and were cut back in the late 1970s and 1980s. A more detailed comparison can be carried out using the same four periods discussed in the last section.

During the first two phases, 1955–1975, the transfer ratios in the two countries followed each other fairly closely. This was also associated with a small or stable unemployment rate differential between the two countries. These similarities changed in the late 1970s and 1980s. The U.S. welfare-adjusted transfer ratio rose steadily after 1975, while Canada stood below 1.0 from 1975 to 1983. During this period, Canada's unemployment rate was much higher than the U.S. rate. The last phase, 1984–1988, is characterized by a steady rise in the Canadian welfare-adjusted transfer ratio (similar to the U.S. ratio) and a steady decline in the unemployment rate differential between two nations.

There are two principal explanations for the divergence between the Canadian and U.S. transfer ratios during the last phase. First, there is an important difference between the unemployment rates in two countries. For most of 1975–1988, the Canadian unemployment rate exceeded the U.S. rate by three to four times its past historical value. Such high unemployment could have accelerated the state's unemployment insurance and welfare payments to labor and therefore reduced the ratio.

Others have rejected this explanation. They claim that deep recessions in the 1970s and 1980s coupled with high unemployment weakened labor's power, saying that the state responded to the crisis by joining the private sector's attack on labor. This "harmonization" assault on labor in the two countries occurred both in expenditure and taxation—shifting the burden more on labor.

Conclusion

Contrary to popular wisdom, the empirical evaluation of Canada during 1955–1988 reveals that "net transfers from labor to the state were used to finance the state transfer payments to families on welfare as well as other state expenditures whose beneficiaries were neither labor nor welfare recipients." [87] If these trends continue, a "negative social wage could be used to improve profitability by reducing capital's responsibility for paying for nonlabor supporting state activities such as for the military, administrative costs or capital grants, by transferring surplus through to corporations and/or by undermining labor's ability to protect its wages and working conditions by reducing unemployment insurance and welfare payments." [87]

Summary of

On Targeting and Family Benefits

by Anthony B. Atkinson

[Published in *Incomes and the Welfare State: Essays on Britain and Europe* (New York: Cambridge University Press, 1995), Ch. 12, 223–261.]

How should government benefits, such as family assistance, be distributed? Targeting, or concentrating benefits on those in need, is an attractive and widely supported idea.

> However, although politically fashionable, calls for greater targeting [of family benefits] need to be treated with caution. The argument in favor has to be made explicit and critically examined. Behind such policy recommendations lie views with regard to (a) the objectives of policy, (b) the range of instruments available to attain those objectives, and (c) the constraints under which policy has to operate. . . . [223–224]

This chapter examines the ambiguities and limitations of common approaches to targeting of benefits, and suggests the need to consider other objectives in designing effective social security programs. (Note that the author, focusing primarily on Britain and Europe, uses "social security" as a generic term for a range of benefit programs, not a specific reference to the American retirement program.)

Targeting and the Objectives of Social Security

Although social security is often linked to poverty alleviation, it has other important functions as well. These include smoothing of income over the life cycle; provision of security against events such as sickness, disability, and unemployment; redistribution toward those with children; and redistribution according to gender or other social criteria. Relief of poverty is only one motive for the introduction of transfer payments, and sometimes not the most important one. In France, social insurance and family allowances, introduced in the 1930s, were intended to create solidarity among different groups of workers and families, not to combat poverty. Universal benefits are more politically popular, and hence may be better funded, than means-tested programs serving only a minority. Nonetheless, poverty alleviation is an important goal of social security, and the remainder of the discussion here concerns the targeting of benefits to help the poor.

Alleviation of poverty can be taken to mean raising people up to the "poverty line," a specified income level. The extent of poverty is often measured by the head count ratio, or proportion of families with incomes below the poverty line. However, this is not the ideal measure. A focus on the head count ratio alone has the perverse implication that the most cost-effective way to reduce poverty is to provide benefits exclusively to those just below the poverty line, since relatively small income supplements will move them above the line; the same total expenditure directed to the poorest of the poor would achieve a much smaller head count reduction.

To avoid such paradoxes, it is more appropriate to use a measure such as the poverty gap—the total income needed to raise the poor up to the poverty line. The effectiveness of an income transfer program can then be measured in two ways: horizontal efficiency, or the percentage of the poverty gap that is filled by the program; and vertical efficiency, or the percentage of program benefits that go toward closing the poverty gap. Vertical efficiency can be less than 100 percent, both because some benefits may go to nonpoor households and because the program may lift some formerly poor people significantly above the poverty line.

The two standards of efficiency measure very different dimensions of programs. At one extreme, Belgium's total social security spending in the 1970s had a horizontal efficiency of 99 percent and a vertical efficiency of 8 percent. That is, government social spending essentially closed the nation's poverty gap, but only about one-twelfth of the total expenditure went for this purpose. At the other extreme, a small means-tested program may have a vertical efficiency of 100 percent, if only those below the poverty line are eligible, but a horizontal efficiency close to zero, if the poverty gap is much larger than the program budget.

Although the poverty gap is an improvement over the head count ratio, it still may not be the correct measure for some purposes. The definition of the poverty gap places an equal value on every dollar of income needed by everyone below the poverty line, while one might believe that there is a greater urgency in providing an additional dollar to the poorest households than to those closer to the poverty line. To reflect this concern, a spectrum of measures akin to the poverty gap can be created, by calculating each poor household's extent of poverty as

$$(\text{the poverty line} - \text{the household's income})^{\alpha}$$

and then summing or averaging across households. With $\alpha=0$, this is just the head count; with $\alpha=1$ it is the poverty gap. With $\alpha>1$, the new poverty measure weights the experience of poorer households more heavily; as α becomes infinite, it approaches a Rawlsian concern with the status of society's least fortunate individual. Academic research has often used $\alpha=2$.

The greater the value of α, the more the optimal policy tilts toward benefits targeted to the very poor. Many different standards can be created with this simple apparatus; for example, to reflect a moderate social value of payments to near-poor households and a greater value of payments to the very poor, one can raise the poverty line, while using $\alpha>1$. Clearly, each variant on the measure of poverty may imply a different optimal policy response. Without a clear agreement about the appropriate measure, it is impossible to say that one program design is more or less efficient than another in alleviating poverty.

Categorical Conditions and Family Benefits

Family benefits, which exist throughout Europe and in Canada and Australia, are a prime example of categorical programs: Benefits are provided to everyone in a certain category, defined on a basis other than income. Categorical programs are often criticized as inefficient, since a means-tested program with the same budget would be more efficient in reducing poverty. In practice, however, families with children, especially single mothers with children, include a disproportionate number of the poor, particularly in the United States but also in other countries. Thus categorical programs for this group may be reasonably effective in targeting the poor.

There are many dimensions and variations to family benefits. Some programs are tied to labor market status, such as parental leave at birth, or child care subsidies for working parents. Child benefits may vary with the child's age; several European countries provide larger benefits for older children, while others give more to parents of younger children, and a third group has the same benefit for all ages of children. Several countries that have worried about low birth rates have larger benefits per child for bigger families, while others have constant benefits per child. The United Kingdom, in the 1990s, provides less per child for bigger families. Benefits end at ages ranging from 14 to 18, and in some countries can be extended for those in school or apprenticeship.

Categorical programs are not simply alternatives to income testing. Several European countries reduce or eliminate child benefits at high incomes. The reduction of benefits occurs more abruptly in some countries than others: A means-tested component of Britain's child benefits offers fairly high payments to the lowest-income families, but tapers off rapidly as income rises; a comparable French program offers a constant payment for all families (less than Britain pays to the poorest), up to well above average earnings.

Problems in Targeting: Information and Incentives

The ability of targeted programs to reach the poor is limited by administrative problems and by their impact on economic incentives. Administratively, any categorical or income-tested program requires information about potential recipients; gathering and verifying this information can be expensive and difficult. Errors are possible in both directions, as eligible households may fail to get benefits while ineligible households may succeed.

When eligibility depends on something as simple as the presence of children in the household, errors may be relatively rare and administrative costs may be low (though not zero). For income-tested transfers, information requirements, administrative costs, and potential for error are all much higher. The stigma attached to participation in such programs, and the demeaning and tedious nature of the application process, often lead to a third or more of the eligible population failing to claim their benefits.

Income-tested programs also create problems of work incentives. If a household loses benefits as its wages begin to rise, the effective tax rate on its earnings may be high enough to discourage work effort—falling into the "poverty trap." In the United Kingdom in 1992/93, the marginal income tax rate on low-income wage earners was 34 percent. However, those who qualified for three major means-tested social programs also faced the loss of those benefits, adding up to an effective tax rate of 96 percent on incremental earnings. Concern about such high effective taxation may arise both from its impact on labor supply and separately from a sense of fairness: It may be regarded as unfair that a person is unable to improve his or her position by working more. These concerns may lead to limits on the extent to which benefits can be means-tested, and therefore limits on targeting of payments exclusively to the poor.

Bibliography

Acemoglu, Daron. "Why Do New Technologies Complement Skills? Directed Technical Change and Wage Inequality." *The Quarterly Journal of Economics* CXIII, 4 (November 1998), 1055–1090.

Ackerman, Frank. *Hazardous to Our Wealth: Economic Policies in the 1980s* (Boston: South End Press, 1984).

Ackerman, Frank. *Still Dead After All These Years: Interpreting the Failure of General Equilibrium Theory* (Tufts University, 1999). Available at www.tufts.edu/gdae.

Adams, Walter, and James Brock. "Bigness and Social Efficiency: A Case Study of the U.S. Auto Industry." Chapter 9 in *Corporations and Society,* ed. Arthur Miller (Greenwich, Conn.: Greenwood Press, 1987).

Adelman, Irma, and Nobuhiko Fuwa. "Income Inequality and Development: The 1970s and 1980s Compared." *Economie Applique* 46, 1 (January 1994), 7–29.

Adler, Moshe. "Stardom and Talent." *American Economic Review* 75 (March 1985), 208–212.

Albelda, Randy, and Chris Tilly. *Glass Ceilings and Bottomless Pits: Women's Work, Women's Poverty* (Boston: South End Press, 1997).

Albelda, Randy, Nancy Folbre, and the Center for Popular Economics. *The War on the Poor: A Defense Manual* (New York: The New Press, 1996).

Alesina, Alberto, and Roberto Perotti. "Income Distribution, Political Instability, and Investment." *European Economic Review* 40 (1996), 1203.

Alesina, Alberto, and Dani Rodrik. "Distributive Politics and Economic Growth." *The Quarterly Journal of Economics* (May 1994), 464–489.

Allen, Polly Wynn. *Building Domestic Liberty—Charlotte Perkins Gilman's Architectural Feminism* (Amherst: University of Massachusetts Press, 1988).

Angle, John. "The Inequality Process and the Distribution of Income to Blacks and Whites." *Journal of Mathematical Sociology* 17 (1992), 77–98.

Angle, John. "Deriving the Size Distribution of Personal Wealth from 'The Rich Get Richer, the Poor Get Poorer.'" *Journal of Mathematical Sociology* 18 (1993), 27–46.

Angle, John. "How the Gamma Law of Income Distribution Appears Invariant Under Aggregation." *Journal of Mathematical Sociology* 21 (1996), 325–358.

Anker, Richard. *Gender and Jobs: Sex Segregation of Occupations in the World* (Geneva: International Labor Office, 1998).

Arthur, W. Brian. "Competing Technologies, Increasing Returns, and Lock-In by Historical Events." *Economic Journal* 99 (March 1989), 116–131.

Atkinson, Anthony B. "On Targeting and Family Benefits." Chapter 12 in *Incomes and the Welfare State: Essays on Britain and Europe* (New York: Cambridge University Press, 1995), 223–261.

Atkinson, Anthony B. "Bringing Income Distribution in From the Cold." *The Economic Journal* 107, 441 (March 1997), 297–321.

Autor, David H., Lawrence F. Katz, and Alan B. Kreuger. "Computing Inequality: Have Computers Changed the Labor Market?" *National Bureau of Economic Research Working Paper* No. 5956 (March 1997).

Autor, David H., Lawrence F. Katz, and Alan B. Kreuger. "Computing Inequality: Have Computers Changed the Labor Market?" *The Quarterly Journal of Economics* CXIII, 4 (November 1998), 1169–1214.

Ayres, R.U., with T. Van Leynseele. *Eco-Efficiency, Double Dividends and the Sustainable Firm* (Fontainebleau, France: INSEAD's Centre for the Management of Environmental Resources, 1997).

Barnet, Richard J., and John Cavanagh. *Global Dreams* (New York: Simon and Schuster, 1994).

Barr, N. "Economic Theory and the Welfare State: A Survey and Interpretations." *Journal of Economic Literature* 30 (1992), 741–803.

Bartel, Anne, and Frank Lichtenberg. "The Comparative Advantage of Educated Workers in Implementing New Technology." *The Review of Economics and Statistics* LXIX, 1 (1987), 1–11.

Becker, Gary. "Altruism in the Family and Selfishness in the Marketplace." In *The Economics of the Family,* ed. Nancy Folbre (Brookfield, Vt.: Edward Elgar Publishing Company, 1996), 97–109. Originally published in *Economica* 48 (February 1981), 1–15.

Been, Vicki. "What's Fairness Got To Do With It? Environmental Justice and the Siting of Locally Undesirable Land Uses." *Cornell Law Review* 78, 6 (September 1993), 1001–1084.

Behrman, Jere R., Nancy Birdsall, and Robert Kaplan. "The Quality of Schooling and Labor Market Outcomes." *Opportunity Foregone: Education in Brazil* (Washington, D.C.: The Inter-American Development Bank, 1996), 246–266.

Bell, Carolyn Shaw. "Economics of Equality: Changes Loom With More Women Attending College Than Men." *Boston Globe* (April 6, 1999).

Bell, Daniel. "The Power Elite—Reconsidered." *American Journal of Sociology* 64 (1958), 238–250.

Bergmann, Barbara. *In Defense of Affirmative Action* (New York: Basic Books, 1996).

Berle, Adolph, and Garginer C. Means. *The Modern Corporation and Private Property* (New York: Macmillan, 1932).

Berman, Eli, John Bound, and Zvi Griliches. "Changes in the Demand for Skilled Labor Within U.S. Manufacturing: Evidence from the Annual Survey of Manufactures." *The Quarterly Journal of Economics* CIX, 2 (May 1994), 367–397.

Bernstein, Jared, and Lawrence Mishel. "Has Wage Inequality Stopped Growing?" *Monthly Labor Review* (December 1997).

Bhalla, Ajit S. "Access to Education." Chapter 10 in *Uneven Development in the Third World: A Study of India and China* (New York: St. Martin's Press, 1995), 255–290.

Bhalla, Ajit S., and Frédéric Lapeyre. "Social Exclusion: Toward an Analytical and Operational Framework." *Development and Change* 28, 3 (July 1997), 413–433.

Björklund, Anders, and Richard Freeman. "Generating Equality and Eliminating Poverty, the Swedish Way." In *The Welfare State in Transition: Reforming the Swedish Model*, eds. Richard B. Freeman, Robert Topel, and Birgitta Swedenborg (Chicago: University of Chicago Press, 1997), 33–78.

Blanchflower, David G., and Andrew J. Oswald. "An Introduction to the Wage Curve." *Journal of Economic Perspectives* 9 (Summer 1995), 153–167.

Blau, Francine D. "The Gender Pay Gap." Chapter 1 in *Women's Work and Wages*, eds. Inga Persson and Christina Jonung (London and New York: Routledge, 1998), 15–35.

Bluestone, Barry. "Old Theories in New Bottles: Toward an Explanation of Growing World-Wide Income Inequality." In *The Changing Distribution of Income in an Open U.S. Economy*, eds. Jeffrey H. Bergstrand, Thomas F. Cosimano, John W. Houck, and Richard G. Sheehan (Amsterdam: Elsevier Science, 1994), 331–342.

Bok, Derek. "Summing Up." Chapter 11 in *The Cost of Talent* (New York: Free Press, 1993), 223–248.

Borjas, George, and Valerie Ramey. "The Relationship Between Wage Inequality and International Trade." Chapter 7 in *The Changing Distribution of Income in an Open U.S. Economy* (New York: Elsevier, 1994), 217–241.

Borjas, George J. "Long-Run Convergence of Ethnic Skill Differentials: The Children and Grandchildren of the Great Migration." *Industrial and Labor Relations Review* 47 (1994), 553–573.

Borjas, George J. "Ethnicity, Neighborhoods, and Human-Capital Externalities." *The American Economic Review* 85, 3 (June 1995), 365–390.

Borjas, George J., and Glenn T. Sueyoshi. "Ethnicity and the Intergenerational Transmission of Welfare Dependency." *Research in Labor Economics* 16 (1997), 271–295.

Boschen, John F., and Kimberly J. Smith. "You Can Pay Me Now *and* You Can Pay Me Later: The Dynamic Response of Executive Compensation to Firm Performance." *Journal of Business* 68 (1995), 577–608.

Bound, John, and Richard Freeman. "What Went Wrong? The Erosion of Earnings and Employment Among Young Black Men in the 1980s." *Quarterly Journal of Economics* 107 (February 1992), 201–232.

Bourguignon, Francois, Jaime de Melo, and Akiko Suwa. "Distributional Effects of Adjustment Policies: Simulations for Archetype Economies in Africa and Latin America." *The World Bank Economic Review* 3, 2 (1991), 339–336.

Bowen, William G., and Derek Bok. *The Shape of the River: Long-Term Consequences of*

Considering Race in College and University Admissions (Princeton, N.J.: Princeton University Press, 1998).

Bowles and Gintis. "Power and Wealth in a Competitive Capitalist Economy." *Philosophy and Public Affairs* 21, 4 (1992), 324–353.

Bowles, Samuel, and Herbert Gintis. "Economy: The Political Foundations of Production and Exchange." Chapter 3 in *Democracy and Capitalism* (New York: Basic Books, 1986).

Bruyn, Severyn. *A Civil Economy: Transforming the Marketplace* (Ann Arbor: The University of Michigan Press, 1999).

Bureau of Labor Statistics, *Monthly Labor Review* (1990–present). Various issues.

Burtless, Gary. "Trends in the Level and Distribution of U.S. Living Standards: 1973–1993." *Eastern Economic Journal* 22, 3 (Summer 1996), 271–290.

Card, David, and Alan B. Krueger. "School Resources and Student Outcomes: An Overview of the Literature and New Evidence from North and South Carolina." *National Bureau of Economic Research Working Paper* No. 5708 (August 1996). (Cambridge, Mass.: National Bureau of Economic Research, 1999).

Card, David, and Alan Krueger. "Is There an Explanation? Alternative Models of the Labor Market and the Minimum Wage." Chapter 11 in *Myth and Measurement: The New Economics of the Minimum Wage* (Princeton: Princeton University Press, 1995), 355–386.

Chandler, Alfred D., Jr. *Scale and Scope: The Dynamics of Industrial Capitalism* (Cambridge, Mass.: Harvard University Press, 1990).

Chandler, Alfred D., Jr. *The Visible Hand: The Managerial Revolution in American Business* (Cambridge: Harvard University Press, 1977).

Chiappori, Pierre-Andre. "'Collective' Models of Household Behavior: The Sharing Rule Approach." In *Intrahousehold Resource Allocation in Developing Countries: Models, Methods and Policy*, eds. Lawrence Haddad, John Hoddinott, and Harold Alderman (Baltimore: The Johns Hopkins University Press, 1997, for the International Food Policy Research Institute), 39–52.

Chung, Kee H., and Raymond A.K. Cox. "A Stochastic Model of Superstardom: An Application of the Yule Distribution." *Review of Economics and Statistics* 76 (November 1994), 771–775.

Clark, Charles M.A. "Inequality in the 1980s: An Institutionalist View." In *Inequality: Radical Institutionalist Views on Race, Gender, Class, and Nation*, ed. William M. Dugger (Westport, Conn.: Greenwood Press, 1996), 197–221.

Clawson, Dan, Alan Neustadtl, and Denise Scott. "Business Unity, Business Power." In *Money Talks: Corporate PACs and Political Influence* (New York: Basic Books, 1992), 158–190.

Coase, Ronald H. *The Nature of the Firm: Origins, Evolution, and Development* (New York: Oxford University Press, 1991).

Cook, Paul, and Colin Kirkpatrick. "The Distributional Impact of Privatization in Developing Countries." Chapter 2 in *Privatization and Equity* (London: Routledge, 1995), 35–48.

Danziger, Sheldon, Sandra Danziger, and Jonathan Stern. "The American Paradox: High Income and High Child Poverty." In *Child Poverty and Deprivation in the Industrialized Countries, 1945–1995,* eds. Giovanni Andrea Corvica and Sheldon Danziger (Oxford: Clarendon Press, 1997), 181–209.

Darity, William A., Jr. "What's Left of the Economic Theory of Discrimination?" In *The Question of Discrimination: Racial Inequality in the U.S. Labor Market,* eds. Steven Shulman and William Darity, Jr. (Middletown, Conn.: Wesleyan University Press, 1989), 335–374.

Darity, William A., Jr. "Intergroup Disparity: Economic Theory and Social Science." *Southern Economic Journal* 64, 4 (April 1998), 805–826.

Darity, William A., Jr., and Samuel L. Myers, Jr. "The Marginalization of Black Men: Impact on Family Structure." Chapter 7 in *The Black Underclass* (New York: Garland, 1994), 143–185.

DeSerpa, Allan C., and Roger L. Faith. "'Bru-u-u-uce': The Simple Economics of Mob Goods." *Public Choice* 89 (1996), 77–91.

Dickens, William T., and Kevin Lang. "A Test of Dual Labor Market Theory." *American Economic Review* 75 (September 1985), 792–805.

Dickens, William T., and Kevin Lang. "Labor Market Segmentation Theory: Reconsidering the Evidence." In *Labor Economics: Problems in Analyzing Labor Markets,* ed. William A. Darity, Jr. (Boston: Kluwer Academic Publishers, 1993), 141–180.

DiNardo, John, and Thomas LeMieux. "Diverging Male Wage Inequality in the United States and Canada, 1981–1988. 80 Unions Explain the Difference?" Unpublished paper (Irvine: University of California, 1994).

DiNardo, John, and Jorn Steffen-Pischke. "The Returns to Computer Use Revisited: Have Pencils Changed the Wage Structure Too?" *The Quarterly Journal of Economics* CXII, 1 (February 1997), 291–303.

Doeringer, Peter B., and Michael Piore. *Internal Labor Markets and Manpower Analysis* (Lexington, Mass.: D.C. Heath, 1971).

Domhoff, G. William. *Who Rules America? Power and Politics in the Year 2000* (Mountain View, Calif.: Mayfield Publishing Company, 1998).

Domhoff, William. "The Control of the Corporate Community." Chapter 3 in *Who Rules America Now?* (New York: Touchstone, 1983).

Drucker, Peter Ferdinand. *The Concept of the Corporation* (New Brunswick, N.J.: Transaction Publishers, 1946).

Dugger, William M. "An Institutional Analysis of Corporate Power." *Journal of Economic Issues* XXII, 1 (March 1988).

Durlauf, Steven N. "A Theory of Persistent Income Inequality." *Journal of Economic Growth* 1 (1996), 75–93.

Esping-Andersen, Gøsta. "The Three Political Economies of the Welfare State." *International Journal of Sociology* 20 (Fall 1990), 92–112.

Esping-Andersen, Gøsta, ed. *Welfare States in Transition: National Adaptations in Global Economies* (London: SAGE Publications, 1996).

Estes, Ralph. Interview. *Corporate Crime Reporter* 5, 41 (Oct. 28, 1991).

Estes, Ralph. "The Solution: A Better Scorecard" and "What the Scorecard Should Contain." Chapters 9 and 10 in *Tyranny of the Bottom Line: Why Corporations Make Good People Do Bad Things* (San Francisco: Barrett-Koehler Publishers, Inc., 1996), 201–231.

Fapohunda, Eleanor B. "The Non-Pooling Household: A Challenge to Theory." In *A Home Divided: Women and Income in the Third World,* eds. Daisy Dwyer and Judith Bruce (Stanford, Calif.: Stanford University Press, 1988), 143–154.

Fields, Gary S. "Income Distribution in Developing Economies: Conceptual, Data, and Policy Issues in Broad-Based Growth." Chapter 4 in *Critical Issues in Asian Development: Theories, Experiences, and Policies* (Oxford: Oxford University Press, 1995), 75–93.

Fischer, Claude S., et al. *Inequality by Design: Cracking the Bell Curve Myth* (Princeton, N.J.: Princeton University Press, 1996).

Folbre, Nancy. "The Pauperization of Motherhood: Patriarchy and Public Policy in the United States." *Review of Radical Political Economics* 16, 4 (1984), 72–88.

Folbre, Nancy. "Gender Coalitions: Extrafamily Influences in Intrafamily Inequality." Chapter 16 in *Intrahousehold Resource Allocation in Developing Countries,* eds. J.H. Lawrence Haddad and Harold Alderman (Baltimore: The John Hopkins University Press, 1997), 263–275.

Fortin, Nicole M., and Thomas Lemieux. "Institutional Changes and Rising Wage Inequality: Is There a Linkage?" *Journal of Economic Perspectives* 11 (Spring 1997), 75–96.

Frank, Robert H., and Philip J. Cook. "How Winner-Take-All Markets Arise" and "The Growth of Winner-Take-All Markets." Chapters 2 and 3 in *The Winner-Take-All Society* (New York: The Free Press, 1995), 23–60.

Freeman, Richard, and Lawrence Katz. "Rising Wage Inequality: The U.S. vs. Other Advanced Countries." Chapter 2 in *Working Under Different Rules* (New York: Russell Sage, 1994).

Freeman, Richard B., and William M. Rodgers III. "Area Economic Conditions and the Labor Market Outcomes of Young Men in the 1990s Expansion." *National Bureau of Economic Research Working Paper* No. 7073 (Cambridge, Mass.: National Bureau of Economic Research, 1999).

Friedman, Benjamin M. "Economic Implications of Changing Share Ownership." *Journal of Portfolio Management* 22, 3 (Spring 1996), 59–70.

Friedman, Milton, and Rose Friedman. *Free to Choose.* (New York: Harcourt Brace Jovanovich, 1980).

Galbraith, James K. "Inequality, Unemployment, Inflation and Growth." Chapter 8 in *Created Unequal: The Crisis in American Pay* (New York: The Free Press, 1998), 133–149.

Galbraith, John Kenneth. *The New Industrial State* (Boston: Houghton Mifflin, 1967).

Garen, John E. "Executive Compensation and Principal-Agent Theory." *Journal of Political Economy* 102 (1994), 1175–1199.

Garner, Thesia I., et al. "Experimental Poverty Measurement for the 1990s." *Monthly Labor Review* 121, 3 (March 1998), 39–61.

Gazel, Ricardo C., and R. Keith Schwer. "Beyond Rock and Roll: The Economic Impact of the Grateful Dead on a Local Economy." *Journal of Cultural Economics* 21 (1997), 41–55.

Gilman, Charlotte Perkins. *The Man-Made World or Our Androcentric Culture* (New York: Charleton Company, 1911; facsimile edition New York: Source Book Press, 1970.)

Gilson, Stuart C., and Michael R. Vetsuypens. "CEO Compensation in Financially Distressed Firms: An Empirical Analysis." *Journal of Finance* 48 (June 1993), 425–458.

Goldin, Claudia. "The Political Economy of Gender" and "Economic Progress and Gender Equality." Chapters 7 and 8 in *Understanding the Gender Gap: An Economic History of American Women* (New York: Oxford University Press, 1990), 185–217.

Gordon, David. "Wielding the Stick." Chapter 8 in *Fat and Mean: The Corporate Squeeze of Working Americans and the Myth of Managerial "Downsizing"* (New York: The Free Press, 1996), 204–237.

Gordon, David M., Thomas E. Weisskopf, and Samuel Bowles. " Power, Accumulation, and Crisis: the Rise and Demise of the Postwar Social Structure of Accumulation." In *Radical Political Economy: Explorations in Alternate Economic Analysis,* ed. Victor D. Lippit (Armonk, N.Y.: M.E. Sharpe, 1996), 226–244.

Gordon, Ian. "The Impact of Economic Change on Minorities and Migrants in Western Europe." Chapter 16 in *Poverty, Inequality, and the Future of Social Policy: Western States in the New World Order,* eds. Katherine McFate, Roger Lawson, and William Julius Wilson (New York: Russell Sage Foundation, 1995), 521–541.

Gottschalk, Peter. "Inequality, Income Growth, and Mobility: The Basic Facts." *Journal of Economic Perspectives* 11 (Spring 1997), 21–40.

Gottschalk, Peter, and Timothy M. Smeeding. "Cross-National Comparisons of Earnings and Income Inequality." *Journal of Economic Literature* 35 (1997), 633–687.

Greider, William. *One World, Ready or Not: The Manic Logic of Global Capitalism* (New York: Simon and Schuster, 1997).

Grossman, Gene, and Alan Krueger. "Economic Growth and the Environment." *The Quarterly Journal of Economics* 110 (1995), 353–377.

Gustafsson, Siv. "Single Mothers in Sweden: Why Is Poverty Less Severe?" Chapter 8 in *Poverty, Inequality, and the Future of Social Policy,* eds. Katherine McFate, Roger Hawson, and William Julius Wilson (New York: Russell Sage Foundation, 1996), 291–323.

Hacker, Andrew. *Money: Who Has How Much and Why* (New York: Touchstone Press, 1997).

Hamlen, William A., Jr. "Superstardom in Popular Music: Empirical Evidence." *Review of Economics and Statistics* 73 (November 1991) 729–733.

Harrison, Bennett. "The Dark Side of Flexible Production." Chapter 9 in *Lean and Mean* (New York: Guilford, 1994).

Harrison, Bennett. *Lean and Mean: The Changing Landscape of Corporate Power in the Age of Flexibility* (New York: Basic Books, 1994).

Harrison, Bennett, and Barry Bluestone. "Wage Polarisation in the U.S. and the 'Flexibility' Debate." *Cambridge Journal of Economics* 14, 3 (1990), 351–373.

Harrison, Bennett, and Barry Bluestone. *The Great U-Turn: Corporate Restructuring and the Polarizing of America* (New York: Basic Books, 1990).

Haubrich, Joseph G. "Risk Aversion, Performance Pay, and the Principle-Agent Problem." *Journal of Political Economy* 102 (1994), 258–276.

Herrnstein, Richard J., and Charles Murray. *The Bell Curve: Intelligence and Class Structure in American Life* (New York: The Free Press, 1994).

Himmelstein, Jerome. "The Mobilization of Corporate Conservatism." Chapter 5 in *To The Right* (Berkeley: University of California Press, 1990).

Himmelstein, Jerome L. *Looking Good and Doing Good: Corporate Philanthropy and Corporate Power* (Bloomington: Indiana University Press, 1997).

Hoff, Karla. "Market Failures and the Distribution of Wealth: A Perspective from the Economics of Information." *Politics and Society* 24 (December 1996), 411–432.

Hout, Michael, Adrian E. Raftery, and Eleanor O. Bell. "Making the Grade: Educational Stratification in the United States, 1925–1989." Chapter 2 in *Persistent Inequality: Changing Educational Attainment in Thirteen Countries,* eds. Yossi Shavit and Hans-Peter Blossfield (Boulder, Colo.: Westview Press, 1993), 25–49.

Howell, David R. "Institutional Failure and the American Worker." *Jerome Levy Economics Institute of Bard College Public Policy Brief* 29 (1997).

Hsieh, Ching-Chi, and M.D. Pugh. "Poverty, Income Inequality, and Violent Crime: A Meta-Analysis of Recent Aggregate Data Studies." *Criminal Justice Review* 18 (Autumn 1993), 182–202.

Huggett, Mark. "Wealth Distribution in Life-Cycle Economies." *Journal of Monetary Economics* 38 (1996), 469–494.

Ichniowski, Casey, Kathryn Shaw, and Giovanna Prennushi. "The Effect of Human Resource Management Practices on Productivity: A Study of Steel Finishing Lines." *American Economic Review* 87, 3 (June 1997), 291–313.

Jacobs, Michael T. "Management Compensation Plans: Panacea or Placebo?" Chapter 7 in *Short-Term America: The Causes and Cures of Our Business Myopia* (Cambridge, Mass.: Harvard Business School Press, 1991), 197–212.

Jensen, Michael C., and Kevin J. Murphy. "Performance Pay and Top-Management Incentives." *Journal of Political Economy* 98 (1990), 225–264.

Johnson, George E. "Changes in Earnings Inequality: The Role of Demand Shifts." *Journal of Economic Perspectives* 11 (Spring 1997), 41–54.

Jones, Charles. "On the Evolution of the World Income Distribution." *Journal of Economic Perspectives* 11, 3 (Summer 1997), 19–36.

Kabeer, Naila. "Benevolent Dictators, Maternal Altruists and Patriarchal Contracts: Gender and Household Economies." In *Reversed Realities: Gender Hierarchies in Development Thought* (London: Verso, 1994), 95–135.

Kaplan, Steven N. "Top Executive Rewards and Firm Performance: A Comparison of Japan and the United States." *Journal of Political Economy* 102 (1994), 510–546.

Kasarda, John. "Joblessness and Poverty in America's Central Cities: Causes and Policy Prescriptions." *Housing Policy Debate* 7, 2 (1996).

Katz, Lawrence F., and Kevin Murphy. "Changes in Relative Wages, 1963–1987." *Quarterly Journal of Economics* 107, note 1 (February 1992), 35–78.

Katz, Michael L., and Carl Shapiro. "Systems Competition and Network Effects." *Journal of Economic Perspectives* 8 (Spring 1994), 93–115.

Kennan, John. "The Elusive Effects of Minimum Wages." *Journal of Economic Literature* 33 (December 1995), 1949–1965.

Kerbo, Harold R., and L. Richard Della Fave. "Corporate Linkage and Control of the Corporate Economy: New Evidence and a Reinterpretation." *The Sociological Quarterly* 24 (Spring 1983), 201–218.

Kim, Kwan. "Income Distribution and Poverty: An Interregional Comparison." *World Development* 25, 11 (1997), 1909–1924.

Korten, David. *The Post-Corporate World: Life After Capitalism* (San Francisco: Barrett-Koehler Publishers, Inc.; West Hartford, Conn.: Kumarian Press, Inc., 1999).

Krieger, Nancy, and Elizabeth Fee. "Social Class: The Missing Link in U.S. Health Data." *International Journal of Health Services* 24 (1994), 25–44.

Krueger, Alan B. "How Computers Have Changed the Wage Structure: Evidence from MicroData." *The Quarterly Journal of Economics* 108 (1993), 33–60.

Krugman, Paul, and Anthony Venables. "Globalization and the Inequality of Nations." *The Quarterly Journal of Economics* 110, 4 (November 1995), 857–880.

Kuttner, Robert. "Markets and Politics." Chapter 9 in *Everything For Sale* (New York: Alfred A. Knopf, 1997), 328–362.

Kuznets, Simon. "Quantitative Aspects of the Economic Growth of Nations." *Economic Development and Cultural Change* 11, 2 (1963), 1–80.

Lambert, Thomas, and Christopher Boerner. "Environmental Inequity: Economic Causes, Economic Solutions." *Yale Journal on Regulation* 1, 1 (1997), 195–228.

Lazear, Edward P., and Sherwin Rosen. "Rank-Order Tournaments as Optimum Labor Contracts." *Journal of Political Economy* 89 (October 1981), 841–864.

Levin, Henry M. "The Economics of Justice in Education." Chapter 5 in *Spheres of Justice in Education (The 1990 American Education Yearbook)*, eds. Deborah A. Verstegen and James Gordon Ward, 129–147.

Levy, Frank, and Richard J. Murnane. "U.S. Earnings Levels and Earnings Inequality: A Review of Recent Trends and Proposed Explanations." *Journal of Economic Literature* 30 (1992), 1333–1381.

Lindbeck, Assar. "The Swedish Experiment." *Journal of Economic Literature* 35 (September 1997), 1273–1319.

MacDonald, Glenn M. "The Economics of Rising Stars." *American Economic Review* 78 (March 1988), 155–166.

MacDuffie, John Paul, and John F. Krafcik. "Integrating Technology and Human Resources for High-Performance Manufacturing: Evidence from the International Auto Industry." In *Transforming Organizations,* eds. Thomas A. Kochan and Michael Useem (New York: Oxford University Press, 1992), 209–225.

Machin, Stephen, and John Van Reenan. "Technology and Changes in Skill Structure: Evidence from Seven OECD Countries." *The Quarterly Journal of Economics* 113, 4 (November 1998), 1215–1244.

Machin, Stephen, Annette Ryan, and John Van Reenan. *Technology and Changes in Skill Structure: Evidence from an International Panel of Industries* (London: Centre for Economic Policy Research Discussion Paper Series #1434, 1996).

Mahnkopf, Birgit. "The 'Skill-Oriented' Strategies of German Trade Unions: Their Impact on Efficiency and Equality Objectives." *British Journal of Industrial Relations* 30, 1 (March 1992), 61–81.

Main, Brian G.M., Charles A. O'Reilly III, and James Wade. "Top Executive Pay: Tournament or Teamwork?" *Journal of Labor Economics* 11, 4 (1993), 606–628.

Massey, Douglas S. "American Apartheid: Segregation and the Making of the Underclass." *The American Journal of Sociology* 96, 2 (September 1990), 329–357.

Massey, Douglas S. "The Age of Extremes: Concentrated Affluence and Poverty in the Twenty-first Century." *Demography* 33, 4 (November 1996), 395–412.

Massey, Douglas S., and Mitchell L. Eggers. "The Ecology of Inequality: Minorities and the Concentration of Poverty, 1970–1980." *The American Journal of Sociology* 95, 5 (March 1990), 1153–1188.

McCrate, Elaine. "Trade, Merger, and Employment: Economic Theory on Marriage." *Review of Radical Political Economics* 19, 1 (Spring 1987), 73–89.

McElroy, Marjorie B. "The Empirical Content of Nash-Bargained Household Behavior." In *The Economics of the Family,* ed. Nancy Folbre (Brookfield, Vt.: Edward Elgar

Publishing Company, 1996), 203–227. *The Journal of Human Resources* 25, 4 (1990), 559–583.

McElroy, Marjorie B. "The Policy Implications of Family Bargaining and Marriage Markets." *Intrahousehold Resource Allocation in Developing Countries: Models, Methods and Policy,* eds. Lawrence Haddad, John Hoddinott, and Harold Alderman (Baltimore: The Johns Hopkins University Press, 1997, for the International Food Policy Research Institute), 53–74.

Miller, David. "Distributive Justice: What the People Think." *Ethics* 102 (April 1992), 555–593.

Miller, Jerome. "Tracking Racial Bias." Chapter 2 in *Search and Destroy: African-American Males in the Criminal Justice System* (New York: Cambridge University Press, 1996), 48–88.

Mishel, Lawrence, Jared Bernstein, and John Schmitt. *The State of Working America 1998–99* (Ithaca, N.Y.: ILR Press, 1998).

Mishel, Lawrence, Jared Bernstein, and John Schmitt. *The State of Working America 1998–99* (Ithaca, N.Y.: Cornell University Press, 1999, for the Economic Policy Institute).

Mitchell, Deborah. "Is There a Trade-off Between the Efficiency and Effectiveness Goals of Income Transfer Programs?" *Journal of Income Distribution 5 (1995),* 111–135.

Moene, Karl Ove, and Michael Wallerstein. "How Social Democracy Worked: Labor-Market Institutions." *Politics and Society* 23, 2 (June 1995), 185–211.

Morgenson, Gretchen. "Stock Options Are Not a Free Lunch." *Forbes* (May 18, 1998).

Moss, Philip, and Chris Tilly. "'Soft' Skills and Race: An Investigation of Black Men's Employment Problems." *Work and Occupations* 23 (August 1996), 252–276.

Nelson, Joan. "Poverty, Equity, and the Politics of Adjustment." *The Politics of Economic Adjustment,* eds. Stephen Haggard et al. (Princeton, N.J.: Princeton University Press, 1992), 221–264.

Nolan, Brian, and Christopher T. Whelan. "Income, Deprivation, and Poverty" and "Implications for Conceptualizing and Measuring Poverty." Chapters 6 and 8 in *Resources, Deprivation, and Poverty* (Oxford: Oxford University Press, 1996), 115–151, 179–201.

Oliver, Melvin, and Thomas Shapiro. "A Story of Two Nations: Race and Wealth." Chapter 5 in *Black Wealth/White Wealth* (New York: Routledge, 1995).

Oorlog, Dale R. "Marginal Revenue and Labor Strife in Major League Baseball." *Journal of Labor Research* 16, 1 (Winter 1995), 26–42.

Øyen, Else, S.M. Miller, and Syed Abdus Samad. *Poverty: A Global Review: Handbook on International Poverty Research* (Oslo and Cambridge, Mass.: Scandinavian University Press, 1996).

Page, Benjamin, and Robert Y. Shapiro. *The Rational Public* (Chicago: University of Chicago Press, 1992).

Parsons, Talcott. "A Revised Analytical Approach to the Theory of Social Stratification." In *Class Status and Power*, eds. Reinhard Bendix and S.M. Lipsit (Glencoe, Ill.: The Free Press, 1953), 92–128.

Persson, T., and G. Tabellini. "Growth, Distribution, and Politics." *European Economic Review* 36 (1992), 593–602.

Pindyck, Robert S., and Daniel L. Rubinfield. *Microeconomics* (New York: Macmillan Publishing Company, 1992).

Piven, Frances Fox, and Richard A. Cloward. "Poor Relief and the Dramaturgy of Work." Chapter 11 in *Regulating the Poor: The Functions of Public Welfare* (New York: Vintage Books 1993), 343–405.

Prag, Jay, and James Casavant. "An Empirical Study of the Determinants of Revenues and Marketing Expenditures in the Motion Picture Industry." *Journal of Cultural Economics* 18 (1994), 217–235.

Pritchett, Lant. "Divergence, Big Time." *Journal of Economic Perspectives* 11, 3 (Summer 1997), 3–17.

Putterman, Louis, John E. Roemer, and Joaquim Silvestre. "Does Egalitarianism Have a Future?" *Journal of Economic Literature* 36 (June 1998), 861–902.

Quinn, Bill. *How Wal-Mart Is Destroying America: And What You Can Do About It* (Berkeley, Calif.: Ten Speed Press, 1998).

Quirk, James P. *Hard Ball: the Abuse of Power in Pro Team Sports* (Princeton, N.J.: Princeton University Press, 1999).

Quirk, James, and Rodney D. Fort. *Pay Dirt: The Business of Professional Sports* (Princeton, N.J.: Princeton University Press, 1992).

Rainwater, Lee. "Poverty and the Income Package of Working Parents: The United States in Comparative Perspective." *Children and Youth Services Review* 17 (1995), 11–41.

Rees, Albert. "The Tournament as a Model for Executive Compensation." *Journal of Post-Keynesian Economics* 14 (Summer 1992), 567–571.

Robinson, John P., and Geoffrey Godbey. *Time for Life: the Surprising Ways Americans Use Their Time* (University Park: Pennsylvania State University Press, 1997).

Robson, Arthur J. "Status, the Distribution of Wealth, Private and Social Attitudes to Risk." *Econometrica* 60 (July 1992), 837–857.

Rodgers, William M., III, and William E. Spriggs. "What Does the AFQT Really Measure: Race, Wages, Schooling, and the AFQT Score." *The Review of Black Political Economy* 24, 4 (Spring 1996), 13–46.

Roldan, Martha. "Renegotiating the Marital Contract: Intrahousehold Patterns of Money Allocation and Women's Subordination Among Domestic Outworkers in Mexico City." In *A Home Divided: Women and Income in the Third World*, eds. Daisy Hilse

Dwyer, Judith Bruce, and Mead Cain (Stanford: Stanford University Press, 1988), 229–247.

Rosen, Sherwin. "The Economics of Superstars." *American Economic Review* 71 (December 1981), 845–858.

Rosen, Sherwin. Review of *The Winner-Take-All Society*, in *Journal of Economic Literature* 34 (March 1996), 133–135.

Roy, William. *Socializing Capital: The Rise of the Large Industrial Corporation in America* (Princeton, N.J.: Princeton University Press, 1997).

Rubury, Jill. "Wages and the Labour Market." *British Journal of Industrial Relations* 35 (1997), 337–366.

Samuels, Warren J., and Arthur S. Miller, eds. *Corporations and Society: Power and Responsibility* (New York: Greenwood Press, 1987).

Sawinski, Diane M., et al. *Encylopedia of Global Industries* (New York: Gate Research, 1996).

Scott, John. "Structures of Corporate Control." Chapter 3 in *Corporate Business and Capitalist Classes* (New York: Oxford University Press, 1997), 35–78.

Scully, Gerald W. *The Market Structure of Sports* (Chicago: University of Chicago Press, 1995).

Sepehri, Ardeshir, and Robert Chernomas. "Who Paid for the Canadian Welfare State Between 1955–1988?" *Review of Radical Political Economics* 24, 1 (1992), 71–88.

Silver, Hilary. "Reconceptualizing Social Disadvantage: The Paradigms of Social Exclusion." In *Social Exclusion: Rhetoric, Reality, Responses*, ed. G.C. Rodgers. (New York: St. Martin's Press, 1995), 57–80.

Simon, Herbert. "Organizations and Markets." *Journal of Economic Perspectives* 5 (Spring 1991), 25–44.

Sorensen, Elaine. "The Crowding Hypothesis and Comparable Worth." *The Journal of Human Resources* 25, 1 (1990), 55–89.

Steinberg, Ronnie J. "Social Construction of Skill: Gender, Power, and Comparable Worth." *Work and Occupations* 17, 4 (November 1990), 449–482.

Steiner, George A., and John F. Steiner. "Corporate Social Responsibility." In *Business, Government, and Society: a Management Perspective* 8th ed. (New York: McGraw-Hill, 1997).

Stephens, John D. "The Scandinavian Welfare States: Achievements, Crisis, and Prospects." In *Welfare States in Transition: National Adaptations in Global Economies*, ed. Gøsta Esping-Andersen (London: SAGE Publications, 1996), 32–65.

Stiglitz, Joseph E. "The Invisible Hand and Modern Welfare Economics." In *Information, Strategy, and Public Policy* (Cambridge, Mass.: Basil Blackwell, 1991), 12–50.

Stiglitz, Joseph E. *Whither Socialism?* (Cambridge, Mass.: MIT Press, 1994).

Stokey, Nancy L. "Shirtsleeves to Shirtsleeves: The Economics of Social Mobility." In

Frontiers of Research in Economic Theory: The Nancy L. Schwartz Memorial Lectures, 1983–1997, eds. Donald P. Jacobs, Ehud Kalai, and Morton I. Kamien (New York: Cambridge University Press, 1998), 210–241.

Streeten, Paul P. "Diversity, Conflict, and Equality of Access." Draft, prepared for the UNESCO annual volume on Culture and Development (March 1999).

Strobel, Pierre. "From Poverty to Exclusion: A Wage-Earning Society or a Society of Human Rights?" *International Social Science Journal* 148 (June 1996), 173–190.

Sturm, Susan, and Lani Guinier. "The Future of Affirmative Action." *California Law Review* 84 (July 1996), 953–1036.

Taub, Amy, et al. "Oligopoly: Highly Concetrated Markets Across the U.S. Economy." *Multinational Monitor* 20, 4 (November 1998), 9.

Taylor, Lance. "Income Distribution, Trade, and Growth." *U.S. Trade Policy and Global Growth,* ed. Robert Blecker (Armonk, N.Y.: M.E. Sharpe, 1996), 240–267.

Thomas, Duncan. "Incomes, Expenditures, and Health Outcomes: Evidence on Intrahousehold Resource Allocation." Chapter 9 in *Intrahousehold Resource Allocation in Developing Countries: Models, Methods, and Policy,* eds. J.H. Lawrence Haddad and Harold Alderman (Baltimore: The John Hopkins University Press, 1997), 142–164.

Tilly, Charles. *Durable Inequality* (Berkeley: University of California Press, 1998).

Tilly, Chris. *Half a Job: Bad and Good Part-Time Jobs in a Changing Labor Market* (Philadelphia: Temple University Press, 1996).

Tilly, Chris, and Randy Aldelba. "Not Markets Alone: Enriching the Discussion of Income." Chapter 10 in *Political Economy for the 21st Century* (Armonk, N.Y.: M.E. Sharpe, 1996), 195–205.

Tilton, Timothy. "What Is Distinctive About Swedish Social Democratic Ideology?" In *The Political Theory of Swedish Social Democracy: Through the Welfare State to Socialism* (Oxford: Clarendon Press, 1990), 248–280.

Topel, Robert H. "Factor Proportions and Relative Wages: The Supply-Side Determinants of Wage Inequality." *Journal of Economic Perspectives* 11 (Spring 1997), 55–74.

Torras, M., and J.K. Boyce. "Income, Inequality, and Pollution: A Reassessment of the Environmental Kuznets Curve." *Ecological Economics* 25 (1998), 147–160.

Towse, Ruth. *Singers in the Marketplace: The Economics of the Singing Profession* (Oxford: Clarendon Press, 1993).

United Nations Development Program. *Human Development Report, 1992* (Oxford: Oxford University Press, 1992).

United Nations Development Program. *Human Development Report, 1995* (Oxford: Oxford University Press, 1995).

United Nations Development Program. *Human Development Report, 1997* (Oxford: Oxford University Press, 1997).

Useem, Michael. *The Inner Circle* (New York: Oxford University Press, 1984).

Vogel, Harold L. *Entertainment Industry Economics: a Guide for Financial Analysis* (New York: Cambridge University Press, 1990).

Waldfogel, Jane. "The Effect of Children on Women's Wages." *American Sociological Review* 62 (April 1997), 209–217.

Wallace, W. Timothy, Alan Seigerman, and Morris B. Holbrook. "The Role of Actors and Actresses in the Success of Films: How Much Is a Movie Star Worth?" *Journal of Cultural Economics* 17 (June 1993), 1–27.

Weed, E. "Income Inequality, Democracy, and Growth Reconsidered." *European Journal of Political Economy* 13 (1997), 751–764.

Weicher, John C. "The Rich and the Poor: Demographics of the U.S. Wealth Distribution." *Federal Reserve Bank of St. Louis Review* (July/August 1997), 25–37.

Weinberger, Catherine J. "Race and Gender Wage Gaps in the Market for Recent College Graduates." *Industrial Relations* 37, 1 (January 1998), 67–84.

Williamson, Jeffrey G. "Globalization and Inequality, Past and Present." *World Bank Research Observer* 12, 2 (August 1997), 117–135.

Williamson, Jeffrey G., and Peter Lindert. "Long-Term Trends in American Wealth Inequality." Chapter 1 in *Modeling the Distribution and Intergenerational Transmission of Wealth,* ed. James Smith (Chicago: University of Chicago Press, 1980).

Wilson, William Julius. "Racial Antagonisms and Race-Based Social Policy." Chapter 7 in *When Work Disappears: The World of the New Urban Poor* (New York: Alfred A. Knopf, Inc., 1997), 183–206.

Wolff, Edward. "International Comparisons of Wealth Inequality." *Review of Income and Wealth* 42, 4 (1996).

Wolff, Edward N. "Recent Trends in the Size Distribution of Household Wealth." *Journal of Economic Perspectives* 12 (Summer 1998), 131–150.

Wolff, Edward N., and Marcia Marley. "Long-Term Trends in U.S. Wealth Inequality: Methodological Issues and Results." In *The Measurement of Saving, Investment, and Wealth,* eds. Robert E. Lipsey and Helen Stone Tice (Chicago: University of Chicago Press, 1989), 765–844.

Wood, Adrian. "Openness and Wage Inequality in Developing Countries: The Latin American Challenge to East Asian Conventional Wisdom." *The World Bank Economic Review* 11, 1 (January 1997), 33–57.

Wright, J. Skelly. "Politics and the Constitution: Is Money Speech?" *The Yale Law Journal* 85, 8 (July 1976), 1001–1021.

Wright, J. Skelly. "Money and the Pollution of Politics: Is the First Amendment an Obstacle to Political Equality?" *Columbia Law Review* 82, 4 (May 1982), 609–645.

Yermack, David. "Good Timing: CEO Stock Option Awards and Company News Announcements." *Journal of Finance* 52 (June 1997), 449–476.

Zeitlin, Maurice. "Corporate Ownership and Control: The Large Corporations and the Capitalist Class." *American Journal of Sociology* 79 (1974), 1071–1119.

Zimbalist, Andrew. *Baseball and Billions: a Probing Look Inside the Big Business of Our National Pastime* (New York: HarperCollins, 1992).

Subject Index

Name Index

Island Press Board of Directors

Susan E. Sechler, *Chair,* Vice-President, Aspen Institute

Henry Reath, *Vice-Chair,* President, Collector's Reprints, Inc.

Drummond Pike, *Secretary,* President, The Tides Foundation

Robert E. Baensch, *Treasurer,* Professor of Publishing, New York University

Catherine M. Conover

Gene E. Likens, Director, The Institute of Ecosystem Studies

Dane Nichols, Chairman, The Natural Step. U.S.

Charles C. Savitt, President, Center for Resource Economics/Island Press

Victor M. Sher, Environmental Lawyer

Peter R. Stein, Managing Partner, Lyme Timber Company

Richard Trudell, Executive Director, American Indian Resources Institute

Wren Wirth, President, The Winslow Foundation